DISCARD

KOREA UNDER ROH TAE-WOO:

DEMOCRATISATION, NORTHERN POLICY,

AND INTER-KOREAN RELATIONS

**edited by
James Cotton**

Allen & Unwin
in association with
Department of International Relations
RSPacS, ANU, Canberra, ACT

First published in 1993

Allen & Unwin Pty Ltd.
9 Atchison St., St Leonards, NSW 2065, Australia

Department of International Relations, RSPacS,
Australian National University, Canberra ACT 2601, Australia

National Library of Australia
Cataloguing-in-Publication entry:

Korea Under Roh Tae-woo: Democratisation, Northern Policy, and Inter-Korean Relations

ISBN 1 86373 397 3

1.Roh, Tae Woo, 1932–. 2. Korea (South)—Politics and government—1988– . 3. Korea (South)—Foreign relations. I. Cotton, James, 1949– . II. Australian National University. Dept of International Relations.

951.95043

Printed by ANU Printery, ANU, Canberra ACT 2601, Australia

Table of Contents

Acknowledgements

Grateful acknowledgement is given to the following periodicals, publishers and organisations for permitting the following essays which they have previously published to be reprinted in this collection:

Basil Blackwell Ltd, publisher of *Political Studies*, for:

James Cotton, 'From Authoritarianism to Democracy in South Korea', vol. 37, no. 2 (1989);

The Hudson Institute, publisher of *Triumph After Trial: East Asia After the Cold War* (Indianapolis, 1992), for:

Perry Wood, 'The Strategic Equilibrium on the Korean Peninsula in the 1990s';

The Center for Strategic & International Studies, Washington DC, publisher of *Economic Development and Democratization in the Asia-Pacific Region* (Washington, 1992) for:

Kim Jae-youl, 'Democratisation in South Korea';

The Japan Institute of International Relations, publisher of *Japan Review of International Affairs*, for:

Okonogi Masao, 'South Korea's Experiment in Democracy', vol. 2, no. 1 (1988);

Kim Hak-joon, 'The Republic of Korea's Northern Policy: Origin, Development, and Prospects', vol. 5 (1991), Special Issue;

Oxford University Press, publisher of *The Pacific Review*, for:

Chalmers Johnson, 'South Korean Democratization: The Role of Economic Development', vol. 2, no. 1 (1989);

James Cotton, 'The Two Koreas and Rapprochement: Foundations for Progress?', vol. 5, no. 2 (1992);

The Institute of Korean Studies, publisher of *Korea Observer*, for:

Dong Won-mo, 'The Democratization of South Korea: What Role Does the Middle Class Play?', vol. 22, no. 2 (1991);

The Regents of the University of California, publisher of *Asian Survey*, for:

Kim Hong-nack, 'The 1988 Parliamentary Election in Korea', vol. 29, no. 5 (1989);

Park Jin, 'Political Change in South Korea: The Challenge of the Conservative Alliance', vol. 30, no. 12 (1990);

© 1989, 1990, The Regents of the University of California. Reprinted by permission of the Regents.

The Research Institute for International Affairs, Seoul, publisher of *The Journal of East Asian Affairs*, for:

Robert E. Bedeski, 'State Reform and Democracy in Korea', vol. 6, no. 1 (1992);

The Research Centre for Peace and Unification of Korea, publisher of *Korea and World Affairs*, for:

Park Sang-seek, 'Northern Diplomacy and Inter-Korean Relations', vol. 12, no. 4 (1988);

Lee Hong-koo, 'Unification through a Korean Commonwealth', vol. 13, no. 4 (1989);

Kim Hak-joon, 'New Political Development with a Vision for the 1990s and Beyond', vol. 14, no. 1 (1990);

Kim Hak-joon, 'Korean Reunification: A Seoul Perspective', vol. 14 (1991), no. 1;

Lim Dong-won, 'Inter-Korean Relations Oriented Toward Reconciliation', vol. 16, no. 2 (1992);

Previously unpublished work is © copyright the authors, 1993

The editor would also like to record his gratitude to the Korea Foundation for supporting the publication of this book, to Professor Kim Hak-joon for his guidance, and to Lynne Payne and Robin Ward for their expeditious processing of the text.

Notes on Contributors

Bae Sun-kwang is a graduate of Yonsei and Waikato Universities. He is presently a PhD student at the Australian National University where he is working on regionalism in Korean politics employing data from two large scale opinion surveys.

Robert Bedeski is Professor of Political Science, University of Victoria, British Columbia. He has served as consultant to the Department of National Defense and Department of External Affairs of Canada. His publications include *The Fragile Entente: The 1978 Japan–China Peace Treaty in a Global Context* (1983), and *Japan's Defense Strategy* (1985).

James Cotton is a Senior Fellow in the Northeast Asia Program, Department of International Relations, Australian National University, and editor of the *Australian Journal of International Affairs*. His publications include *The Korean War in History* (editor, 1989), *Asian Frontier Nationalism: Owen Lattimore and the American Policy Debate* (1989), *James Harrington's Political Thought and Its Context* (1991), and *The End of the Cold War in Northeast Asia* (edited with Stuart Harris, 1991).

Dong Won-mo teaches and directs the Asian Studies Program at Southern Methodist University in Dallas, Texas. His field of speciality is modern Korean politics. His most recent publications include 'Domestic Politics in 1990, A Year of Crisis', in Donald N. Clark (ed.), *Korea Briefing* (1991), and 'Generational Difference and Political Change in South Korea', *The Journal of Korean Studies*, vol. 22 (March 1993).

Chalmers Johnson is Rohr Professor of Pacific International Relations, Graduate School of International Relations and Pacific Studies, University of California, San Diego. His many publications on Northeast Asian politics and political economy include *Politics and Productivity: How Japan's Development Strategy Works* (co-editor, 1989), *MITI and the Japanese Miracle. The Growth of Industrial Policy, 1925-1975* (1982), and *Peasant Nationalism and Communist Power. The Emergence of Revolutionary China 1937-1945* (1962).

Okonogi Masao is Professor of Political Science, Keio University, Tokyo, and Research Director of the Northeast Asian Division, The Japan Institute of International Affairs. His publications include *Japan and North Korea: The Next Five Years* (1991), *North Korea at the Crossroads*

(1988), and *The Korean War: The Process of American Involvement* (1986).

Kim Hak-joon is Spokesman and Senior Press Secretary to President Roh Tae-woo. He was Professor and Chairman of the Department of Political Science, Seoul National University, and a member of the 12th National Assembly of the Republic of Korea. His publications include *Unification Policies of South and North Korea: A Comparative Study* (second edition 1986), and *Korea in Soviet East Asian Policy* (1986).

Kim Hong-nack is Professor of Political Science at West Virginia University. He has published very widely on Japanese and Korean politics and foreign policy, and his publications include *Korean Reunification: New Perspectives and Approaches* (co-editor, 1984) and *Korea and the Major Powers After the Seoul Olympics* (co-editor 1989).

Kim Jae-youl holds a position at the Johns Hopkins University School of Advanced International Studies, and is a contributor to the Asian Studies programme of the Center for Strategic and International Studies, Washington DC. He has published on Korea's political economy and foreign policy.

Lee Hong-koo taught for twenty years at Seoul National University as Professor of Political Science and Director of the Institute of Social Sciences. In 1989 he joined the cabinet as Minister of National Unification, and since 1991 has served as Korean Ambassador in London.

Lim Dong-won is Vice-Minister of the National Unification Board, Republic of Korea and also a delegate at the Inter-Korean High-level Talks. A retired Army major-general, Lim served as ambassador to Nigeria and Australia, and also as chancellor of the Institute of Foreign Affairs and National Security, Ministry of Foreign Affairs. He is the author of *Communist Revolutionary War and Counterinsurgency* (1967).

Park Jin is a lecturer at the East Asia Centre, University of Newcastle upon Tyne. He has published a number of studies of Korean domestic politics and international relations, and of Japanese politics.

Park Sang-seek is the Republic of Korea Consul General in Boston, USA. He has been a university professor at Hampton University, Virginia, and has served as director-general of the Office of Research, Institute of Foreign Affairs and National Security, Ministry of Foreign Affairs. He has published widely on international politics and the politics of Africa.

Perry Wood is a research fellow at the Hudson Institute, Indianapolis. He is a political scientist specialising in Asian politics and security issues. His publications include *Multinational Naval Cooperation in the Southwest Pacific* (1993), *ASEAN: New Challenges, New Directions* (co-author,

1990), and *Beyond Recrimination: Perspectives on US–Taiwan Trade Tensions* (co-author, 1987).

Yoo Jang-hee is President of the Korea Institute for International Economic Policy. He was formerly a professor at Virginia Commonwealth University and Clark University, and his publications include *Macroeconomic Theory* (1975).

Introduction

JAMES COTTON

It is now almost two decades since the Republic of Korea came to be regarded as something of a model in economic development. The export led industrialisation strategy initiated under the presidency of Park Chung-hee, achieving rapid and relatively equitable growth from 1963 onwards, seemed to indicate the way forward for other resource poor but labour surplus economies. But into the 1980s, Korea was far from being considered a model in political affairs. On the one hand the domestic political system was still disfigured by authoritarianism, while on the other Korea's external and security relations were dominated by that national division which was the inheritance of the Cold War.

In the last five years, in a period largely coinciding with the tenure in office of President Roh Tae-woo, Korea's domestic and international political character have undergone a remarkable transformation. Roh Tae-woo, then presidential candidate for the Democratic Justice Party, defused with his eight-point declaration in favour of democratisation the crisis of mid-1987 which threatened to abort the process of peaceful regime succession. The democratic constitution approved by national referendum in October 1987 laid the foundation for orderly political competition, Roh then becoming president in the first substantive political contest to have occurred since 1971.

Although a close colleague of the former president, Roh did not obstruct a thorough review of some of the abuses of power associated with the Fifth republic. His administration was also instrumental in augmenting the independence of the judiciary and ensuring that the military and security organs did not exercise that power of veto over the political process which they had long possessed. President Roh presided over a political system in which power was not held exclusively by the executive but was increasingly diffused among the other branches of government. Elections to the National Assembly were held in 1988 and again in 1992, and the legislature emerged as a significant contributor to policy making and the oversight of the administration. Meanwhile the lifting of restrictions upon the operations of the media ensured the emergence of a vigorous national debate on a wide agenda of social, economic, and political issues. And some commentators detected, in the formation of independent labour unions and a variety of citizens groups, the beginnings of an autonomous Korean civil society.

Roh has been able to hand power on to a democratically elected successor. Though in recent years the tide of democratisation has swept across Eastern Europe and also has had its impact in Asia, the institutionalisation of stable successor regimes to the former authoritarianisms has been notoriously difficult. Korea, however, has been singularly successful in this latter task. Roh's particular contribution to this process was evident in his decision in October 1992 to choose as the members of his final cabinet genuinely non-partisan figures who would supervise the presidential elections and the transfer of power in an impartial way.

If the changes in the domestic affairs of Korea in this period have been remarkable, the transformation of Korea's place in the Northeast Asian region has been nothing less than revolutionary. During President Roh's administration, South Korea has successfully courted its erstwhile communist antagonists, opening official relations with China and developing a close relationship first with the Soviet Union under Mikhail Gorbachev, and then with President Yeltsin's Russia. At the same time, Korea has been successful in pursuing increasingly important commercial ties with the former socialist bloc. On the international stage, Korea has entered the United Nations and President Roh has been able to put forward in the General Assembly concrete proposals for enhancing the security of the Northeast Asian region.

Seoul has also offered a policy of conciliation towards Pyongyang. Though the two Korean states have been engaged in a dialogue intermittently from 1971, in the past they have never been able to institutionalise this dialogue nor develop mechanisms for exchange. Early in his administration Roh moved to announce explicitly that he considered that the era of competition and antagonism between the two states should come to an end. Further initiatives resulted in 1991 in the adoption of the South–North Korean agreement on reconciliation, non-aggression, and cooperation. As a consequence, there are now in existence joint South–North committees tasked with the business of achieving the goals specified in the 1991 agreement. South Korea has also hosted visits from North Korean officials concerned to pursue collaborative economic activities, which will undoubtedly proceed once security problems have been addressed.

This volume brings together the work of Korean and foreign scholars and commentators, all of whom consider aspects of the Roh Tae-woo era. Democratisation has clearly been a consequence of a complex of factors: the emergence of appropriate social and economic conditions, the formation of stable political institutions, and the manoeuvres and decisions of political leaders and parties. The essays in the first part of this book consider all the elements of this equation. The second part is devoted to issues related to the political process, including elections to the legislature, party realignment, economic policy, and the problems associated with regionalism. The third part reviews Korea's diplomatic revolution and the beginnings of reconciliation with Pyongyang. The book concludes with a selection of the most significant documents of the Roh administration.

To the extent that Korea becomes a model in politics as it has in economics, the Roh Tae-woo era will be regarded as that period when the essentials of the model were institutionalised. This collection therefore offers perspectives on a time of significance not just for Korea but also for the world community.

PART I

DEMOCRATISATION: PREREQUISITES

1 South Korea's Experiment in Democracy

OKONOGI MASAO

In the six months from the 29 June 1987 announcement by ruling party head Roh Tae-woo of support for democratic reforms, including direct elections for the presidency, and the holding—and Roh's winning—of the presidential election on 16 December, South Korea experienced a major political upheaval, one that rivals the events of 1960 and 1961 in its significance for the country's history.

The 1960–61 episode began with a transfer of the reins of power brought on by a student uprising, and it ended with a military coup. This time, the changes started with a call for liberalisation from moderates within the government and culminated in a change of administration by popular election. However one chooses to interpret them, the importance of these developments, in which South Korea achieved political reform through non-violent means, ought not to be underestimated.

As indicated by the way events unfolded, this accomplishment was not the result of a smooth process planned in advance but the outcome of trial and error and courageous determination. Roh Tae-woo won the election, but ultimately the success cannot be credited to any single party. It was the joint product of the labours of the government, the ruling and opposition parties, students, intellectuals, and—above all—the people of the nation. Here, while retracing the course of events, I will examine this Korean experiment in democracy and consider the prospects for President Roh's new administration.

Chun's 13 April Speech: Background

On 13 April 1987, President Chun Doo Hwan addressed the nation, announcing that since no agreement had been reached on constitutional reform even after a year of talks between the opposition and the ruling Democratic Justice Party, the reform process would have to be shelved. This meant that his successor would be selected under the existing electoral college system before the end of the year. Chun's speech was a surprise attack on the opposition. The government had clearly decided to take the offensive and quickly started to prepare for a presidential election, using its might to suppress the objections of the opposition. On 10 June the DJP nominated Roh Tae-woo, its chairman, as its candidate to succeed Chun as president.

In retrospect, we can see that the position of the government and ruling party on the constitutional reform issue had been hardening ever since the end of the September–October 1986 Asian Games in Seoul. The government criticised the opposition's insistence on direct presidential elections and rejection of the ruling party's proposal that most of the president's power be shifted to the Prime Minister and that both be elected by the National Assembly. It claimed that this showed a lack of respect for the legislature and prepared to counterattack. In October Assembly member Yu Sung Hwan of the New Korea Democratic Party was arrested on charges of violating the National Security Law. This was followed in November with the jailing of over 2,000 students who had occupied Konkuk University and orders for the dissolution of the opposition People's Movement for Democracy and Unification.

The government and DJP were encouraged to adopt an even more aggressive stance by the split in the ranks of the opposition that started to surface at the end of 1986. On 24 December New Korea Democratic Party President Lee Min Woo indicated willingness to consider the ruling party's formula for reform. This caused great dissent within the party, ultimately leading to the decision the following 8 April by Kim Young Sam and Kim Dae Jung to leave the NKDP and unite their factions in a new party. The government saw this as an irresistible chance to pounce, and on 13 April President Chun dropped his bombshell.

But the administration had overestimated its power to control the situation. After Chun's speech, groups of university professors published statements in rapid succession deploring the shelving of constitutional reform. Journalists joined in this protest, and religious leaders began a hunger strike. Within Korean society, where religious feelings run deep and intellectuals are highly respected, these actions had a great impact.

Two more developments shook the government's hold. One was the April suicide of the president of a major shipping company in a scandal involving the disappearance of 10 billion won in political contributions and the spiriting abroad of another 100 billion won, which sapped public trust in the authorities. The second was the disclosure of new evidence about the January torture death of a university student in police custody, directly implicating the superiors of the two officers previously charged with responsibility for the case. This major coverup scandal naturally led to sharp criticism of both the police and the government prosecutors, in the end forcing Chun to ask for the resignation of his entire cabinet on 26 May.

As a long-term development, the demand for democratic reforms had been gradually spreading among the general public. The question that an increasing number of people were asking was why their country, which had achieved phenomenal economic growth, had successfully staged the Asian Games, and would soon be hosting the Olympics, should be unable to succeed in the realm of political development. And they noted that they had not had the chance to elect their own president directly since 1971.

Over the short-term, meanwhile, the debate over constitutional reforms starting in the spring of 1986 had greatly fanned hopes for democratisation. President Chun had in fact only promised to revise the constitution provided the ruling and opposition parties could reach agreement on the conditions. But the general public had not fully noted the proviso in the president's promise, and to them his 13 April announcement appeared to be a betrayal of sorts.

Not only the urban unemployed but even the self-employed and office workers cheered on the students who took to the streets, and some actually joined in the demonstrations themselves. This can only be explained as a reflection of these people's disappointment at the dashing of their short- and long-term hopes for reform and the disillusionment brought on by the two scandals that had rocked the administration. The nation-wide anti-government movement that reached a crescendo late in June 1987 may be considered a revolution of rising expectations with which reality had failed to keep pace.

The government and DJP should have been more sensitive to this popular sentiment. As early as in the National Assembly elections of February 1985, many members of the new urban middle class had supported the just-formed New Korea Democratic Party, allowing it to win 29 per cent of the votes and sixty-seven seats and holding the ruling DJP's share of the votes to 35 per cent. The opposition was especially strong in the big cities. In Seoul 43 per cent of the votes went to the NKDP, while only 27 per cent went to the DJP and in Pusan the returns were 37 per cent for the NKDP and 28 per cent for the DJP.[1]

Shortly after President Chun's 13 April announcement of the decision to shelve the constitutional reforms, I wrote, 'How will the government and ruling party react if they find the movement for constitutional reforms gaining momentum again as it did last spring? Since they have suspended the reform process, all they will be able to do is rely on might [to suppress

---

[1]   *Chosun Ilbo*, 14 February 1985.

the opposition]. But I cannot believe that Kim Dae Jung or Kim Young Sam will yield'.[2]

The movement for constitutional reforms had the backing not just of the opposition parties but also of students, intellectuals, and the new urban middle class. What were these people after? Simply stated, what they wanted was to curtail the military's role in politics. In the 1960s and early 1970s reasons could be found for having the military play a role in South Korea that went beyond defending the nation. Without General Park Chung Hee's *coup d'état* in 1961 and his assumption of political leadership, the country could most likely not have achieved industrialisation and the restoration of normal relations with Japan. And at least for the former part of his years in power, much of what Park did was in accordance with the will of the public. We should not forget, after all, that he won three presidential elections.

In the later years of the Park regime, however, the political role of the military grew to mammoth proportions, particularly in the period from the institution of the Yushin, or Revitalisation, system in 1972 until the president's assassination in 1979. Following Park's death, in the 'Seoul spring' period of 1980, the military upheld the provisional administration of Choi Kyu Hah, who had made a declaration of political neutrality, but in return for this support it had the government proclaim martial law across the nation. In May 1980 the army violently crushed an insurrection in Kwangju, and in September of that year General Chun Doo Hwan became president. (The Kwangju incident has ever since been a persistent issue between the government and its opponents, who have demanded that the authorities acknowledge their responsibility for the carnage.)

It would be difficult to say to what extent the military played a political role under Chun's administration. But with the rapid strengthening of the nation's defence capacity and the reconfirmation of its security agreement with the United States, it was not unreasonable for the South Korean public to aspire for the normalisation of their political situation. The people were hoping to achieve a gradual and legitimate reduction of military power through a presidential election under a new constitution. The turmoil into which the nation fell in June 1987 attests to the greatness of these popular expectations, which Chun's 13 April speech had dashed.

Roh's 29 June Declaration

The political turmoil that broke out in the wake of the convention of the ruling Democratic Justice Party on 10 June was brought under control on 29 June, when DJP Chairman Roh Tae-woo, whom the convention had

---

2 *Ekonomisuto*, 28 April 1987, pp. 30–31.

chosen as the party's presidential candidate, came out with his declaration of support for liberalisation. Roh's declaration covered eight points, among which were calls for direct presidential elections, a large-scale pardon and rehabilitation of political criminals—including Kim Dae Jung—the restoration of freedom of the press, and respect for the autonomy of local governments and of universities.

There were reasons, of course, for Roh's offer of these and other concessions. First of all, the demonstrations against the government during the month had escalated beyond mere student unrest. On 18 and 19 June protests took place on a nation-wide scale in Seoul, Pusan, Taegu, Inchon, Taejon, Kwangju, and other large cities. This and the 'Peace March' of 26 June made it clear that it was not practical for the government to go forward with its plans for an indirect presidential election.

Secondly, there was growing concern over the possible adverse effect of this political unrest on the 1988 Seoul Olympics. People in other countries had begun to talk about holding the games in Los Angeles or Berlin instead, and prospects were uncertain for the North Korea–South Korea sports talks to be held in Lausanne in July. If these talks should cause doubts to arise about Chinese and Soviet participation in the Seoul games, it was feared that the blow to the government might prove fatal.

Thirdly, the repeated diplomatic efforts of the United States can also be said to have had a major impact. President Ronald Reagan wrote Chun a personal letter on 19 June. On 20 June Under Secretary of State Edward Derwinksi visited Seoul, followed by Assistant Secretary Gaston Sigur three days later—each held talks with Chun, Roh, and others. The Americans pressed for a compromise settlement between the government and the opposition parties, made clear their support for freedom of peaceful assembly, and indicated that they were strongly against the involvement of the military.

Roh's 29 June declaration was not, however, simply a set of unilateral concessions, let alone an admission of defeat. Rather, it was an indication of his determination to bring the political turmoil under control by abandoning the electoral college format and thereby achieving a historical compromise with the opposition; and, at the same time, it was a declaration of his intent to run as a candidate in direct elections for president. The major concessions that Roh unveiled represented the first stage of a massive counter-attack on his part.

If we examine the political transformation that took place in South Korea after Chun's 13 April speech in terms of comparative politics, Roh's declaration appears profoundly significant as a dramatic manifestation of the beginning of a shift away from authoritarianism by moderate forces within the system. His move was clearly a response to the resistance of the public to the drastic hardening of the government's position as announced in the president's speech. But it was also meaningful as an expression of the support for liberalisation among moderates within the government. Roh Tae-woo saw clearly that the authoritarian system had reached its limits, and he decided to employ the initiative of the moderates to break the deadlock.[3]

At the outset of Chun's administration, just as at that of other authoritarian regimes, there was no distinct group of moderates within the ruling circles. Following the assassination of President Park Chung Hee in October 1979, hard-liners had moved to crush all experimentation with democracy, in the name of law and order and of national security. And Chun had taken power in what was virtually a *coup d'état*.

It was only with the February 1985 National Assembly elections that moderates within the system began to raise their voices. The great support that the opposition won raised doubts about the future of authoritarianism. President Chun's selection of Roh Tae-woo to head the ruling DJP may have been part of his groundwork for the party politics that would ensue after his administration. And after his selection, Roh worked to develop a position of his own as a leader of the moderates in the party as distinct from the hard-line advisers surrounding the president.

But the road leading to Roh's presidential nomination at the June 1987 party convention was not a smooth one. Serious splits emerged between the hard-liners and moderates at first in the summer of 1985 when the government tried to put through a law to control student demonstrations (including provisions for 'ideological reorientation' for violent demonstrators), and again starting in the fall of 1986 when it tried to crush antigovernment forces. In many cases, the president's administration and the DJP found themselves in opposition to each other.

The rift between the two reached a climax in the spring of 1987. Chun's 13 April speech appeared to signal the victory of the hard-liners, people like Chang Se Dong, director of the National Security Planning Agency, and Hu Moon Do, head of the National Unification Board. Some younger voices in the military even suggested that Chang should be designated to succeed Chun as president. Hu, meanwhile, slapped a 'procommunist' label on the two Kims' new Reunification Democratic Party in an effort to break it up.

The irony is that what finally guaranteed Roh's victory was the outburst of student protests set off by the 13 April speech, as well as by the two scandals that had come to light shortly thereafter. The reshuffling of the cabinet in late May saw the departure of Home Minister Chung Ho Yong, a moderate, but with him he took both Chang Se Dong and Prime Minister Lho Shin Yong, Roh Tae-woo's major civilian rival. As after the February 1985 National Assembly election, the strength of the anti-

---

3   See Guillermo O'Donnell and Philippe Schmitter, *Political Life After Authoritarian Rule* (Washington: Woodrow Wilson Center, 1985).

government movement played into Roh's hands as leader of the moderate faction within the government.

What is especially interesting is that Roh addressed his 29 June declaration to President Chun, suggesting that if his proposals were not accepted he would step down from his position as party chairman and presidential candidate. This may be seen as a well-timed push at Chun, who had been carefully balancing himself on the fence between the moderates and hardliners.

Constitutional Reform and the Split of the Opposition

If we assume that Roh saw establishing his distance from the president as necessary for his credibility as a candidate, then we may also view the subsequent series of liberalisation measures that were adopted by the government and ruling party as a desperate effort to regain the trust of the estranged public. Chun endorsed Roh's proposals; on 9 July, Kim Dae Jung and well over 2,000 other political prisoners were granted amnesty, and the following day Chun handed over his post as president of the ruling party to Roh, stating his intention to lead the country from a position above the political fray. On 13 July he reshuffled the cabinet again, attempting to reduce its factional colour.

In spite of these moves, however, it remained unclear whether it would be possible to achieve liberalisation in a politically stable environment. Actually, there existed two distinct scenarios for South Korea in the period following Roh's declaration. According to one scenario, anti-government forces would remain dissatisfied with the authorities' moves and continue their attacks on the government, leading ultimately to intervention by the military. These anti-government forces did in fact seek the release of the 200 or so remaining political prisoners, the truth concerning the Kwangju incident, complete freedom to hold demonstrations and meetings, as well as a ban on the use of tear gas. During the summer there were also coal strikes, along with labour disputes at Hyundai Motor and Daewoo Shipbuilding and Heavy Machinery, which spread to other firms across the nation, finally affecting buses, taxis, and other forms of public transportation. And rumours were flying about a 'September crisis', in which students and workers would join forces at the start of the new school year, creating a situation that could not be brought under control without military intervention.

But the leaders of the ruling and opposition parties, especially Roh and Kim Young Sam, were envisaging a second, quite different scenario. They believed that the turbulent situation would be settled quickly if their two groups cooperated in achieving constitutional reforms and making it clear to the public exactly how and when a change of administration would take place. In other words, they were hoping that by gaining the support of the public for constitutional reforms and a presidential election, they would be able to restore political stability and minimise the interference from extremists on both the right and left, namely, the military and the students. After 29 June, the opposition and ruling party leaders clearly had interests in common.

The turning point came around the end of August. A general strike planned by Opposition forces failed to occur, and labour–management disputes began to subside. In other words, the student–worker solidarity movement fizzled out before it really even got off the ground. Furthermore, by 30 August, the opposition and ruling parties managed to reach an agreement concerning the framework of the new constitution and the timetable for the presidential election. This meant that the two sides had agreed on the how and when of the shift away from authoritarianism.

With this issue settled, the public turned their attention to the biggest remaining question, that is, whether the opposition would be able to choose between Kim Dae Jung and Kim Young Sam and arrive at a single presidential candidate. They realised that the answer would have a major bearing on the outcome of the presidential election.

When Roh made his 29 June declaration, he was clearly anticipating that the two Kims would split their forces. If one of them quit the race in favour of the other, Roh would be at a definite disadvantage. But for each of the two, the very strength of his prospects of being elected if he could persuade the other to withdraw made him that much more eager to run. There were also major differences between their political positions, support groups, and regional affiliations.

Kim Young Sam was from Koje Island in North Kyongsang Province and had made his political base in Pusan; Kim Dae Jung hailed from Mokpo and had formed his base in Kwangju in the province of South Cholla. In South Korea politicians' native districts tend to become the focal points of their support, and so it was significant that the two had their respective bases in Kyongsang and Cholla, two antagonistic provinces. Furthermore, Kim Young Sam's supporters consisted mainly of middle and upper middle-class white-collar workers, intellectuals, and Protestants, while Kim Dae Jung's support came largely from the lower-income sector, blue-collar workers, students, and Catholics.

There were also distinct political differences between the two Kims. Kim Young Sam clearly took the compromise between Roh and the opposition very seriously, intending to see to it that the accord survived until the election. His intention was to win the presidency on the basis of popular support, and he did not want a revolution or *coup d'état* to interfere with this process. He was also a party politician who was very concerned about the organisation and wanted to see party politics take root in South

Korea regardless of who won the race. And in the eyes of the public he enjoyed an image as a middle-of-the-roader.

Kim Dae Jung, on the other hand, rather than hold back from attacking the government, continued to cooperate with other anti-government forces to press for even greater concessions. His hope was to orchestrate a sort of 'Kim Dae Jung boom' in the midst of swelling opposition to the government. His position was that of a populist more than a party politician. Direct democracy was his creed, and he staked his political life on exploiting his charisma to the utmost.

Although the two Kims had promised to agree between themselves on a single candidate, neither one was willing to give up his own stake in the race. After Kim Dae Jung's visit to Kwangju on 8 September, they delayed the decision even further and for a month both candidates travelled across the country giving speeches and vying for the people's support. And by the time the new constitution was accepted in a national referendum on 27 October, Kim Dae Jung had decided to form a separate party of his own, marking the failure of efforts to produce a single opposition candidate.

The Presidential Election

The presidential election campaign was officially opened on 16 November 1987. The race was between Roh Tae-woo, Kim Young Sam, Kim Dae Jung, and the New Democratic Republican Party's Kim Jong Pil, who served as prime minister during the Park administration. Given the upsurge of the anti-government movement in the months since April, the prospects for Roh as candidate of the ruling Democratic Justice Party were clouded. In the circumstances, it was reasonable to expect victory to go to the opposition forces.

In spite of the opposition's built-in advantage, however, it was by no means certain that Roh could be defeated. The split between the two Kims was clearly something he could benefit from. Kim Jong Pil's entry into the race was another factor to be considered. It was predicted that whoever got 35 per cent of the votes would win; this was just the share that the ruling party had won in the two previous National Assembly elections.

If Kim Young Sam and Kim Dae Jung both ran, it was likely that they would split the opposition vote in half, making it difficult for either of them to win. But there was the possibility that one would out-poll the other significantly; there was also the chance that Roh would fail to garner 35 per cent of the votes, leaving all three with about 30 per cent each. Finally, the possibility could not be excluded that one of these two Kims would pull out in the middle of the campaign, making possible a dramatic unification of the opposition behind a single candidate.

As of mid-October, the conventional wisdom had been that Roh, with his organisational support, and Kim Dae Jung, with his ability to mobilise the people, were the leading candidates. But the success of Kim Young Sam's 17 October rally in Pusan showed that his power to mobilise popular support was no weaker than Kim Dae Jung's. He was also successful in laying the blame for breaking up the opposition on Kim Dae Jung. And he further consolidated the position of his Reunification Democratic Party as the leading opposition party when Chung Song Hwa, a retired four-star general, became a member at the party convention on 9 November. Thus, by the time the official race began on 16 November, Kim Young Sam had managed to put quite a bit of distance between himself and Kim Dae Jung.

The appearance of Chung Song Hwa at the RDP convention was an even greater shock to Roh than to Kim Dae Jung. On 12 December 1979, Roh, along with Chun Doo Hwan and other junior generals had arrested Chung, who at the time was army chief of staff and martial law commander, in order to seize control of the army. After the convention Kim Young Sam, calling this 1979 incident a 'rebellion within the military', began to attack Roh heavily. The print media played up this story, and unofficial polls showed Kim Young Sam's popularity surging.

This popularity, however, proved short-lived. A 14 November speech by Kim Young Sam in Kwangju was cut short because of rock throwing, and then there was a disturbance at a Kim Dae Jung rally in Taegu two days later. This made voters begin to worry about the violently emotional struggle between Kyongsang and Cholla, the two Kims' home provinces. The massive confusion arising at Roh Tae-woo's two rallies in Cholla, namely, in Kwangju on 29 November and Chonju on 10 December, was considered to have had an especially large effect on the outcome of the election.

For one thing, the outburst of regional emotions clearly worked to Roh's advantage. Seeing the endless violence reported on television, voters began to worry whether things would settle down after the election. This pushed them to become more concerned about stability than the movement for democracy. The bombing of the Korean Air Lines jet on 29 November further accelerated this shift in sentiment.

The anxiety of the voters was certainly not without reason. If Roh Tae-woo were to win by only a slim margin, leaving the three major candidates within a million votes of each other, the two Kims could persuasively claim that the election had been rigged and throw the political situation into turmoil. The dispute could be expected to grow increasingly bitter in the period leading up to the spring 1988 National Assembly elections, and student and labour unrest would be likely to ensue.

Another point was that the violence in Cholla ended up hurting Kim Dae Jung's prospects. This display of the Cholla people's hostility toward the military regime and their sense of rivalry with Kim Young Sam's

Kyongsang Province served to drive voters in other districts away from Kim Dae Jung In fact, as the election returns showed, though Kim Dae Jung monopolised the vote in Cholla and among former Cholla residents in the big cities, he was unable to broaden his support beyond this regional base. This was the greatest reason for Kim Dae Jung's defeat.

Interestingly, Roh was not just strong in rural areas but also did better than expected in urban districts as well. Returns showed that in Pusan, Taegu, Inchon, Kyonggi, urbanised areas, Roh won a higher percentage of the vote than the Democratic Justice Party had received in the 1985 National Assembly elections, suggesting that some of the urban voters who had voted for the opposition in the National Assembly elections turned to Roh in this one. In other words, Roh succeeded in partially regaining the support of the urban middle class.

In the end, Roh's 29 June declaration brought about much more than just an election. It triggered the breakup of an opposition that lacked cohesiveness and led to an outpouring of regional emotion. In the midst of such a state of affairs, voters became strongly inclined to choose the candidate who promised stability. The final outcome of this first direct presidential election in sixteen years was a replay of the pattern of the Park Chung Hee era, when the closely-knit minority in power was able to defeat the divided opposition majority.

After the Election

In the period since Roh's victory in the election, South Korea has been moving rapidly toward political stability. The movement of support toward Roh Tae-woo in the latter half of the campaign period, which reflected the public's yearning for stability, continued even after the election and Roh's inauguration as president on 25 February. The people of South Korea handed down a carefully deliberated verdict in their first direct presidential election in sixteen years, and they were hardly about to overturn this decision in the National Assembly elections of April 1988 and wreak political havoc all over again.

Of course the resentment felt in Kwangju, where over 90 per cent of the vote went to Kim Dae Jung, will not easily die out. And anti-government demonstrations by radical students will probably continue. But it seems unlikely that those raising objections to the outcome of the presidential election will win general public support. If this prognosis is correct, then we can assume that South Korea is at least for the present heading toward political stability.

The real pinch now is that felt by the opposition parties. The position of Kim Dae Jung, who came in third, is especially grave. Seeing the 'Kim

Chart 1.1   Presidential Election Results by Region, December 1987 (share of valid votes cast, %)

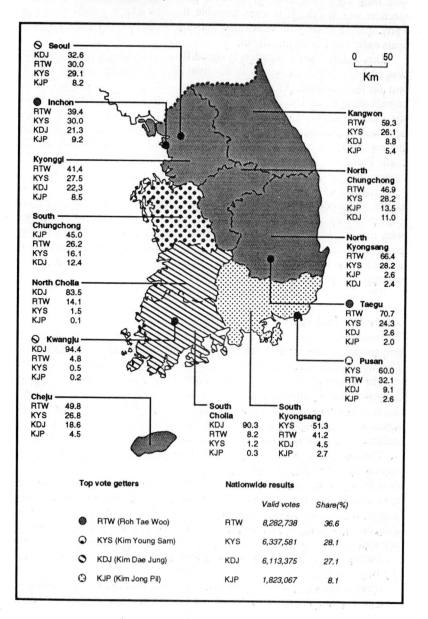

Seoul
KDJ	32.6
RTW	30.0
KYS	29.1
KJP	8.2

Inchon
RTW	39.4
KYS	30.0
KDJ	21.3
KJP	9.2

Kyonggi
RTW	41.4
KYS	27.5
KDJ	22.3
KJP	8.5

South Chungchong
KJP	45.0
RTW	26.2
KYS	16.1
KDJ	12.4

North Cholla
KDJ	83.5
RTW	14.1
KYS	1.5
KJP	0.1

Kwangju
KDJ	94.4
RTW	4.8
KYS	0.5
KJP	0.2

Cheju
RTW	49.8
KYS	26.8
KDJ	18.6
KJP	4.5

Kangwon
RTW	59.3
KYS	26.1
KDJ	8.8
KJP	5.4

North Chungchong
RTW	46.9
KYS	28.2
KJP	13.5
KDJ	11.0

North Kyongsang
RTW	66.4
KYS	28.2
KJP	2.6
KDJ	2.4

Taegu
RTW	70.7
KYS	24.3
KDJ	2.6
KJP	2.0

Pusan
KYS	60.0
RTW	32.1
KDJ	9.1
KJP	2.6

South Cholla
KDJ	90.3
RTW	8.2
KYS	1.2
KJP	0.3

South Kyongsang
KYS	51.3
RTW	41.2
KDJ	4.5
KJP	2.7

0   50
Km

Top vote getters

- RTW (Roh Tae Woo)
- KYS (Kim Young Sam)
- KDJ (Kim Dae Jung)
- KJP (Kim Jong Pil)

Nationwide results

	Valid votes	Share(%)
RTW	8,282,738	36.6
KYS	6,337,581	28.1
KDJ	6,113,375	27.1
KJP	1,823,067	8.1

Dae Jung myth' crumble, all he could find to do was complain that the election was unfair. It is even possible that the Peace and Democracy Party that he leads will deteriorate into a local party unable to win any seats except in Cholla and Seoul.

Kim Young Sam's situation is also difficult. During the campaign, he was perhaps overly conscious of his rival, Kim Dae Jung, and may have lost on this account. As he reflects on this, he will probably attempt to remain aloof from Kim Dae Jung and reaffirm his position as a middle-of-the-road politician. It is unlikely that he will be as uncompromising in his approach to dealing with the Roh administration as his rival. His goal for the present is probably to ensure the survival of his Reunification Democratic Party and, through a regrouping of the opposition, bring a two-party system into being.

Criticism of the two Kims' failure to decide between themselves on a single candidate is spreading, and we can expect demands for a new generation of leaders. But a change of leadership will be difficult. No matter who may be blamed for the presidential election defeat, the opposition parties can hardly campaign without using the renown of Kim Dae Jung and Kim Young Sam. Furthermore, neither the RDP nor the PDP have younger leaders capable of replacing the two Kims.

The blow dealt to the opposition in being defeated was considerably greater than generally thought; in fact, questions have been raised about whether the road to political power has been cut off to them completely. The most urgent issue for the opposition parties now is to emerge as modern, solidly organised political groups that represent the people's interests. This will be no easy task for them.

The likelihood that Roh's new administration will return to authoritarianism is low. First of all, objective conditions do not allow it to. The reaction to Chun's address last April showed the strength of the public's hopes for liberalisation, and there can be no backtracking. Roh Tae-woo, author of the 29 June declaration understands this very well.

The support given to Roh in the last election was by no means unreserved. The majority of those who voted for Roh were merely expressing their tentative approval of his promise of reform with stability and of his openness to dialogue. As long as Roh continues to act according to the wishes of the public, he will earn their support, but any deviation from that course back to authoritarianism would be considered an act of betrayal.

Furthermore, Roh's message of 'patience and self-control' is probably the best way of dealing with the opposition as well, and he will also want to avoid a relapse into authoritarianism in order to strengthen the political base of the ruling party. Roh, by calling out to opposition leaders to hold a conference for 'democratic reconciliation', has already set up the DJP in a favourable position. As long as he continues to show a conciliatory attitude and a willingness to arrive at solutions through discussion, he should be able to hold on to his lead.

The position of the Roh administration resembles that of Japan's Prime Minister Hayato Ikeda after the violent clashes over the renewal of the Japan–US security treaty in 1960. If Roh maintains his accommodating posture and keeps his promise of democratisation, the opposition will be unable to function just on the plank of resisting authoritarianism. This is why, in order to avoid falling apart, the opposition will have to reform itself into a modern political organisation or organisations.

Roh's slogans about doubling the income of rural villagers and raising the average national income to $5,000 also call to mind the Ikeda administration and its 'income-doubling' plan. These targets give hope to a people devastated by political turmoil. Achieving these goals is just what is needed to win the solid support of the urban middle class for the DJP. The new administration is not without its problems, however. In particular, the anti-government feelings that erupted among residents of Kwangju and Cholla during the campaign have roots that go deep. And some radical students continue to oppose the government on the basis of ideologies like dependency theory, liberation theology, and Marxism. The government will be hard pressed to quell this deep-seated resentment and opposition, and problems will no doubt continue to surface from time to time.

On the economic front, meanwhile, the trillion won in campaign funds spent on the presidential election will most likely cause a rise in the rate of inflation, which is already uncomfortably high. Higher prices, along with a possible rise in the value of the won against the dollar, will cause South Korean exporters to lose some of their competitive edge and will hinder progress in carrying out Roh's campaign promise of improvements in the welfare system.

The possibility of renewed labour disputes is another worry. Before he was elected Roh promised to ensure workers' basic rights, and so his administration cannot resort to force in order to suppress demands for wage increases. Doing so would only encourage the politicalisation of the labour movement. The problem is that large wage hikes will hurt the competitive position of Korean manufacturers in international trade and put a brake on the country's export-dependent economic growth. This may also trigger serious joblessness in the affected industries.

What is encouraging for the new administration, however, is that Japan and the United States, and even socialist countries like China and the Soviet Union, have reacted favourably to Roh's victory and consequently decided to participate in the Olympics. Progress is also being made in agreements between South Korea and socialist countries like Hungary, Poland, and Yugoslavia to set up private trade offices. After the Olympics, these trade ties may spread to encompass China and the Soviet Union.

The greatest problem with Roh's Olympic diplomacy was that it assumed the improvement of relations with North Korea could wait until after the games were over. The bombing of the Korean Air Lines jet made better ties impossible for the time being. But the dimmer the prospects for a North–South thaw, the more serious the danger that Pyongyang would view the Seoul Olympics as a form of provocation from the South. How to handle this extremely touchy area is the most serious issue confronting the president.

2 From Authoritarianism to Democracy in South Korea

JAMES COTTON

The emergence of citizen political participation within recognised and generally agreed parameters may be taken as the best indicator of the movement from an authoritarian to a more democratic if not fully democratised form of government. Although the fundamentals of the political system are still in a state of flux, the government of the Republic of Korea (South Korea) after decades of quasi-military rule is now popularly constituted and opportunities are unfolding for citizen political activity and dissent which are unprecedented in the nation's history. Given the contemporary economic and social resurgence of East Asia and the durability in that region of elements of Confucian political culture, this is a development of great theoretical and comparative interest. In this chapter the conditions which have made this transformation possible will be reviewed from the comparative and historical viewpoints. This will be followed by an analysis of events since 1985, and a prognosis for the new Korean democracy.

The Path From Authoritarianism

As Huntington and Nelson have pointed out the process of development requires the balancing within the political system of goals and characteristics—socio-economic development, stability, equality, and participation—which can and have easily come into conflict.[1] Development

---

[1]   Samuel P. Huntington and Joan M. Nelson, *No Easy Choice. Political Participation in Developing Countries* (Cambridge, Mass.: Harvard University Press, 1976), pp. 17–41.

without a degree of equality and participation can generate pressures which may undermine stability, thus vitiating the whole process. Alternatively, strategies aimed at producing equality and participation may threaten socio-economic development.[2] Of all these goals or features, it can be maintained that political participation which is not of the strictly mobilised kind is the least predictable in terms of its effects on rulers and ruled alike.

Huntington and Nelson suggest that political participation may be advocated or may develop as

a. a primary goal of the political elites, social forces, and individuals...;

b. a means by which elites, groups, and individuals achieve other goals that they value...; or

c. a by-product or consequence of the achievement of other goals...[3].

If these alternatives are a correct and complete account, how are the sources of the growth in political participation in South Korea to be assessed?

Until recently South Korea did not seem an exception to the rule that élites in authoritarian systems do not value political participation as a goal in itself. Quite apart from the fact that this would likely have undermined their power, the Confucian elements present in the political culture compelled the élites to adopt a moralistic and severely hierarchical view of their role. Such a conception tends to preclude extensive participation by the ordinary citizen though of course it is not inconsistent with a degree of orchestrated popular involvement.[4] The international predicament of the political system has also impeded the growth of participation. However, the evolution of Korean labour organisations since 1987 may mark the emergence of independent social groups.[5]

There is a further element to the perspectives and purposes of the South Korean élites. Aside from the fact that they share national and international aspirations to be perceived as modernising and rational political actors, they are aware that their political system confronts a dilemma which is a product of its origins. However much its practice has varied,

---

2   This is the conclusion of Harry Oshima's comparative analysis of Sri Lanka's development strategy: Harry T. Oshima, *Economic Growth in Monsoon Asia. A Comparative Survey* (Tokyo: University of Tokyo Press, 1987), pp. 235–62.

3   Huntington and Nelson, *No Easy Choice*, p. 40, cf. pp. 159–71.

4   Lucian W. Pye, *Asian Power and Politics. The Cultural Dimensions of Authority* (Cambridge, Mass.: Harvard University Press, 1985), pp. 215–36.

5   Asia Monitor Resource Centre, *Min-ju No-jo. South Korea's New Trade Unions* (Hong Kong: Asia Monitor Resource Centre, 1988).

the Republic of Korea since its inception has been ruled under a constitutional order more or less modelled upon that of the United States and in which explicit statements of citizen sovereignty have been incorporated. When Roh Tae-woo, then the ruling Democratic Justice Party's candidate for the presidency, made it clear in 1987 that he wished to move Korea out of the authoritarian military based politics of the past, he was forced to embrace some further elements of popular participation. To the extent to which he was sincere in his declaration, he therefore was forced to accept and promote new forms of participation beyond those political and parapolitical means that have been long used to mobilise mass opinion. There is no doubt that some at least of the various groups that constitute the opposition have also committed themselves to the goal of a greater role for the ordinary citizen as a good in itself and as an indicator of modernisation and political progress.

Political participation as a goal in itself is a rather rarefied notion, connected with questions of legitimacy and ultimate political values. It is much more likely to be embraced when circumstances are propitious or compelling as a means to some more concrete goals, and here it can be seen that most social and political élites and forces have accepted it, though with varying degrees of enthusiasm, as a way of achieving (often conflicting) objectives. For the ruling élites it is evidently seen as a strategy for bolstering their rule in new times. For opposition élites it provides at a minimum an avenue to displace the existing rulers, and perhaps a way also to incorporate previously dispossessed or denied groups by according them a positive role in the state. Other interests, notably labour and the farming lobby, are beginning to employ participatory (or confrontational) strategies in order to have addressed their particular needs and demands.

Finally, demands for political participation may be seen to flow from the process of socio-economic modernisation itself. This is a generally acknowledged consequence of development[6], and the degree to which South Korea has been transformed in the last four decades suggests that such demands will be manifest however much the prevailing political culture causes them to take on unique and perhaps muted forms.

In the case of Korea this topic has been far from thoroughly researched. However, one study maintains that the variable found to give the highest correlation with the possession of democratic values is education[7],

---

6   Samuel P. Huntington, 'Social and Institutional Dynamics of One-Party Systems', Samuel P. Huntington and Clement H. Moore (eds), *Authoritarian Politics in Modern Society. The Dynamics of Established One-Party Systems* (New York: Basic Books, 1970), pp. 18–19.

7   Lee Nam Young, 'The Democratic Belief System: A Study of the Political Culture in South Korea', *Korean Social Science Journal*, vol. 12 (1985), pp. 66–8.

a fact which suggests that the expansion of education which accompanied (and even anticipated) modernisation has led to an increased desire for political participation. There is also preliminary evidence in surveys by the Korean press which shows that those groups most likely to vote for the Democratic Justice Party are older people and those with rural occupations. This implies that to some extent the DJP represents the politics of the past.

The most comprehensive survey of this question, by Kim and Choe, finds that rates of political participation, as measured by voter turnout, are higher in rural than in urban areas, though the evidence they consider offers no conclusive reason as to why this is so. The authors prefer the 'decline of community' hypothesis put forward by Verba, Dahl and others, though it is equally possible that high rural turnout rates are a result of a combination of traditional deference towards the state and mobilised voting.[8] On the related phenomenon of 'cities for the opposition, villages for the government party', a pattern which they see manifest as far back as 1963, Kim and Choe regard developments associated with urbanisation and industrialisation as crucial to any explanation. The growth of cities itself appears to foster dissent, either through the opportunities afforded by personal proximity or communications, or because the cities house those most adversely affected by government orchestrated programmes for rapid growth. And the cities are more likely to contain the better educated who, survey evidence shows, are more inclined to vote for the opposition than the governing party.

In the context of the findings of the theory of political development, Huntington[9] has maintained that South Korea is to a degree anomalous in that it has the economic foundations, both the wealth and its distribution, which in other parts of the world have produced democratic political systems. Market relations, another apparent precondition for democracy, have also had a profound impact on the social structure. However the cultural obstacles to a movement towards democracy are considerable, particularly as this is manifest in the political values of the ruling élites.[10] Huntington

8   Hong Nack Kim and Sunki Choe, 'Urbanization and Changing Voting Patterns in South Korean Parliamentary Elections', *Journal of Northeast Asian Studies*, vol. 6, no. 3 (1987), pp. 31–50; Sidney Verba, Norman H. Nie & Jae-On Kim, *Participation and Political Equality. A Seven Nation Comparison* (Cambridge: Cambridge University Press, 1978), pp. 269–85; Robert A. Dahl and Edward R. Tufte, *Size and Democracy* (Stanford: Stanford University Press, 1973), p. 43.

9   Samuel P. Huntington, 'Will More Countries Become Democratic?', *Political Science Quarterly*, vol. 99 (1984), pp. 193–218.

10   On this point see the remarks on East Asia in: Myron Weiner, 'Political Change: Asia, Africa, and the Middle East' in, Myron Weiner and Samuel P.

recognises, however, that one of the two alternative routes to democratisation proceeds from the realisation by the élites in an authoritarian polity that 'that system which they have led and presumably benefited from no longer meets their needs or those of their society'.[11] This observation seems to accord with the experience of South Korea, though it perhaps understates the failure of existing corporate and other controls to stem the crisis of legitimacy which fed upon popular dissent and forced the political élite to accept the need for a modification of the political structure.

This approach to the preconditions and nature of change in such a previously non-democratic system raises in turn the question of how it is to be characterised in theoretical terms. What kind of system has the initial capacity to incorporate both a consistent policy emphasis upon rapid social and economic transformation and apparent élite autonomy, but has now reached a period of political transition?

To an extent Perlmutter's notions of the 'new corporatism' and 'praetorian corporatism' might be thought applicable to the past if not to the future of the South Korean political system.[12] In systems of this type 'authority remains patrimonial-clientalistic; the organisation, however, is modern, bureaucratic, and even technocratic'. Perlmutter, however, is of the opinion that such authoritarian systems are incapable of accommodating the emergence of pluralities of opinion or of overseeing reforms which would dilute their authoritarian fundamentals.[13] And the adoption of such an approach could well obscure the tension that exists in these cases— described by Perlmutter as 'true developmental regimes'—between these two characteristics.[14]

Although there have been some attempts to develop parallels between the authoritarian character of systems of this type and the 'bureaucratic' authoritarianisms of Latin American experience, these efforts are now regarded as of limited theoretical value particularly in the light of the

---

Huntington (eds), *Understanding Political Development* (Boston: Little, Brown, 1987), p. 45.

[11] Huntington, 'Will More Countries Become Democratic?', p. 213.

[12] Amos Perlmutter, *Modern Authoritarianism* (New Haven: Yale University Press, 1981), pp. 122–35.

[13] Perlmutter, *Modern Authoritarianism*, pp. 122, 169–70.

[14] In one of his few concrete references to Korea, Perlmutter describes it as 'state capitalist' (p. 156) a less appropriate label than a 'true developmental regime' (p. 159). It should be recalled that Perlmutter is writing largely with Central Europe and Latin America in mind. For a defence of the view that patrimonialism can be rendered consistent with modernisation (but not 'development') see Norman Jacobs, *The Korean Road to Modernization and Development* (Urbana: University of Illinois Press, 1985).

democratic evolution seen in recent times in the Latin American southern cone.[15] However, such comparisons have highlighted the importance of that confluence of historical conditions which has made the emergence of contemporary South Korea possible. According to the approach adopted by Hagen Koo, South Korea took on its present form through the interplay of three factors, the condition of the world system, the configuration of indigenous social classes and forces, and the programme and backing of the emergent state. While this approach is perhaps too schematic, with the addition of a greater emphasis upon the institutional autonomy and political strategy of the state (as exemplified in the argument presented by Frederic Deyo), and allowing for the indisputable role of cultural variables, it provides a useful starting point.[16]

Owing its creation ultimately to United States' geo-political interests, South Korea evolved from the first into a bureaucratic entity unchallenged by old domestic classes or strata as a result of comprehensive land reform policies, the impact of the Korean war, and the exigencies of survival. While continuing confrontation with its communist sibling and legitimacy problems required it to maintain strong military forces, the lack of other institutions allowed the military to assume a direct political role. The Park regime having chosen (at least partly for cultural reasons) the path of rapid transformation, the combined influence of indigenous and historical factors (including the heritage of Japanese rule as well as the need to satisfy the United States as the source of external assistance) led to the creation of a bureaucratic state with extensive powers. An ever more technocratic bureaucracy, its tasks facilitated by further elements of Confucian political culture, evolved to transform the social and economic character of South Korea under the stimulus of external threats and the opportunities afforded by free access to the Pacific economy. The 'strong' and 'hard' character of

---

15 On the question of the parallel between East Asian and Latin American newly-industrialised countries (NICs), see Thomas B. Gold, *State and Society in the Taiwan Miracle* (Armonk: M.E. Sharpe, 1986), pp. 3–20; Peter Evans, 'Class, State, and Dependence in East Asia: Lessons for Latin Americanists', in Frederic C. Deyo (ed.), *The Political Economy of the New Asian Industrialism* (Ithaca: Cornell University Press, 1987), pp. 203–26; Stephen Haggard, 'The Newly Industrializing Countries in the International System', *World Politics*, vol. 38 (1985–86), pp. 343–70; Daniel H. Levine, 'Paradigm Lost: Dependence to Democracy', *World Politics*, vol. 40 (1988), pp. 377–96; Richard E. Barrett and Martin King Whyte, 'Dependency Theory and Taiwan: Analysis of a Deviant Case', *American Journal of Sociology*, vol. 87 (1982), pp. 1064–89.

16 Hagen Koo, 'The Interplay of State, Social Class, and World System in East Asian Development: The Cases of South Korea and Taiwan', and Deyo, 'Coalitions, Institutions, and Linkage Sequencing—Towards a Strategic Capacity Model of East Asian Development', in Frederic C. Deyo (ed.), *The Political Economy of the New Asian Industrialism*, pp. 165–81, 227–48.

this bureaucracy permitted it at once to maintain sufficient local autonomy to assert national over external interests and to inhibit, through a strategy of 'political exclusion', most non-state actors from a role in the formation of national policy.

For almost three decades this situation prevailed, but now all three of Koo's factors appear to point towards a different trajectory. Trade imbalances and technological maturity as well as the opening of the Northeast Asian communist systems to reform now prescribe a new world role for South Korea, and indeed the East Asian NICs as a group. Meanwhile the rigours of state policy have produced both an increasingly independent capitalist stratum as well as a new and ever growing middle class of educated urban dwellers, with attitudes sometimes at variance with their Confucian heritage. Political exclusion, while possible and perhaps even appropriate in a condition of labour abundance, is less and less sustainable, practically as well as ethically, once this condition is superseded.[17] While confrontation with communism remains, the strength of the economy has led to the eclipse of military preparedness as the most important aspect of national policy. A complete explanation of the democratising trends manifest in South Korea would need to take account of other circumstances and contingencies, but this undoubtedly comprises the background to recent events.

Participation Without Democracy

A multiplicity of cultural and historical influences have conspired to frustrate the emergence of a democratic political system in South Korea.[18] Although differences exist regarding the precise weighting to be given to these influences, it is not in dispute that the long history of patrimonial-bureaucratic government, and the subsequent experience of colonial rule under Japan (1910–1945), were a poor preparation for the emergence of an autonomous national and modernising political consciousness. The division of the peninsula, brought into being by the Cold War and deep-

---

[17] Hyug Baeg Im, 'The Rise of Bureaucratic Authoritarianism in South Korea', *World Politics*, vol. 39 (1987), pp. 231–57; Hyun-Chin Lim, *Dependent Development in Korea 1963–1979* (Seoul: Seoul National University Press, 1985); Dal-Joong Chang, *Economic Control and Political Authoritarianism. The Role of Japanese Corporations in Korean Politics 1965–1979* (Seoul: Sogang University Press, 1985).

[18] Gregory Henderson, *Korea: The Politics of the Vortex* (Cambridge, Mass.: Harvard University Press, 1968) *passim*; Young Whan Kihl, *Politics and Policies in Divided Korea: Regimes in Contest* (Boulder, Col.: Westview, 1984), chs. 2, 5; Norman Jacobs, *The Korean Road to Modernization and Development* (1985), chs. 2, 3.

ened by the fratricidal conflict of the Korean War, polarised political attitudes and led to the emergence of powerful military and security establishments. After 1961 under the regime of Park Chung Hee these establishments became primary political actors whose bureaucratic administrative style and economic policy priorities did nothing to encourage notions of citizen consultation or participation. The change of regime in 1980, with the coming to power of another former general, Chun Doo-hwan, did little to change this pattern.

However, institutions and organisations have not been lacking in recent years for civilian political activity. Under the successive constitutions of the six Korean republics since 1948 there have been a hundred or more political parties.[19] For the most part they have not had a profound political impact, due to the fact that many of them have been transient entities brought into being as the organisational expression of personal followings. Where they have been more substantial movements they have been hampered by their limited constitutional role and by the lack of institutionalisation in the political system. This latter factor is reflected in the frequency with which there have been major constitutional revisions in South Korea; the six republics have been governed under nine distinct constitutional orders, the most recent approved by national referendum in October 1987.[20]

Unfair and corrupt practices have often distorted such electoral competition as has been permitted. In the era of President Rhee (1948–1960) and again in the later years of President Park certain opposition politicians were banned from political activity, and voting returns were sometimes inflated so as to ensure majorities for the ruling party. Government interference in the media, and latterly control over television broadcasting, have led to distorted reporting of opposition election campaigns. The superior resources of the government have also been used for the direct as well as indirect purchase of voting support. Indeed, it has been government policy to place impediments in the way of citizen support and funding for opposition parties, thus not only leaving them short of money but thereby encouraging them to remain personal followings of prominent

---

19 Sung M. Pae, *Testing Democratic Theories in Korea* (Lanham, Md.: University Press of America, 1986), p. 155.

20 Pae, *Testing Democratic Theories in Korea*, ch. 7; Han Sung-joo, 'Political Institutionalization in South Korea, 1961–1984', in Robert A. Scalapino and Jusuf Wanandi (eds), *Asian Political Institutionalization* (Berkeley: University of California, Institute of East Asian Studies, 1986), pp. 116–37; Ahn Byung-joon, 'Political Changes and Institutionalization in South Korea', *Korean Social Science Journal*, vol. 10 (1983), pp. 41–65.

figures.[21] This latter tactic has also served to radicalise groups which might otherwise have evolved a role as interest or pressure groups working through parliamentary institutions.

Such obstacles and discouragements have not prevented Korean voters from engaging in political participation to a surprising degree. This has not, moreover, been simply mobilised participation, since candidates and parties avowedly critical of authoritarian politics and ostensibly standing for policies of democratisation have secured large followings. Thus in the presidential elections during the Park era (1963, 1967, and 1971) the opposition candidates (in 1971, Kim Dae-jung) received between 41 per cent and 45 per cent of the valid votes cast.[22] More recently elections to the National Assembly have shown strong followings for the opposition. Thus in 1978, despite the fact that under the Yushin constitution of 1972 the government of Park Chung Hee was guaranteed an almost permanent majority through the president's power to appoint additional members, the New Democratic Party (led by Kim Young-sam) received a plurality of the popular vote (34.7 per cent, against 30.9 per cent for the governing Democratic Republican Party). Again in 1985 the New Korea Democratic Party (NKDP), though newly formed and competing in an electoral contest marked by many of the old abuses, received 29.2 per cent of the popular vote against the ruling Democratic Justice Party's 35.3 per cent.[23]

Government Response to the Crisis of Legitimacy

The elections of 1985 marked the return of a genuine opposition to Korean politics. From that time the strategy of the NKDP in South Korea, formally led by Party President Lee Min-woo but in substance an alliance of the personal retainers of the two Kims, was to make the legitimacy question the only political issue. In pursuit of this strategy the party was helped by the activities of a congeries of radical student and Christian groups. It was clear to the opposition that the longer the political system of the Fifth Republic was permitted to exist the more likely it would be that the Democratic Justice Party (DJP) would provide a successor to Chun in 1988. To prevent such an eventuality the opposition launched a petition

---

21   Gregory Henderson, 'The Politics of Korea', in John Sullivan and Roberta Foss (eds), *Two Koreas—One Future?* (Lanham, Md.: University Press of America, 1987), pp. 109–10.

22   Joungwon A. Kim, *Divided Korea: The Politics of Development 1945–1972* (Cambridge, Mass.: Harvard University Press, 1976), ch. 7.

23   Chong-sik Lee, 'South Korea 1979: Confrontation, Assassination, and Transition', *Asian Survey*, vol. 20 (1980), p. 67; B.C. Koh, 'The 1985 Parliamentary Election in South Korea', *Asian Survey*, vol. 25 (1985), pp. 888–9.

campaign in February 1986 to push for the immediate introduction of a new constitution incorporating provision for direct elections to the presidency.[24] The government's initial response was hostile, but the evident popularity of this proposal and the example of the demise of the Marcos administration in the Philippines led Chun to drop his original insistence that the transfer of power would proceed in 1988 under the (manifestly non-democratic) rules established at the outset of his administration. At this time a series of violent rallies (most notable that at Inchon on 3 May) revealed not only the extent of support for the NKDP, but the growing radicalism and anti-Americanism of some opposition groups. Chun perhaps felt it wiser to deal with the political machine of the two Kims than hazard a later confrontation with even more dangerous opponents.

Following a period of intensive political wrangling the question of constitutional revision was turned over to a special committee of the National Assembly constituted for the purpose. Little progress was made in this forum, however, as the major participants differed from the first on the fundamentals of the new constitution. Nor were Chun or DJP Chairman Roh Tae-woo prepared to resolve the issue, as the opposition suggested, by putting the question to a national referendum. Government opinion and tactics hardened with the boycott by the NKDP on 30 September 1986 of these deliberations in the National Assembly. Chun was evidently signalling his intention to accept democratisation only on terms chosen by and advantageous to the regime. The president was also hoping that a tough stance would weaken the internal unity of the opposition.

As a result of government implacability, tensions within the NKDP caused the emergence in public of differences of opinion within the leadership. The response of Kim Dae-jung and Kim Young-sam was to adhere rigidly to their original insistence that a democratised constitution could only incorporate a directly elected presidency. Consistent with the fundamentals of the political culture they regarded compromise as symptomatic both of weakness and of lack of moral rectitude. Amidst opposition

---

24 On the campaign for constitutional revision see, James Palais et al., *Human Rights in the Republic of Korea* (New York: Asia Watch, 1986); C.I. Eugene Kim, 'South Korea in 1986: Preparing for a Power Transition', *Asian Survey*, vol. 27 (1987), pp. 64–74; Tim Shorrock, 'The struggle for democracy in South Korea in the 1980s and the rise of anti-Americanism', *Third World Quarterly*, vol. 8 (1986), pp. 1195–218; Selig S. Harrison, 'Dateline South Korea: A Divided Seoul', *Foreign Policy* (Summer 1987), pp. 154–75. I have also drawn in this account on the excellent coverage of events since 1985 in Korea by Shim Jae Hoon, John McBeth, Adrian Buzo and Mark Clifford published in the *Far Eastern Economic Review*, and additional reportage in *Korea Herald* and *Korea Newsreview*.

rancour they withdrew their followers from the NKDP in March 1987 to form a new grouping, the Reunification Democratic Party (RDP).

It is clear that Chun regarded this event as a vindication of his strategy. Rather than move forward with his own plans for democratisation he adduced the disarray of the opposition as the pretext for a return to his former policy of arranging a political transition under the ground rules of the Fifth Republic. This revealed perhaps his own priorities, but did not restore his authority. Rather it provoked an unprecedented coalition which took on increased solidity when the DJP was induced to accept Roh as the party's nominee for the presidency.

The previous rules of political engagement were broken in May and June of 1987 with the appearance of many new political actors. The political climate now produced the beginnings of an unprecedented struggle in the larger *chaebol* (industrial conglomerates) between labour and management which threatened the government's corporatist labour strategy.[25] Spokesmen for the various religions (including, in a parallel with the Philippines not lost on the government, the Catholic primate Stephen Souhwan Kim) became more vocal in their appeals for the government to return to the path of democratisation. The managerial and professional classes of Seoul also played their part by joining in increasing numbers student led protests which grew in scale and in national and international impact. This last development was perhaps of greater moment than any other. Chun and Roh had clearly hoped that the economic record of the DJP administration would have been sufficient to carry the middle ground of Korean political opinion in any confrontation with dissenters. But authoritarianism was evidently out of favour with an increasing proportion of the normally quiescent citizenry.

Chun's efforts to assuage his critics proved fruitless, and it was left to Roh Tae-woo to announce to the astonished members of a press conference on 29 June that he was now prepared to accept the major demands of the opposition. His eight point democratisation package included measures to release political prisoners, to restore Kim Dae-jung's civil rights, and to remove restrictions on the press, but the greatest concession lay in the promise to conduct free and fair direct presidential elections by the end of the year. It appeared to many commentators that the opposition had won the day, and that only the unlikely step of army intervention would prevent rapid democratisation.

---

25 Choi Jang-jip, 'A Corporatist Control of the Labour Union in South Korea', *Korean Social Science Journal*, vol. 9 (1984), pp. 25–55; Shim-han Young-hee, 'Social Control and Industrialization in Korea—On the Corporatist Control of Labour', *Korean Social Science Journal*, vol. 13 (1986–87), pp. 95–123; Moon Kyu Park, 'Interest Representation in South Korea: The Limits of Corporatist Control', *Asian Survey*, vol. 27 (1987), pp. 903–17

Roh Tae-woo's Decision to Back Democratisation

Roh's shrewdness at this juncture cannot be denied. Although confronted by a deeply divided opposition he could see that time was running out for the old form of authoritarian politics. He must also have weighed carefully opinion in the United States administration (conveyed directly by a series of high level delegations) as well as in Congress which was in favour of a new beginning in Korean politics. To handle the growing tide of civil disorder Roh may have considered the possibility of a further spell of military administration. But there were signs that the military were unhappy with the prospects of taking yet again a direct role in politics, a role that would undoubtedly have led to severe domestic and international censure.

Seoul's role as host for the 1988 Olympics was probably the major consideration in Roh's decision. Continuing civil unrest would have sabotaged the Games, thereby tarnishing the image of the nation and making a mockery of the regime succession. The Olympiad was seen as a source of prestige for Chun and his successor. It was also sought as a means of opening contacts with North Korea's erstwhile communist patrons, and as a message to the international community (reminiscent of that of the 1964 Tokyo Games) that Korea was now a nation to be reckoned with.

By presenting the initiative for democratisation as his own personal contribution to Korean political development Roh hoped also to win some credibility on his own account. At this point he could see that, notwithstanding his many efforts to win a reputation as a personable and approachable individual, Roh needed to break free of his close association with Chun if he was to have any hope of winning the middle ground of popular opinion. He was aware also that there was a considerable body of voters, particularly in the new industrial areas of the southeast as well as in the capital and in the countryside, prepared to vote for the governing party either through fear of the likely chaos of any alternative or because of the government's able handling of such vital issues as South Korea's security and economic development. Nor was he unaware of the availability to him of the advantages of his party's incumbency, many of which could be manipulated even under more liberal rules.

It may be surmised, though conclusive evidence is lacking, that Roh's choice of the democratisation alternative was made ultimately over Chun's protests. At several points in the period prior to the breakthrough Chun's clumsy hand could be detected in plans to thwart dissidents and the opposition. Thus he announced in August 1985 a scheme to defuse student activism by holding protesters for prolonged periods without trial for 'ideological remoulding', and in October 1986 riot police stormed the National Assembly to arrest an opposition member for breaking anti-communist security laws in a speech. When the death by torture of a student in police custody and the subsequent attempts at a cover-up became public knowledge Chun reshuffled his cabinet as an act of contrition in January 1987, but the incoming Interior Minister was none other than former Special Forces General Chung Ho-yong who had been instrumental in the president's initial scramble to power. A further cabinet reshuffle in May may have marked the turning point as it removed not merely Chung and Agency for National Security Planning head Chang Se-dong, Chun's closest ally in the security establishment, but also the competent and relatively blameless Prime Minister Lho Shin-yong who was Roh's chief civilian rival.[26] In clearing the way for Roh, Chun was perhaps signalling his willingness to allow the latter to determine the character and pace of reform.

By passing the initiative to the opposition Roh knew that he would thereby put their fragile unity to the test. Though they were then allied in a newly formed party Roh was aware that there was little prospect of either opposition Kim allowing the other to run alone in a presidential race. Their rivalry extended back at least to 1971 and had taken first place on several previous occasions even at the expense of the furthering of democratisation. Here indeed opposition tactics actually improved Roh's chances. Under any constitutional arrangements other than those which provided for a strong presidential executive, cooperation between Kim Dae-jung and Kim Young-sam might have been possible.

In the event the 1987 presidential elections in South Korea were a major watershed in the evolution of the political system. Neither the presence of electoral abuses nor the superior resources of the DJP could negate the role of the opposition forces. However, regionalism and personal rivalry conspired to deflect the opposition impulse from victory when the Kim Dae-jung and Kim Young-sam factions found it impossible to agree on a single candidate for the office, the former breaking from the RDP to form the Peace and Democracy Party (PPD) for the contest.

With an extraordinarily high turnout of over 89 per cent of the registered voters Roh won a plurality with 35.9 per cent.[27] As expected Kim Jong-pil made little headway, with 7.9 per cent, but the followings of Kim Dae-jung and Kim Young-sam were of similar dimensions, being 26.5 per cent and 27.5 per cent respectively. The provincial distribution of this vote was particularly noteworthy since it demonstrated clearly that regional loyalties were the strongest determinant of voting behaviour in much of the country. Thus Kim Dae-jung received 93.4 per cent of the vote in

---

26 Han Sung-joo, 'South Korea in 1987: The Politics of Democratization', *Asian Survey*, vol. 28 (1988), pp. 52–61; Masao Okonogi, 'South Korea's Experiment in Democracy', *Japan Review of International Affairs*, vol. 2 (1988), pp. 24–41.

27 These figures have been computed from the official election returns in *Korea Herald*, 20 December 1987, p. 2.

Kwangju, Kim Young-sam 55.2 per cent in Pusan, and Roh Tae-woo 69.8 per cent in Taegu. In South Chungchong Kim Jong-pil also managed to secure 43.8 per cent. In the capital which alone accounted for 24.8 per cent of the votes cast the candidates were more evenly matched, undoubtedly because none could claim special ties there. Kim Dae-jung received 32.1 per cent of the vote in Seoul, Roh Tae-woo 29.4 per cent, and Kim Young-sam 28.6 per cent. Although the regional power bases of both of the opposition Kims were insufficient to give them victory, particularly in the light of the apparently wide distribution of Roh's supporters, the opposition would in all probability have triumphed if they had offered a single candidate to the electorate. Whilst acknowledging the long and arduous struggles both Kims have made for the democratisation of Korea, their inability to cooperate in 1987 may well be seen as their most influential contribution to Korean politics.

The Division of the Opposition

The reasons for this momentous fragmentation of the opposition, viewed by many in Korea as nothing short of a national tragedy, must be sought in both historical and personal factors.

From the beginning the NKDP was an alliance of convenience. The chief faction leaders in the party, the two Kims and Lee Chul-seung, had long been rivals. In 1970 at the opposition New Democratic Party convention Lee, contrary to an earlier agreement, instructed his supporters to shift their allegiance from Kim Young-sam to Kim Dae-jung in order for the latter to receive party nomination as the official presidential candidate. A similar factional alliance, this time between Lee and Kim Young-sam, denied Kim Dae-jung the party presidency the following year, despite his impressive showing in the presidential competition against Park.[28] Such manoeuvring exacerbated divisions within the opposition and thereby strengthened Park's hand for the introduction of the authoritarian Yushin constitution of 1972. There was a repetition of these unseemly struggles, this time on the eve of Chun's seizure of power, over the terms on which Kim Dae-jung (his civil rights having been restored by the interim administration) could make common cause with the New Democratic Party, now led by Kim Young-sam. In the event the two Kims could not agree and within three months Chun, now president, was able to sweep aside all opposition. Kim Dae-jung was sentenced to death (a sentence later commuted) after his trial on charges of sedition in connection with the

---

28 Joungwon A. Kim, *Divided Korea: The Politics of Development 1945–1972*, p. 282; Chae-jin Lee, 'South Korea: Political Competition and Government Adaptation', *Asian Survey*, vol. 12 (1972), p. 41.

Kwangju incident, during which paratrooper units brutally crushed a civil rebellion.[29]

Provincial loyalties lie behind the rivalry of the two Kims. The Cholla provinces of the southwest, traditionally the richest agricultural area, were bypassed in the development plans of both Presidents Park and Chun who being natives of the southeast (Kyongsang) favoured their home region. Kim Young-sam also being from the southeast renders it difficult for the Cholla political élites to support him in preference to their own native son. The depth of this inter-regional animosity has been ascribed by some commentators to differences which go back to the regional power bases of contending mediaeval bureaucratic cliques, and perhaps even to the three kingdoms era of Korean history (before 668 AD) when the Paekche state arose in Cholla while Shilla developed in Kyongsang.

Ideological differences are also evident within the opposition ranks. Although Kim Young-sam has been an implacable opponent of authoritarianism he has not been inclined to question the fundamentals of the South Korean state: opposition to communism, export led rapid industrialisation funded by international borrowings, and close relations with the United States. Kim Dae-jung, on the other hand, has from time to time given expression to more radical ideas and has received support from radical groups. His opinions on economic questions, though not well defined, call for a 'mass participatory economy', and in a recent collection of his writings he expressed the view, perceptive given the subsequent presidential election result, that the sole force for progress in Korean history has ever been the popular masses though they have always been betrayed by their leaders.[30] Kim Dae-jung also is the political figure most likely to be invoked by student dissenters and by contributors to the populist *minjung* (masses) cultural and social movement which had its origins in his native Cholla.

If historical, regional, and personal factors have conspired to divide the opposition it must be conceded also that factionalism has long been an essential part of the political culture.[31] Authoritarian rule has reinforced that tendency by obstructing the formation of mass parties and other autonomous social and political agencies, thereby forcing opposition

[29] Chong-sik Lee, 'South Korea in 1980: the Emergence of a New Authoritarian Order', *Asian Survey*, vol. 21 (1981), pp. 123–43.

[30] Kim Dae-jung, *Mass Participatory Economy: A Democratic Alternative For Korea* (Lanham, Md.: University Press of America, 1985); Kim Dae-jung, *Prison Writings* (Berkeley: University of California Press, 1987).

[31] Jacobs, *The Korean Road to Modernization and Development*, pp. 23–8; Pae, *Testing Democratic Theories in Korea*, pp. 27–41; Henderson, *Korea: The Politics of the Vortex, passim*; Han Sung-joo, *The Failure of Democracy in South Korea* (Berkeley: University of California Press, 1974), pp. 75–6.

political activity back onto the resources of personal followings. This observation is supported by the fact that factionalism has also undermined the political machine of the ruling groups on more than one occasion. The various political vehicles created by President Rhee all suffered from rivalry and divisions of this kind, the democratic regime of Chang Myon (1960–61) was paralysed because of them, and one factor in the long reign of President Park was the inability of his Democratic Republican Party to agree to the naming of a successor. Indeed, one of the reasons for the comparative ease with which Chun Doo-hwan achieved power was the fact that the DRP was divided by the contention of Park's lieutenants Kim Jong-pil and Lee Hu-rak, both of whom as a result fell easy victims to Chun's political purge of May 1980. Kim Jong-pil's insistence on pursuing his own political ambitions in 1987 rather than ally with the forces of the establishment can be traced to these events.

The magnitude of the gulf which divides the opposition can be seen in the manoeuvres which led up to the National Assembly elections of April 1988. The new constitution held out the prospect that Roh's administration could be held in check by a united body of opposition assemblymen. Having failed to form a combined leadership or even a joint slate of candidates, the PPD and the RDP were then incapable even of agreeing on a joint approach to electoral reform, with the result that all the circumstances favoured the DJP. Thus the elections largely reproduced the results of the previous year. The Democratic Justice Party secured a purality of the seats (87, plus 38 on a proportional representation basis, to give 125 of a total of 299 seats) and votes (33.96 per cent), though it failed to achieve an overall majority. The Reunification Democratic Party received a higher proportion of the vote (28.83 per cent) than the Peace and Democracy Party (19.26 per cent) though with the electoral system favouring the geographically more concentrated following of the latter, the PPD secured a larger number of seats (70 to 59). Kim Jong-pil's New Democratic Republican Party (largely composed of remnants of the Park regime) also demonstrated a good following (with 15.59 per cent of the popular vote).[32]

Dilemmas of Democracy

Following the National Assembly elections, there was a sharp acceleration in the pace of political change. Indeed, the changes have been such that some commentators have been inclined to see in them a new beginning in Korean politics. Thus, in May 1988 the Chief Justice, Kim Yong-chul, stepped down after a petition calling for his removal received the support

---

[32] *Korea Herald*, 28 April 1988, p. 1; *Korea Newsreview*, 30 April 1988, p. 6.

of a large number of members of the judiciary. Kim's greatest demerit was undoubtedly his participation in the trial of Kim Dae-jung in connection with the Kwangju incident, but his removal was a sign that there would need to be a searching appraisal of personnel inherited from the Chun administration. In August, the chief of the Army Intelligence Command was dismissed, and two brigadier-generals under his command arrested, after it became known that personnel from that unit were responsible for an assault on a journalist who had published a critical account of the armed forces. In the following month Chun's younger brother, Chun Kyung-hwan, was sentenced to a seven-year term of imprisonment for embezzlement and corruption. Other family members, in-laws, and associates have also been paraded through the courts. Meanwhile Chun Doo-hwan himself, forced to face many allegations of malfeasance, including charges involving the funding of his Ilhae Foundation and in connection with influence buying in former government circles by the Northrop Corporation, finally offered a public apology for his errors and returned his wealth to the state.

Despite the new political atmosphere, it must be emphasised nevertheless that for progress towards democratisation to continue an extremely divergent set of interests must be satisfied within a relatively stable set of political and constitutional rules.[33]

President Roh, although now disposed of a strong executive machine and serving for a single five year presidential term, must maintain the general support of a body of interests including members of the senior military and security establishments, the bureaucracy, and inhabitants of his regional base and rural areas. He must also remain sensitive to the aspirations of the growing middle class while continuing at the helm of an administration devoted to managing rapid development. The opposition, for their part, while in competition for middle class support need also to serve their regional bases while fostering links with the newly independent labour sector.

The pace of democratisation, the character of regional development, the nature and extent of social disparities of wealth, not to mention such external issues as relations with the United States and North Korea will all provide Roh with the familiar democratic difficulty of pleasing both opposition and supporters. In a political culture where compromise is too often regarded as a sign of weakness or moral uncertainty this will be no easy task. But it is the past rather than the future which threatens to arrest the emergence of more democratic institutions and attitudes.

---

33 See further, Han Sung-joo, 'Political Institutionalization in South Korea, 1961–1984', in Robert A Scalapino and Jusuf Wanandi (eds), *Asian Political Institutionalization*, pp. 116–37.

Roh's association with Chun and the Chun era could not be closer. A boyhood friend, he was a key figure in the coup within the military in December 1979 which cleared the way for Chun's rise to power, and he was a senior military commander when the army carried out the bloody suppression of the Kwangju insurrection in May the following year. He then held important state and party posts, and was Chun's hand-picked successor, prevailing over some within the DJP who could see the desirability of a candidate with a civilian background. Yet for democratisation to proceed with public credibility Roh must permit some retrospective judgement of the acts of his predecessor. Indeed he has been forced to take such steps as a response to the constituting by the National Assembly of seven panels (the members of which are empowered to call witnesses or request any evidences deemed pertinent) to investigate specific aspects of the Chun administration including cases of corruption and the Kwangju incident.

So far, Roh has done little to impede investigations concerning Chun's closest associates and family members. It has even been reported that Chun's apology was scripted by Roh who reneged on an earlier promise to protect members of Chun's circle. He has also moved to replace some of those personnel still in the service of the state but tainted by former practices. But there are some past acts of the Korean state regarding which compromise will be extremely elusive. There are many well documented allegations of torture and victimisation, and of unexplained deaths while in security or military custody, which occurred during the fifth republic. Victims and relatives now seek redress and the punishment of those responsible. Some recent cases have demonstrated how quickly responsibility for such acts can be pursued to the senior ranks. This prospect has undoubtedly given rise to considerable unease amongst senior members of the armed and security forces. It must also be borne in mind that blameless members of these forces are aware that vigorous and undiscriminating National Assembly investigations of their activities may produce a security paralysis which, in the circumstances of continuing confrontation with North Korea, could invite hostile and potentially disastrous intervention. As Roh is assuredly committed not only to avoiding this scenario but also to conserving his support from within the military and security sectors he will be hard pressed to protect their interests while meeting the legitimate claims of those with grievances.

A further requirement of democratisation is the emergence of political parties not crucially dependent on government largesse and at least partly free of ties to particular and sectional interests. So far, in Korea only a start has been made in this direction. Although the Japanese form of democracy demonstrates that the dominance of personalities is not inconsistent with the creation of stable political parties, the conditions under which this came about—the long reign of a hegemonic party staffed by former bureaucrats and financed by a powerful business sector—do not yet exist in the Korean case. The opposition parties particularly remain heavily dependent upon single individuals whose first priorities have not always been to further democratisation.

The institutionalisation of democracy is also dependent upon constitutional stability and predictability. While it is clear that the present division of labour between the presidency and the legislature is fraught with potential difficulties, these must be borne for a time. Already a proposal to introduce a parliamentary based executive has been floated within the ruling party, a fact which suggests that this point has not been grasped. In addition, President Roh must be permitted to serve out his existing term, presiding over an executive which is permitted to discharge its regular business and suffering neither impeachment nor personal disgrace. Here again opposition insistence on a comprehensive review of the past, and their preparedness to offer non-cooperation on present and future issues as leverage, renders this prospect less than completely assured.

The survival of the new Korean democracy rests ultimately on the government's capacity to foster in the population a sense of its legitimacy. Although the constituting of a popularly elected administration and the recognition of many rights and freedoms is a necessary step in that direction, legitimacy inheres neither in political structures nor in procedures themselves, but in opinions. The coming into being of the Korean republic in 1948 was accomplished only by ignoring deep divisions in the body politic. Neither the brief democratic experiment of 1960–61, nor the military based administrations of Presidents Park and Chun were successful in bridging them. Indeed, as a result of their policies as well as incidentally they may be said to have created new divisions. In the circumstances and given his background President Roh has made a promising start, but fundamental historical and cultural issues will need to be addressed before the new political system is capable of an identity distinct from its predecessors. An initiative that would greatly simplify Roh's task would be the forging of a new relationship with North Korea, but given the complexion of the regime in Pyongyang this remains as yet a distant prospect, though one which preoccupies many of the policy-makers in Seoul given the rapid changes elsewhere in the socialist countries.

Conclusions

The greatest challenge Roh will have to meet will be the need to alter political attitudes while managing the new political environment. Although the architect of modern Korea, Park Chung Hee, did enjoy in his earlier days a form of electoral mandate his status as the citizens' choice was always dubious. Roh has the opportunity to oversee the emergence of institutions and procedures which appear now to be required by Korea's external and domestic circumstances. Building such political structures will introduce some stability and the beginnings of a spirit of compromise into what has often been a volatile and confrontational political system. To do so will require humility as well as patience and statesmanship. But Roh has succeeded where Park, despite repeated efforts, failed abjectly. He has led to electoral victory and regime succession a political machine created by the military. This speaks not only for his ability and shrewdness but also, to a degree, for his public credibility. In the estimation of his chances, however, some caution is required. On an earlier occasion, Huntington, in assessing Park Chung Hee's prospects after his success in the elections of 1963, observed:

> In three years a military junta had transformed itself into a political institution. In three years, military intervention in politics with power based on the praetorian use of force had been converted into military participation in politics with authority based on popular support and legitimated by electoral competition.[34]

The advent of the authoritarian Yushin system in 1972, after the wielding of lesser controls proved insufficient for Park's purposes, revealed this episode as a false dawn. If he is to respond constructively to South Korea's new role and character, Roh will need to restrain powerful forces unaccustomed to democratic scrutiny, not to mention his own military inclinations.

---

[34] Samuel P. Huntington, *Political Order in Changing Societies* (New Haven: Yale University Press, 1968), p. 260.

3 Democratisation in South Korea

KIM JAE-YOUL

In the past few years, the Republic of Korea (ROK) has attracted world-wide attention as an emerging economic power with great promise of becoming a democratic nation. Beginning as a war-torn country in virtual ruin and with few resources, South Korea has achieved astonishing economic growth over the subsequent four decades. It has averaged an annual gross national product (GNP) growth of 8.6 per cent in the period between 1961 and 1991, and its per capita income increased from $US450 (in 1987 prices) in 1953 to $6,253 in 1991. Today, South Korea is considered by the World Bank as a high-income economy.[1]

The economic 'miracle' has contributed to a political transition in South Korea. Improvements in living standards and the expansion of educational opportunities have allowed a prosperous and growing middle class to add demands for democratisation to traditional bread-and-butter interests. In 1987, the public threw its support behind the democracy movement led by university students and opposition leaders, ultimately inducing the ruling élites to accommodate growing public expectations for democratisation. Since then, South Korea has made great strides, breaking away from the four-decade old authoritarian tradition and moving in the direction of democracy.

---

[1] John T. Bennet, 'Korea Adopts Seventh Five-Year Plan' in *Korea's Economy*, no. 8 (1992), p. 4; Korea Economic Institute of America, *Korea Economic Update* (Spring 1992), p. 1.

South Korea's Undemocratic Past

After thirty-five years of colonial rule, Korea was liberated in 1945 following Japan's defeat in World War II. Shortly thereafter, the country was divided into North and South Korea. The ROK was founded in the south on 15 August 1948, with Rhee Syngman as the first president. The Rhee government initially attempted to establish a constitutional democracy modelled on that of the United States. President Rhee, however, drifted gradually towards authoritarianism, and his administration was toppled by the democracy movement in 1960.

Following the Rhee administration, South Korea enjoyed a brief period of democracy that was abruptly put to an end on 16 May 1961 by a military *coup d'état* led by General Park Chung Hee. The 1961 coup marked the beginning of the eighteen-year reign of the authoritarian Park.

From the moment of the coup, Park was determined to lead Korea to rapid economic development and social order. Because Park came to power without the fiat of a popular election, he needed to imbue his regime with legitimacy. He chose to find this legitimacy by restoring order in the country and making it wealthy. He reiterated that rapid industrialisation and social stability were necessary to protect South Korea from the powerful enemy to the north and emphasised traditional Confucian values of social harmony and totality to realise these ends. In Park's *Weltanschauung*, political dissidents were an obstacle to the realisation of the 'ultimate national interest' that did little but engender cynicism and distrust toward the ruling élite. Park's military-backed government manipulated the constitution, the police, and the Korean Central Intelligence Agency (KCIA) to force political conformity. Park even made himself eligible for life-time presidency through the implementation of the 'October Revitalizing Reforms' of 1972.

The Park Chung Hee regime came to an end on 26 October 1979 when he was assassinated by the Chief of the KCIA. With Park's death, it seemed that South Koreans would finally see the rebirth of the long-awaited democracy, absent since its brief flowering in 1960. Prime Minister Choi Kyu Ha assumed the presidency in accordance with the constitution, and the new government led the country towards political liberation. As in 1961, however, a military coup again shattered hopes for a democracy in 1980. This time, the coup's instigator was General Chun Doo Hwan.

Chun was determined to assume supreme leadership. When students in Kwangju protested the declaration of martial law in May 1980, Special Forces were deployed to quell demonstrators. The result was the Kwangju tragedy, which left some 200 killed and more than 1,000 injured—the country's worst civil insurrection in modern history.[2] After making himself president in 1981, Chun Doo Hwan followed in the footsteps of his predecessor, Park, attempting to establish his legitimacy through successful economic development. He also implemented various repressive measures to respond to the growing democracy movement.

Anti-government sentiments reached their peak toward the end of Chun's presidency. In June 1987, Chun's decision to name his close military colleague and personal friend Roh Tae-woo as his successor enraged students and opposition leaders. They immediately organised massive demonstrations to condemn Chun and demanded open and fair elections. The government initially took harsh measures, but failed to deter the angry dissidents. On the contrary, governmental repression provoked greater civil unrest and fuelled popular expectations of democratisation, ultimately resulting in a wider range of participation in the pro-democracy movement. Under mounting public pressure, Roh announced on 29 June 1987 an eight-point proposal for sweeping democratic reforms, including the guarantee of fair presidential elections later that year, freedom of the press, and the relaxation of restrictive labour controls.

Post-June 29 Democratisation

The June 29 Declaration opened the floodgates to a new era of political change, an era of rapid, massive democratisation. Individuals and groups previously denied a political role added their views to the growing panoply of voices. Today, South Korea enjoys an unprecedented degree of political pluralism, public political participation, and freedom of the press and of labour activity.

Political pluralism and public participation

In the post-June 29 Declaration era, the South Korean public has relentlessly pressed the ruling élites to accommodate popular demands for democratisation. In October 1987, the lame-duck Chun administration enacted a new constitution incorporating Roh's eight-point proposal. Two months later, South Korea held the first open presidential elections in sixteen years. In these democratic elections, Roh Tae-woo obtained a plurality (36 per cent of the votes) and managed a marginal victory over the two strong opposition leaders—Kim Dae-jung (27 per cent) and Kim

---

2   *Far Eastern Economic Review* (hereafter *FEER*), 30 May 1991, p. 31.

Young-sam (28 per cent)—who had failed to form a united front against the ruling party candidate.[3]

Following its assumption of power in February 1988, the Roh administration carried out a series of political reforms. Shortly before the National Assembly elections of April 1988, the government adopted a single-member system in place of the existing two-member one, which had previously provided the ruling Democratic Justice Party (DJP) with substantial advantages. In part due to this change, the DJP failed to secure a majority, winning only 125 of the 299 seats in the National Assembly. By contrast, the three opposition parties received far more seats than warranted by the percentage of votes each received. Kim Dae-jung's Party for Peace and Democracy (PPD) and Kim Young-sam's Reunification Democratic Party (RDP) won seventy-one and fifty-nine seats respectively, while another political organisation, Kim Jong-pil's New Democratic Republican Party (DRP), secured thirty-five seats.[4]

The outcome of the April elections created a *yoso-yadae* (or small ruling party, big opposition) National Assembly. The *yoso-yadae* phenomenon conferred independence upon the law-making body, bringing an end to its days as a rubber stamp for the ruling party. Moreover, the strength of the opposition-dominated National Assembly continued to increase at the expense of the Roh administration. The National Assembly's August 1988 rejection of Roh's nomination of Chung Ki-seung as Supreme Court chief justice—on the grounds that Chung was politically 'tainted'—was a telling sign of the changing power dynamic between the newly-independent National Assembly and the executive branch.[5]

The National Assembly again indicated its increasing political clout in late 1988 in disclosing the wrongdoings of the Chun administration. From October to December that year, the legislators held hearings on forty-four major scandals allegedly committed by the previous regime, including the Kwangju tragedy and the suppression of the press in 1980. Although critics found these hearings inconclusive and unsatisfactory, that the National Assembly could exercise power in such sensitive issues was an unprecedented sign of change.

Despite the on-going trend of democratisation, vestiges of authoritarianism may still be found in South Korea today. The Roh administration, like the authoritarian governments of the past, at times attempted to monopolise political power. On 23 January 1990, the ruling DJP announced its decision to merge with Kim Young-sam's RDP and Kim

---

3   Bret L. Billet, 'South Korea at the Crossroads: An Evolving Democracy or Authoritarianism Revisited?' in *Asian Survey*, vol. 30 (March 1990), p. 302.

4   Han, Sung-Joo, 'South Korea in 1987: The Politics of Democratization' in *Asian Survey*, vol. 28 (January 1988), pp. 30–1.

5   Ibid., p. 31.

Jong-pil's DRP. The merger led to the founding of the Democratic Liberal Party (DLP), a Korean version of Japan's mammoth ruling party, and was denounced by a large segment of the society as unethical.

The merger reversed the *yoso-yadae* phenomenon in the National Assembly. Now enjoying over a two-thirds majority, the ruling party reportedly adopted autocratic methods to meet its ends. In June 1990, when opposition law-makers opposed major bills proposed by the government such as the supplementary budget bill and a controversial bill for reparations to victims of the Kwangju massacre, DLP members 'railroaded bills through the Assembly by relying on *blitzkrieg* tactics'. The National Assembly enacted twenty-three bills without the participation of the opposition law makers.[6]

The administration also manipulated an army counter-intelligence corps to monitor political activists. In early October 1990, an army deserter revealed that the Defense Security Command (DSC) conducted illegal surveillance on about 1,300 civilians. The DSC's secret file included the names of prominent opposition politicians, academics, journalists, labour activists, and student leaders characterised as potential threats to the government.[7]

The administration has reportedly attempted to circumscribe political participation. When Chung Ju-yung, founder of the Hyundai Group and one of the wealthiest men in Korea, rebelled against the existing political system and formed the United People's Party (UPP) in January 1992, the Roh administration allegedly imposed financial sanctions against Hyundai in an attempt to induce the tycoon out of politics. The DLP was particularly concerned because the *chaebol*-backed political party had the potential to attract conservative support.[8]

On the other hand, however, Chung's debut to politics itself indicates increased democracy in South Korea. The establishment of the UPP not only meant increased competition for conservative votes but also less political funds for the ruling party, considering Hyundai largesse in the past, including a $US13.24 million contribution to the president as recently as 1990.[9]

Against the government's will, moreover, an active and aware public has strengthened the system of political pluralism and mass participation. The Roh administration was unable to protect Chun Doo-hwan from an angry public—most notably the university students—demanding the

---

6   Kihl, Young Whan, 'South Korea in 1990: Diplomatic Activism and a Partisan Quagmire' in *Asian Survey*, vol. 31 (January 1991), p. 66.

7   Ibid. p. 67.

8   *Hankuk Ilbo*, 4 March 1992.

9   *FEER*, 23 January 1992, p. 11.

prosecution of the former president. Chun made a humiliating public apology for his misdeeds and asked for forgiveness on 23 November 1988. Chun also surrendered most of his wealth to the state and went in disgrace to a self-imposed exile at a remote Buddhist temple. Two years later, Chun was forced to return to Seoul to testify before a National Assembly panel investigating irregularities during his rule.[10]

The public also shattered the DLP's ambition to control the National Assembly. South Korea's voters, dissatisfied with the current domestic conditions, delivered a stunning rebuke to the ruling party, reducing its share of seats in the National Assembly to less than 50 per cent—far less than the expected two-thirds majority—in the March 1992 elections. The outcome of the March elections reminded the DLP of the increasing strength of the people and their growing willingness to cast individual votes. With their exceptionally high political expectations and awareness, the people of South Korea will continue to direct the country towards democracy, and the prospects for the consummation of a genuine democracy seem bright.

Freedom of the press

Roh Tae-woo's 29 June 1987 democratic reform package guaranteed the freedom of the press. Prior to the recent political liberalisation, freedom of the press was merely *de jure*, not *de facto*. Rhee, Park, and Chun found suppression of the press necessary for the consolidation of their power because uncontrolled newspapers could instigate the masses and vocally challenge the legitimacy of their undemocratic governments.

Upon his seizure of power, Chun Doo-hwan acted promptly to undermine the press. In July 1980, the government brought about the dismissal of 711 outspoken journalists as a warning against those who would denounce the Chun regime. The government also reduced the number of existing newspapers. The *Shin-a Ilbo* was forcefully taken over by the pro-government *Kyunghyang Shinmun*, while two economic newspapers were absorbed by force into the remaining two economic dailies. In addition, six provincial newspapers were forced to close down permanently.[11]

The government enacted the Basic Press Law specifying the rights and restrictions of the press. While the law provided nominal rights, it ultimately imposed various constraints on the newspapers. It included a clause prescribing numerous, restrictive facility requirements for publication intended to restrict the growth of existing newspapers and the founding of new ones. Not surprisingly, not a single newspaper was

---

10 Kihl, 'South Korea in 1990', p. 64.
11 Billet, 'South Korea at the Crossroads', p. 303.

established between the enactment of the law and its repeal in November of 1987.[12]

The Basic Press Law also empowered the Ministry of Culture and Information (MOCI) to cancel the registration of publications and to suspend them for various reasons, such as 'encouraging and praising violence or other illegal acts disrupting public order'.[13] This clause imposed a high degree of restriction on the press because the government considered countless activities—such as anti-government student demonstrations—disturbing.

The Chun government established the systematic control of the press by forcing newspapers to follow the 'guidelines' provided by the MOCI. One constant guideline was to label all anti-government protesters as 'pro-communist'. Daily guidelines were more specific. In late February of 1986, for instance, the MOCI instructed the newspapers not to elaborate on the collapse of the Marcos regime in the Philippines on the front page. Instead, the press was told to highlight Chun's visit to Europe.[14]

The government also relied heavily on extra-legal means to silence the press. The Korean National Security Planning Agency (KNSPA), the former KCIA, often intimidated and assaulted outspoken journalists. In May 1983, for instance, the intelligence agency arrested and battered a *Chosun Ilbo* reporter for breaking a forced silence on the ongoing hunger strike of Kim Young-sam.

Even after the June 29 Declaration, the lame-duck Chun administration tried to control the press, creating the '*Shin Dong-a* Crisis' in September 1987. The government was not pleased with an article that the *Shin Dong-a*, a monthly periodical published by the *Dong-a Ilbo* (a daily newspaper), was preparing and requested the periodical to omit that piece. The *Shin Dong-a*'s refusal to comply with the government led to serious tension between the two. The KNSPA threatened and intimidated the newspaper's management and editorial board.

This development attracted national attention because it was the first sober test of the sincerity of the ruling élites' vow for democratisation. Opposition politicians, university students, the press, and citizens supported *Shin Dong-a*'s cause, and under this public pressure, the govern-

---

12 Kim, Dong Son, 'Che 5 Konghwaguk-ui Onlon Tongje Siltae' (The State of the Press Regulation in the Fifth Republic) in *Shin Dong-A*, November 1987, p. 522.

13 Ibid., p. 522; Youm, Kyu Ho, 'Press Freedom Under Constraints: the Case of South Korea' in *Asian Survey*, vol. 26 (August 1986), p. 872.

14 Youm, Kyu Ho and Salwen, Michael B., 'A Free Press in South Korea: Temporary Phenomenon or Permanent Fixture?' in *Asian Survey*, vol. 30 (March 1990), p. 314.

ment apologised for the 'unnecessary dispute and inconvenience' and repealed its restrictions on the publication of the periodical.[15]

The resolution of the *Shin Dong-a* crisis ultimately marked the beginning of the free press era in South Korea. As the International Press Institution reported, 'visible and invisible restrictions imposed on the (Korean) press have been abolished in favor of a greater freedom of information and the right of the people to know has been guaranteed'.[16] The revised constitution of 1987 explicitly guarantees freedom of expression and prohibits censorship. In November 1987, the Basic Press Law was replaced by the Act on Registration of Periodicals and the Broadcast Act. This change repealed various rights that the MOCI had used to restrict the press. The ministry, for instance, no longer prescribes a press 'guideline'.

The Act on Registration of Periodicals and the Broadcast Act allow anyone meeting the basic registration requirements to start a printing business. Not surprisingly, the new law has engendered a proliferation of publications. The total number of South Korean dailies soared from thirty-two in June 1987 to 111 in March 1992.[17] The government has even tolerated the publication of progressive newspapers such as the *Han Kyoreh Shinmun*, whose senior editorial staff consists mainly of journalists who were either imprisoned or dismissed in 1980.[18]

Furthermore, the KNSPA no longer practices extra-legal tactics to silence the press. Consequently, with a few exceptions[19], South Korean newspapers have been free from governmental influences. Naturally, the press was exceptionally effective and critical in its investigation of the numerous abuses of the Chun Doo-hwan regime, including the Kwangju tragedy and the press repression of 1980. As one journalist comments, 'there certainly exists an unprecedented freedom of the press in contemporary South Korea'. Today, the Korean press serves its proper function of informing the public and keeping the government in check.

The Labour movement

The Korean work force made an extensive contribution to the country's remarkable economic growth by working diligently and efficiently for low

---

15 Kim, 'Che 5 Konghwaguk-ui Onlon Tongje Siltae', p. 519.

16 Youm and Salwen, 'A Free Press in South Korea', p. 312.

17 Information Office, Embassy of the Republic of Korea.

18 Billet, 'South Korea at the Crossroads', p. 304.

19 Exceptions are the *Seoul Shinmun* and a few other pro-government newspapers. However, the exertion of government influence on these papers cannot be regarded as press control because the government owns the *Seoul Shinmun* and has several intimate ties to other (independently owned) pro-government newspapers.

wages. Despite the country's economic 'miracle', however, workers reaped only few of the benefits prior to the recent political liberalisation. Undemocratic governments in the past viewed labour unions as unproductive and disruptive and imposed a high degree of control on the labour movement. The Rhee administration restricted labour activism on the presumption that labour unions were composed of left-wing activists. Park Chung-hee decided to take advantage of Korea's specific factor endowment—the abundance of educated, skilled, and inexpensive labour—to promote an export-oriented economy, and thus saw restrictions on the labour movement as a vital necessity. He implemented many arbitrary policies to suppress growing labour unionism, which, had it been allowed to organise and mature, would have demanded wage increases.

Like Park, Chun placed economic development first and created an arbitrary 'industrial peace'. The constitution of 1980 guaranteed workers the three rights of union formation, collective bargaining, and leading strikes—but only 'within the scope defined by law'. This ambiguous statement made it almost impossible for labourers to organise a union or to strike without their employer's approval. The 1980 constitution also empowered the government to dissolve unions and dismiss union activists if they were perceived to be 'harmful to the public interest'. The Fifth Republic labelled countless union activists as 'left-wing insurrectionists' and harassed them.

The surging pro-democracy movement of 1987 opened a new chapter in Korea's labour activism. In accordance with Roh's democratic reform package, the Chun administration overhauled the system of labour laws in October 1987. The new constitution guarantees workers the three basic rights with virtually no restrictions. Also repealed were many arbitrary rights that the government had enjoyed, including the power to dissolve unions.

Since then, the government has demonstrated an increased tolerance towards the wave of labour activism. It is true that the Roh administration has occasionally intervened in labour strifes. But generally speaking, the government has taken a relatively hands-off approach towards the labour movement in spite of pleas of entrepreneurs.

As anticipated, workers immediately took advantage of the political liberalisation to press their demands. Among the 3,617 labour disputes in 1987, approximately 3,500 of them broke out after 29 June. Nearly twice as many labour disputes occurred after Roh's announcement than in the previous ten years combined.[20] The number of labour unions doubled

---

20 Han, 'South Korea in 1987', p. 58.

from just 4,000 in 1987 to nearly 8,000 in 1990[21], while union membership nearly tripled from 775,000 in 1985 to 2.1 million in 1991.[22]

Korean labourers have reaped many benefits. The average work week for large companies was decreased to 48.3 hours in 1990 from fifty-seven hours in 1985[23], while labour wages more than doubled in the past five years.[24] The government's show of tolerance towards militant labour activism—in spite of South Korea's deteriorating international competitiveness partially as a result of soaring wages—indicates increased civil rights in South Korea.

Prospects for the Future

There is a well known Korean proverb which states: 'After a decade, even a landscape changes'. South Korea, however, endured four decades of unremitting authoritarianism (excluding two brief periods of democracy) before it witnessed the swift introduction of democratic processes in 1987. Since then, the country has made substantial progress towards democracy and now enjoys an unprecedented degree of political pluralism, public political participation, and freedom of the press and of labour activism.

The consummation of democracy is an important issue to all forty-two million South Koreans, and its international significance should not be overlooked. South Korea's dynamic economic growth has served both as model and catalyst for market-oriented reforms in developing countries such as China. Similarly, a successful political transition in South Korea could have parallel ripple effects in the developing world.

The presidential elections, scheduled for mid-December 1992, will open an important chapter in South Korea's democratisation. The December elections are likely to lead to the first genuine, peaceful transfer of power in the country's history. Unlike his predecessors, President Roh is not expected to leave office disgraced or dead. The elections will also mark the historic transfer from military to civilian power, putting an end to three decades of military-based authoritarianism. None of the three major presidential candidates—Kim Young-sam, Kim Dae-jung, or Chung Ju-yung—has a military background.

More importantly, the military is highly unlikely to intervene in politics after the elections. Roh has been advocating the professionalisation and depolitisation of the military, stating that he 'should be the last

---

21 Information Office, Embassy of the Republic of Korea, *Korea: Background Information*, 22 June 1992, p. 2.

22 *FEER*, 23 May 1991, p. 30.

23 *FEER*, 23 May 1991, p. 28.

24 *Wall Street Journal*, 1 July 1991.

president to come from the army'.[25] He dissolved *hanahoe*, an élite army organisation that played a crucial role in Chun's 1980 coup. Moreover, he redefined and reduced the Defense Security Command's (DSC) main functions to be the prevention of the penetration by left-wing students into the military and the prevention of a military coup.[26]

Today, the military is no longer impelled to intervene in politics to secure its own well-being by preventing a possible seizure of power by an opposition party. Under the historical system of politico–military rule, opposition leaders called for the emasculation of the military and its exclusion from government. Today, as the military is being depoliticised and as the government is being democratised, the various opposition groups have begun to concede the importance of a strong military for national defence and internal stability and have focused their disapprobation on other areas. Even Kim Dae-jung, the harshest critic of the military in the past, has recently recruited a number of former generals to his party.

Most importantly, South Korea is now politically too sophisticated to allow another military intervention. Today's increased public desire for political pluralism, a free and outspoken press, and firmly established opposition activism will not allow further authoritarianism, unless justified by a national crisis that endangers the future of the country. Prospects for further political transition in South Korea seem bright.

The US can facilitate Korea's democratisation, and thereby promote global democracy, by maintaining close bilateral security and improving economic ties between the two countries. Such a policy would eliminate any possibility of recurring instability that may serve as the pretext for a revival of authoritarianism.

---

25 *FEER*, 25 April 1991, p. 16.
26 *FEER*, 14 March 1991, pp. 23–4.

4 State Reform and Democracy in South Korea

ROBERT E. BEDESKI

Introduction—The International Setting

In retrospect, the 1980s will be remembered as a decade of democratisation and political reform in a number of dictatorial states. These far-reaching reforms generally began as structural modifications in which the leaders resolved to make changes that would reinforce their power under changing conditions, and in some cases, to meet promised commitments to elections. Few had imagined that once unleashed, these changes would lead to the breakdown of presumably impregnable systems of repression. Even today, the list of reforming and liberalising regimes continues to grow. East Germany is extinct as a state. Even long-isolated Mongolia has moved ahead with liberalising changes. Myanmar and Nicaragua held elections in the belief that their outcome would favour the status quo—indicating that repressive regimes are far less informed about the psyche of their own people than we had imagined.[1]

The beginnings of these changes can perhaps be traced to the reform movement initiated by China, and pressed further by the USSR. In both cases, there was the unmistakable message that centrally planned socialism was a road to nowhere—especially in light of the examples of the newly-industrialising countries (NICs) and other successful market economies.

In late 1978, Deng Xiaoping, the Chinese supreme leader, embarked on a series of reforms that were primarily economic and legal. The

---

1   Despite an overwhelming rejection of the military government in Myanmar, it continues to stall the transfer of power to the victors. *Far Eastern Economic Review*, 21 June 1990, pp. 20–1.

reforms were more easily implemented because of the years, as well as human and material resources, wasted by the Cultural Revolution. China had to embark on a radically new direction to survive. Ideology provided no solution—it was part of the problem that had blighted China during the Mao years. Deng and his group introduced radical (by communist standards) market and legal reforms which were standard fare in many capitalist countries—but insured that the Communist Party remained dominant. Political reforms remained secondary, and were limited to increasing bureaucratic efficiency and the gradual separation of party and government functions. By 1989, inflation and popular demonstrations for democratic reform led to a party backlash and halted progressive reforms, illustrating the risks of introducing changes.

Mikhail Gorbachev has dominated implementation of legal and political reform—setting the agenda, selecting key personnel, and ordering the sequence of policy. Political *perestroika* has set off in directions confirming the worst nightmares of party conservatives—the loss of the leading position of the Communist Party of the Soviet Union (CPSU) and the possible dissolution of the USSR through secession or autonomisation of the Republics. The Soviet state[2] has also seen the emergence of splinter groups which could form the core of opposition groups. Eastern Europe was written off to the Soviets when Shevardnadze announced that the Red Army would not intervene if the 'People's Republics' wanted to pursue their own *perestroika*. It was not imagined that the various communist parties would fall so quickly.

In contrast to China, the Soviets have moved very slowly in the realm of economic reform. A binge of consumer buying has contributed to swollen debt and defaulting on foreign obligations—the first time in many years.[3] The long-awaited set of economic reforms to move the Soviets toward a market economy has been blunted by fears of the Polish example of high inflation. There, the Solidarity government enjoys a large reservoir of support—something Moscow lacks, and therefore fears that strong

---

2   The concept of the state remains a troublesome one in political science. During the heyday of the systems approach, the concept was largely eclipsed as unscientific. In recent years, it has been resurrected, almost with a vengeance. For all its limitations, the notion of the state does convey the reality of an organised power structure, although there is a frequent tendency to use 'state' as a synonym for government. In communist systems, government has been largely an administrative apparatus for carrying out party decisions, with little or no existence as an independent entity. Likewise, the police and army in a large number of authoritarian systems have considerable autonomous power. In the present chapter, I use the term 'state' to refer to the sum of those power structures which exercise physical, psychological, legal, and administrative power of coercion over members of the society

3   'Russia's Latest Queue: for Creditors', *Economist*, 19 May 1990, p. 75.

measures would endanger social order and the remaining authority of the party.

Given these experiences and precedents, it is not strange that the North Koreans refuse meaningful reforms—political or economic. It may be that these regimes are unreformable, and significant modification of their power structure may be the first step to dissolution.[4] This growing number of regimes forced to accommodate unwelcome and unanticipated reforms (from their ideological standpoint) raises the question of the relationship between political reform and democratisation.

In the momentous changes underway in the communist world, the liberalising reforms of South Korea are usually overlooked, or treated as a special case. While these reforms admittedly do not have the international implications of the Soviet and Chinese events, they are significant in providing a case study of how political reform may be carried out successfully in an authoritarian state. When political reform appears to liberalise a regime, it inevitably creates the possibility of instability.[5] Neither the Soviet Union nor the People's Republic of China (PRC) have been able to deal with this risk without eroding the foundations of state authority. South Korea, on the other hand, has been reasonably effective in containing the side-effects of reform.

Part of the success or failure in implementing reforms can be attributed to the scale and heterogeneity of the states involved, to the totalitarian[6] structure of the communist regimes, to revolutionist and dogmatic ideology, and to accumulated bureaucracy in the Soviet Union and China. Comparisons must take these factors into account. Nevertheless, the statecraft of Gorbachev, Deng Xiaoping, and Roh Tae-woo seeks to transform inadequate centralised systems into polities that are able to respond to challenges of modernisation and rising public demands for responsive government.

---

4   Albania is one of the latest communist countries to pursue modest reforms, but even small steps in this isolated, Stalinist state have produced tensions and conflict—as well as an exodus of thousands. *Korea Herald*, 5 July 1990, p. 5.

5   See *China Daily*, 3 January 1990, p. 4, 'State control urged while pursuing policy of reform'.

6   This term is frequently avoided because of its 'cold war' and polemical connotation, or evidence that systems so described are not monoliths. But the aspects of single party radical penetration of society and illegitimacy of all political opposition remain characteristics of a group of Marxist–Leninist states in common with Italian and German fascism which are qualitatively different from ordinary authoritarian systems analysed by Jua Linz and others. For an exposition and critique of the totalitarian model, see Philip G. Roeder, *Soviet Political Dynamics, Development of the First Leninist Polity* (New York: Harper & Row, 1988), ch. 9, 'The Political Process'.

For purposes of comparison, the term 'dictatorship' will be used to refer to strong states which exercise centralised authority with relatively little concern for societal preferences.[7] Within this category, I include authoritarian and totalitarian systems. Scholars have either rejected this dichotomy, or have invested it with varying definitions.[8] For present purposes, the major structural difference between them is the existence of a visible, autonomous and organised legal opposition in authoritarian polities, and their absence in the latter.

Political Reform and Liberalisation

Political reform can be tentatively defined as the purposive structural modification of state institutions and their authority relationship with the social system, initiated and implemented by a dominant political élite. This modification of political institutions and their relations with society is a fairly continuous feature of states—especially non-dictatorial ones. But in dictatorial states, political reform may be more episodic and visible because it publicly announces that the old relationship between state and society is defective and therefore must be amended.

Raising questions about the legitimacy of authority in a dictatorial regime is corrosive to its power and must be minimised if the regime is to survive intact. A prolonged period of political reform must also be avoided. Political reform is a compression of adaptive restructuring by a current élite, and is often triggered by a current of impending authority crisis. To prolong the period of reform can invite further erosion of regime credibility. Political reform may be accompanied by economic reform, or may be influenced by economic restructuring, or it can have considerable impact on economic structures. But as Soviet *perestroika* has demonstrated, it can also remain relatively independent of the economic system.

Liberalisation in a dictatorial state is a specific type of political reform involving a redefinition of the relationship between state and society by reducing the coercive interference of the state apparatus. This often entails restructuring state institutions in a manner that diminishes their autonomy

---

7 In this approach, I follow what Eric A. Nordlinger has termed a 'state centered perspective' in which the state acts on its own policy preferences, and translates them into public policy. 'Taking the State Seriously', in Weiner, Myron and Samuel P. Huntington (eds), *Understanding Political Development* (Boston: Little, Brown, 1987), p. 353.

8 Frederick C. Barghoorn and Thomas F. Remington, for example, write that because of important changes that have taken place since Stalin's death, 'it may be more accurate to regard the Soviet system as a modernised variant of authoritarianism'. In Gabriel A. Almond and G. Bingham Powell, Jr. (eds), *Comparative Politics Today: A World View* (Glenview, Illinois: 1988), p. 318.

without reducing their authority. Genuine liberalisation is not easily reversible, and can lead to democratisation—the meaningful participation in elections by individual citizens and organised groups. A key characteristic of democratic elections is that they provide genuine choices of parties and candidates to the electorate to determine actual distribution of power in government which has actual power.[9] Liberalisation is antithetical to dictatorship because it requires loss of control over society and surrender of privilege and may be destabilising. The preferred path of dictatorship is political reform without liberalisation.

Another type of political reform is decentralisation in which decision-making power is delegated to lower levels of the administrative apparatus. When this decentralisation is largely administrative, it does not directly affect state autonomy and therefore differs from liberalisation.[10] However, some degree of local autonomy does act as a brake on central power. In the USSR, Boris Yeltsin's calls for the Russian Republic's sovereignty, if realised, will introduce genuine federalism into the political realm. Canadian federalism is undergoing its recurring crisis as Quebec increasingly feels its aspirations and Francophone culture are inadequately served in a largely Anglophone nation. Thus, changes in central-republic, or federal-provincial relations, may significantly alter the character of state power.

On the Dilemma of Liberalisation

Colossal changes currently underway in the communist world are redefining the international system. What began as structural reforms in two refractory systems has now accelerated into potential imperial dissolution in the Soviet case, and actual conservative backlash in the PRC which has arrested further political reform for the present. These two cases emphasise the dilemma of tolerating or initiating liberalisation in political reform: once reform is undertaken in a dictatorial system, it takes on a life

---

9 The mere existence and occurrence of elections does not equate with democracy, as previous Chinese and Soviet systems of single party, single candidate elections illustrate. There must be significant alternatives in opposing parties, and relatively free entry of candidates into the process, as well as a certain level of non-interference by the government and the ruling party.

10 One of the major reasons that West Germany is a federal republic is the postwar constitutional design to provide the ten *Länder* with sufficient power to prevent a centralised dictatorship of the type that emerged under Hitler. One debate on German reunification now centres on whether the five *Länder* to be recreated in former East Germany (plus one for Berlin) will complicate the federal state unnecessarily. *Economist*, 2 June 1990, p. 45.

of its own, raising popular demands for even further changes. The predicament consists in attempting to balance the demands for closer harmony between state and society without eroding political order beyond the point where anarchy and social cooperation begin to erode the supervisory role of the state.

Political reform is a major structural adjustment of the state in its relations with society. The political reforms of the Soviet Union, China, and South Korea have taken place in strong states with government and party possessing a relatively high degree of autonomy from society. This autonomy means that political structures are fairly insulated from social pressures, and can carry out reforms without significantly compromising their authority.

Political reform can be distinguished from administrative reform, which alters government management practices, organs, and jurisdiction, without modification of authority relationships between state and society. The vehicles of political reform in modern states may include the formal constitution, the legal system, the institutions of representation, the executive organs, the party system, and other politically relevant structures and processes in the state. By definition, political reform is government-initiated. It may be in response to popular dissatisfaction[11] or to a failing economy, or it may reflect sensitivity to international pressures. A principal goal of political reform is to consolidate the structure of authority in the state where it is weakening or under attack. The penalty of inadequate, or failed, political reform is what Chalmers Johnson has termed, 'deflation of authority'. It may result in revolution or *coup d'état* or major restructuring of the state far beyond the original intentions of the reformers.

Elements of political reform

Political reform represents a significant departure from previous patterns of authority distribution in the state, and therefore involves several novel elements:

1. *New leadership.* Death or retirement of supreme leaders, or appointment of new top personnel in the state hierarchy provides an occasion for embarking on new initiatives. The new leadership emerges from the old

---

11 The Japanese government is currently formulating legislation on political reform of the election system in response to public outcry over the Recruit Scandal, inequitable distribution of seats, a confusing system of multi-member districts, and expensive election campaigns which corrupt the political process. See Prime Minister Kaifu's press conference, *Asahi Shimbun*, 11 May 1990, p. 2, translated in *Daily Summary of the Japan Press* (US Embassy, Tokyo), 19–21 May 1990, pp. 1–2.

and so can presumably be trusted to conform to old obligations and values. The new is also less encumbered by political debts to vested interests so that it may set off in new directions. The occurrence of a change in leadership may be the best and only opportunity for a regime to embark on major political reform. In the case of China, the succession from Mao Zedong provided the 'window of opportunity' for Deng Xiaoping to begin rapid economic, and limited political, reforms once the leadership question was settled. Gorbachev's accession to power and the transition from Chun Doo-hwan to Roh Tae-woo both supplied occasions for reform in their respective systems.

2. *Inclusion of new social groups in the formal constituency of the state.* Political reforms change the mix of who has access to state power. Old groups, such as the government ruling party may be forced to address the concerns of emerging social groups. A reforming leadership must establish links with the new groups which will provide support and possibly share in setting policy agendas. In China, intellectuals and a new managerial–technological élite were provided more freedom than at any time since 1949. Soviet political reforms allowed freer elections, and allowed a multitude of new interests to be expressed. In South Korea, journalists and intellectuals have seen improvement in the late 1980s over previous periods. Also, with the 13th National Assembly, the two Cholla provinces have had their demands taken more seriously. Labor, which had been suppressed under the Fourth and Fifth Republics, has fought for and won significant economic concessions.

3. *Abandonment of structures and processes which were proven to be unworkable or dysfunctional.* Political reform would not be necessary if old structures had been sufficiently flexible to adapt to changing conditions. Old symbols of ideology and styles of ruling behaviour—which may have been previously sacrosanct—are eroded and even derided and humiliated. This allows fresh perceptions to emerge and new prototypes of institutions to be experimented.

In this, an element of scapegoating is often present; past mistakes may be blamed on previous regimes—Stalin or Brezhnev or Mao Zedong or Chun Doo-hwan. Blaming predecessors for excesses and abuses may provide a certain psychological purging and facilitate introduction of new patterns of politics. In China, the Deng reforms were undoubtedly expedited by popular revulsion against the Cultural Revolution and contributed to de-Maoisation. In December 1989, demands for testimony from ex-President Chun before the National Assembly certainly had an element of vengeance coming from the opposition parties which had suffered under his regime.

4. *Establishment and implementation of new patterns and structures.* This requires strengthening of the legal system so that impersonal struc-

tures can acquire credibility. The state constitution exists as the convergence of law and state structures and must be changed in light of new directions. Political reform tied to legal change must therefore also strengthen the state organ of legislation—the Supreme Soviet, the National People's Congress in China, or the National Assembly in South Korea. Membership in these parliamentary organs will be defined by new election laws.

Totalitarian vs authoritarian reforms

Up to this point the government is generally in control of the direction and rate of reform. A crucial difference between communist totalitarianism and the South Korean authoritarian system was the presence of organised opposition in the latter. In South Korea the opposition parties shared a major role in determining the content of reform, and pressing the government for liberalisation. In China, decades of repression have eliminated most vestiges of potential organised opposition, and reforms have proceeded with relatively little input from social groups. In the Soviet Union, Gorbachev's apparent toleration of limited opposition resembled the technique used by Mao Zedong in the Cultural Revolution—going outside the party and creating a strong non-party position of leadership in order to make a flanking attack on the individuals and groups inhibiting reforms. In Gorbachev's case, however, it appears that this technique has gone out of control, and fragments of genuine opposition are emerging.

This characteristic of totalitarian/authoritarian states suggests that political reform remains confined to limited political restructuring, and stops short of liberalisation, which requires institutionalised accountability of the state to society. With no organised opposition, there is little possibility of the regime losing its control of the state, and so it is in the interest of the regime to eliminate or undermine any tendency for the emergence of an organised opposition. The alternatives to political reform may be stagnation, revolution, or collapse.

To summarise the discussion thus far, political reform is a process of structural change which alters the distribution of state power. This affects the legal system, the constitution, the legislature, and other organs of power. In totalitarian dictatorships, the process of reform is monopolised by the regime, while authoritarian dictatorship may be forced to consult with an organised opposition, whose demands include liberalisation beyond institutional reform.

In order to illustrate and refine this hypothesis, the South Korean state provides a case study of reform and liberalisation in the transition from the Fifth Republic to the Sixth. In this instance, the regime's legal and political reforms were pushed into liberalisation by an organised and determined opposition. By reviewing and dissecting the South Korean experience in political reform, perhaps a few broader insights may be derived.

Characteristics of the South Korean State

The quasi-sovereign nation-state in South Korea is a modern development—established in the aftermath of World War II. Unlike the Russian or Chinese multi-ethnic empires, Korean kingdoms in the pre-modern period were largely composed of a single national group.[12] Over the centuries, the Korean Peninsula has provided a bridge between the East Asian mainland and Japan, a knife pointed in two directions—toward Manchuria and toward the Japanese archipelago. With this strategic position and importance, it is a remarkable achievement that Korean society has been able to survive, much less to flourish, as it has during different periods.

In 1910, Korea became part of the Japanese Empire under direct Tokyo rule. After World War II, the peninsula was divided into a communist north and non-communist south, which became the Republic of Korea (ROK). The Korean War, 1950–1953, hardened the division which has persisted to the present day. The Japanese colonial legacy and subsequent division of the country had the effect of expunging the traditional political institutions from Korea.[13] The Korean War and the continued threat of renewed war reinforced the authoritarianism of Syngman Rhee[14], and assured that the military forces would have a major share in political power. Under the presidency of Park Chung-hee, military leadership pushed economic growth and laid the foundations of export oriented industrialisation. According to Henderson, 'The Park era saw the rebirth

---

12 See Andrew C. Nahm, *Korea: Tradition and Transformation; A History of the Korean People* (Seoul: Hollym, 1988), *passim*.

13 Yang Sung-chul has written a convincing essay on the persistence of traditional political culture in contemporary Korea, which will require reformulation of many of our assumptions about Korean behaviour. See his article, 'The Korean Political Culture and Traditions: A Historical Analysis', *Journal of Social Sciences and Humanities*, vol. 66 (June 1988), pp. 23–77.

14 The roots of postwar authoritarianism started in Syngman Rhee's rejection of the responsible cabinet system in the draft constitution drafted by Dr Yu Chin-o and the Drafting Committee. At his insistence, the presidency was strengthened at the expense of the cabinet. Henderson and others find it ironic that in the 1980s, the opposition parties demand the popularly elected president, while the government attempts to introduce the cabinet system. Gregory Henderson, 'Constitutional Changes from the First to the Sixth Republics: 1948–1987', in Ilpyong J. Kim and Young-whan Kihl (eds) *Political Change in South Korea* (New York: Paragon House, 1988), pp. 22–43.

of a kind of Japanese colonial-style politics of firm, somewhat militarised control, decisive economic planning, widespread mobilisation techniques, and political desiccation'.[15]

After the assassination of President Park in October 1979, a brief move toward civilian constitutionalism ended with the Kwangju incident, where the army suppressed an incipient rebellion with considerable force, resulting in hundreds of casualties. Military intervention helped to install Chun Doo-hwan as president in the new Fifth Republic of 1980. Under the new constitution, Chun could serve only a single seven-year term, unlike the successive terms followed by Park. As the nation prepared for the 1987 succession and 1988 Olympics, all groups and parties seemed to focus their attention on these twin events as anticipated turning points in South Korea's political life.

The Authority Crisis of 1985

1985 elections

The authority crisis which led to the collapse of the Fifth Republic began in 1985 as the opposition parties gained more strength. The February parliamentary election was preceded by the establishment of the New Korea Democratic Party (NKDP), led by politicians who had been removed from a political blacklist. Its roots were in the major opposition party of the 1970s—the New Democratic Party. Lee Min-woo, a close associate of Kim Young-sam, was elected party president. The two major opposition figures, Kim Dae-jung and Kim Young-sam, were still barred from political activity, and the new party rejected the legitimacy of the current government and constitution. The other opposition parties were considered to be creations of the government. The NKDP was expected to win a sizable share in the National Assembly election, although the ruling party was assured of at least 150 of 276 seats. In preparation for the 1987 elections, the NKDP sought to change the constitution to allow direct popular voting for the president.[16]

In the 1985 election, the NKDP became the largest opposition bloc in the Twelfth National Assembly, sweeping the urban centres of Seoul, Pusan and Inchon. It captured seats in fifty out of ninety-two local constituencies, and 30 per cent of the national vote, winning a total of sixty-seven out of 276 seats. In the campaign, the opposition parties constantly referred to Chun as a military dictator. The government's Democratic Justice Party (DJP) received 35 per cent instead of the 38 per cent target.

---

[15]   Ibid., p. 33.

[16]   *Christian Science Monitor*, 25 January 1985, p. 13.

The Democratic Korea Party (DKP), suffering from the perception that it was a government-created party, received 20 per cent. On 6 March, the government removed the ban on several prominent politicians, but not Kim Dae-jung. A cabinet shakeup also followed, and Roh Tae-woo was named as party chairman. In early April, thirty legislators left the opposition DKP to join the NKDP. Subsequently, the NKDP absorbed the DKP to form a united bloc of 106 seats against the DJP's 147 seats.[17]

Constitutional changes

With growing opposition strength, constitutional change was more likely. But the government stated it had no intention to change the indirect presidential system into a direct one before 1988.[18] In the spring of 1986, the government adopted a more tolerant attitude toward popular demonstrations, but still ordered the house arrest of some 200 opposition party members. The crackdown was denounced by the US State Department, and was extremely unpopular at home. Events in the Philippines raised the cry of 'people power' in Seoul.[19] This set the stage for the opposition parties to organise a popular movement to pressure the authoritarian government for radical reforms.

On 13 April 1987, Chun Doo-hwan halted the debate on constitutional revision until after the 1988 Olympics to be held in Seoul. He claimed that consensus among the opposition parties was not possible, and time was running out before the elections.[20] The government offered a parliamentary system as a compromise, while the opposition wanted a return to direct presidential election. Lee Min-woo, president of the NKDP, said that his party would consider the government's offer if the ruling party adopted seven major political reforms. This initiative was rejected by Kim Dae-jung and Kim Young-sam, who broke away and formed their own party, once again splitting the opposition and raising doubts over their ability to handle power responsibly.

Opposition parties

A major hurdle which opposition parties face in general is their credibility when they have never had the responsibility of government. They may be popular as expressions of protest against existing injustices, and threaten the dominant party, but there is often reluctance among voters to entrust

---

17 *Christian Science Monitor*, 5 April 1985, p. 12.

18 *Korea Herald*, 2 March 1984, p. 1.

19 *Christian Science Monitor*, 14 March 1986, p. 14.

20 *Korea Report* (Embassy of the Republic of Korea, Ottawa, Canada), 13 April 1987, p. 1.

an untested organisation with the reins of power. Moreover, if an opposition party is perceived to behave in a way that indicates an incapacity to provide orderly government, its chances at the polls will be decreased. The slow progress of the Japan Socialist Party toward winning the confidence of the electorate, despite the relatively low popularity of the governing LDP, reflects some of this burden of opposition parties.

By 1986, it was apparent to the government that the opposition parties in South Korea had to be taken seriously as potential rivals for power. The presidential election was scheduled for the end of 1987, and the two Kims were the strongest opponents against the DJP. Both had worked in the opposition during the postwar period and had strong popular appeal—in contrast to the stern Confucian military leadership provided by Park Chung-hee and Chun Doohwan.

Party organisations have not been very durable in South Korean political life. Even ruling parties have not lasted much longer than their leader's hold on power.

The major issue in 1987 was over the method of election of the president. The government insisted on an indirect election, while the opposition wanted a direct election since this would be a more accurate representation of public opinion, and also favoured the opponents of the DJP. Lee Min-woo's compromise formula for democratisation only succeeded in weakening his own position. The two Kims feared that any appearance of compromise would weaken their party *vis-à-vis* the DJP.[21]

Street demonstrations in the spring of 1987 faced large numbers of riot police. To the rest of the world, it appeared that the stability of the Olympics' host country was very much in question. The government pondered its international image, but also feared student-led riots of the type which had overthrown Syngman Rhee in 1960. Demonstrators were also supported by the growing labour movement, which long felt it had not shared in the fruits of the Korean economic miracle. The government feared recriminations over the Kwangju incident, which had discredited the Fifth Republic domestically and internationally. Demands for democracy were mixed with yearning for justice and retribution, and South Korean society seemed to be drifting into two mutually antagonistic camps in early 1987. An official half-joked to this writer in late 1986 that his country seemed to face two choices, either a military republic or a student republic.

The opposition dealt from a position of weakness—against the entrenched government and its use of officials in its service. A $1.2 billion loan to fishermen and farmers in 1987 did not hurt the government in the countryside. A viable opposition required unity of the two Kims. Before leaving the NKDP, Kim Dae-jung had backed the more moderate Kim

---

21 *Far Eastern Economic Review*, 16 April 1987, p. 24.

Young-sam to replace Lee Min-woo as party president. Internal squabbling would only further raise doubts over whether the opposition party could form an effective government.

Other issues of contention between the government and opposition included the demanded release of political prisoners, reintroduction of the local government system which had been suspended in 1961, press freedoms, an end to police brutality, and the repeal of draconian anti-communist laws.[22] The opposition also demanded redistricting to reflect population changes. A drift of immigrants into the cities since 1981 strengthened the popular support of the opposition parties but this would not be translated into National Assembly strength without district changes.

Roh Tae-woo's June 1987 eight-point declaration

The DJP convention of June 1987 was scheduled to be a smooth transition of power from Chun to Roh. Within his own party, Chun heard a strong consensus for conciliation and resumption of talks on constitutional reform. The US was also calling for dialogue between the rival forces to avert a breakdown which might invite North Korean intervention. The atmosphere was one of increasing public violence—students were joined by other groups in urban Korea. Without a solution to the impasse, the Olympics were hostage to political instability.

On 29 June Roh Tae-woo reversed years of refusal to compromise with the opposition, and conceded to their major demands, including direct presidential elections and amnesty for the leading dissident, Kim Dae-jung. Two days later, Chun gave his blessing to the reforms which he had so long refused. Other items of Roh's eight-point package of reforms included the freeing of all political prisoners except those charged with serious crimes; guaranteed human rights; a free press; local autonomy; freedom for political parties; and a campaign against crime and corruption.[23] The abrupt change in the government policy was undoubtedly influenced by over two weeks of clashes. Rallies on 26 June had drawn hundreds of thousands of demonstrators and there was also a growing revolt within the DJP.

By adopting the main demands of the opposition, Roh had seized the initiative in the approaching election. He had turned mass opposition to his candidacy into a new legitimacy, and isolated the radical students from the Catholic church and middle class support. In addition, by granting amnesty to Kim Dae-jung, he indirectly intensified the rivalry between the two Kims which paralysed their efforts to unite in the presidential election.

---

22 Ibid., p. 25.
23 *Asiaweek*, 12 July 1987.

The 1987 presidential contest

Negotiations between the government and opposition party cleared several major obstacles during the nineteen rounds of closed-door talks by the eight-member negotiating panel. The opposition wanted the president to serve a four-year term, with the option of running for a second term; the DJP wanted a single six-year term. The panel compromised on a single five-year term. In a major concession, the ruling party agreed to drop the president's power to dissolve the National Assembly. The Reunification Democratic Party (RDP) wanted the voting age lowered to eighteen to give university students, who were in the vanguard of the movement for democratic reform, the right to vote. However, the DJP remained firm, and the opposition agreed to leave the issue until new election laws were drawn up.[24] The voting age was later set at twenty. In late October the new constitution was approved by 93 per cent of voters.

The two Kims ran against Roh as well as against each other. Kim Dae-jung was the favourite son of south Cholla—the rice basket of the nation and a southwest province frequently bypassed in the past two decades of industrialisation. The incident in Kwangju, the major city in the province, had further increased hostility toward the government. The people of Cholla clearly perceived Kim as their regional saviour.[25] Both Kim Dae-jung and Kim Young-sam called for the end of military rule, referring to the army background of Chun and Roh. Nevertheless, Kim Young-sam was supported by former four-star General Chung Sung-hwa—a signal that he could work with the military establishment more effectively than the Kim from Cholla.

As the race heated up, other elements sought recognition of grievances. Labour became more militant, and staged over 3,500 strikes and demonstrations in the three months after 29 June. Wages rose by 20 per cent, and business feared the end of Korea's successful export drive.[26]

In the election scheduled for 16 December, Roh was the only candidate heading a party he had not founded to further his political ambitions. Kim Young-sam and Kim Dae-jung held leadership positions in the newly formed RDP and failed to agree on a single candidate to oppose Roh. Kim Dae-jung later told me that he could not guarantee that his followers would support Kim Young-sam even if he did. The fierce loyalty of his Cholla backers was expressed in the landslide he received there, and could not be traded away. Kim Dae-jung formed his own Party for Peace and Democracy (PPD). Many Koreans were frustrated by the perceived

---

24 *Asiaweek*, 13 September 1987, p. 24.

25 *Far Eastern Economic Review*, 24 September 1987, p. 12.

26 David I. Steinberg, *South Korea: Economic Transformation and Social Change* (Boulder: Westview, 1989).

inability of opposition candidates to allow national interest to transcend individual aspirations of growing regionalism. Roh was virtually assured of election when the two Kims failed to cooperate. Between them, they won and split 55 per cent of the popular vote to Roh Tae-woo's plurality of 37 per cent. Strong regional loyalties to Kim Young-sam and Kim Dae-jung reduced their respective ability to cooperate.

The opposition parties were determined not to repeat their mistakes in the coming April 1988 election for the National Assembly.[27] Under the new constitution, the legislature regained the powers lost under previous regimes. Once again, the election system, which favoured the government party, through the proportional representation scheme, had to be revised. Negotiations broke down and the DJP rammed through a law based on single-member districts, calculating that the PPD and RDP would split the opposition vote. A system was set up in which the National Assembly consists of 299 seats, with 224 to be filled through the single-member district system and the remaining seventy-five at-large seats to be allocated by a proportional representation scheme.[28]

After a lively campaign—not clean, but one of the freest[29]—75.8 per cent of the eligible voters cast their ballots. It was a stunning setback for the government party, which won only eighty-seven of the 224 constituencies, against fifty-four for the PPD[30], forty-six for the RDP, twenty-seven for the New Democratic Republican Party (NDRP), and nine for the independents. In popular votes, the DJP won 34 per cent, the RDP 23.8 per cent, the PPD 19.3 per cent and the NDRP, formed by former Premier Kim Jong-pil, 15.6 per cent. Kim Dae-jung's PPD emerged as the largest opposition party, replacing his rival Kim Young-sam.

Voter turnout was higher in rural areas, and lower in urban areas. The pattern of partisan support was for rural voting in favour of the government party and urban endorsement for the opposition—*yochon yado*. Kim Hong-nack's analysis indicates that the government's unilateral change in the election system was not a major factor in its defeat.[31] (Park Chan-wook, however, considers that Kim Young-sam was hurt by the changed rules.[32]) Rather, there appeared to be a strong desire among voters to strengthen the opposition in the legislature. Other factors

---

27 Kim Hong-nak, 'The 1988 Parliamentary Election in South Korea', *Asian Survey*, vol. 39, no. 5 (May 1989), pp. 480–95.

28 Ibid., p. 482.

29 Ibid., p. 486.

30 One member of the Hangyore party was elected but switched to the PPD. Ibid.

31 Kim Hong-nack, 'The 1988 Parliamentary Election in South Korea', p. 480.

32 'The 1988 National Assembly Election in South Korea: The Ruling Party's Loss of Legislative Majority', *Journal of Northeast Asian Studies*, vol. 7, no. 3 (Fall 1988), p. 67.

included revelations about corruption in the DJP, the inability of the government party to attract the support of young and well-educated urban voters, and candidate blunders. A deepening sense of regionalism, evident in the 1987 elections also affected the government's fortunes.

After the election, the government faced a National Assembly dominated by the opposition parties. President Roh's attempts at consultation and reconciliation eased some friction but did not spare his government setbacks and demands for the settlement of abuses suffered in the Fifth Republic—especially the Kwangju incident.

Testimony and apology by former President Chun Doo-hwan in December 1989 cleared away this logjam, and set the stage for a new realignment in South Korean politics. The DJP, RDP, and NDRP decided in January 1990 to merge into a single megaparty—the Democratic Liberal Party (DLP), which reduced the PPD to a minority opposition in the National Assembly. Domestically the move reduced the choices available to voters in the next election, and could be viewed as a backward step from the process of democratisation underway in 1987 and 1988. Externally, the consolidation could improve the ability of the National Assembly and executive branch to cooperate more in reviving a slowing economy and provide a more unified front in diplomacy with the US and the communist world. But the deep-seated factionalism of Korean politics may also erode the stability of this new alignment.

Analysis

Over the past four years, a major transformation of the South Korean political system has taken place. A rigid—but not totalitarian—government has modified its authoritarian autonomy from society, and upgraded the legislature to a more equal status with the executive branch in the new constitution. Repressive laws have been revised and the opposition party is now closer to influencing legislation and holding the government accountable for its actions. In the future, much will depend upon whether actual and prospective party coalitions cooperate or refragment.

We can recapitulate the stages of South Korean liberalisation as follows:

1. *First preparatory stage: Authoritarian regime control of state and society.* The state apparatus consisted of coercive institutions, including the police and army, to protect the polity from North Korean invasion and subversion within. It also included the state bureaucracy which coordinated economic development. This period lasted from the early 1960s through 1987. Although opposition parties existed in the National Assembly, their impact on government policy was minimised by the legacies of Rhee, Park and the interference of the army.

2. *Second preparatory stage: Popular reaction against the government.* Through the years of the South Korean Republic, opposition was frequently expressed by student demonstrations. But by early 1987 they were joined by a broader cross-section of society. This probably helped to convince the regime leadership that they could not maintain social order and control during the coming election of in the 1988 Olympics. Public opinion was increasingly rejecting the dominant DJP, and would consign it to the role of opposition party unless reforms were initiated.

3. *Political reform, stage one: Government takes the initiative and negotiates with the opposition.* Faced with increasing social disruption and the prospect of economic difficulty, the government leadership acknowledged the crisis. Roh Tae-woo's Eight Point Proposals for reform on 29 June was a major tactical shift. To resume control, the government opened contacts with representatives of the opposition, thereby granting them and their grievances a greater degree of legitimacy. This stage saw negotiations and consultations over changing the rules of the political system—especially the electoral process and the distribution of power, while the government tried to minimise risk to its monopoly of power.

4. *Political reform, stage two: Implementation.* Having agreed to make changes, the government provided a clear agenda of its intentions and was obligated to implement them and abide by the outcomes of the new rules. Several crucial keys to South Korean political reforms have been the existence of a viable opposition which pressured for reform and liberalisation, and an urban citizenry which was cynical and antagonistic toward continued authoritarianism. Without popular pressure, mediated by the opposition parties and often led by student radicals, political reform would probably have been postponed, or been slow in implementation, or even sabotaged by military and reactionary elements.

5. *Liberalisation: Widening the power base.* Liberalisation occurred in South Korea when the political reforms were seen to encourage responsible government and increased the possibility of a power transfer to an opposition-dominated government. This possibility was indicated in the 1987 presidential election, and nearly realised in the April 1988 parliamentary election. That the transfer has not occurred was due more to the divided opposition than to any aborted liberalisation in the South Korean state. Now that two major opposition leaders, Kim Young-sam and Kim Jong-pil, have joined the DLP, the likelihood of a transfer of power to an active opposition party is even more distant. The South Korean DLP is consolidating and coopting the moderates into a single, Japanese LDP-style, coalition. While the long-run impact of the new super-party remains unclear, it does not seem to bid well for democratic institutions in the sense of a system in which a political opposition aggregates demands, holds the government accountable for its actions, repre-

sents various interests in a plural society, and offers an alternative set of personnel and policies to voters. At the moment, it appears that the South Korean political reforms have led to liberalisation, but not democratisation.

Liberalisation of a modern dictatorship can be understood as a late stage in the significant reduction of state autonomy from society. An organised opposition is crucial as a counterweight to the state power of the government. Without it, as in the Soviet Union or China, the state remains the instrument of the regime with little prospect of change except through violent revolution or grudging concessions which may be withdrawn when crisis has passed. The expression of this liberalisation is expressed, enshrined and implemented in the constitution, the legal system and its enforcement, the accountability of government to a free electorate, the redistribution of power, and the possibility of a non-regime group taking control of the government.

Authoritarian liberalisation may also be characterised as the change from 'hard' to 'soft' authoritarianism. It has already occurred in Taiwan where elections in December 1989 increased the number of opposition representatives in the legislature. To be sure, it stops short of liberal democracy, but it is an important step toward full democracy. Without justifying authoritarianism, it should be kept in mind that both South Korea and Taiwan have been in a state of semi-war with highly militarised states, and cannot be expected to allow full democracy to emerge until unification or stabilisation/normalisation has been completed.

Conclusions

Historical oligarchies have sought to retain power with all means at their disposal. Today, whether the oligarchy is North or South Korean, Soviet or Chinese Communist, this remains constant. No government is so altruistic that it will step down from power in admission of failure without significant pressure from outside, nor will it voluntarily share power with its opponents. In this light, political reform in strong autonomous states can be seen as a process consisting of compromises designed to prolong the power of the ruling oligarchy.

Political reform is not inevitable when governments fail or lose their legitimacy. The North Korean system has stagnated for decades without facing any major authority crisis. The Myanmar generals are resisting any change despite widespread revulsion and rebellion, and even defeat in national elections.[33]

---

[33] The voters nearly annihilated the official government party in the 27 May elections, 1990. Even in constituencies with a large number of soldiers, the

The South Korean liberalising reforms are significant because of their success in facing up to the authority crisis by making fundamental changes in political regime, and bringing part of the opposition into government via elections. Through the changes of the past four years, the economy has maintained growth, but at a declining rate. Presidential succession occurred on schedule, and the Olympics were held with hardly a flaw. In the six years since the 1985 legislative elections, a strong and responsible opposition facilitated the reforms by negotiating with the government as potential partners in the state. To be sure, liberalisation cannot be guaranteed as permanent. Much has depended upon the character of the major actors—a cast which could change at any moment. But it has gone too far to be turned back easily, and this is no small accomplishment.

In considering political reform on a broader scale in the context of modern oligarchies, South Korea represents a relatively successful case of reform and liberalisation. There are several characteristics which make its experiences unique—including its ethnic homogeneity, geographical compactness, tradition of factionalism, and vulnerability to US influence. Unlike communist authoritarian systems, South Korea has avoided totalitarian methods of a single-party dictatorship and a single utopian ideology which rule out any role of legitimacy for opposition parties.

At present, communist systems are seeking to deal with new realities: in Mongolia, a new election law has been drafted and an opposition party has been established.[34] New opposition organisations are emerging in the Soviet Union and Eastern Europe. On the anti-*perestroika* side, China has tried to breathe new life into its moribund united front, the Chinese People's Political Consultative Conference (CPPCC), as a substitute for multi-party competition, and Vietnam rejects any hint of a multi-party system. It is abundantly clear that communist parties have failed to maintain legitimacy and must deal with political reform in a way that acknowledges an alternative to single party dictatorship. This must occur before any hope of liberalisation can be entertained.

We can also assume that a similar opposition may be a crucial ingredient for liberalisation in other authoritarian countries including the Soviet Union and the People's Republic of China. Currently, Soviet opposition has been emerging as ethnic nationalism. The rivalry between Boris Yeltsin and Mikhail Gorbachev may be personal and concerned with the pace of reforms, but it also expresses the growing distance between Russian nationalism and a united, centralised USSR. This ethnic/linguistic type of opposition, which is growing in other regions of the Soviet empire,

---

opposition League for Democracy candidates received 75 per cent of the vote. *Economist*, 2 June 1990, p. 21.

34 'Sodnom Says Mongolia Seeks Multiparty Reform', *Daily Report: East Asia*, 20 February 1990, p. 19.

may soon erode the fragile unity of the state. It is opposition which is ultimately anti-(Soviet) state, desiring new institutions to be dictated by national identities. It differs from the partisan opposition familiar in South Korea, Japan, and other relatively democratic polities where the boundaries and membership of the state are generally accepted and agreed upon. Two antagonistic visions of the state confront each other. Gorbachev's is that of the Stalinist, cosmopolitan pan-nation whose citizens are an artificial nationality, the 'Soviet people'. Yeltsin is the Russian patriot, whose idea of the state conforms to the nineteenth century nationalisms that have been unleashed in Eastern Europe and the corners of the USSR. To him, ideology is an artifice and cannot create a new sense of loyalty to supersede the centuries of language, art, religion, culture and other ingredients of national consciousness. He has perhaps more in common with the Lithuanian separatists than with Gorbachev.

To the Chinese communists, the idea of a loyal opposition is a contradiction. How can an individual or a group be loyal to the party or government or a principle (which is what the party claims to represent), and still play a role in opposing authority? Fang Lizhi personified the anti-party opposition type so abhorred by Beijing. His critiques of the Communist Party and Maoism were devastating and played no small part in inspiring the democratic dissidents in the spring of 1989. His sanctuary in the US Embassy in Beijing until late June 1990[35] symbolised his enthrallment to foreign ideas and that he was an alien intellectual who had betrayed his country. Similarly, the Chinese authorities have treated dissidents as criminals—anti-social and anti-socialist deviants who are either punished and allowed to repent, of are driven abroad—'proving' that their true loyalties are not to China, but to 'international bourgeois capitalism'. Savage reprisal has also been visited upon the Tibetans, who seek some autonomy from the Chinese suffocation of native culture. They are not merely opposition, but 'rebels'.

There seems to be no place in the PRC for any opposition—in contrast to Taiwan, where a healthy opposition flourished for years in the *dangwai* and more recently, the Democratic Progressive Party (DPP). With the lifting of martial law in 1987, there has been a decline in social order, and some members of the DPP have participated in violent demonstrations. Should violent opposition get out of hand, the PRC has reserved the right to intervene and restore order. Thus the appointment of a former general as premier may be meant to prevent such an opportunity to the mainland communists.

The hard fact that the mainlanders are a small minority on the island played some part in convincing the Guomindang to make some accommodations to the majority Taiwanese, who tended to support the opposition.

---

35 *Korea Herald*, 26 June 1990, p. 1.

Had the Guomindang defeated the communists in 1949, it is likely that some sort of opposition parties would be flourishing on the mainland today. Although the party is loosely based on Leninist principles, adherence to the ideas of Sun Yat-sen has a moderating influence on its totalitarian tendencies.

Today, the Taiwan government is cautiously seeking reconciliation with the mainland. Taiwan tourism to the mainland as well as business investment has increased since the Tiananmen massacre of 4 June 1989—rather surprising in light of the Guomindang's obdurate anti-communism since 1928. Perhaps Taipei senses—at least hopes for—the imminent collapse of Chinese communism, and plans to step in with money, ability, and a more genuinely Chinese ideology than Marxism–Leninism. In the present weakened stage, Beijing needs all the help it can get. Its own unification schemes in the recent past have called for a renewal of the United Front, which collapsed in 1940, between the CCP and Guomindang. Under this plan, the two parties would remain separate but cooperate in governing the country. In the recent past, Beijing's intention was for the Guomindang to rule Taiwan, but Taipei may be thinking in larger scope—Guangdong and Fujian as starters, perhaps.

The purpose of this chapter has been to distinguish political reform from political liberalisation, and to identify and explain how both have occurred in South Korea in recent years. From a comparative perspective touching on reforms in the USSR and the PRC, we can see that political resolution and authority alone can produce political reform, but the existence of a strong and autonomous opposition party seems to have been a precondition of political liberalisation in South Korea—and the same condition is possibly true elsewhere. While it is premature to say that the strength of the opposition in the National Assembly is the independent variable in Korean democratisation, its role is undoubtedly crucial.

5 The Democratisation of South Korea: What Role Does the Middle Class Play?

DONG WON-MO

One of the most controversial topics in the study of political change in South Korea is how and to what extent the middle class has contributed toward the democratisation process of the country, including the remarkable 'Democratic Revolution of 1987'. What is so striking about this ongoing debate is the fact that there is no agreement on either the meaning or the size of the middle class in the Korean context.

One school of thought contends that the emergence of a politically-conscious middle class (*Chungsanch'ung*), serving as a force of change for democracy and political pluralism, is an empirically-unfounded assumption based on suspicious government economic data. Some of the Korean scholars tilting toward this view concede that there may be something of a middle class in Korea, in smaller numbers than are often reported by mass media and the academic community. But they contend that the so-called middle-class citizens of the country are mostly opportunistic fence-sitters in the democratic struggle.

Others suggest that the Korean middle class may be materially better off than the low-wage strata (*Chosodukch'ung*), but that they are politically very conscious and active. When the issues are right, according to this school of thought, members of the middle class do not hesitate to take sides with the radical university activists of the ideological left in support of the cause of Minjung (People's) Democracy.

Among those who positively evaluate the role of the middle-class sector in the democratisation process, opinions vary considerably as to why its members become politically active, either continuously or intermittently.[1]

---

[1] For a critique of the ambivalent role of the middle class of South Korea, see the special April 1987 issue of the *Wolgan Choson*, which focuses on the topic

This study seeks to examine the validity of some of these contrasting views and theories of the politics of the middle class. It also attempts to assess the *actual* role of the middle class in the democratisation process of the country in recent years. In particular, this study directs its special attention to some primary motivating factors for an increasing and intermittent involvement of middle-class citizens in the anti-authoritarian political movement of the 1980s.

South Korea has emerged as a focal point of the international economic community. It is a dynamic, newly-industrialised country averaging a double-digit annual GNP growth rate during recent years. The country also has received considerable global attention for its traumatic but significant democratisation process since the summer of 1987. The quantitative economic growth and increase of political pluralism in the Republic of Korea has, thus, become a topic of increasing research interest among students of both economic and political development.

In South Korea the two-and-a-half decades of rapid export-oriented economic growth under the military-led authoritarian regimes since the early 1960s have brought a pace of social change never before experienced by the people of the country. Between 1960 and 1980 the population living in cities of over a half-million population increased from 61 to 77 per cent. Today more than seven-tenths of all South Koreans are engaged in industrial and service occupations, compared to two-fifths in the mid-1960s.

From 1965 to 1985, the number of Korean youths enrolled in secondary schools rose from 35 per cent to above 90 per cent. The college enrolment exceeded 1 million in 1984—a 370 per cent increase over 1974.[2] As of 1985, 33.9 per cent of high school graduates in South Korea entered a four-year college or university, compared with 28.6 per cent in Japan and 15.1 per cent in West Germany. The only industrialised country

---

of 'Chungsanch'ung ui hosang kwa silsang' (The False Image and Reality of the Middle Class), pp. 354–69. Several published works representing a cross section of divergent viewpoints are: Han Sangjin, *Minjung ui sahoe kwahakjok insik* (Understanding of the People by Social Science) (Seoul: Munhak kwa Jisongsa, 1987); Kim Jin-kyun, et al., *Han'guk sahoe ui kekup yon'gu* (Study of Social Classes in Korea) (Seoul: Hanul, 1985); So Kwan-mo, 'Pinbu kyokch'a wa kegup kaldung' (Rich–poor Gap and Class Conflict), *Shin Dong-a*, November 1987, pp. 552–61; Choe Jae-hyon, 'Han'guk ui chungsanch'ung: wae pigop'han'ga?' (Why Is the Middle Class in Korea Timid?), *Wolgan Choson*, April 1987, pp. 354–63; and Zinn Dokyu, 'Chungsanch'ung ui posuhwa munje' (Problem of Conservative Tendency among the Middle Class People), *Wolgan Choson* (February 1987), pp. 114–19.

2   Wonmo Dong, 'Students and S. Korea's Middle-class Revolution', *Dallas Morning News*, 20 July 1987.

with a higher rate of post-secondary school enrolment is the United States, where the 1985 figure was 37.5 percent.[3]

South Korea's real GNP increased at the average annual rate of 8 per cent[4] in 1967–1987, and the GNP per capita increased from $US278 in 1971[5] to almost $US5,000 in 1989.[6]

In light of these dimensions of rapid economic and social change, it is hardly surprising that the role of the middle class as an emerging social force of political change and democratisation has received increasing attention in social science literature in South Korea.

Defining the Middle Class

A basic problem in the study of the middle class in South Korea is that, because there are so many definitions of the Korean middle class, the estimated percentage of the people belonging to this socio-economic class ranges from a low of 23 per cent of the adult population to a high of 72 to 84 per cent—a whopping differential of a 1-to-4 ratio.[7]

While this great discrepancy in the estimated size of the middle class in South Korea is caused mainly by the different definitions used, another reason is the ideological underpinnings of contending theories of the middle class. Some university activists and the young academics who are ideologically sympathetic with them tend to exclude most of the self-identified middle-class citizens from that class category. They contend that unless people are in alliance with the Minjung (People Power) movement, they are for all practical purposes the political preys of the

3   Wonmo Dong, 'Why Radical Students in South Korea Are Rebelling', *Chronicle of Higher Education*, 20 July 1988.

4   *Time*, 29 June 1987.

5   Choo Hakchung, 'Development Strategies: The Korean Experiences' (Seoul: Korean Development Institute, 1982), p. 17.

6   According to a Bank of Korea report, South Korea's GNP per capita in 1989 was $US4,968. *Chungang Ilbo*, 27 March 1990.

7   The low estimate of Professor So Kawn-mo is reported in Pak Hyong-jun, 'Chungsanch'ungron ul tasi saeng'gak handa' (Rethinking About the Middle-class Theory), *Wolgan Chungang* (August 1988), pp. 592–3. Also see Han Sang-jin's estimates that the middle class comprises 48 per cent of the population. The high estimate is based on the spring 1987 survey of the Dong-a Ilbo (see *Dong-a Ilbo*, 4 April 1987). Han'guk Ilbo, *Han'guk ui chungsangch'ung* (The Middle Class of Korea) (Seoul, 1987) found that the percentage of the respondents who self-identified as the middle class in the joint survey of the daily paper and the Seoul National University's Social Science Research Center (4–13 May 1987) ranged from 72 to 84 per cent. See, ibid., pp. 11–12.

upper ruling class and that their temporary 'middle-classness' is of a marginal utility for the democratisation process of the body politic.[8]

According to the Economic Planning Board of the South Korean government, a middle-class citizen by definition should meet the following criteria:

1. Have a family income of at least 2.5 times as much as that of the legally-defined minimum living cost;

2. Own and dwell in a separate house or apartment, or rent a house or apartment with a deposit to be repaid on leaving;

3. Be employed on a full-time basis or own his/her enterprise(s); and

4. Attain high school graduation or above in education.[9]

On 22 November 1988 the Economic Planning Board announced that in 1980 an estimated 35 per cent of the population was middle class or above and that by 1985 the middle and upper classes comprised 43 per cent of the total population.[10] In other words, by 1985 the size of the middle-class population was approximately 38 per cent, if an estimated 5 per cent presumed to belong to the upper class is excluded.[11] At the rate at which the middle class was increasing in 1980–1985, therefore, it can be estimated that by 1988 the percentage of middle-class citizens (according to the EPB definition) reached between 40 to 45 per cent of the adult population in South Korea. This estimate conforms to the results of a detailed 1983 study of class structure conducted in the city of Taegu by the Christian Institute for the Study of Justice and Development. It reported that the two middle-class groups, salaried intellectuals of the middle strata and self-managed proprietors, constituted 38.3 per cent of the economically-active population[12]:

1. Capitalists   1.1

2. Salaried intellectuals of the middle strata   5.9

3. Self-managed proprietors   32.4

4. Working class   60.6

---

8   For this assessment from university activists of the evanescent nature and the 'political unreliability' of the middle class, see Han'guk Kidokkyo Sahoemunje Yon'guso, *Gisayon ripot* (Gisayon Report), (April 1988), pp. 213–4.

9   Han'guk Ilbo, *Han'guk chungsanch'ung*, p. 10.

10 *Saege Ilbo*, 23 November 1988.

11 *Dong-a Ilbo*, 4 April 1987, reported that 5.1 per cent of the respondents in its spring 1987 survey identified themselves as belonging to the upper class.

12 See Han'guk Kidokkyo Sahoemunje Yon'guso, *Taegu/Ulsan jiyok silt'aewa nodong undong* (The Situation in the Taegu/Ulsan Region and the Labor Movement), (Seoul: 1988), especially pp. 101–4.

The two estimates of the size of the middle class in South Korea cited above generally agree with the figure reported by Professor Han Sangjin of Seoul National University. According to Han, about 48 per cent of the Korean population can be classified as middle class in terms of both subjective identification and objective criteria.

The four socio-economic criteria Han used in his designation of the middle class are:

a. family income exceeding 75 per cent of the government-reported average family income;

b. job security (proprietorship and full-time employment);

c. educational attainment (at least high school graduation or above for those in their twenties, middle school or above for those in their thirties and no reference to education for those in their forties or above), and

d. housing index of house ownership for those in their forties (house ownership or two persons per room in case of a rented house).[13]

Based on these indices and the subjective class identification of his respondents, Han arrived at the following breakdown of the four subgroups of the respondents:

Table 5.1   Identification of Middle-Class Persons by Self Report and Objective Criteria (Unit: %)

Classification	Per cent
1. Self report	54.8
2. Self report but without objective criteria	22.3
3. No self report but met objective criteria	12.5
4. Self report and also met objective criteria	35.0

Source: Han Sangjin, 'Han'guk chungsanch'ung ui kaenyomhwa rul wihan sido' (Toward the Conceptualisation of the Middle Class in Korea), *Han'guk Sahoehak*, vol. 21; cited in Pak Hyonjun, 'Chungsanch'ungron ul tasi saeng'gak handa', pp. 592–5.

According to the above data, Han concludes that the middle class in South Korea can be estimated at 47.5 per cent of the total. Of the 54.8 per cent who subjectively identified themselves to be the middle class, 22.3 per cent did not meet the objective criteria. The total percentage of the middle class was based on combining the difference between (1) and (2)

---

13   Pak, 'Chungsanch'ungron ul tasi saeng'gak handa', pp. 592–3.

above—that is, 32.5 per cent—and (3) those meeting the objective criteria, 12.3 percent.

The above estimates of the percentage of the middle class for the late 1980s may be compared with the distribution of income and index of concentration, which is based on the income data provided by the Economic Planning Board. Table 5.2 shows that between 1965 and 1985 the general pattern of income distribution in the Republic of Korea did not change radically, although in the late 1970s the portions of the national income going to the upper 20 per cent of the population increased considerably—from 41.6 per cent in 1970 to 45.4 per cent in 1980.

Table 5.2   Distribution of Income and Index of Concentration (1965–1985)

10 groups	1965	1970	1976	1980	1985
1	1.32	2.78	1.84	1.57	2.06
2	4.43	4.56	3.86	3.52	4.02
3	6.47	5.81	4.93	4.86	5.24
4	7.12	6.48	6.22	6.11	6.39
5	7.21	7.63	7.07	7.33	7.47
6	8.32	8.71	8.34	8.63	8.76
7	11.31	10.24	9.91	10.21	10.21
8	12.00	12.17	12.49	12.38	12.14
9	16.03	16.21	17.84	15.93	15.42
10	25.78	25.41	27.50	29.46	28.29
GC[*]	0.3439	0.3322	0.3908	0.3891	0.3631
DDR[**]	19.34/41.81	19.63/41.62	16.85/45.34	16.06/45.39	17.71/43.71
9+10/1+2	7.27	5.83	7.95	9.04	6.37

Source: Economic Planning Board, Social Indicators in Korea 1987, p. 80.

* Gini Coefficient

**Decimal Distribution Ratio

Figure 5.1 demonstrates the persistence of a fair stability of income distribution during the two-decade period of high economic growth from 1965 to 1986. While the rich got richer, the middle-income group did not proportionally dwindle.

One group that did relatively poorly was the lowest 40 per cent of the income groups. But even that group did not do as poorly as most critiques of the government's development policy have argued.

Figure 5.1 Ratio of Income Possession by Income Group

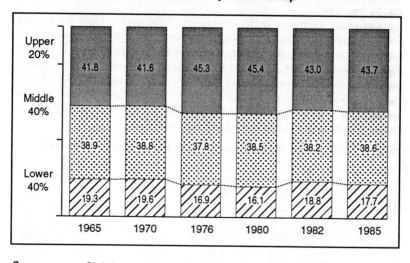

Source: Christian Institute for the Study of Justice and Development, *Social Justice Indicators in Korea* (Second Edition), (Seoul: 1987), p. 45.

Table 5.3 also indicates that the relative rates of growth in the average monthly income between 1980 and 1985 were remarkably close among

Table 5.3   Distribution of Income Decile (1980, 1985) (Unit: %)

Year	1985		1980	
Income group	Average monthly income	Share	Average monthly income	Share
1st	95,500 Won	2.06%	38,000 Won	1.57%
2nd	186,400 Won	4.02%	85,000 Won	3.52%
3rd	242,700 Won	5.24%	117,000 Won	4.86%
4th	295,900 Won	6.39%	147,000 Won	6.11%
5th	346,000 Won	7.47%	176,000 Won	7.33%
6th	405,300 Won	8.76%	208,000 Won	8.63%
7th	473,000 Won	10.21%	246,000 Won	10.21%
8th	561,400 Won	12.14%	298,000 Won	12.38%
9th	713,600 Won	15.42%	383,000 Won	15.93%
10th	1,310,300 Won	28.29%	709,000 Won	29.45%
		100.00%		100.00%

Source: Economic Planning Board, *Social Indicators in Korea 1986*; quoted in *Dong-a Ilbo*, 24 January 1987.

the three income brackets of the lower 40 per cent, middle 40 percent and upper 20 per cent—2.1 per cent, 1.9 per cent and 1.8 per cent, respectively.

Looking at the income distribution picture of 1982 (Figure 5.2), however, one is struck by the fact that among the self-employed managers, the upper 20 per cent, which includes the country's large enterprises, earned more than half of the total income for the sub-group while the bottom 40 per cent, representing mostly semi-subsistent, small self-employers, earned less than 15 per cent of the national income. In the agricultural sector, the lowest 40 per cent did somewhat better than their counterparts in the self-managed jobs.

Figure 5.2 National Income Distribution and Income Distribution by Householder's Occupation in 1982

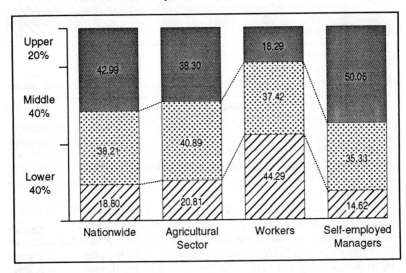

Source: Choo Hakchung and Yuon Juhyun, 'Distribution of Income in Korea, 1982: Its Estimation and Causes of Change', *The Korea Development Review*, vol. 6, no. 1 (Spring 1984), p. 7.

Needless to say, one can place too much emphasis on these income data provided by the economic bureaucracy of the government. But for the purpose of this study, it seems that the government income data generally support the two estimates (Dong and Han) of the relative size of South Korea's middle class, which will serve as the basis for examining several dimensions of the political attitudes and behaviour of the middle class.

Income distribution in South Korea lags somewhat behind Japan and the United States (see Table 5.4) The upper 20 per cent income bracket in

Korea had access to 44 per cent of the national income, as compared to 38 per cent in Japan and 40 per cent in the United States. However, the middle 40 per cent group in Korea compared favourably with its counterpart in Japan in the mid-1980s, as the proportion of the national income to which each group had access in Korea and Japan stood at 39 per cent and 41 per cent, respectively. The United States, as well as Canada, had a stronger middle 40 per cent group than did South Korea. As Table 5.4 reveals, however, South Korea was far ahead of Mexico and the Philippines in terms of overall income distribution—especially in terms of the strength of the middle 40 per cent bracket.

Table 5.4 Income Distribution: An International Comparison (Unit: %)

Income Brackets	Country						
	ROK ('85)	US ('80)	Japan ('79)	Canada ('81)	Italy ('77)	Mexico ('77)	Philippines ('75)
Upper 20%	43.7	39.9	37.5	40.0	43.9	57.7	53.3
Middle 40%	38.9	42.9	40.6	42.9	38.6	32.4	32.0
Low 40%	17.7	17.2	21.9	17.1	17.5	9.9	14.7

Source: World Bank, *World Development Report 1988*, p. 273; and Economic Planning Board, *Social Indicators in Korea 1987*, p. 80.

In studying the middle class in Korea, it is interesting to note that the proportion of survey respondents who subjectively identify themselves with the middle class far exceeds their numbers and percentages based on objective criteria.

One national survey that surprised many students of social stratification in Korea was the *Han'guk Ilbo* survey of 13 April 1987, which that reputable daily newspaper conducted in cooperation with Seoul National University's Social Science Research Center. The total number of respondents in this study was 1,043. They were asked rather bluntly whether they thought they belonged to the middle class, and 79 per cent answered that they did. Asked to indicate to which of the five groups they belonged in terms of their living standards, 16 per cent said they belonged to the group that 'lived well' and 68 per cent picked the group that 'lived fairly (moderately) well'. A total of 84 per cent thus responded that their living standards were above the middle level. Further, 31 per cent of the workers surprisingly said that they lived above the level of the middle group.[14]

---

[14] See Han'guk Ilbo, *Han'guk ui chungsangch'un*, pp. 9–11. For a summary of the findings, see *Han'guk Ilbo*, 9, 17 June and 15 July 1987.

Likewise, the *Dong-a Ilbo* survey of April 1987 found the self-identification with the five classes of the respondents as follows (in percentages)[15]:

1.	Upper class	5.1
2.	Middle class	38.4
3.	Low middle class	38.3
4.	Lower class	18.2
	TOTAL	100.0

It is noteworthy that a combined total of 76.6 per cent of those interviewed considered themselves either middle or lower middle class, which was very similar to the results of the *Han'guk Ilbo* survey of May 1987.

In 1988 the Economic Planning Board took another national sample of opinions and reported that 60 per cent thought they were in the middle class on 'the basis of income, education, property and living standards'.[16] The 1988 EPB figure is about 20 per cent lower than the one reported by the *Han'guk Ilbo* findings of May 1987. Be that as it may, it can be said that from three- to four-fifths of South Koreans like to think that they have joined or are on the verge of joining the ranks of the middle class.

This perception of the middle class among the Korean public has important implications for the political attitudes and behaviour of the middle class, as it is after all their own opinion of the 'political self' and their sense of group identity that largely determine how they act and interact in the political process.[17]

Some Korean analysts maintain that the actual size of the middle class is a small fraction of the numbers of self-identifiers. In fact, some of them estimate far below the approximately 40–50 per cent figure cited in this study. One *Dong-a Ilbo* economic reporter, in taking exception to the EPB report that 60 per cent of South Koreans consider themselves to be in the middle class, argued that this figure could not be correct, considering the fact that 48 per cent of all households and 60 per cent of urban households live in rented properties. The same journalist warned against the misinterpretation of the term *Chungch'ung*, the intermediate class, which he contends is mistakenly assumed to mean the middle class.[18]

Professor So Kwan-mo of Ch'ungbuk University, a well-known young political sociologist with a rising reputation among the student activists, takes issue with the 40 to 50 per cent middle-class figure based on the use of objective socio-economic criteria, let alone the much larger percentage

---

15 *Dong-a Ilbo*, 4 April 1987.

16 Ibid., 25 January 1989.

17 Ibid.

18 Pak, 'Chungsanch'ungron ul tasi saeng'gak handa', p. 593.

of self-identified middle-class persons reported in the *Han'guk Ilbo*, the *Dong-a Ilbo* and the EPB surveys. So maintains that as of 1987 the family income of 6.48 per cent of Korean households was below W500,000 ($US588)—the minimum monthly income for a family of four. 'How could any family possibly belong to the middle class while failing to earn the minimum income for survival?' asks So. With reference to the educational level of a middle-class person, he also finds serious flaws in Han's classification method whereby if a person is forty or above, he can be classified middle class even when he has attained no education at all.[19] Rejecting the general validity of Han's figures, So contends that according to his own survey administered to a male sample in 1985, the percentage breakdown of the different classes in South Korea was as follows:

1. Capitalist class	2.0%
2. New intermediate strata	15.0%
3. Old intermediate strata	9.0%
SUB-TOTAL (1, 2, and 3):	26.0%
4. Working class	43.0%
5. Urban semi-proletariat	9.0%
6. Farmers/fishermen	22.0%
SUB-TOTAL (4, 5 and 6):	74.0%
TOTAL:	100.0%

The new intermediate strata in So's study are mainly white-collar workers (both technical and clerical). They differ from the old intermediate strata, who are professionals in medicine and law and small and medium-sized self-employed proprietors. It is particularly significant that the principal reason for the low estimate by So—which turns out to be about one half of Han's figure—is the narrow basis of So's composite index. It excludes a sizable number of respondents from the middle-class category on the basis of several particularistic criteria such as the income level, house ownership and educational attainment.

The Middle Class and Politics

The political role of the middle class and the extent to which it can influence the democratisation of South Korea depends upon such variables as: the actual and relative demographic size of the group; its ideological commitment to the cause of political liberalisation and democratic institution-building; the quality of leadership and the capability for citizen mobilisation. In addition, the dynamics of coalition politics with other

---

[19]   So, 'Pinbu kyokch'a wa kegup kaldung', p. 554.

social strata significantly determine its effectiveness as a force for democratic change. During the past two years, social science literature in South Korea has been inundated with conflicting theories, new and contradictory findings and vastly contrasting prognoses. The 'middle-class theory' (Chungsanch'ung-ron) has emerged as a hot topic of contentious and heated debates in intellectual and political circles as well as among young activists.

In my survey of a large body of scholarly and semi-scholarly writings in Korea, I have been struck by the fact that until the summer of 1987 a majority of the students of the middle-class theory tended to show great scepticism, doubts and reservations about whatever positive roles the middle class was presumed to be playing in the democratisation of South Korean society.

For example, in an April 1987 article entitled 'The Middle Class of Korea: Why Is It Timid?', Choe Jai-hyon of Sogang University reported his criticism of the 'silent middle class' of Korea, by pointing out that the Korean middle class was interested in the promotion of private interests in the individualist mode over the advancement of social justice (communitarianism). In the Korean context, he observed, the old middle class (those engaged in professional and self-managed occupations) has sharply decreased while the numbers of the new middle class—mostly clerical and technical white-collar workers—have rapidly increased. But this 'new' and 'fragile' middle class of Korea fell far short of living up to societal expectations as an important force for social change and political liberalisation.

Choe maintained that the 60 to 90 per cent rate of middle-class self-identifiers greatly exaggerates the actual strength of this class in Korean society and that it would be better to refer to these self-styled middle-class individuals as the intermediate group (Chun'gang chipddan). Also Choe warned that 'depending on circumstances, the middle-class people do not hesitate to sacrifice workers' interests to promote their private interests'.[20]

Professor Choe's sceptical assessment of the role of the Korean middle class was reinforced by Professor Im Hyon-jin of Seoul National University. Im, who authored Modern Korea and Dependency Theory, wrote that 'the middle class of South Korea lacked substantive contents' in spite of their outward appearances of affluence and social consciousness. He contended that the faulty image of this class can be shown by the fact that it has thrived in the midst of a total absence of social movement and political struggle. Given these facts, Im concluded, it is premature and indefensible to call South Korea a middle-class society.[21]

---

20 Wolgan Choson (April 1987), pp. 345–63.

21 Ibid., pp. 364–9.

Two months before the articles by Choe and Im appeared in the *Wolgan Choson*, Professor Zinn Dokyu of Ehwa Womans University went a step further and argued that one major stumbling block in the democratisation process of South Korea was 'the conservative tendency of the middle class'. He observed: 'The people who are referred to as the middle class today are the "rootless entities" in Korean society; they are proud to exhibit their [improved social] position [but without real substance to it]'.[22] In essence, Zinn contended that the appearance of material abundance and heightened social consciousness among the Korean middle class is deceptive.

The above three views are but a small indication of the prevailing opinion among Korean intellectuals about the slight political consciousness of the Korean middle class. To the extent that this middle class in South Korea was preoccupied with the material improvement of their immediate private interests, the arguments of these observers seem to be well taken.

But what such scholars did not anticipate, even in March 1987 when the articles were submitted by Choe and Im, was a latent and potential political power of the outwardly apathetic middle class. This awakened power was soon combined with the 'physical' (*mullijok*) power of the university activists, the more determined and cohesive opposition politicos, and other dissident elements who coalesced in the 'Democratic Revolution of 1987'.

As shown in another recent study of mine[23], the primary issues that brought together the middle class with these other elements of political opposition were not the sense of economic justice and the depth of ideological commitment that the sceptics of the middle class seemed to have had in mind.

The important questions that we now need to raise are: What initially caused the 'Democratic Revolution of 1987' and the subsequent political events, which have arguably ended the continuation of the military-controlled authoritarian regime in Korea? Why did the 'conservative' and 'privately motivated' middle class of Korea join the university activists and other dissidents in the late spring and summer of 1987? And what motivated the white-collar people of the middle class, more than the factory and underpaid workers, to turn from the posture of idle bystanders to that of active participants in the political struggle of June 1987, which

---

22 Ibid. (February 1987), pp. 114–19.

23 See Wonmo Dong, 'Juridical Culture and the Rule of Law in South Korea: From Rulers' Law To Citizens' Law?' unpublished paper presented to the U.S. Constitution Bicentennial Symposium on Comparative Constitutionalism Perspectives on Civil Liberty in East Asia and the United States, Baylor University, 13–14 March 1989, especially pp. 25–31.

forced the Chun Doo Hwan regime to capitulate to the popular demands for direct presidential election and other democratic reforms?

First, the end of the authoritarian political order—marked by the 29 June 1987 declaration of Roh Tae-woo as leader of the governing Democratic Justice Party and the presidential successor hand-picked by Chun—was not due to a bad economy; it in fact came about in spite of a good economic performance. Secondly, labour unrest was not a principal cause, although since July 1987 the country saw rising demands for wage increases and unionisation. Thirdly, the militant and radical students alone were not capable of forcing the Chun regime and the governing Democratic Justice Party to agree to democratic reforms.

Furthermore, it would not be correct to attribute the downfall of military-authoritarianism primarily to the radical militancy of anti-American campus activists. They were supported by the urban poor, exploited farmers and disaffected intellectuals, but were shunned by an absolute majority of the middle-class people, at least until the early spring of 1987.[24]

Although a chain of important events in 1986 and 1987 indirectly contributed to the rapid disintegration and the eventual collapse in June 1987 of the Chun regime, perhaps the two most dramatic and critical blows to the political longevity of the Chun regime were the Sexual Interrogation Incident of July 1986 and the Pak Jong-ch'ol Torture Death incident of January 1987. They are referred to as the 'Korean Dreyfus Affairs'.

The former incident took place at the Puchon police station near Inchon, where a former Seoul National University coed named Kwon In-suk, who was employed in a factory under the pretence of high school graduation, was sexually assaulted while undergoing police interrogation. This incident literally shocked the whole nation and quickly became a political wildfire, which the Chun regime was not able to extinguish until on 29 June Roh Tae-woo accepted the opposition demands for democratic reforms, including direct presidential elections.[25]

The second incident that caused havoc for the Chun regime was another explosive case involving an extreme human rights violation. On 14 January 1987 the torture death of Seoul National University activist Pak Jong-ch'ol at the hands of several police interrogators was reported in the Korean and foreign daily papers. This tragic incident, caused by the

24 For this analysis of the South Korean political situation in the spring and summer of 1987, see Wonmo Dong, 'Students and S. Korea's Middle-class Revolution', *Dallas Morning News*, 22 June 1987.

25 Yi Sang-su, 'Puch'on songkomun sakon' (The Sexual Interrogation Incident of Puchon) in *Hyondae han'guk ul dwihundun yuksipdaesakon* (The Sixty Major Incidents That Shook Modern Korea) (Seoul: Dong-a Ilbo, 1988), pp. 324–7.

abuse of state power by police, became an instant *cause célèbre* of the democratic movement, which was now joined by the middle class.

It was an open secret that since the early 1970s, police, prosecution and security agencies in South Korea had practised political torture and forced interrogation. In the spring of 1987, however, the abuse of state power in violation of constitutionally guaranteed human rights went one step beyond the outer limits of people's tolerance and patience. The middle class had been heretofore lukewarm and aloof, if not outright silent, on other issues (especially economic issues). However, it became so agitated that many among the middle class joined the activist student demonstrators, taking to the streets with their shared indignation and frustration in more than thirty major cities in late June.[26]

On 13 April 1987 President Chun made a fateful mistake, which brought about the beginning of the end of his regime. Reversing his spring 1986 pledge to consider a constitutional amendment for direct presidential elections, he made an ill-advised announcement that he was absolutely opposed to any constitutional amendment for that purpose and would impose a moratorium on the matter until after his term of office expired in February 1988. This poorly-timed presidential decision precipitated an escalating nationwide protest movement, which was actively joined by the country's middle class.[27]

On 9 June the widely-read *Han'guk Ilbo* reported the result of the 4–13 May national opinion survey in which 85.7 per cent of the self-identified middle-class respondents were found to agree with the statement: 'We should promote human rights even if it delays economic growth'.[28]

Other important findings of the *Han'guk Ilbo* survey included the following (in percentages)[29]:

	Agreed	Disagreed
1. The middle class is the leading force of democratisation	75.9	23.5
2. The middle class considers political freedom more important than economic growth	52.1	47.7
3. The presidential power is too strong	89.4	1.4
4. The constitution should guarantee the people's right to rebel against undemocratic government	95.7	3.8

---

[26] Kim Ilsu, 'Pak Jong Ch'ol kun komunsagon' (The Torture Incident of Pak Jong Ch'ol) in ibid., pp. 340–5.

[27] The middle class participation was prominently reported by most papers both foreign and domestic. See *Yomiuri Shimbun*, 19 June 1987; *Dong-a Ilbo*, 29 and 30 June 1987.

[28] *Han'guk Ilbo*, 9 June 1987.

[29] Han'guk Ilbo, *Han'guk ui chungsangch'ung*, pp. 61–2 and 66–7.

Two principal issues motivated more than one million citizens in all major cities to join the spontaneous nationwide protest movement: the violation of human rights and the constitutional issues pertaining to the people's right to choose the President in the manner they determined. The rationale by the ruling regime of the *de facto* suspension of these constitutionally-guaranteed rights, on the grounds of national security and economic development, had outlived its legitimacy and persuasiveness as an acceptable government policy.

The Middle Class and Democratisation

In assessing the role of the middle class in the democratisation of South Korea, it is important to delineate the specific issues that motivate different segments of the population, including the middle class, to become involved in participatory democracy. A key factor influencing the activation of middle-class people in South Korea is their sensitivity to a stable social order. They are willing to support political and constitutional reforms, but not at the expense of the basic equilibrium and balance in the body politic. In their minds their political involvement is legitimate to the extent that it enhances the general cause of citizens' democracy *(simin minjujui)*, but not necessarily the particularistic political interests of the very poor or the very rich. This is why most of the middle class withdrew from involvement when the ideological rhetoric of *minjung minjujui* (people's democracy) was overplayed by the opposition movement.

Han Sangjin is very much on the mark when he writes: '[The Korean] middle class benefited economically, but was politically alienated'. He is very persuasive when he says that, although middle-class individuals are objectively better off, they may feel relatively more deprived than the workers.[30] According to one of Han's studies, 49.9 per cent of the new middle-class respondents felt that they benefited from the existing economic system in Korea, as compared to 50.1 per cent who reported a measure of relative deprivation.[31] In this regard, one interesting result of the 4–13 May 1987 survey of the *Han'guk Ilbo* is that a clear (62.9 per cent) majority of the middle-class interviewees said that in their opinion the middle class was more critical of the privileged class than was the lower class.[32]

In summary, the middle class of South Korea, however defined, is in favour of consensual political culture, as opposed to conflictual political

---

30 Han Sangjin, *Minjung ui sahoekwahakjok insik*, p 107.

31 Ibid., p. 11.

32 Han'guk Ilbo, *Han'guk chungsangch'ung*, p. 62.

culture[33], which proponents of the minjung democratic ideology have advocated in recent years. There is no denying that the quantitative size—and qualitative political consciousness—of the middle class is slowly and steadily increasing, the claims of the radical Left notwithstanding. According to some objective indicators, the size of the middle class has reached approximately 40 to 50 per cent of the economically-active population. At present, the Korean middle class appears to be more concerned about issues of democratic constitutional order and the rule of law than with issues of distributive justice and class cleavage.[34] While this does not mean that they do not suffer from a deep sense of relative deprivation, the political issues that engage their immediate attention, let alone active participation, have to do with 'freedoms from arbitrary and repressive rule and human rights violations' (*negative freedoms*), that is, the democratic political order of their society. For the most part, the middle class tends to shy away from the revolutionary ideology of the far left, which is more concerned about issues of *'positive freedoms'*—the people's substantive rights to fair wages, decent housing, stable commodity prices and affordable education. It should be anticipated, however, that in the future the middle class will turn its main attention more and more toward these matters of *'positive freedoms'*.[35]

In the spring and summer of 1987, the university activists successfully coalesced with the middle class in ending the quarter-century-old political order of military-authoritarianism. A common set of timely issues united these two powerful groups and brought about the downfall of the military-led dictatorial regime. But, after the 26 April 1988 National Assembly election, the coalition politics of student–middle-class solidarity largely disappeared until the post-Olympic struggle to resolve the irregularities and end the corruption of the Fifth Republic brought them together again.[36]

---

[33] For a comparison of these two types of political culture, see Gabriel Almond and G. Bingham Powell, Jr. (eds), *Comparative Politics Today* (Glenview: Scott, Foresman, 1988) pp. 446.

[34] For an indepth analysis of this topic, see Dong, 'Juridical Culture and the Rule of Law in South Korea', especially pp. 27–31.

[35] For articulation of the contrasting concepts of negative freedom and positive freedom, I am indebted to Richard M. Battistoni, 'American Civil Liberties: Ongoing Tensions Between Private Rights and the Public Good', unpublished research paper presented to the United States Constitution Bicentennial Symposium on Comparative Constitutionalism: Perspectives on Civil Liberty in East Asia and the United States, Baylor University, 13–14 March 1989, especially, pp. 2–7.

[36] See Wonmo Dong, 'In Seoul, Real Question Is: What After the Olympics', *Atlanta Constitution*, 20 September 1988.

What is remarkable about the characteristics of the middle class in South Korea is that they 'took to the streets to demand democracy, [but] they also chanted "order" in the midst of demonstrations'.[37] In this regard, it can be assumed that the Korean middle class believes in the continuum of *communitarianism* and *individualism*, rather than preferring one over the other. They seem to be neither for *liberal democracy* in the individualist mode nor for the *minjung* (people's) *democracy* in the communitarian mode. They are for *citizens' democracy*, which transcends class cleavage and the dichotomy of privatism and communitarianism.

Today South Korea is at a critical crossroads in its democratic transition away from the authoritarian dictatorship of the past forty years. The slow rise and the resilience of the middle class are underlying reasons for guarded optimism for the future of democratic change in South Korea. In this regard, a comparison of Korean democracy with the democracy of post-World War II Japan is instructive. In the words of Christena Turner: '[T]he Japanese people never fought for democracy...[It] was handed to them by the Americans [during the 1945–51 occupation period]'. Chalmers Johnson goes on to say[38]:

> A final factor working in favor of Korean democratisation is that the people took direct action in a revolutionary situation and forced political reform. It was not something bestowed by a foreign conqueror (as in Japan) or from above by a liberalising but still dominant élite (as in Taiwan).[39]

As the people—the middle class in alliance with the young university activists and other reform-oriented citizens of all social strata—have fought for democracy and political pluralism, they are likely to support and nurture the new democratic institutions and the newly-found rule of law which they themselves must struggle to achieve.

---

[37] *New York Times*, 13 March 1989.

[38] Cited in Chalmers Johnson contribution to this volume, p. 104.

[39] Ibid., p. 104.

6 South Korean Democratisation: The Role of Economic Development

CHALMERS JOHNSON

Modern East Asia is a junkyard for Western theories of economic development and political modernisation, and it is wise to remind ourselves of the area's profound exceptionalism whenever approaching a theory-intensive subject like democracy. Marx's great scheme of a progression from primitive communism to slave society and then on to feudalism, capitalism, socialism, and communism cracked on its obvious irrelevance to the history of classical Asia (viz. Oriental despotism, the Asiatic mode of production, and all that), which suggests that Marx's analysis of the role of classes in development and revolution is equally overgeneralised.[1] Similarly, Weber's discovery of the Protestant ethic as the lynchpin of capitalism in the West led him to write what may well be the world's most interesting wrong book, *The Religion of China*, in which Confucianism is held to be a major obstacle to the development of capitalism.[2] Needless to say, the spate of books claiming that there is a positive correlation between Confucianism and East Asian capitalism is a tribute to Weber's influence, not necessarily to the insight of the authors.[3] My own view is

---

[1] The *locus classicus* is Karl A. Wittfogel, *Oriental Despotism* (New Haven: Yale University Press, 1957), chap. 9.

[2] Max Weber, *The Religion of China*, trans. Hans H. Gerth (Glencoe, IL: Free Press, 1951), chap. 8 'Confucianism and Protestantism'. For the latest effort to save Weber from himself, see Andreas E. Buss (ed.), *Max Weber in Asian Studies* (Leiden: E.J. Brill, 1985).

[3] See, e.g., Kim Il-Gon, *Jukyo bunka-ken no chitsujo to keizai* (Order and Economy in the Confucian Cultural Area) (Nagoya: Nagoya Daigaku Shuppankai, 1986).

close to that of Winston Davis: religion, race, and primordial characteristics have practically nothing to do with economic development except
insofar as they can be used to justify the inequalities it produces.[4] In more
recent times so-called *dependencia* and World Systems theories foundered
on the economic performances of South Korea, Taiwan, Hong Kong, and
Singapore.[5] And now the appearance of democracy in many different East
Asian contexts is again posing anomalies for Western theory.

The area's, perhaps the world's most advanced industrial nation,
Japan, shows many signs of pluralism but at best only a weak and attenu-
ated democracy; whereas the Philippines, one of the area's poorer per-
formers economically, has undergone a genuine democratic revolution.[6]
At the same time, two of the most authoritarian regimes in East Asia and
arguably the two most successful cases of intentional economic development in human history, Taiwan and South Korea, are starting to
'democratise' (in quotes because we have not yet indicated what that
might mean). When they think about it at all, Westerners suppose that this
democratisation is occurring because these Asian nations are in some
sense capitalist countries like themselves, despite the long histories of
bureaucratic authoritarianism and single-party rule in all of them, including Japan.[7]

Economic Development and Democratisation

Does the degree of economic development achieved in Taiwan and South
Korea explain the timing of their movements toward democracy? Do their
high degrees of economic development offer propitious circumstances for
the establishment of democracy? Despite the contrary cases of Japan,
where democracy seems to recede as the nation gets richer, and India, the
Philippines, Costa Rica, and Colombia, where economic prosperity has

---

4   Winston Davis, 'Religion and Development: Weber and the East Asian Exper-
    ience', in Myron Weiner and Samuel P. Huntington (eds), *Understanding
    Political Development* (Boston: Little, Brown, 1987), pp. 221–80.

5   See Kim Kyong-Dong, 'Socio-cultural Aspects of Political Democratization in
    Korea', paper prepared for the Conference on Development and Democracy in
    East Asia: Taiwan, South Korea, and the Philippines, American Enterprise
    Institute, Washington, D.C., 18–19 May 1988; and Thomas B. Gold, *State and
    Society in the Taiwan Miracle* (Armonk, NY: M.E. Sharpe, 1986).

6   On the Philippine revolution, the best available account is Bryan Johnson, *The
    Four Days of Courage: The Untold Story of The People Who Brought Marcos
    Down* (New York: Free Press, 1987).

7   See, e.g., Milton and Rose Friedman, *Free to Choose* (New York: Harcourt,
    Brace, Jovanovich, 1980).

not accompanied democracy, many observers think there is a positive correlation between economic growth and democracy. John T. Bennett, after some initial reluctance, accepts that 'economic growth, at least that which is widely shared, promotes democracy'; and he quotes the *Wall Street Journal* in commenting on Korea's new democracy, 'You can't sustain economic growth over the long run without relaxing political restrictions'.[8] These views reflect in part the Western theory that the emergence of a true *bourgeoisie* (literally 'people of the cities' but in context meaning middle classes) provides the foundation and chief cause of political democracy. Barrington Moore is categorical on the subject: 'We may simply register strong agreement with the Marxist thesis that a vigorous and independent class of town dwellers has been an indispensable element in the growth of parliamentary democracy. No bourgeois [sic], no democracy'.[9] Thus, according to at least one version of common Western theory, economic growth in Taiwan and Korea has probably led to the emergence of a middle class in each country and that is why democracy is starting to appear there.

But there are problems with this theory, particularly as it relates to the most advanced capitalist countries, the United States and Japan. American democratic theory does not prescribe any particular level of economic development or the existence of a middle class for democracy to flourish. The Americans are, in fact, largely silent on the relationship, if any, between economics and democracy. This may, of course, merely reflect American myopia. Tocqueville thought that democracy succeeded in America for two reasons: the place was naturally rich, and the United States lacked a heritage of feudalism. The latter condition was important to help distinguish it from Latin America, which was equally rich but a failure at democracy. Reflecting on Tocqueville, Arthur Schlesinger came to this generalisation: 'Democracy is unlikely to last without economic progress, but economic progress does not guarantee democracy'.[10]

Japan appears to be an illustration of Schlesinger's point. Japan's attempts at democracy, as periodised by Rokuro Hidaka, break down into the following pattern of three failures:

---

8   John T. Bennett, 'Political and Economic Development in Korea', paper prepared for the A.E.I. Conference (n. 5); *Wall Street Journal*, 3 May 1988.

9   Barrington Moore, Jr, *Social Origins of Dictatorship and Democracy* (Boston: Beacon Press, 1966), p. 418.

10 Arthur Schlesinger, Jr, 'Democracy: The American Experience', in Kim Kihwan (ed.), *Progress in Democracy: The Pacific Basin Experience* (Seoul: The Ilhae Institute, 1987), p. 13.

- *First phase*: Meiji Restoration, 1868 to c. 1890. A period of 'enlightenment', with movements toward liberty, people's rights, and democracy.

- *Second phase*: 1890 to c. 1912. A period of nationalism and imperialism in which democracy waned.

- *Third phase*: 1912 to 1931. A period in which attempts were made to bring the absolutist system (*tennosei*) under democratic constraints, known as the era of Taisho Democracy.

- *Fourth phase*: 1931 to 1945. A period of militarism, ultra-nationalism, and the suppression of all democratic tendencies.

- *Fifth phase*: 1945 to 1960. A period of intense democratisation in the wake of Japan's defeat and the reforms of the Allied occupation.

- *Sixth phase*: 1960 to the present. A period of high-speed economic growth based in part on single-party government and the avoidance of political problems.

Throughout this 120-year period Japan continued to experience significant economic progress, but capitalism in the Japanese form does not produce or even seem to need political democracy in order to function. Contrary to Western bourgeois theory, capitalism in Japan seems to have flourished when democracy was weakest. Hidaka explains:

In the prewar period, the state unified the Japanese people by fostering loyalty to the Emperor. Today, the state coopts the people by elaborately redistributing profits to meet the people's expectations.

...The high-growth economy made this ability to redistribute profits possible...The postwar period can be divided into two phases: the phase of postwar democracy and the phase of high economic growth...The high-growth economy of Japan which began in the 1960s created a new state completely different in quality from the Japanese state during or immediately after the war.[11]

In other words, the periods of greatest economic growth coincide with periods of growing authoritarianism, not with periods of democracy, as Western theory suggests.

If the link between economic growth and democracy is problematic, i.e., not obvious, and the evidence from the major East Asian cases (Japan, Korea, and Taiwan) ambiguous, then let me turn to a direct analysis of the relationship between economic growth and democracy. First, however, what do I mean by democracy? It is necessary to answer this question as

---

11 Rokuro Hidaka, 'Personal Retrospective', in Gavan McCormack and Yoshio Sugimoto (eds), *Democracy in Contemporary Japan* (Armonk, NY: M.E. Sharpe, 1986), pp. 228–46.

specifically as possible because the concept of democracy is buried under so many layers of philosophy, description, and propaganda as to make it almost meaningless.

Definitions of Democracy

I follow Karl Popper's distillation of the essence of democracy for three reasons: (1) it is parsimonious; (2) it does not depend on a particular culture or religious heritage (e.g., a Periclean Age, Judeo–Christian ethics, or the Natural Law); and (3) it is very relevant to the transition from authoritarianism to democracy as it is encountered in East Asia today. Popper writes,

> How is the state to be constituted so that bad rulers can be got rid of without bloodshed, without violence?...The modern so-called democracies are all good examples of practical solutions to this problem...[They all adopt] the principle that the government can be dismissed by a majority vote...Nowhere do the people actually rule. It is governments that rule, [including] our civil servants—or our uncivil masters, as Winston Churchill called them...[Democracy thus means] not a theory of the 'rule of the people', but rather the rule of law that postulates the bloodless dismissal of the government by a majority vote.[12]

Popper's principle can be stated positively. What democracy requires is the institutionalisation of a competitive process by which people choose their leaders. Competition involves a rule-bound contest in which both sides recognise the legitimacy of the other side's interests and strategies so long as both sides obey the rules. Such institutions as the rule of law, bills of rights, constitutions, judicial review, and legislative oversight are devices to set, maintain, umpire, and when necessary change the rules of political competition. Democracy is the set of institutions that allows the citizens to hold their governments accountable for what they have done and what they propose to do. In a democracy, election day is judgement day.

Democracy in this specific sense should be distinguished from two related concepts—namely, pluralism and liberalisation. Pluralism refers to a state of a society that is commonly, but not exclusively, caused by processes of economic development (it may also be caused by immigration, acculturation, regionalism, and other non-economic forces). The advent of a pluralistic society often has the effect of increasing demands for democracy, since majoritarianism and the consensus building it entails coheres better with pluralism than any other form of government. Pluralism thus may be a cause of democracy, but not all democracies are necessarily

---

[12] 'Popper on Democracy', *Economist* (London), 23 April 1988, pp. 19–22.

pluralistic regimes (e.g., ancient Athens was not pluralistic in any contemporary sense of the term).

Liberalisation refers not to pluralism or democratisation but to the process of granting or establishing rights that protect individuals and social groups from arbitrary or illegal acts committed by the state or other citizens. Such rights include habeas corpus, security in one's home, protection of private property, and freedom of movement, speech, and religion. These rights may come from tradition, the common law, a fundamental grant of liberties such as the Magna Carta (1215), struggles between the executive and legislative branches of government, developments in the criminal law, and so forth.

In very general terms, pluralism promotes demands for liberalisation, and liberalisation is conducive to democratisation. The American revolution at the end of the eighteenth century, for example, was caused in part by a process of liberalisation that had gone on for the previous two centuries. The purpose of the revolution was to establish democracy in order to secure preexisting liberal rights against encroachments by (in the eyes of the Americans) English tyrants. When democratisation takes place before the development of either pluralism or liberalisation, the resultant democracy may fail—as in China in 1912, or most Latin American countries during the nineteenth century, or in Korea in 1960–61. But, again, liberalisation is not the same thing as democracy; one may cause the other and vice versa. Until very recently both Taiwan and South Korea have been more pluralistic and liberal than, for example, mainland China, without being democracies.

Keeping these fundamental distinctions in mind, let me try to relate the occurrence of democracy to various economic influences. It is possible for democratising movements to have no connection at all to the economy. A people may have ample reasons for wanting to judge and to be rid of its government other than economic reasons: Manila, February 1986, offers a good example. But there *are* cases in which people strive for democracy precisely to check the economic power of the state and to advance their own economic interests instead. These are the classic cases of the West associated with the concept of 'bourgeois revolution'. In these cases the capitalists opposed the monopoly or predominance of the state in economic affairs; and they were able to prevail against the state because they did not require state assistance in capital accumulation or in breaking up potentially socialist workers' movements and because the traditional landlord class had lost its potency. The industrial bourgeoisie of the West thus developed strong economic interests in restricting state power and in promoting a *laissez-faire* (i.e., government free) economy. It sought and defended democracy as a way to achieve these ends and to prevent political power from being used against it by groups with different economic interests. In this way the concept of democracy came to be associated with the interests of the middle class, but it actually refers only to the development of democracy and capitalism in some countries of the West. To make a general principle out of the particular bourgeois–democratic relationship that developed in Europe in the nineteenth century is to overgeneralise the experience of the West—but that is what virtually all Western social science theory does.

The Capitalist Developmental State

The relationship between democracy and the economy obviously changes when the state leads economic development, when it directly mobilises and allocates capital, when it licenses or subcontracts its projects to private entrepreneurs, and when it plays the predominant role in controlling the organisation of workers. This is the pattern that prevails under the 'capitalist developmental state' (CDS), a configuration which Japan invented and of which Korea since 1961 is a prime example.[13] In these cases very high levels of economic development can be achieved without eliciting any so-called bourgeois pressure to liberalise or democratise, and a collaborative but illiberal relationship between the state and private capital can persist for long periods of time. In the CDS, the role of entrepreneurship is largely preempted by the state, and private capitalists in effect fulfill contracts authorised by the state. Even so, as the CDS progresses to advanced levels of capital-intensive and knowledge-intensive industrialisation, the resulting high levels of pluralism will create a crisis of stability that *can* lead to democracy. There are various configurations that this crisis will take, and the process of resolving the crisis has as much to do with the occurrence of a democratic or a non-democratic outcome as the causes of pluralism itself. Before I turn to those configurations, let me briefly review the theory of intentional economic development in order to show the place of the CDS in it.

From a contemporary political economy perspective, the theory of intentional economic development is composed of four broad elements, the most important aspect of which is that they must occur in the following order: (1) a receptive social environment; (2) determined leadership;

---

13 See Chalmers Johnson, *MITI and The Japanese Miracle* (Stanford: Stanford University Press, 1982), and 'Political Institutions and Economic Performance: The Government–Business Relationship in Japan, South Korea, and Taiwan', in Frederic C. Deyo (ed.), *The Political Economy of The New Asian Industrialism* (Ithaca, NY: Cornell University Press, 1987), pp. 136–64. For a discussion of South Korea as a CDS, see Ahn Byung-Joon, 'Korea's Political Economy and International Environment', paper prepared for the A.E.I. Conference (n. 5).

(3) technical competence and (4) money (i.e., capital). The order is important: pouring aid money into places without either a receptive social environment or determined leadership of technical competence will not produce development but only corruption. Let me expand on each of these elements.

The idea of a receptive social environment is the broadest and least well-formulated aspect of the theory. It is merely a catch-all category to take into account the influence of cultural factors. The theory argues (or acknowledges) that intentional development cannot succeed in a culture that is hostile to economic activities or is so riven with ethnic, religious, caste, or tribal disputes as to put economic affairs on a low priority. Iran during and after 1979 offers an example of a culture that stood in the way of economic development, as does Spain during much of the nineteenth and twentieth centuries. Generally speaking, all of the countries of the Sinitic cultural area have societies that are conducive to development, although in several cases ideology and extreme forms of nationalism have been as severe obstacles to development (e.g., Vietnam, North Korea) as culture is elsewhere.

The second element of the theory, 'determined leadership', means something very specific. It refers to a draconian process of priority setting and maintaining. The theory holds that the overall process of development must be disaggregated into economic development, social development, and political development, each of which can be understood in *per capita* terms. Economic development means *per capita* increases in productivity. Social development means *per capita* increases in such measures as life expectancy at birth, basic education, health care, access to media of communication, and leisure time. Political development mean *per capita* increases in access to forums where binding decisions for the society as a whole are made. Political development is not synonymous with democratisation—access and the ability of a majority to dismiss the government are not the same—but the existence of democracy is evidence of advanced levels of political development.

The role of leadership in a campaign of intentional development is to promote one aspect of development, usually economic development, at the expense of the other two. (One can imagine a situation in which first priority is given to either political or social development at the expense of the other two, but these cases are less common. Mao's policies during the Chinese Cultural Revolution are an example of political development being advanced at the expense of social and economic development.) Giving priority to the economic sector requires that the leadership develop intrusive and preemptive capacities that can demobilise the social and political sectors while pouring resources into the economic sector. Based on the important historical cases (primarily Japan and the Soviet Union), the theory holds that only unbalanced schemes of development can succeed. Attempts at balanced development will only frustrate all development as resources will be spread too thinly into welfare schemes or politically popular projects. Determined leadership presupposes the existence of a serious, ruthless, informed élite—a Meiji oligarchy, a communist party politburo, or a military junta such as that of Park Chung-Hee—that can force these priorities on the society. Needless to say, to the extent that the developmental élite succeeds in its task, it will produce a seriously unbalanced society, one that is highly developed economically, moderately developed socially, and deeply underdeveloped politically. It is this imbalance that produces the ultimate crisis of legitimacy for developmental élites.

The third element of the theory, technical competence, refers to the need to educate enough members of the society to be able to staff the factories, offices, and governmental bureaux of a modern economy. Determined leadership without technical competence is not enough; that is what mainland China has had since its First Five-year Plan (1953–1957). All of the East Asian CDSs are heavy investors in education. Of course, this commitment to education leads to a contradiction: the greater the degree of education the harder it is to keep the social and political sectors demobilised. A strong nationalistic content to the education and controls over private contacts with the external world can mitigate its effects, however. Both Japan and the Soviet Union illustrate the point that the unbalanced configuration even with high levels of education can last longer than many Western critics of the these systems believe.

The final element of the theory, money, means that even the society perfectly organised for development must still find, squeeze out, or borrow funds that it can invest in more productive facilities. The ultimate need of the developing society is capital, that is wealth in whatever form that is not consumed but used to produce more wealth. The normal sources of developmental capital are forced savings, borrowing, and international aid. Another duty of determined leadership is to force savings from the population by restricting its consumption.

Nation-states undertaking programmes of intentional economic development usually do so for non-economic motives—national security, political ideology, overcoming neo-colonialism—and are therefore more concerned with the effectiveness of their programmes than with their efficiency. This is one of the reasons that they usually do not pay much attention to the advice of professional economists. At some point, however, very inefficient schemes of state entrepreneurship become ineffective and must be reformed. Generally speaking, there are three broad patterns of state-initiated economic development—those in which the state monopolises ownership and control of all productive assets, those in which the state retains ownership but decentralises control to the level of enterprises and households, and those in which the state eschews ownership but exercises control through the manipulation of incentives, rationing of resources and capital, cartels, and so-called 'administrative guidance'. Examples of the first are the true 'command economies' (e.g., the Soviet Union), examples of the second are the reformed command economies (e.g., Hungary, mainland China), and examples of the third are the CDSs (e.g., Japan, South Korea, and Taiwan). Economies in which both ownership and control are in private hands and the state is restricted to a regulatory role approximate the *laissez-faire* model of neo-classical economic theory (e.g., the United States, Hong Kong). It is also only the latter to which neo-classical economic theory is relevant.[14] Of these four types the CDS is historically the most successful in terms of the levels and pace of economic development actually achieved. It is not without its human costs, but in general it is also less costly in human suffering than the Soviet-type command economy.[15]

The Crisis of Unbalanced Development

A successful CDS, that is, one that has broken economic growth, sooner or later must face a crisis caused by its extreme imbalance. Japan during the 1920s displayed this configuration in an acute form: high economic development, fair social development, and poor political development. During the decade Japanese élites undertook various reforms intended to correct the imbalance in the society, but these were eventually overwhelmed by an international crisis. There is nothing predetermined about the outcome of the crisis of imbalance: it may lead to renewed authoritarianism (as in Japan in the 1930s), it may lead to democratisation (perhaps contemporary Spain and Portugal are examples), and it may lead to an indefinite postponement of any resolution so long as the élites are able to 'manage' the crisis (e.g., Russia under Brezhnev, Japan today).[16]

---

14 I am indebted to Wu Yu-shan for these distinctions based on ownership and control. See his *Leninist State and Property Rights: Economic Reform in the People's Republic of China* (Ph.D dissertation, political science, University of California, Berkeley, forthcoming). On the relevance of neo-classical economic theory to the CDS, see Chalmers Johnson, 'The Japanese Political Economy: A Crisis in Theory', *Ethics and International Affairs*, vol. 2 (1988), pp. 79–97.

15 For a listing of some of the human costs of Japanese development, see Mikiso Hane, *Peasants, Rebels, and Outcasts: The Underside of Modern Japan* (New York: Pantheon, 1982).

16 Note that Professor Hidaka refers to Japan today as a *kanri kokka*, which he tranlates as 'control state' but might more accurately be rendered 'managerial state', *Democracy in Contemporary Japan*, p. 244

The breakdown of authoritarian regimes is contingent on a host of factors. One of the most important is leadership errors by the élite that make the crisis situation worse. This is the most common final cause of revolution.[17] If, for example, the élite is constituted as an exclusive body, e.g., a military élite, it cannot use its greatest potential weapon in attempting to defuse the situation—namely cooption of protest leaders into the status quo élite. The Mexican ruling party has used this gambit for years, and the Kuomintang in Taiwan has largely defused the Taiwanese separatist issue by coopting Taiwanese into the party and the government. A regime that cannot coopt protesters is much more fragile than one that can. Some classic examples of leadership errors that deepened the crisis include Louis XVI's calling the estates general in 1789; Ferdinand Marcos calling a snap election in February 1986; and Chun Doo-Hwan's decision of 13 April 1987, to suspend further debate on the Korean constitution.

The transition from authoritarian rule to more popular forms of government, when it occurs, usually occurs for one of three reasons. The first is international factors, commonly defeat in war. Japan owes its democracy today to its losing a big war to 'the right people at the right time'. Similarly, contemporary Argentine democracy came about because Argentina lost the Falklands War, thereby discrediting its military regime. The second reason is a decision unilaterally by the authoritarian regime to liberalise, which often leads to democratisation. It may do so because it recognises that the success of its economic development programme has produced many medium and smaller enterprises that are beyond its control. Both because it trusts the moderation of these bourgeois forces and to avoid seeing them radicalised, the regime decides to liberalise. Something like this is occurring in Taiwan today. The third reason for the transition is the development of a true revolutionary situation. These cases will be resolved either through revolutionary violence or else one side or the other, usually the one with the least legitimacy, will back down and undertake reforms.

The Case of South Korea

South Korea offers a vivid illustration of these generalisations about intentional economic development and the crisis of unbalanced development that it produces when it succeeds. Let me therefore try to place the Republic of Korea in the perspective outlined here. All CDSs are authoritarian (explicitly or covertly) but not all authoritarian regimes are CDSs.

---

17 See Plato, *Republic*, Book 8. Cf. Chalmers Johnson, *Revolutionary Change* (Stanford: Stanford University Press, 1982), chap. 5

Some authoritarian regimes are merely preservative.[18] South Korea has experienced both kinds: under the First Republic of Syngman Rhee (1948–1960) and under the Third (1962–1972) and Fourth Republics (1972–1980) of Park Chung-Hee. The Masan Revolution of 19 April 1960 that overthrew Rhee, was a straightforward democratic revolution without economic causes. It has strong similarities to the Aquino Revolution of 1986 in the Philippines and illustrates again that a people may want democracy—the ability to dismiss their government bloodlessly—regardless of their economic interests. Nonetheless, the Korean revolution of 1960 was important for later events because of the dramaturgy and precedents it established: it was led by students, a major student martyr was created (in 1960 Kim Chu-Yol was tortured to death by the police just as in 1987 Park Jong-Chul died under similar circumstances), and authoritarian arrogance inflamed non-participants and caused them to rally behind the students.

The 1960 revolution and the subsequent 1961 military *coup d'état* led to the creation in South Korea of a true CDS. Between 1962 and 1987 the Korean economy grew at an average rate of 8.9 per cent per year, and for the years 1986 and 1987 it grew at 12.6 per cent and 12.3 per cent respectively. These growth rates have political significance in that they show that Korea could *afford* to bring its CDS into greater balance even if that caused its growth rate to fall into the 6 to 8 per cent range. This economic development had the effect of shifting the composition of the Korean labour force from 79 per cent engaged in the primary sector in 1961 to 70 per cent engaged in the secondary and tertiary sectors in 1988. Nonetheless, this shift did not produce a large middle class independent of the state, as in Taiwan, because the Korean CDS followed the Japanese model closely in its reliance on large, state-supported conglomerates *(zaibatsu* in Japan, *chaebol* in Korea). Professor Kim Kyong-Dong notes the political consequences:

> The entrepreneurial–managerial élite initially emerged in the early period of the new republic in close collaboration with the politico–bureaucratic sector, and has maintained the relationship essentially the same way throughout...The role played by the entrepreneurial–management sector as far as the process of political democratization is concerned has been passive, if not negative. By actively leading the way to economic growth, it has provided soil for rising aspirations among the people for greater amounts of democracy. Nonetheless, this sector has not actively sought to

---

18   For further details, see Barry Rubin, *Modern Dictators* (New York: McGraw-Hill, 1987).

persuade the governing politico-bureaucratic élite to pursue democratization programs.[19]

So much for the Western theory of a middle-class vanguard leading the way to democracy. One important difference between the Korean CDS and military regimes in South America is that General Park civilianised his junta and operated the CDS under a facade of democracy and constitutionalism. Park and his allies replaced their uniforms with civilian clothes, and they worked through political parties (the Democratic Republican Party and its contemporary successor, the Democratic Justice Party) to control the National Assembly. Equally important, Korea's generals-turned-politicians placed their cadres in the party and the secret police, and they dominated the armed forces, not the other way around. In Latin America the survival of the governments run by generals depended almost entirely on the support of fellow military officers. Park's civilian front allowed him to coopt many technical élites, including those educated abroad. When the crisis of imbalance came to Korea, it did not directly discredit the armed forces thereby allowing them to remain neutral.

The crisis in Korea was precipitated by the February 1985 elections for the National Assembly, in which the New Korea Democratic Party, led by Kim Young-Sam and Kim Dae-Jung, emerged as the largest and most articulate force in the legislature. And this election was in turn conditioned by the approach of the 24th Olympiad, scheduled for Seoul in 1988, which focused international attention on Korea's economic successes and its political shortcomings. Sensing that he could not reestablish the bases of legitimacy of the Park regime for his own government, President Chun tried to win popular endorsement through support of Korean nationalism. Clearly he could not take credit for economic development (Chun's coup of 1980 had, in fact, threatened it), and the alleged threat from the North was beginning to wear thin as an excuse for military rule in the South. Thus, Chun sponsored Korean nationalism in the form of the Asian Games of 1986 and the Seoul Olympics of 1988.

The 24th Olympiad

The Olympics proved to be a great constraint, opening a window of opportunity for protest. If the government had declared martial law to stop

---

[19] Kim Kyong-Dong, 'Socio-cultural Aspects of Political Democratization in Korea' (n. 5). On the Korean conglomerates, see Fukagawa Yukiko, 'Keizai o saseru zaibatsu pawa' (Zaibatsu Power that Maintains the Economy), *Chuo koron*, March 1987, pp. 220–1. This is one of 13 articles in a special collection entitled 'Nikkan shinteikei jidai no makuake' (Opening of a New Era of Japanese–Korean Cooperation), pp. 172–231.

the protests, which began in 1985, the International Olympic Committee would have been forced to shift the games elsewhere. That would have humiliated the nation and discredited Chun. Thus the demonstrations went ahead in favour of a constitutional amendment authorising the direct election of the president. The intent of this change was to prevent Chun and his colleagues from perpetuating their rule through a Japanese-style singleparty regime. In order to stop the demonstrations, Chun in April 1986 unexpectedly made a concession and declared that he would support any constitutional change endorsed by the National Assembly, where his party had *de facto* control. Chun himself promised to leave office in February 1988 in any case.

This concession ended the demonstrations and led to protracted squabbling and ultimate deadlock among the various political parties and factions. Then Chun misread the public mood and made a fatal blunder. Hoping to reverse his earlier concession and using the Olympics and his own departure from office as excuses, on 13 April 1987, President Chun said that he had decided 'to put constitutional change on hold'. A month later, on 10 June, the national convention of the Democratic Justice Party nominated former general Roh Tae-woo as its candidate to succeed Chun in an indirect election. The country erupted in violent street demonstrations. A revolutionary situation existed in the sense that the protesters sensed public support shifting to their side and the government dared not use its ultimate weapons of coercion, the armed forces, because that would also have scuttled the Olympics. On 29 June candidate Roh split with Chun, accepted the opposition's demands for constitutional reform and an end to police surveillance of opposition politicians, and promised investigations of long-standing grievances. It was a masterful political move. The subsequent presidential election of 16 December 1987, and the parliamentary elections of 26 April 1988, ended the authoritarian regime in Korea, ushered in the Sixth Republic, and inaugurated parliamentary democracy. What are its chances of surviving? In a broad socio-economic sense chances are good because the Korean CDS was badly imbalanced and its degree of development and the consequent pluralism of the society called for compensatory political development. But the relationship between economic and political development is in no sense deterministic. There are several contingent factors, some working for Korean democracy and some working against it. Among the negative factors one is that the vanguards in the street battles of June 1987 were composed almost entirely of students and not substantial elements of the middle class. Student nationalism in Korea goes back at least to the 1919 demonstrations against the Japanese occupation, and it is therefore autonomous from the changes wrought by Korea's economic development. Given enough time the student movement will probably break down from within, particularly as it comes more and more to be dominated by intransigent radicals (the Minmintu, Sanmintu, and Chamintu factions). There may not be enough time, however, given that politically and economically Korea cannot afford the luxury of ceaseless street battles.[20]

One possible solution would be an American military withdrawal from Korea, which would defuse the main nationalistic issue that the students are attempting to exploit (American pressures for Korean reciprocity in terms of market access, the belief that the United States tacitly supported the Chun regime, including its use of force at Kwangju in May 1980, and the feeling that the American presence blocks progress toward negotiations with the North and improved relations with the Communist nations). Korea no longer needs American ground forces based inside the country to guarantee its security, and the growth of the Korean economy has caused the military budget to drop from 6 per cent to 5 per cent of GNP even as it is being expanded. American withdrawal could save the United States as much as $23 billion per annum, an important consideration given the American fiscal imbalances, and guarantees of air and naval protection from American forces in the area could be continued. Perhaps most seriously, a continued presence of American ground forces inside Korea could damage Korean democracy because it both fuels student nationalism and perpetuates Korea's dependent position as an American protectorate. The case for American withdrawal is strong.[21]

Another negative factor in preserving Korean democracy is the apparent unwillingness of all parties in Korean politics to abide by the rules of democratic competition and to compromise their differences. Even though Roh Tae-woo made the first compromise in his historic declaration of 29 June 1987, his subsequent cabinet appointments of 19 December and

---

20 On the Korean student movement, see Wonmo Dong, 'Students and Politics in South Korea', *Journal of International Affairs*, vol. 40, no. 2 (Winter/Spring 1987), pp. 235–55; and 'Student Activism and the Presidential Politics of 1987 in South Korea', in Ilpyong Kim (ed.), *Political Change in South Korea* (New York: Paragon House Press, 1988).

21 For the figure of $23 billion, see 'Cut South Korea's Umbilical Cord', *New York Times*, 31 March 1988. In a recent study of Korean–American relations, the Council on Foreign Relations opposes an American withdrawal, but it acknowledges that the relationship will worsen so long as the American presence continues. It also argues that the Koreans can avoid economic liberalisation so long as the American protectorate is maintained since it also protects Korean vested interests from change. Liberalisation up to now has been only *pro forma* because of the preference for government control of the economy on the part of bureaucrats and the businesses that benefit from it, the anti-import bias built into the system (import liberalisation is carefully planned in consultation with the businesses that will be affected to minimise the impact), and the fear of political repercussions. *Korea at the Crossroads* (New York: Council on Foreign Relations, 1987), p. 33.

his forcing through a new election law at 2.10 a.m. on 18 March 1988, revived fears among the public that the government hopes to rig democratic procedures. Equally seriously, the inability of the opposition to unite behind principles rather than personalities and the extreme regionalism displayed in the elections of 26 April suggest that democracy may only be a slogan among many opposition politicians. If the Korean National Assembly, much like the Japanese Diet, proves unable to supervise and hold accountable Korea's formidable bureaucracy, democracy may prove to be only formal and empty.

On the positive side, the election of 26 April advanced the chances of political stability because it brought all the major dissidents and critics of the government into the National Assembly. If the government party had triumphed, this would have produced an explosive polarisation in society between the 'ins' and the 'outs'. The election, together with the discrediting of ex-President Chun following the arrest in March 1988 of his brother on corruption charges, means that the National Assembly has become the locus of Korean politics. Behind the scenes manipulation has become less important than parliamentary politics. Parliament is the great school of democracy, and Korea now has a healthy one.

A final factor working in favour of Korean democratisation is that the people took direct action in a revolutionary situation and forced political reform. It was not something bestowed by a foreign conqueror (as in Japan) or from above by a liberalising but still dominant élite (as in Taiwan). A persistent source of weakness in Japanese democracy is the feeling that it lacks grass roots. This shows up in many different places in Japan. In Christena Turner's study of labour disputes, for example, one labour leader said to her that the problem with democracy in Japanese unions is the same as for democracy in Japan as a whole:

> The Japanese people never fought for democracy. They have never had to insist on their rights to participation. It was handed to them by the Americans and now we are all trying to make it work. But unless you know how to insist, how to fight, on your own behalf it can't really work.[22]

The best thing going for democracy in Korea is that the people themselves were involved in its creation and have a stake in its survival.

---

22 Christena Turner, 'The Phoenix Falters', paper presented at the Colloquium of the Center for Japanese Studies, University of California, Berkeley, 20 April 1988.

PART II

DEMOCRATISATION: PROCESS

7 The 1988 Parliamentary Election in South Korea

KIM HONG-NACK

The results of the 13th National Assembly election on 26 April 1988, stunned political observers in Korea and abroad, for many expected the ruling Democratic Justice Party (DJP) to win a comfortable majority in the unicameral legislature. The two major opposition parties, the Reunification and Democracy Party (RDP) and the Party for Peace and Democracy (PPD), continued to be hopelessly divided even after their defeat in the December 1987 presidential election and the new president, Roh Tae-woo, was gaining popular support in the country.[1] Contrary to predictions by many observers, when the ballots were tallied the government party, for the first time since 1950, failed to capture a majority of seats in the Assembly. As a corollary of the changed constitutional status and power of the parliament under the Sixth Republic, winning a majority in the election was important both for the government party and the opposition. For the former, it would be difficult to push through key legislative programmes without controlling the National Assembly. For the opposition, control of the legislature was needed in order to check the DJP government. The opposition was particularly concerned about the prospect that majority control in the Assembly by the ruling DJP would impede, if not endanger, the process of democratisation in South Korea, a process begun in earnest after the bloody constitutional crisis in the spring and summer

---

[1] According to an opinion survey conducted jointly by the *Hankuk Ilbo* and a Sogang University research team on 31 March–1 April 1988, 55 per cent of the respondents indicated their satisfaction with the performance of the Roh government. See *Hankuk Ilbo*, 5 April 1988.

of 1987. Thus, the stakes were high for all parties. This essay analyses the results of the 1988 election, emphasising factors that contributed to bringing about the so-called *yadae yoso* (large opposition and small government party) phenomenon in the parliamentary election. In addition, it attempts to evaluate the implications of the election results for the future of the South Korean party system.

Revising the Election Law

In drafting the new constitution of the Sixth Republic in the fall of 1987, the DJP and its opposition were generally in agreement on the need to strengthen the power of the National Assembly, which, under the Fifth Republic, was disproportionately weak *vis-à-vis* the executive branch of government. Thus, under the new constitution, the National Assembly regained all of the powers it had lost under the Park and Chun regimes. No longer relegated to the position of ratifier of policy, it is now empowered to check effectively the executive branch; it has the power to legislate, approve the national budget, investigate wrongdoings of government officials, audit government agency expenditures, adopt a vote of no confidence against the prime minister and cabinet members, and impeach executive and judicial officials by a majority vote and the president of the Republic by a two-thirds vote. By majority vote, it can suspend martial law proclaimed by the president. Moreover, unlike under the Fourth and Fifth republics, the president has no power to dissolve the National Assembly.

Following the bitterly-fought presidential election in December 1987, preliminary negotiations were conducted between the government party and the opposition to revise the parliamentary election law and to set a date for National Assembly elections. Initially, the DJP wanted to hold the election in February 1988, for the ruling party would benefit from the bandwagon effect of its victory in the presidential election as well as disarray in the demoralised opposition resulting from continuing discord between the RDP led by Kim Young Sam and the PPD led by Kim Dae Jung. Opposition parties favoured delaying the election until April to give them more time to regroup and organise candidates and a campaign. Eventually, the DJP agreed to the April date, due to an unexpected delay in revising the election law. Besides, scheduling the election in February would have enabled incumbent President Chun to handpick many parliamentary candidates for the government party at the expense of incoming President Roh.

A more difficult problem for the parties was overhauling the parliamentary electoral system. Under the Fifth Republic (1980–February 1988), two-thirds of the 276 National Assembly members were elected from 92 two-member districts. The remaining one-third (or 92 seats) were elected through a proportional representation system. Two-thirds of these seats were allotted to the party winning the largest number of district seats, while one-third was allocated in proportion to the seats won by the other parties. The system as a whole favoured the government party, assuring it a comfortable majority in the National Assembly. In the 1985 parliamentary election, for example, the ruling DJP won 46 per cent of the district seats with 35.4 per cent of the popular vote, but the seats available through proportional representation boosted the party's share to a 54 per cent majority. The system was not only regarded as undemocratic by the opposition parties but also was unpopular with the voters.

In approaching the problem of overhauling the electoral system, the DJP initially favoured a combination of single-member districts in rural areas, two- to four-member districts in urban areas, and a reduction in the number of at-large seats available under proportional representation. When protracted negotiations failed to produce a necessary compromise, the DJP on 8 March rammed a bill through the National Assembly to amend the election law on the basis of a single-member district (SMD) system. Its decision was based on shrewd calculations that the SMD system would be best for the party due to strong popular support for such a system and especially in view of the continuing rivalry between the RDP and the PPD that was sure to split the opposition vote. Among the opposition parties, the PPD supported the SMD system, expecting to capitalise on its highly concentrated support in the southwest (Cholla) provinces and part of Seoul. The RDP, on the other hand, initially favoured a multi-member district system, because its vote was more evenly scattered throughout the country. However, it too eventually leaned toward the SMD system.[2] The only party that maintained uncompromising opposition was the New Democratic Republican Party (NDRP) headed by former Premier Kim Jong Pil.

Under the new DJP-sponsored electoral system, the National Assembly consists of 299 seats: 224 to be filled through the SMD system, and the remaining seventy-five at-large seats to be allocated by a proportional representation scheme. If a party wins a majority of the 224 district seats, the seventy-five at-large seats must be allocated in proportion to the share of the district seats won by each party. If no party wins a majority of the district seats, the party with the largest number of seats is entitled to thirty-eight of the seventy-five at-large seats. The remaining thirty-seven seats are then allocated to other parties winning five or more district seats in proportion to each party's share.

---

2   John McBeth, 'Hats in Their Hands', *Far Eastern Economic Review* (hereinafter *FEER*), 7 January 1988, p. 16, and John McBeth, 'Electoral Expectations', *FEER*, 21 January 1988, p. 35.

Candidates and the Campaign

Following the announcement of the 26 April election date, the DJP nominated its candidates for each of the 224 electoral districts. Many influential lawmakers, including former DJP Chairman Kwon Ik Hyun, former Secretary-General Kwon Jung Dal, and Kim Sang Koo, former President Chun's brother-in-law, were denied renomination. The party dismissed twenty-eight of the eighty-six incumbent local chapter chairmen (32.6 per cent), while nominating 125 new individuals as candidates. The denial of renomination to key figures of the Fifth Republic power group was apparently engineered to consolidate the power of the party's new president, Roh Tae-woo.[3] In addition, the DJP named sixty-two candidates for the at-large seats available under proportional representation.

The RDP, the major opposition party, fielded 202 candidates, including forty-one incumbents. It denied renomination to twelve incumbents who had tarnished the party's image by collaborating with the government party. The PPD nominated 168 candidates, including twenty incumbents. Five incumbent lawmakers were denied renomination, while most of the former dissident figures aspiring to run in the election were named. The PPD did not field candidates for many constituencies in Kyongsang and Chungchong provinces where the party was weak and unpopular. Former Premier Kim Jong Pil's party, the NDRP, fielded 181 candidates. By 9 April, altogether 1,045 candidates had registered in 224 electoral districts.[4] The average competition rate per seat was 4.7 to 1, and in terms of the number of candidates it was the largest field since 1961. Most ran under the auspices of one of the fourteen political parties participating, but 111 ran as independents.

With the start of the eighteen-day official campaign period on 9 April 1988, both the government and opposition parties launched massive efforts to win popular support. They intensified their political offensives against each other, trading fierce charges and countercharges over the 1980 Kwangju incident in which nearly 200 people had been killed, the *Saemaul* (New Village) Movement scandal involving embezzlement of millions of dollars by former President Chun's brother, Chun Kyong-hwan, and other major irregularities and corruption perpetrated by powerful elements including Chun and his family. Opposition parties also raised questions about the legitimacy of the Roh government, which they

---

3 *Dong-a Ilbo*, 22 March 1988. See also, *Korea Newsreview*, vol. 17, no. 13 (1988), pp. 4–5.

4 Chang-hee Kim, '13-dae Chongson Kyolkwa, Cholmyo han Sontaek, Cholmyo han Kudo', *Shindong-a* (June 1988), p. 171. See also, *Korea Newsreview*, vol. 17, no. 16 (1988), p. 5.

regarded as an extension of the illegitimate Fifth Republic.[5] The 'three Kims', namely Kim Young Sam, Kim Dae Jung, and Kim Jong Pil, all unsuccessful candidates for the 1987 presidential election, spearheaded the opposition campaign to expose the 'corrupt nature of the ruling party'.[6] President Roh appealed to voters to support the government party and thus aid him in carrying out his election pledges of continued economic and political development amid stability. The election, then, became another showdown between Roh Tae-woo and the three Kims.

The opposition's attack on the ruling party for the scandals of the Fifth Republic heated up as election day drew closer. Contending that the DJP had been systematically abusing its political power, Kim Young Sam called for popular support of the RDP, saying that such massive irregularities as were committed by leaders of the Chun government could have been avoided had there been a powerful opposition party. Meanwhile, Kim Dae Jung denounced the DJP for the Kwangju incident. Speaking at a rally in Kwangju, he demanded that the government reveal the truth of the incident and restore the honour of the victims as well as all Kwangju citizens. He called for a fact-finding investigation by a parliamentary task force after the election. Kim also demanded that property holdings of Chun Doo-hwan and his relatives be made public 'to clear mounting public suspicion'.[7] In a similar vein, Kim Jong Pil declared at a party rally in Seoul that the next National Assembly should invoke its investigative power to look into the Chun family's financial scandals. He criticised the government's announced measures of healing the wounds of the Kwangju incident as 'well short of public expectation'.[8]

To counter the opposition's criticisms, DJP Chairman Chae Mun Shick announced on 6 April that the major scandals of the Fifth Republic would be thoroughly reinvestigated after the election, although he charged that the opposition was exaggerating the facts. As for the opposition charge that the ruling party was using money to buy votes in the election, Chae promised that the DJP would do its best to make it the cleanest election in the nation's history. And the DJP chief spokesman, You Kyung Hyun, dismissed as 'baseless' Kim Dae Jung's charge that the 1987 presidential election had been rigged with the use of computers.

As the election entered its closing stage, the ruling party focused on 'floating votes', again stressing the need for a DJP majority to ensure political stability, while the opposition parties lashed out in a chorus of complaints about alleged illegal campaign activities and hammered away

---

5   A detailed analysis of major campaign issues is in *Dong-a Ilbo*, 8 April 1988.

6   *Korea Newsreview*, vol. 17, no. 15 (1988), p. 4.

7   Ibid., p. 5.

8   Ibid.

at their earlier themes of corruption and wrongdoing in the Chun Doo-hwan government. In fact, several opposition parties and groups launched a nationwide campaign in April to collect a million signatures to petition for an investigation of Chun and his wife. Kim Young Sam demanded that President Roh conduct such an investigation, and he also called for an immediate end to what he contended were the government party's illegal activities to utilise the local government infrastructure to mobilise voters on behalf of DJP candidates. Meanwhile, Kim Dae Jung expressed concern to voters in the Cholla provinces that President Roh was conspiring to secure more than two-thirds of the total parliamentary seats in order to renege on his earlier pledge to hold a referendum on his performance as president after the Seoul Olympics in the fall. Kim said that if Roh won an overwhelming victory in the coming parliamentary elections, he would use that as an excuse not to hold the referendum. Kim Young Sam, on the other hand, warned that the ruling party was trying to capture more than a two-thirds majority in a plot to revise the constitution to perpetuate its power through introduction of a parliamentary cabinet system of government. In his campaign, Kim Jong Pil declared that the NDRP would abolish the controversial Advisory Council of Elder Statesmen headed by former President Chun and the monthly neighbourhood meetings called *pansang-hoe*. In a press conference at Puyo, Kim also pledged that his party would strive for the abrogation of all 'undemocratic' laws and for improvement in the protection of human rights. Similar pledges had been made earlier by the other two Kims. Candidates of the major opposition parties, in their own campaigns, generally echoed their leaders' views on the main issues, while the DJP candidates took defensive postures on many issues in efforts to blunt opposition criticisms.

To be sure, voters did not make their choices in the parliamentary election strictly on the basis of issues; other variables such as party identification and candidate orientation also played an important role. An opinion survey conducted jointly by a Sogang University and *Hankuk Ilbo* research team on 1 April showed that 38.6 per cent of the respondents indicated 'personal qualities and character of the candidate' as the most important criterion in making their choice, 20.2 per cent mentioned 'past contributions to the development of their electoral districts and their future promises and pledges', and 16.5 per cent said 'the candidate's commitment to democratization' was the most important. Only 11.4 per cent said that the candidate's party affiliation was the principal criterion.[9]

According to another survey conducted by the same team less than a week before the election, 26.1 per cent now indicated that 'personal qualities of a candidate' was their main criterion, 25.6 per cent said it was the

---

9   *Hankuk Ilbo*, 5 April 1988.

likelihood of a candidate's contribution to democratic political development, and 17.8 per cent said it was the likelihood of a candidate's contribution to political stability. The same survey found 40.1 per cent of the respondents indicating they had not yet decided how to vote. Among those who had, 31.6 per cent indicated support for the DJP candidates, 25.1 per cent for the RDP, 20.9 per cent for the PPD, and 13.1 per cent for the NDRP. Of the remainder, 4.9 per cent said they planned to support other minor party candidates or independents and 4.5 per cent said they would abstain.[10]

On the eve of the election, numerous irregularities—threats and use of force, vote buying, spreading false rumours to defame opponents—were reported by candidates and supporters of both government and opposition parties. It was not a clean election, but it was one of the freest ever held in South Korea.

The Election

On 26 April 1988 a total of 19,853,890 out of 26,198,205 eligible voters, or 75.8 per cent, cast their ballots. The results stunned many who had predicted the government party's victory by an overwhelming margin. The DJP had won only eighty-seven of the nation's 224 constituencies, against fifty-four for the PPD, forty-six for the RDP, and twenty-seven for the NDRP. Independents won nine seats, and a candidate of the Hangyore Democratic Party was elected in South Cholla Province but quickly switched to the PPD. In the popular vote, the DJP garnered 34 per cent, the RDP 23.8 per cent, the PPD 19.3 per cent, and the NDRP 15.6 per cent. In a major upset, Kim Dae Jung's PPD emerged as the largest opposition party, replacing archrival Kim Young Sam's RDP. It swept all but one of the thirty-seven seats in Kim Dae Jung's home region, and seventeen of the forty-two seats in Seoul. The RDP was relegated to third place largely because of its lack-lustre performance in Seoul and other cities except Pusan, Kim Young Sam's political bastion. The NDRP chalked up a strong showing in Kim Jong Pil's native South Chungchong Province (see Table 7.1). The three Kims, all candidates in the 1987 presidential election, were elected to the National Assembly after long absences. As the DJP failed to win a majority of the 224 electoral districts, it was awarded thirty-eight of the seventy-five at-large seats under the proportional representation system, giving it a total of 125 of the 299 seats in the National Assembly. Sixteen of the at-large seats were allocated to the PPD, thirteen to the RDP, and eight to the NDRP (see Table 7.2).

---

10 Ibid., 23 April 1988.

Table 7.1   Final Election Returns, Number of Seats Won by Parties in Special Cities and Provinces (1988)

	DJP	PPD	RDP	NDRP	Other	Total
Seoul	10	17	10	3	2	42
Pusan	1	-	14	-	-	15
Taegu	8	-	-	-	-	8
Inchon	6	-	1	-	-	7
Kwangju	-	5	-	-	-	5
Kyonggi-do	16	1	4	6	1	28
Kangwon-do	8	-	3	1	2	14
Chungchongbuk-do	7	-	-	2	-	9
Chungchongnam-do	2	-	2	13	1	18
Chollabuk-do	-	14	-	-	-	14
Chollanam-do	-	17	-	-	1	18
Kyongsangbuk-do	17	-	2	2	-	21
Kyongsangnam-do	12	-	9	-	1	22
Cheju-do	-	-	1	-	2	3
Subtotal	87	54	46	27	10	224
Proportional representation	38	16	13	8		75
Total	125	70	59	35	10	299

Source: Korea Newsreview, vol. 17, no. 18 (1988), p. 7.

Table 7.2   Results of the 13th National Assembly Election: Representation Rate

Party	% Vote (A)	Number of Seats Won			% of Seats Won		Representation* Rate	
		District (B)	At-large (C)	Total (B+C)	District (D)	Total (E)	D/A	E/A
DJP	34.0	87	38	125	38.8	41.8	1.1	1.2
PPD	19.3	54	16	70	24.1	23.4	1.3	1.2
RDP	23.8	46	13	59	20.5	19.7	0.9	0.8
NDRP	15.6	27	8	35	12.1	11.7	0.8	0.8
Minors	2.5	1	0	1	0.5	0.3	0.2	0.1
Independent	4.8	9	0	9	4.0	3.0	0.8	0.6
Total	100.0	224	75	299	100.0	99.9**		

Sources: Compiled and calculated from election data reported in Dong-a Ilbo, 28–30 April 1988.
* Percentage of seats divided by percentage of popular votes won   by each party.
**Does not total 100 due to rounding.

There were more newcomers than incumbents among the winners: 167 of 299 Assembly members, or 55.9 per cent of the membership. Only seventy-three incumbents were re-elected from the 224 electoral districts, while twenty-eight former lawmakers made comebacks. In addition, sixty-four winners of district seats were party bureaucrats. Thus, professional politicians filled 165 (73.7 per cent) of the district seats. Most of the newly elected had attended institutions of higher education, including eight who held doctorates and thirteen who were lawyers. At the time of the election, 102 members were in their fifties, ninety-four in their forties, fifteen in their sixties, and thirteen in their thirties. None of the twenty-six female candidates was successful in winning a district seat, but six were elected at-large members under proportional representation.

The voter turnout rate (75.8 per cent), relatively low compared to previous elections, was generally and substantially higher in rural districts. The voting rate was lowest in Seoul and other metropolitan areas, indicating that the pattern established in several elections held from 1963 to 1985 is continuing. In other words, the more urbanised a district, the lower the voter turnout has been.

Insofar as partisan support is concerned, the so-called *yochon yado* pattern (villages for the government, cities for the opposition) was clearly evident, as it had been in all but one (1981) of the parliamentary elections held since 1963. Compared to the rural electorate, urban voters were generally younger, better educated[11], more critical about politics, and less vulnerable to governmental pressures, and they provided more support to the opposition. The level of support for the government party was inversely related to the degree of urbanisation: a 30.1 per cent share of the vote for the ruling DJP in metropolitan and urban districts and 40.7 per cent in semi-rural and rural districts. The only exception to this general pattern was Taegu, Roh Tae-woo's hometown, where the DJP garnered 48.4 per cent of the vote and won all eight seats. With the opposition parties as a whole doing much better in urban and metropolitan districts and since there were more of these than rural and semi-rural districts (54 per cent vs. 46 per cent), the DJP's relatively good performance in rural and semi-rural districts was not sufficient to overcome the party's poor showing in more urbanised areas (see Tables 7.3 and 7.4).

---

11 Kap Yun Lee, 'Chae 13-dae Kukhoe Uiwon Sonko ae so ui Tupyo Hyongtae wa Minjuhwa', paper presented at the first workshop on Democratization in Korea: Problems and Prospects, sponsored by the Institute for Far Eastern Studies, Kyongnam University, Seoul (July 1988), pp. 8–9.

Table 7.3   Percentage of Major Parties Vote by Type of District in the 1988
National Assembly Election

District Type	DJP	RDP	PPD	NDRP
Metropolitan (77)	30.03	29.61	20.99	14.75
Urban (44)	30.63	18.54	19.81	21.86
Semi-rural (23)	40.49	26.55	16.42	9.82
Rural (80)	40.37	18.05	17.13	17.51
Nation (224)	33.97	23.91	19.27	16.49

Source: Calculated from Central Election Management Committee (ROK), *Chae
13 dae Kukhoeuiwon Sonko Chiyokku Hubocha-pyol Tukpyo
Sanghwang* (Seoul: Central Election Management Committee, 1988).

Table 7.4   Percentage of the DJP's Vote and Seats Won by Type of District in
the 1988 National Assembly Election

District Type (N)	% DJP Vote	Number of Seats Won	% DJP Seats
Metropolitan (77)	30.03%	25	32.5
Urban (44)	30.63%	11	27.3
Semi-rural(23)	40.49%	11	43.5
Rural (80)	40.37%	40	50.0
Nation (224)	34.00%	87	38.8

Source: Same as Table 3.

Factors in the DJP Losses

The DJP's stunning defeat not only shocked the nation but also aroused
much speculation as to its causes. Some observers maintained that the
party lost because of the introduction of the single-member district (SMD)
system.[12] Such a contention is untenable, however, when we analyse the
representation rate of popular votes to seats (i.e., the ratio between the
popular vote and the seats won) of each party. As Table 7.2 indicates, the
DJP's representation rate is 1.1, using seats won by popular vote, and rises
to 1.2 when the at-large seats available under the proportional representation are added, giving the DJP 41.8 per cent of the total Assembly
seats. The only opposition party that fared slightly better in the
representation rate was the PPD, whose rate is 1.3 according to seats won

---

[12]   *Yomiuri Shimbun*, 28 April 1988.

in the popular vote, but when the at-large seats are added the overall representation rate drops to 1.2. The other two major opposition parties, the RDP and the NDRP, did not fare well in the representation rate—0.8 is the overall rate for both based on total seats (see Table 7.2). It is clear that the SMD system favoured the government party. Even with 34 per cent of the popular vote, the DJP could have won a majority of seats in the National Assembly, as the ruling Democratic Republican Party did in the 1963 general election under the SMD system[13], if the DJP votes were distributed somewhat differently among 224 electoral districts. Thus, one cannot attribute the DJP's defeat to the introduction of the SMD system, but rather to other factors.

First, there was a desire among the voters to check the ruling party by strengthening the opposition in the National Assembly. The government party also failed to convince voters that a stable parliamentary majority was necessary. Although the DJP's Roh Tae-woo won the 1987 presidential election with 36.7 per cent of the popular vote, it was more a victory by default resulting from the disunity between Kim Young Sam and Kim Dae Jung, who between them won 55 per cent of the popular vote. Although many were disappointed by the opposition's inability to close ranks both during and after the presidential election, the popular desire for democratisation of the South Korean political system remained strong. To many voters, President Roh's announcement of his new cabinet in February 1988 was a disappointment, for it retained seven holdovers from the discredited Chun government. Cynical journalists quickly characterised the Roh government as 'the 5.5th Republic'[14], and under such circumstances the voters' desire to check the government of the Sixth Republic was stronger than their willingness to give it a free hand.

Second, the exposure of several major scandals and widespread corruption in the Fifth Republic, all of which implicated Chun Doo-hwan and his family, not only alienated voters from the DJP but also fuelled a growing popular concern about the need to investigate corruption and irregularities perpetrated by Chun and his cronies. Popular demand for an investigation became stronger, especially in the wake of the arrest of Chun's younger brother in March 1988, and it was generally assumed that for an effective investigation the National Assembly had to be controlled by the opposition rather than the government, which retained many key power holders of the Fifth Republic.

---

13   Eugene C.I. Kim, 'The Meaning of Korea's 12th National Assembly Election', *Korea Observer*, vol. 16, no. 4 (Winter 1985), p. 372.

14   Chang-hee Kim in *Shin Dong-a*. See also *New York Times*, 27 March 1988; John McBeth, 'Rough Road Ahead', *FEER*, 3 March 1988, p. 30; and John McBeth, 'Problems of Power', *FEER*, 10 March 1988, p. 12.

Third, the DJP's defeat should be attributed to the party's inability in 1988 to draw the support of young and well-educated urban voters. According to a study by Kap Yun Lee of Sogang University based on the opinion survey conducted by the Sogang team, there was an inverse relationship between the age of voters and their support for the DJP: the younger the voter, the less support for the government party. Furthermore, there was also an inverse relationship between a voter's degree of education and support for the DJP: the more educated, the less support. Since 64.1 per cent of voters in the urban districts are in their twenties and thirties with relatively more formal education (52.4 per cent had more than nine years schooling) than their peers in rural areas (25.1 per cent had more than nine years schooling), who constitute about 47 per cent of the rural electorate[15], it is not too difficult to understand why the DJP lagged behind the opposition in metropolitan and urban districts.

Fourth, the party's prospects were adversely affected by a number of blunders committed by its candidates and supporters. In an incident two days before the election in Andong, North Kyongsang Province, a DJP candidate was caught attempting to mail over 3,700 envelopes each containing 20,000 won ($28) to constituents.[16] The incident shocked the nation, tarnished the government party's image, and undermined voter confidence in the DJP's assurances of an honest election. Another serious incident involved a report broadcast by a government-controlled local television station on Cheju Island claiming on the eve of the election that the DJP candidate was the 'winner' in a local district. Apparently this report was taped during a rehearsal to acquaint anchormen with new computers to be used for live broadcasting of election returns and was not produced for actual use. Inadvertently, however, it was shown, giving credence to the opposition charge that the DJP was attempting to rig the elections by manipulating computers.[17] Undoubtedly, these shocking incidents did serious damage to the ruling DJP. Earlier, virtually all observers predicted that the DJP would win the election—as of 18 April it was projected to win 120 to 128 of the 224 district seats—but it ended up winning only eighty-seven seats.[18]

Last but not least, the DJP's electoral fortunes were affected by a deepening sense of regionalism, a factor that always has been significant in South Korean politics in direct presidential elections. However, it was not an important factor in parliamentary elections until 1988 (see Table 7.5).

---

15 Kap Yun Lee, workshop paper.

16 *Dong-a Ilbo*, 25 April 1988; *Washington Post*, 26 April 1988.

17 *Washington Post, Wall Street Journal*, and *Hankuk Ilbo*, 27 April 1988.

18 *Hankuk Ilbo*, 19 April 1988.

Electoral districts for the National Assembly are small and most parliamentary candidates are closely tied to districts by birth or other linkages. Regional support for candidates was quite strong in the 1987 presidential election, particularly demonstrated by the voters of the Cholla provinces who gave Kim Dae Jung nearly 90 per cent of the popular vote in the region. It is generally believed that Cholla region voters were resentful of discriminatory treatment of them in regional economic development and government personnel recruitment under the Park and Chun regimes[19], both of which favoured the natives of the Kyongsang region. The victory of Roh Tae-woo aggravated the situation, for Roh, like Park and Chun, was a native of Kyongsang. Apparently that regionalism spilled over to the parliamentary election, as the four major candidates in the presidential race came to control the four major parties. As the parliamentary campaigns heated up, nominees tried to utilise the coat-tail effects of their party's leader in a particular region.

Table 7.5   Percentage of the Vote and Seats Won by Parties in the Party Leader's Home City or Province

Party and Leader	Home City or Province	% Vote (Home Region)	% Seats (Home Region)	Nation (% vote)	Nation (% Seats)
DJP* Roh Tae-woo	TAEGU: North Kyongsang	48.4 51.0	100.0 81.0	34.0	38.8
PPD* Kim Dae Jung	KWANGJU: North Cholla South Cholla	88.6 61.5 67.9	100.0 100.0 94.4	19.3	24.1
RDP* Kim Young Sam	PUSAN: South Kyongsang	54.1 36.9	93.3 40.9	23.8	20.5
NDRP* Kim Jong Pil	South Chungchong	46.5	72.2	15.6	12.1

Sources: Calculated from the election data reported in Central Election Management Committee (ROK), *Chae 13 dae Kukhoeuiwon Sonko Chiyokku Hubocha-pyol Tukpyo Sanghwang* (Seoul Central Election Management Committee, 1988).

*DJP = Democratic Justice Party; PPD = Party for Peace and Democracy; RDP = Reunification and Democratic Party; NDRP = New Democratic Republican Party; minor parties are excluded from the analysis.

19   An analysis of regionalism in Korean politics is provided by Wonmo Dong in 'Regionalism and Electoral Politics in South Korea: A Comparative Analysis of the Direct Presidential Elections of 1971 and 1987', paper presented at the annual meeting of the American Political Science Association, Washington DC, September 1988.

The region-party alliance was most conspicuous in the Cholla provinces where Kim Dae Jung's PPD swept all but one of the thirty-seven district seats. Indeed, it captured all five of Kwangju city's seats with an incredible 88.6 per cent of the vote. Since the winner of a minor opposition party joined the PPD immediately after the election, the PPD made a clean sweep of the Cholla region: thirty-seven out of thirty-seven seats contested. A somewhat similar situation developed for Kim Jong Pil's NDRP, which won thirteen of eighteen seats in South Chungchong Province, and in Kim Young Sam's RDP, which won fourteen of fifteen seats in Pusan. The RDP, however, did not fare quite as well in Kim's native South Kyongsang Province where it won only nine of twenty-two seats. Nevertheless, the twenty-three seats the RDP won in Pusan and South Kyongsang represented exactly one-half of the forty-six seats it secured in the election.

The DJP had a clean sweep in Taegu, Roh Tae-woo's home city, where it captured all eight seats contested, the first time the government party had ever captured all the seats allotted to the city. In Roh's native North Kyongsang Province, the DJP again did exceptionally well by winning seventeen of twenty-one seats. However, none of the other parties recorded as large a popular vote majority as did the PPD in the Cholla provinces. Regional voting resulted in the DJP's failure to win a single seat in the Cholla region. It captured only two of eighteen seats contested in South Chungchong Province and only one seat in the city of Pusan. It did considerably better in South Kyongsang Province where it took twelve out of the twenty-two seats contested. In short, the DJP won only fifteen of seventy-eight seats contested in the three major opposition leaders' home regions. The lopsided support given by voters to native son-led opposition parties in the Cholla region, Pusan, and South Chungchong Province nullified many of the advantages the DJP was supposed to enjoy under the single-member district system.[20]

Conclusion

From the foregoing analysis, a few basic conclusions can be drawn with regard to the 1988 parliamentary election in South Korea. First, the 13th National Assembly election ushered in a new era of legislative politics in South Korea. Not only was the Assembly significantly strengthened to perform its constitutional functions as a legislature, but it also emerged free from the domination of the government party for the first time since the Republic was established in 1948. As a result of the so-called *yoso*

---

20 Kap Yun Lee, workshop paper.

yadae (small government party, big opposition) in the National Assembly, the government could no longer push any measure through without winning the support of at least one of the three major opposition parties. On the other hand, the opposition parties could not push their legislative programmes at will either, for there was no consensus or unity among them. Furthermore, even if united on a particular bill, there was no guarantee that it would be enacted into law because the president could still exercise his veto power. To override a presidential veto, the opposition needed to muster a two-thirds majority in the National Assembly, which was virtually impossible because the DJP controlled more than one-third (41.8 per cent) of the 299 seats. Thus, neither the government nor the opposition could enact any law unilaterally, and unless there was compromise there would be political stalemate in the Assembly. Although such a situation was not ideal either for the government or the opposition, it provided a good training ground in the art of negotiation and compromise for South Korean politicians. Viewed in such a perspective, the election results may be regarded as a positive sign for political development in South Korea. The emergence of a powerful legislative opposition brought about not only livelier and more active debates over policy issues but also effective checks against the executive branch, ending the Assembly's disgraceful reputation as a 'maid' of the government.

Second, the election outcome constituted a political setback for Roh Tae-woo, who won the presidential election with a 36.7 per cent plurality in December 1987. The general elections had been regarded as a key popularity test of Roh's new government, inaugurated on 25 February 1988. Without a stable majority in the National Assembly, it was apparent that Roh would face difficulties in pushing through his legislative programmes. Control of the Assembly by the opposition parties also signalled rough sailing for the Roh government, as they vowed to bring to light all 'irregularities' of the Fifth Republic.

Third, the strong regionalism displayed by voters for the opposition parties led by the 'three Kims' nullified whatever advantages the government party might have enjoyed under the single-member district system. Under the SMD system, it was quite possible for the DJP to win a majority in the National Assembly with 34 per cent of the popular vote. In the 1963 parliamentary election under the SMD system, the government party (Democratic Republican Party) won a two-thirds majority of the Assembly seats with 33.5 per cent of the popular vote. The DJP failure in 1988 should be attributed primarily to the region–party alliance that adversely affected the party's fortunes in important regions and caused it to lose its normal share of seats in these regions.

Fourth, in terms of electoral participation and partisan support, the 1988 elections did not deviate from traditional patterns. With the higher voter turnout rate and greater support for the government party in rural areas, the pattern of *yochon yado* (villages for the government party, cities for the opposition) remained in effect in the 13th National Assembly election as had been the case with most of the parliamentary elections in South Korea since 1963.

Fifth, in terms of the implications of the 1988 elections for the development of the South Korean political party system, one can say that it resuscitated the political lives of the 'three Kims' who emerged as the leaders of three major opposition parties in the National Assembly. To a great extent, therefore, party politics in South Korea both within and outside the National Assembly, continued to be shaped largely by 'one Roh and three Kims'.

Finally, the opposition's control of the majority in the parliament helped the process of democratisation of the country's political system. Under the leadership of opposition parties, a series of parliamentary investigations were conducted since the fall of 1988, which not only exposed the corrupt nature of the Chun government, but also the incredible abuse of power by Chun and his powerful lieutenants under the Fifth Republic (1980–1988). As the demand intensified for the trial and punishment of these officials, including Chun and his wife, the former president was compelled to return some $20 million worth of assets to the government, and deliver an apology to the people of South Korea in a nationally televised speech. Furthermore, as a result of the investigations, numerous Chun cronies and relatives were arrested and indicted, developments that would not have been possible if the National Assembly were controlled by the DJP which still had many powerful former lieutenants and followers of Chun among its members. Undoubtedly, the investigations contributed to strengthening South Koreans' determination not to repeat the same mistakes by allowing the emergence of a dictatorial regime, but to strive for the development of a democratic political system which could effectively check the abuse of power by government leaders.

8 Reform With No Caprice: Economic Performance of the Roh Administration

YOO JANG-HEE

Introduction

An economy will always have two faces. Light and dark sides, gains and losses are part of its infrastructure. One major problem in evaluating a country's economy is to misguide peoples' expectations by over-emphasising the bright aspects or gains. At the same time, however, it is also problematic to discourage a positive approach towards future economic development by overshadowing the bright prospects with the dark sides or losses.

In evaluating the current economic situation, both sides of an economy should be weighed equally. Another consideration to be made is that the entire economy should be collectively evaluated rather than approached in a fragmentary manner and the flow and trends rather than a particular section of the economy should be appraised. Thirdly, in evaluating today's economy, a wider, more global perspective is absolutely necessary since no economy can stand alone in the intertwined world economic structure.

Past Versus Present

Korea's economic development in the past two decades has been a transitional phase that has allowed the country to progress from a state of underdevelopment to a developing state. In the past four years, however, Korea has been moving from this developing phase to a state of full development. Data (Table 8.1) illustrates this phenomenal growth that has enabled the Korean economy to roughly double in size during the past four years.

Statistics show that the GNP of Korea has more than doubled from $US130 billion in 1987, when Korea was ranked as having the nineteenth highest in the world, to $US280 billion in 1991, when it was ranked as having the fifteenth highest GNP in the world. The per capital GNP has also doubled from a mere $US3,000 in 1987 to over $US6,000 in 1991, taking the first step towards achieving status as a fully developed country.

The living standards in Korea have correspondingly improved. In particular, blue-collar households' average monthly disposable income has more than doubled during the past four years, reaching one million and eighty thousand won in 1991.

Table 8.1   Korea's GNP and Income, 1987 and 1991

	1987(A)	1991(B)	B/A
GNP (US billion dollars)	128.9	280.8	2.18
Per Capita GNP (US dollars)	3,110	6,498	2.09
Blue-collar Households' Disposable Income (thousand won/month)	516	1,079	2.09

Source: Korean Government, Economic Planning Board, *Economic Trends*, September 1992.

Globalisation Policies

Various economic open-door and globalisation policies are currently being promoted in Korea. Moreover, through active diplomatic efforts to promote cultural and economic exchanges with countries in the eastern socialist bloc, Korea has been able to open doors that have long been closed to the Northern continent. Such economic growth in Korea has made the concurrent adherence of both South and North Korea to the UN possible and has established a firm stepping stone for the future unification of Korea.

Social, Economic and Political Achievements and Reform

While many countries of the world are worrying about their respective high unemployment rates, Korea has recorded an unemployment rate of 2.3 per cent, the lowest in its history, thanks to its high average annual growth rate of over 9 per cent. One might say that Korea is close to a state of full employment where anyone who wishes to work can find a job.

Korea has encountered numerous difficulties but economic growth in recent years, which has been promoted concurrently with democratisation, has proven to be more valuable than past economic growth which was achieved at the sacrifice of democracy. The 1980s experienced a wave of democratisation that crashed over the continents of Asia and South America as well as over Eastern Europe. During this time Korea was the only country to successfully achieve both democratisation and high economic growth, simultaneously. Notably, the fact that blue-collar workers have most benefited from this high economic growth is quite significant especially when one considers how this marks a drastic change from the past.

Significant improvements have also been made in Korea's welfare system and housing development projects. In terms of housing, the annual average number of new houses built between 1981 to 1987 was 220,000. In 1988, however, an ambitious project to build two million additional homes was implemented. The annual average number of new houses built has jumped to 540,000. Thus, the ratio of aggregate houses to the total number of households in Korea rose from 69.1 per cent in 1987 to about 76 per cent in 1992 (see Table 8.2). Housing prices, on the other hand, which had been skyrocketing due to the imbalance between supply and demand, have started to fall and this declining trend is expected to continue.

Table 8.2 Housing Constructions in Two Periods (Unit: thousands, percentage)

	81 – 87	88 – 91
Number of New Houses Built (Annual Average)	1,550 (220)	2,140 (540)
Percentage Ratio of # of Houses/Total Households[a]	69.1	about 76[b]

Note: a. Based on the end of the period of concern.
          b. An estimate for 1992; 74.2 per cent in 1991.
Source: Ibid.

The medical insurance, pension, and minimum wage systems, which had been deferred during the era of economic development, have been implemented by the Roh administration. Additionally, the establishment of the aforementioned foundation for the social welfare system is another noteworthy milestone in Korea's economic history.

The government has made serious attempts to promote a balanced distribution of income and to balance the differences in regional economic development. Thanks to its determined efforts, speculation in real estate has receded and a substantial improvement in balanced taxation has been achieved through government-sponsored tax reforms. A structural reform plan for farming and fishing villages is also being promoted, the purpose of which is to invest forty-two trillion won in such rural areas for the next ten years beginning in 1992.

A full-scale effort to reform fundamentals and to ease economic concentration is actively being promoted by the government. In the future this will be noted as an epochal achievement in this era of economic development. In sum, the past four years marked a very important period for Korea, ending an era of concentrating exclusively on rapid economic growth, and establishing a firm ground for further social development towards the achievement of full development.

Economic Problems

Koreans, by their own choice and initiative, are prepared for an advanced economic society with hopes of promoting and establishing a framework for democracy, freedom, and globalism. It is, unfortunately, also true that negative aspects lie behind the positive. In particular, as the per capita GNP exceeded $US5,000, a rapid rise in the consumption of goods prevailed in the society, a phenomenon also seen in several other countries.[1] Wages have also risen dramatically due to a very tight labour supply caused by the nearly full employment level.

While social welfare has been vastly improved by the government's initiative the extra cost needed for this has put a major financial burden on the government, thus restricting investments made for the social overhead capital. To some degree, this hinders the country's growth potential, preventing it from expanding. Additionally, in the process of democratisation and liberalisation in which individual interests rather than national objectives are emphasised, it is also true that the general will or national

---

[1] This is compatible with the basic-need paradigm in which it was asserted that, as economic growth reaches a certain level, consumption spending accelerates due to the need of a more qualitative life, demanding a healthy, humane and freer society. See D. Hunt, *Economic Theories of Development: An Analysis of Competing Paradigms* (Hemel Hampstead, Herts: Harvester Wheatsheaf, 1989; B.S. Sul, 'Economic Growth and Basic Needs Paradigm', *Kyongie Nonmoon Jie* (Chung Ang University, ERI, No. 5, 1991).

consensus for charged economic growth has greatly diminished in the Korean society.[2]

Recent problems with consumer prices and trade imbalances are derivatives of the country's transition towards an advanced economy which is exemplified by such characteristics as rapid economic growth, high income level, and expanding consumption spending. However, since such problems as rising consumer prices and trade imbalances could possibly be exaggerated or misrepresented, the matter should be investigated from a general, more global perspective.

Consumer Prices

The past four years have experienced a rise in consumer prices of about 9 per cent and a stabilisation of wholesale prices at a rise of about 3 to 4 per cent. The principal reasons for this rise in consumer prices are high growth, high income, and rapid increase in consumption from the demand and expenditure sides. This is exemplified in the dramatically high annual average growth rate of wages which reached 20 per cent since 1988. On this note, wholesale prices which mainly refer to manufactured goods did not rise much since improvement in productivity absorbed the rise in wages. However, since consumer prices which also consist of the prices of agricultural products and services can greatly be affected by the rise in wages, the wage hike during the period directly resulted in the rise in consumer prices.[3]

Regarding consumer prices, some argue, however, that the price of necessities has risen about 50 to 100 per cent, a conclusion drawn from scrutinising the difference between the prices consumers perceive and the price index. However, since the overall price index is derived by a statistical inference using all individual prices, it is not adequate to argue that some prices are not properly reflected in the price index.

While it is true that prices of some items (such as beef, 'Sullungtang', tuition for private colleges, etc.) rose about 50 to 100 per cent during the past four years, some items' prices such as those for television sets and washing machines, fell about 10 per cent during the past four years.

---

2   S. Cho, 'Development Strategy for the Korean Economy', *Korea's Economic Development* (Seoul: Seoul National University, ERI, 1991) (in Korean).

3   It has been estimated that the increase in the consumer price index in Korea is affected more directly by wage hikes adjusted by the labour productivity increase than by an increase in the money supply. See J. Yoo and W. Lee, *Price Determination and the Money Supply in Korea* (Korean Economic Research Institute monograph 29-89-02, 1989.3) (in Korean).

Moreover, some members of society including policy-makers argue that if there is a strong will to control prices from the government's side, the rate of increase in consumer prices can be lowered to about a 3 per cent level. For obvious reasons, no-one can argue that the inflation rate of consumer prices should not be lowered or stabilised. The government, however, is not trying to implement controlling measures, but is letting the market mechanism work by itself. Thus, problems may arise in the difficulty of achieving the so-called target rate of inflation within a short period of time.

Price Stabilisation

Of course, if all other economic concerns are thrown to the wind and Korea concentrates exclusively on the stabilisation of prices, there may actually be a way to lower the rate of increase in consumer prices to the desired 3 per cent level. For example, along with a freeze in wages, the development of a contractionary monetary policy and a low economic growth rate (made feasible if the government were to manipulate the price level rather than leaving it to the market) could lower the inflation rate of consumer prices to the proposed level of about 3 per cent.

However, in such a case, although the price level might be stabilised, a tremendous social burden would have to be borne since such a policy would cause bankruptcies among many firms as well as a sudden rise in unemployment.[4]

Thus, the stabilisation of the price level should be promoted consistently and gradually along with a careful coordination of various sectors of the economy. In order for the government to stabilise consumer prices and maintain the inflation rate within 3 to 4 per cent after a coordination period extending over the next three to four years, stability in wages ought to be emphasised; the government should require big companies, which traditionally pay high wages, to place a ceiling on wage increases and limit the growth rate to within 5 per cent of the total annual salary. At the same time, real estate pricing stabilisation policies and policies designed to slow the economic growth rate down to a 7 per cent level should be implemented for the stabilisation of consumer prices.[5]

---

4 It is a well-known fact that an artificial price–wage control will eventually bring about another round of inflationary pressures. The Nixon administration adopted a wage–price control in 1971 which resulted in double-digit inflation in 1974 albeit the Arab oil embargo also took place in 1973.

5 According to a study by the Bank of Korea based on its model of aggregate production function, the potential growth rate of the Korean economy in the 1990s would be about 7 per cent. See *Josa-Tongye-Wolbo* (Monthly Statistical

Trade Balance and Foreign Debt

In the past when the foreign debt was mounting and the credibility of the country was low due to the chronic trade deficit, the total amount of foreign debt, itself, was a serious concern for Korea. Since the amount of foreign lending has risen significantly, net foreign debt rather than the absolute amount, should be considered. In the case of Japan, although it is a net lender country, the country's total foreign debt amounts to $US1.5 trillion, which is over 50 per cent of the GNP.

The net foreign debt of Korea had almost reached zero in 1989; however, as the trade balance turned into a deficit again after 1990, the debt once again turned around to increase. The net foreign debt at the end of 1991, on the other hand, was $US12.5 billion or 4.5 per cent of the GNP. It was significantly lower than that at the end of 1987, which was recorded at 17.4 per cent of the GNP (see Table 8.3).

Table 8.3   Korea's Foreign Debt Situation, 1981–1991

	81	85	87	89	91
Total Foreign Debt	324	468	356	294	393
Assets Abroad	80	112	132	264	268
Net Foreign Debt	244	355	224	30	125
(Share in GNP, %)	(36.6)	(39.6)	(17.4)	(1.4)	(4.5)

Source: Korean Government, Economic Planning Board, *Nara-Kyungie* (Nation's Economy), various issues.

For obvious reasons, the foreign debt problem should not be overlooked. At the same time, however, one should be careful not to hinder growth potential by restricting investments due to unnecessary anxieties over a mounting foreign debt.

Research), Bank of Korea, February 1992. For the definition of potential GNP, see fn 6.

Recent Economic Trends—Economic Overview
January–August 1992

Recent inflation and the trade imbalance in Korea resulted from the process of high economic growth that exceeded the country's growth potential over the past few years. Determined that structural reform cannot be deferred any more even at the cost of a slower economic growth, the government has endeavoured to stabilise the economy and, at the same time, reform the industrial structure through contractionary policies initiated in 1991. The relevant consequences of such policies have become apparent since the beginning of 1992.

First, regarding the price level, as of August 1992 consumer prices rose just 4.5 per cent compared to the end of the previous year, and about 5.9 per cent with respect to the same time in 1991. The wholesale price level also exhibited a mere 2.3 per cent rise. In particular, prices of twenty necessities and fresh food products became very stable compared to 1991 and the difference between the price index and prices felt in real life diminished. Moreover, because real estate prices stabilised at a lower level (i.e., the housing price has been declining since May 1991 and land prices fell about 0.5 per cent during the second quarter of 1992), speculations for land and housing inflation which have long prevailed throughout Korea have gradually diminished as shown in Table 8.4.

Table 8.4 Korea's Inflation Rates, 1990 and 1991 (Growth rate during the period, %)

	1990	1991	91.1–8	92.1–8
Consumer Price	9.4	9.3	7.8	4.5
(Twenty Necessities)	(-)	(-)	(9.0)	(4.7)
(Fresh Food Products)	(-)	(-)	(20.4)	(0.9)
Wholesale Price	7.4	3.1	2.1	2.3
Housing Price	21.0	Δ0.5	4.8[a]	Δ4.4[a]

Note: a. Based on the period January–July.
Source: Korean Government, Economic Planning Board, *Economic Trends*, various issues.

However, since housing prices in some areas did show an upswing during the recent moving season, the government should effectively coordinate the supply of new houses in order to stabilise prices of houses in such areas. This should be done by carefully investigating regional housing supply and demand.

Secondly, with respect to the trade balance, from January to August 1992, exports showed a consistent growth of about 9.0 per cent while the growth rate of imports fell substantially from 16.7 per cent in 1991 to a mere 2.4 per cent in 1992. This higher growth rate of exports over imports, for the first time since 1988, represents a strong sign of an improving trade balance.

From January to August 1992, the trade deficit (based on customs clearance) had been reduced by about $US3 billion compared to the same period last year; in particular the month of August alone showed a trade surplus of about $US100 million.

Table 8.5   Growth Rates of Exports and Imports and Trade Balance, 1990 and 1991.

	90	91	91.1–8	92.1–8
Export Growth Rate (%)	4.2	10.6	11.3	9.0
Import Growth Rate (%)	13.6	16.7	23.6	2.4
Net Export (in 100 million dollars)	Δ48	Δ97	Δ87	Δ59

Source: Ibid.

Thirdly, as the overheated domestic construction and service industries stabilised, the economic growth rate in the first half of 1992 recorded 6.7 per cent, about the same as the level of potential growth rate of the Korean economy.[6] The growth rate which was under 7 per cent in the first half is a result of the growth rate during the second quarter having recorded a low 6.0 per cent which is lower than both that of the first quarter's 7.4 per cent and the estimated annual growth rate of 7.0 per cent.

The major underlying factor for such a low growth rate was the slowing of the domestic economy: the growth of construction investments fell from 4.0 per cent in the first quarter to -2.9 per cent in the second quarter and the growth in consumer expenditures slowed from 8.6 per cent in the first quarter to 7.0 per cent in the second.

On the other hand, while the domestic market was slowing, the growth rate of the manufacturing sector rose from 7.8 per cent in the first quarter

---

6   Potential GNP is defined by the amount of goods and services that the economy would be able to produce if the labour force were fully employed. In Korea's case, the potential growth rate of GNP should be the one that covers a natural increase in the labour force and the increase in labour productivity.

to 8.6 per cent in the second quarter due to the rise of 11.2 per cent in the export volume.

Table 8.6   Economic Growth Rates, 1990 and 1991

	90	91	1st half, 91	1st half, 92
Economic Growth Rate (%) (Excluding Investments in Construction)	9.3 (5.1)	8.4 (7.6)	9.3 (7.6)	6.7 (8.5)

Source: Korean Government, Economic Planning Board.

Investigating recent economic trends, one can evaluate the economic performance of the Roh administration in terms of the following three characteristics. First, compatible with democratisation, the government has basically promoted the autonomous industrial system, respecting the self-adjusting mechanism of the market. No strong, visible policy stimulants which may deter the private sector autonomy, have been implemented.

Second, the price level and trade balance are improving sooner than expected due to a relatively rapid fall in the economic growth rate. Some, unable to endure the lower growth rate of 6.5 to 7 per cent, may argue for the need of an expansionary policy. However, considering the state of development of the Korean economy as well as rapid changes in the world economy, the government has realised that what is more important for Korea is to induce economic growth accompanied by structural change rather than concentrating on the absolute growth rate driven by government or consumer spending. Korea must also strengthen its competitiveness through the stabilisation of price levels as well as structural reform.

Third, for about a year, the Korean economy has gone through a painful phase of structural reform in order to improve the weakened economic structure which has long been neglected due to the overheated domestic market during the past three to four years. Thus, if the government intervenes again to hastily stimulate the domestic economy in order to increase the growth rate within a shorter period of time, the effectiveness of the stabilisation policy and structural reform will be minimised significantly and Korea will move a step away from its original goal of joining developed economies.

General Projections for the Future

Therefore, it is not desirable at this stage to implement an expansionary policy to stimulate the domestic economy. Instead, a firm foundation for a stable economy must be established. On the basis of such a sound background, a consistent policy which can strengthen industrial competitiveness, expand exports, and, subsequently, improve the growth potential is desirable.

The government, however, should be careful not to restrict investments which are directly related to improvements in productivity such as investment in production facilities and related equipment. It should also be prepared for the expected recovery of the world economy in the future.

Conclusion

Korea has faced cataclysmic economic changes in its recent past, most of which have boosted the country's growth, prosperity and success. It is clear that an increasingly global perspective is necessary for Korea to adapt to the equally sudden changes in the world economy and to remain competitive as one of the thriving dragon countries of East Asia. A detailed outline of statistics amply proves that Korea has experienced exponential growth in the recent past. While this optimistic surge in economic prosperity has been a long awaited beacon of light for Korea, extreme care must be taken by the government and private companies to maintain this tenuous success. Clearly, darkness lurks behind each ray of light and Korea must strive very hard to avoid activity and attitudes, particularly from the government's side, that might shadow the country's bright economic upswing and future. The Roh administration should be evaluated as having been quite successful in this respect.

Korea's major goal is to achieve full development, not exclusively economic, but also encompassing the country's fundamentals including social and ideological standards. Problems have sprouted up in the wake of great success such as the instability in the labour market and a rapid increase in consumption spending that could potentially erode the country's social fibre. Steps, however, are being carefully planned by the government to avoid such forms of erratic instability provoked by sudden changes in economic policies and/or regulations. Most importantly, stability as well as continued growth in both the near and far future are the highest priorities on Korea's economic and developmental agenda. A combination of pragmatic foresight, adaptability, and stabilisation hopefully will continue Korea's bright path towards full development.

9 Political Change in South Korea: The Challenge of the Conservative Alliance

PARK JIN

A revolutionary change occurred in the politics of the Sixth Republic at the beginning of 1990. On 22 January, President Roh Tae-woo and the two opposition leaders, Kim Young Sam and Kim Jong Pil, jointly announced the creation of a new governing party, the Democratic Liberal Party (DLP), thus leaving the largest opposition party, led by Kim Dae Jung, in isolation. The precarious 'one-Roh, three-Kim' four-party system, which had lasted for almost two years, was suddenly abandoned, and a new asymmetric three-party system in the form of a 'one-Roh, two-Kim' grand alliance versus 'one Kim' (and 'one Lee') emerged.[1] Given the traditional pattern of hostile zero-sum confrontation between the government and the opposition, the new political experiment signified drastic chemical as well as physical changes in South Korea's body politic.

The impact of the surprise merger was indeed far-reaching. Domestically, the pace of the 'democratisation' process now became dominated by the new ruling party with its nearly three-quarters parliamentary majority. Inter-Korean relations came to be more regulated by the new conservative alliance in the South, as the influence of the opposition diminished. Externally, South Korea's relations with the US became more subtle as the political base of Seoul's bargaining position was strengthened commensurately. On the other hand, its relations with Japan began to develop in a more pragmatic direction as the two governments came under comparable political structures. In addition, the *Nordpolitik* of South Korea acceler-

---

[1] Lee Ki Taek succeeded Kim Young Sam by choosing to remain in the opposition rather than joining the new ruling party with Kim. His faction subsequently joined Kim Dae Jung's party.

ated because of reduced concern about the negative domestic political feedback.

The challenge of the conservative alliance in South Korea, however, carried with it potential sources of instability. First, it reflected as much a strategic concord as an ideological unity. The new ruling tripartisan solidarity, therefore, was not immune to immobilism nor to reversion. Second, it could bipolarise South Korean politics in the short term by radicalising the remaining opposition sectors. Third, Seoul's enhanced bargaining position could spark further economic tension with Washington at a time when the issues of security burden sharing and US troop withdrawal are high on the agenda. Fourth, the growing chance of Japan's diplomatic normalisation with North Korea could strain the Seoul–Tokyo partnership because of the continuing uncertainty of inter-Korean relations. This article, based on the above perspective, explores the background of the epoch-making political change in South Korea and examines its future implications for the country's democracy, prosperity, security, and diplomacy in the 1990s.

The 1988 System: The Four-Party Stalemate

Ever since the April 1988 parliamentary elections in South Korea introduced a competitive four-party system, it had been cautiously predicted that the then-ruling Democratic Justice Party (DJP) would coalign with one of the three opposition parties. The major reason was that the conservative DJP, which had suffered a defeat in the elections, could find no better alternative than to share power with the opposition side. For the first time in South Korean politics since 1954, the ruling party's parliamentary majority collapsed, thus creating the new phenomenon of a 'ruling minority and opposition majority' (*yoso yadae*). Despite the representational electoral advantage, the DJP could secure only about 42 per cent of the vote, winning 125 of the 299 seats in the expanded National Assembly.[2]

On the other hand, the electoral advances made by the centrist Party for Peace and Democracy (PPD), led by Kim Dae Jung, were significant. By gaining seventy seats, it surprisingly outrivalled the centre–right Reunification Democratic Party (RDP), led by Kim Young Sam, which won only fifty-nine seats. At the same time, the most conservative New Democratic Republican Party (NDRP), led by former Prime Minister Kim Jong Pil, also made headway by winning thirty-five seats. Considering the DJP's previous 58 per cent majority in the parliament, the new electoral verdict was nothing short of a legislative 'power transfer'.

---

2   In terms of popular vote, the DJP attained about 34 per cent of the total, which was even lower than the 36.6 per cent it got in the presidential election result.

With hindsight, the main reason for the DJP's electoral setback was the change in the election system.[3] But the cause of the defeat was more than institutional. The DJP's assumption that the continuing opposition fracture would allow it at least a marginal victory proved to be wishful thinking. Instead, the regionally polarised voting pattern sharply disadvantaged the DJP. The most significant aspect of the electoral verdict can, however, be found in the popular 'sense of balance'. The DJP's prediction of a conservative swing did partially materialise, but it was the minor opposition NDRP that attracted those floating voters who preferred political stability but simultaneously wanted to contain the Roh government. As President Roh himself acknowledged later, the South Korean voters, in the wake of the divided opposition's bitter defeat in the December 1987 presidential elections, refused to allow the emergence of a 'too-strong' government.

The momentum for the realignment of power

The 'Olympic truce' provided a political breathing space for the Roh government during 1988. The internal exile of former President Chun Doo-hwan in November also seemed to help the Roh government to distance itself from the shadow of the previous regime. But the Roh presidency was soon overridden by the collective offensive of the three opposition parties. Among others, the key issue of 'liquidating the Fifth Republic' (*ogong chongsan*) not only constrained the government's ability to build its popular power base but also created a serious schism within the ruling party itself. For the ruling side, therefore, it was imperative to break through the 'one-Roh, three-Kim' impasse to secure the ability to govern.

On the other hand, it became quite evident to the three opposition leaders that their anti-Roh cooperation could only be a limited strategy. Apart from their common animosity toward the government, the three Kims were no more able to work with one another than with the ruling side. To be sure, Kim Dae Jung and Kim Young Sam shared some liberal political programs, but the former's populist call for 'mass democracy' clearly differed in substance from the moderate parliamentarian approach taken by the latter. Moreover, the personal as well as political mistrust between the two precluded united action against the government. The frustration was particularly strong for Kim Young Sam whose élitist appeal to the political middle ground was overshadowed by the progressive image of Kim Dae Jung. The momentum for change, therefore, came from both the government and the opposition side.

---

[3] The previous double-member constituency system (under which two parliamentary seats were assigned to each electoral constituency) was changed into single-member constituencies.

A DJP coalition with either of the two main opposition parties, however, seemed unnatural, if not unthinkable. For the DJP, doing so was tantamount to denying its own political *raison d'être*, not to mention its political confidence. For the two opposition Kims, such a coalition was even more unjustifiable. Both had been endeavouring to mould their political identities as the 'pro-democracy fighters' since the late 1960s when the Park Chung-hee regime began to turn explicitly authoritarian. As the rival anti-power symbols in South Korea, therefore, both Kims could hardly afford to risk a unilateral, pro-government move because a compromise of one Kim with the ruling side would automatically be condemned by the other as outright collusion.

By contrast, a DJP coalition with the NDRP was easily conceivable. All three Kims had been politically ostracised by the previous Chun regime. But Kim Jong Pil had a far less heterogeneous political orientation towards the post-Park power élite, including both Presidents Chun and Roh, than had the other two Kims. As a soldier-turned-politician and the leading heir-apparent under the Park presidency, Kim Jong Pil continued to take the most conservative political stance, especially toward North Korea. Also, as a well-known 'Japan hand,' Kim Jong Pil, like President Roh, openly favoured a parliamentary system of government.[4]

A Roh Tae-woo–Kim Jong Pil coalition, therefore, was the most imaginable scenario for power realignment. Second to this was a Kim Young Sam–Kim Jong Pil partnership. Given the serious political rivalry between Kim Young Sam and Kim Dae Jung, and the obvious ideological incongruity between Kim Dae Jung and Kim Jong Pil, such an intra-opposition conservative coalition seemed increasingly likely. The third possibility was a Roh Tae-woo–Kim Young Sam grand coalition excluding both the most 'right' NDRP and the most 'left' PPD. In the event, all three scenarios took place, and this was the least likely outcome.

The 1990 System: The Conservative Alliance

The creation of the conservative alliance (DLP) between the three parties, however, came as a *blitzkrieg* to the vigilant political circles as well as to the uninformed public. Given the dramatic shift of the political power balance, it was in fact nothing short of a peaceful revolution launched by 'one-Roh and two-Kims'. The timing of the conservative alliance was most significant. Domestically, the Roh government's need to offer a 'new

---

4   In his 'June 29 Declaration' of 1987, which introduced the direct presidential election system, DJP presidential candidate, Roh Tae-woo, made it clear that he personally preferred a parliamentary system of government, like the official position of the DJP, for reason of political stability.

course' after the parliamentary testimony of former President Chun provided a major incentive. Also, the government and the two Kims' strategic concern about the coming local government elections and the growing anxiety about the country's economic crisis contributed to the making of the grand alliance. Externally, the impact of the breathtaking democratic convulsions in Eastern Europe, in particular the historic crumbling of the Berlin Wall and the catastrophic collapse of the Ceausescu regime in Romania at the end of 1989, stimulated a rightward shift of the political mood in South Korea.

On balance, however, the core reason for creating the conservative alliance can be found in the commonality of interests between the three merged parties. The common reckoning that the 'one-Roh, three-Kim' stalemate, if continued under the presidential system, would not guarantee a confident power succession by any of the three parties, might have encouraged the three leaders to opt for the second-best alternative, e.g., a stable conservative power sharing, presumably under the parliamentary system of government. The least desirable scenario for the three merged parties would be to see the PPD led by Kim Dae Jung monopolise power through direct presidential elections.

The viability of the new 'Ruling Majority'

Yet the viability of the restored ruling majority is uncertain as the partners of the DLP do not necessarily share common political calculations and strategic goals. For the former DJP, the new alliance signifies power managing by power merging. In return for the partial concession on power monopoly, the previous ruling party has solved its main dilemma—the four-party impasse. The two opposition parties also brought with them an expanded legitimacy for the government. In terms of the political balance sheet, therefore, the DJP may have gained the most among the three parties by expanding its political base without losing its power position.

For the former RDP on the other hand, the merger means power securing through power sharing. By entering the alliance, Kim Young Sam has departed from the lackluster, second-opposition status, thus out-manoeuvring Kim Dae Jung. Also, as the only career civilian politician within the new power *troika*, Kim Young Sam can expect to appeal to the public as an alternative leader during his 'cohabitation' with the Roh presidency. Kim, however, can lose his whole political future if the alliance should disintegrate. The political stake in merging, therefore, is highest for Kim Young Sam.

For the former NDRP, the integration signifies, *inter alia*, power building through power brokering. It means the party's return to the political centre stage after a decade of alienation in the post-Park era. The main political asset of the NDRP is that the party, and especially its leader Kim

Jong Pil, possesses two decades of experience in governing. As the strategic balancer and vote caster within the new DLP, the Kim Jong Pil group will, therefore, pursue its own strategy of post-Roh power expansion. In short, Kim Jong Pil has nothing to lose in the new political experiment.

Future implications

Whatever the main reasons for the three-party merger, there is no question that 'the 1990 system' in South Korea is having profound implications for the country's domestic affairs, inter-Korean dialogue, and foreign relations. First, political regionalism is shrinking in favour of political 'coloring'. The conservative integration is transforming the previous quadri-polar regional rivalries into that of a new tripartisan system reflecting the ideological discrepancies. But the regional antagonism of the Cholla provinces may intensify. The PPD moved to challenge the new power structure by withdrawing en masse from the parliament and tilting toward the more progressive extra-parliamentary opposition sectors.

Second, the Japan model is having relevance for South Korea. The analogy, however, is only partially valid. In Japan, the main stimulus to the making of the conservative Liberal Democratic Party (LDP) came from the growing influence of the two Socialist parties, which, when merged in October 1955, occupied about one-third of the Diet; by contrast, in South Korea, although the centrist PPD has been occupying one-quarter of the National Assembly seats, it is arguable whether it ever posed an urgent ideological challenge to the government comparable to the spectre of the 'Socialist take-over' in post-Occupation Japan.

Third, the factional politics within the DLP is becoming noticeable. The first and largest faction is the 'neomainstream' (shin-juryu) group that supports the current leadership of President Roh. The second is the 'indigenous' (tochak) group that is composed of the original members of the former DJP. The third is the 'progressive' (jinbo) group that has been identified with the moderate and liberal line within the former ruling party.[5] The fourth is the Kim Young Sam group, which, as the main alliance partner, wants to exercise substantial power within the DLP as well as in the Roh government. The last is the Kim Jong Pil group, which, as the strategic balancer within the power triumvirate, wants to have its voice heard in the major political and policy decision-making process.

The above categorisations, however, are conditional. Unlike Japan's consensual politics characterised by systemic power diffusion, the political structure of South Korea has been built around a centralised

---

5   For a South Korean media analysis of the factional alignment within the ruling DLP, see *Chosun Ilbo*, 12 January 1990, and also *Dong-a Ilbo*, 15 January 1990.

presidency. The function of the 'middle boss' as a faction manager, therefore, can only be nominal in South Korea. Given the continuing weight of the presidency, the actual political process under a cabinet system, if introduced, will be more similar to that of West Germany or France, depending on the scope of the prime ministerial mandate. Meanwhile, the winner-take-all political culture of South Korea will also have to change into one of pragmatic bargaining and compromise.

Nevertheless, there are potential sources of conflict. First of all, the prospects for a consensual power sharing within the DLP are not certain. The contention between the status quo advocates and the reformists will continue. The government's indecision about introducing the reformative 'real-name transaction' system as well as local government autonomy presents the hard evidence. Second, the post-Roh power structure is even less predictable. For long, Kim Young Sam's power succession was not a *fait accompli*. The interfactional clash of interest, especially between the neo-mainstream and the Kim Young Sam groups, will remain as the most divisive issue within the DLP. The resignation in mid-April 1990 of the leading neo-mainstream influential, Park Chol Un, minister for Political Affairs, after his publicised criticism of Kim Young Sam, provides a graphic illustration. Third, it is debatable whether South Korean politics are mature enough to digest the merits (e.g., stability) and demerits (e.g., inefficiency) of the parliamentary system of government. The absence of a supra-political national symbol, such as a constitutional monarch; the need for more effective civilian control; and the underlying tension of negative regionalism differentiate the South Korean case from either the British or Japanese model.

Meanwhile, the popularity of the conservative alliance itself had not registered any improvement.[6] Instead, the DLP's surprise defeat by the RDP, now led by Lee Ki Taek, in the April 1990 by-election in the conservative Chungchong area indicated the popular interest in checking the 'mammoth' government. The political 'paralysis' caused by the DLP's unexpected legislative offensive in July, which prompted the opposition PPD to leave the National Assembly, was partly relieved in October by the conciliatory approach taken by the government. But the contentious issues of local government autonomy and constitutional revision remained at the centre of South Korean democratisation.

---

6 In early February, the popular perception of the conservative alliance was relatively favourable with only 38.4 per cent opposing the merger. *Chosun Ilbo*, 11 February 1990. In a mid-April opinion survey, however, 55.8 per cent or those South Koreans questioned replied that the DLP was not performing up to popular expectations at the time of the merger. *Chosun Ilbo*, 15 April 1990.

The economic dimension

The Roh government sought to shift its main political energy toward economic recovery in order to prevent a further downturn of the industrial situation. In fact, the popular perception of the conservative alliance hinges first on the improvement of economic conditions.[7] In 1989, South Korea's economy grew by 6.7 per cent, and its per capita GNP nearly reached the $5,000 level. But relatively, the economy stagnated. Its trade surplus of $1 billion was only about 11 per cent of that of the previous year. Also, the annual ratio of the country's exports in terms of real quantity recorded about a minus 6 per cent decrease in 1989, which was the worst economic performance by South Korea since the country introduced the export-oriented growth policy in 1962.[8]

The major problem that the South Korean economy now faces is the double pressure of labour wages and trade frictions. A generous labour policy with competitive export pricing will be the best answer to the problem. But in order to do that, the government needs to deal not only with the rising expectation on the part of the industrial working force but also with the American demand for a strong South Korean won *vis-à-vis* the dollar. The average labour cost has roughly doubled, in won terms, during the past three years as a result of industrial disputes. The government's cabinet reshuffle in mid-March brought in a growth-oriented policy team in order to boost exports and expand the country's economic pie at the risk of further inflation. The won–dollar exchange rate was also readjusted to help restore the price advantage of the export sector.[9]

The labour issue has relatively eased since 1990. But the industrial wage dispute remains the potential epicentre of South Korea's economic trouble. The country's double-digit wage increase of 10.1 per cent in 1987 and 15.5 per cent in 1988 was about ten times that of Japan.[10] Within the newly-industrialising countries (NICs) group, Taiwan had displayed similar quantum leaps in labour costs, but the Taiwanese economy decisively diverged from the South Korean model in 1989 when the average wage in

---

7   In an early March 1990 opinion survey, the largest proportion (32.8 per cent) singled out economic policy as the most unsatisfactory area of the Roh government's performance. *Chosun Ilbo*, 6 March 1990.

8   The data are quoted from *Chosun Ilbo*, 4 January 1990, and also *Dong-a Ilbo*, 3 January 1990.

9   The overvalued won, which rose to its peak of 666-per-dollar level in April 1988 came down to 680 level by January 1990, and again rose to the 700 level in late March. *Chosun Ilbo*, 27 March 1990.

10   The data are quoted from *Nihon Keizai Shimbun*, 11 January 1990.

South Korea rose by 18.7 per cent, about twice that of Taiwan and more than triple that of Japan and Singapore.[11] Searching for a stable balance between economic recovery and workforce control, the Roh government set the goal of restoring the single-digit wage increase for 1990. But the government's decisive shift to the reflationary economic policy and the increasing difficulty in securing low-cost labour are constraining such a possibility. The labour issue also reflects the structural problem of the growing perception of income disparity in the country. The major task for the new conservative alliance, therefore, will be to set an optimum balance between industrial growth and social welfare. The launching of Japan's '1955 system' benefited from the timely emergence of the country's high economic growth period. The disadvantage of South Korea is that its 'second take-off' in the 1990s has to be carried out under a relative economic slowdown.

Inter-Korean relations

Inter-Korean relations have also been significantly affected by the new political change in South Korea. The expanded Roh government has sought to upgrade its dialogue with North Korea in order both to reduce national security tension and to pre-empt the radical opposition's demand for prompt reunification. In his 1990 New Year's press conference, President Roh reiterated his proposal for inter-Korean summitry while reacting positively to the earlier proposal of Kim Il Sung to 'open up the inter-Korean border for mutual free visits'. President Roh also emphasised the need for establishing the Korean Economic Community based on the idea of a 'Korean National Community' proposed in September 1989. Against this, the North Korean position continues to revolve around the idea of a Koryo Confederal Republic, which was officially adopted by the North Korean Workers' Party in October 1980. Despite the difference of approaches, however, the two Koreas have agreed to hold high-level, politico–military talks with each other, and in fact the premiers of both sides began reciprocal visits to Seoul and Pyongyang in September and October 1990, respectively.

The two Koreas thus agree on the principle to reunify the divided nation, but below the surface a fundamental philosophical difference exists. While the South Korean side wants to stabilise the national division first before talking seriously about reunification, the North invariably wants to change the status quo before addressing practical ways to regularise inter-Korean relations. While the inter-Korean competition for

---

[11] By contrast, the industrial productivity of South Korea, which reached a peak of 16 per cent increase in 1987, gradually fell to 7.8 per cent in the first half of 1989. Ibid.

power and prestige has decisively turned in favour of the South during the last decade, the basic strategic difference remains unchanged today.

Now that a conservative alliance has been created in the South, North Korea's 'unification card' has less disturbing political effect in the South. Seoul's active *Nordpolitik* toward major socialist countries has further pushed Pyongyang into a diplomatic corner. But the Kim Il Sung regime is not likely to miss the new window of opportunity opening in the South presented by the possible escalation of political confrontation between an expanded government and an embittered opposition. Particularly, the radical student groups in South Korea, for whom pan-Koreanism began to overshadow anti-communism, will be the major target of a North Korean propaganda campaign. Pyongyang's continuing demands for a single entry to the United Nations, the cessation of the South Korean–US Team Spirit military exercise, and the release of dissident figures in the South who made unauthorised visits to the North, are clear signs of such propaganda.

It is North Korea, however, that is facing a critical dilemma. The widening inter-Korean GNP gap, which is now about ten to one, the domestic political problems of North Korea itself, and the changed external situation are further isolating Pyongyang from the mainstream of the new East–West relations. 'New thinking' will be hardly conceivable under the totalitarian rule of Kim Il Sung, but Pyongyang knows that its final choice will be either hopeless isolation or risky liberalisation. Under these circumstances, the best that South Korea can do is to expand its channels of dialogue with the North. Besides having talks on the political, military and humanitarian issues, the proposed 500 billion won (c. $730 million) inter-Korean joint project on the development of the eastern coastal area of Korea, ranging along Mt. Kumgang to the south and Wonsan beach to the north, will be a major practical step forward for Seoul–Pyongyang rapprochement.

The alliance with the United States

South Korea's relations with the United States are becoming more subtle and reciprocal. The US is now perceived by many South Koreans not so much as a beneficent patron as a self-interested partner. In the 1980s, because of the alleged American implications in the Kwangju incident and growing bilateral trade frictions, the rise of anti-Americanism in South Korea added a new dimension to the Seoul–Washington alliance. According to a January 1990 opinion poll, 64 per cent of South Koreans interviewed believed that US–South Korean relations were in trouble, and 41 per cent responded that anti-Americanism was a serious phenomenon as against 39 per cent who disagreed.[12]

---

12 *Dong-a Ilbo*, 1 January 1990.

South Korea, however, unlike security-allergic Japan, is still security conscious. The popular concern about the immediate physical threat from the North has weakened. But the fact that Seoul lies within twenty-six miles of the Demilitarised Zone across which massive numbers of regular North Korean troops are deployed, gives South Koreans enough reason to be extra-sensitive to any major change in their security conditions. In the same survey, only 10 per cent of the South Korean public demanded the withdrawal of American forces, while 55 per cent wanted no change in the US military presence, and 27 per cent favoured some reductions.

Given North Korea's continuing offensive posture, the Roh government will prefer a burden-sharing arrangement with the US to a massive troop withdrawal. But under the East–West *détente* of the post-Malta era, Korean Americanism and American globalism will clash more easily than under the Cold War. Already, the Pentagon has established a three-stage plan for scaling down American forces in South Korea as part of its global military reductions. The three US air bases in South Korea at Kwangju, Suwon, and Taegu will soon be deactivated while a total of 7,000 non-combatant air and ground troops will leave the country by the end of 1993. Seoul will have to accept the initial cuts. But the next stage in the possible reduction of US combat forces could strain bilateral relations.

The scheduled joint production of the FX fighter planes by the two countries will substantially enhance South Korea's self-defence capability. It can, however, provide excuses for North Korea to ask for more advanced offensive armaments from the Soviet Union. Moreover, there is no guarantee that a desperate Kim Il Sung regime will not 'go nuclear' in order to compensate for the widening inter-Korean economic gap.[13] A hasty American troop withdrawal from South Korea, in this context, can spark off competitive nuclear nationalism in the divided peninsula.

On the economic dimension, there are positive signs for bilateral conflict resolution. The thorny issues related to the US 'Super 301 Clause' were successfully negotiated last year between Seoul and Washington. As a result, the size of the bilateral trade imbalance that rose to a near $10 billion level in South Korea's favour in 1987 has now been reduced by nearly half. But the rapid diminution of South Korea's trade surplus with the US in the areas of automobiles and electronics is constraining the country's exports industry. The issue of further opening of the agricultural sector, which employs about one-fifth of South Korea's population, also presents a sensitive political as well as economic agenda for Seoul. A flexible approach by the administration in Washington to these issues will

---

[13] For evidence of North Korea's growing nuclear ambitions, see *Far Eastern Economic Review*, 2 February 1989, p. 15; *International Herald Tribune*, 30 July 1989, and also 8 January 1990.

be crucial for both the moderation of anti-Americanism and promotion of political stability in South Korea.

The partnership with Japan

The South Korean government's relations with its Japanese counterpart is becoming more pragmatic and even closer. Now that the two countries are going to share similar political dynamics under a conservative institutional dominance, the degree of political and economic interdependence will increase. The channels of bilateral political communications will also be diversified between Seoul and Tokyo because of the possible emergence of multifactional party diplomacy.

On the whole, the relationship between the two countries has visibly improved on the governmental level during the last decade. The reciprocal summit diplomacy, the political democratisation of South Korea, and the reduced bilateral trade imbalance all contributed to the cordial partnership between the two sides. There are, however, clear limitations to the growing Seoul–Tokyo cordiality. Most of all, South Korea's popular antipathy toward Japan is still higher than toward other major powers. In a recent opinion poll, 36 per cent of the South Koreans interviewed replied that Japan's foreign policy was 'hostile' to South Korea, one per cent higher than the figure for the Soviet Union. The relevant figures for China and the United States were 28 per cent and 16 per cent.[14] South Korean apprehension about Japan's regional economic domination and 'encroaching rearmament' will also continue.

A direct Seoul–Tokyo security partnership is politically out of the question given the strong historical anti-Japanism in South Korea. The US role as the strategic linchpin in the triangular cooperation has also been reducing the need to conceptualise such an unrealistic scenario. The long-term trends of American military disengagement from the Korean Peninsula, however, is posing a new uncertainty to the South Koreans as well as to the Chinese. For South Korea, as long as inter-Korean relations do not deteriorate to a critical level, a direct security cooperation with Japan will be one of the last policy options to consider. The new vigorous peace initiative from Moscow in the Asia–Pacific region is making such a possibility even less likely.

Meanwhile, the Roh government will continue to take issue with Japan about the latter's discriminatory treatment of the 650,000-strong resident Korean minority, including the issue of 'third-generation' Koreans, and the various trade and non-trade barriers to South Korean exports. Also in the longer term, the South Korean perception of Japan's attitude toward inter-Korean relations can pose a potential source of bilateral conflict of

---

14 *Dong-a Ilbo*, 1 January 1990.

interest. According to the same 1990 opinion poll it was found that 55 per cent of South Koreans thought that Japan was 'opposing' Korean reunification. The figure marked the highest level next to that of the Soviet Union, among the four major powers. The respective figures for the Soviet Union, China, and the United States were 59 per cent, 48 per cent and 38 per cent.[15] But as long as Japan's approach toward North Korea contributes to the inter-Korean *détente* and the liberalisation of the latter, the above issue will not surface.

The 'Nordpolitik'

Finally, South Korea's new *Nordpolitik* has been further activated. South Korea entered into diplomatic relations with Hungary, Poland, Yugoslavia, Czechoslovakia, Bulgaria, Mongolia, and finally the Soviet Union in 1989–90. The expansion of the diplomatic horizon in the socialist world has not only added to the post-Olympics international prestige of South Korea but has also enhanced Seoul's political leverage with Pyongyang. Most importantly, South Korea's entering into a diplomatic relationship with the Soviet Union, the principal guardian of North Korea in the communist world; then negotiating relations with the People's Republic of China, the closest ally of North Korea in Asia; and also opening a diplomatic relationship with Algeria, the principal spokesman of Pyongyang in the non-alignment world, resulted in an effective diplomatic 'encirclement' of North Korea by the South.

North Korea's erstwhile socialist patrons remain the central targets of Seoul's *Nordpolitik*. Kim Young Sam's second visit to Moscow in late March 1990 and President Roh's surprise meeting with Mikhail Gorbachev in San Francisco in June of the same year, marked major junctures in the expanding South Korean–Soviet relations. On the economic dimension, the incentive to sustain South Korea's industrial growth by entering the 'northern markets' well matches Sino–Soviet interests in absorbing the capital, marketing skills, and industrial technologies from South Korea under more favourable conditions than Japan can offer. On the political dimension, benefits are also mutual. For Seoul, the creation of diplomatic ties with both Moscow and Beijing are a *sine qua non* for consolidating a Korean peace under a dwindling US security presence. For the two mainland Asian powers, on the other hand, the 'South Korea card' means more than prodding Pyongyang or countering Washington. It also means checking Tokyo's resurging influence.

There is no question, however, that the *leitmotif* of Seoul's *Nordpolitik* is to induce greater flexibility in Pyongyang on eventual national reunification. It is apparent that domestic political factors and the

---

15   Ibid.

'Koreanisation' of inter-Korean relations are more important for the success of South Korea's *Nordpolitik* than the external factors, which have already turned favourable. As the South Korean experience in 1989 clearly proved, the pursuit of a 'Northern policy' without sufficient domestic preparations to support it can incur a negative backlash against inter-Korean relations as well as the *Nordpolitik* itself.[16] The American and Japanese approach to North Korea also poses a potential dilemma for the South. Washington sees the improvement of relations with Pyongyang as an essential precondition for further troop withdrawals from South Korea. For Tokyo, its corresponding approach to Pyongyang would at least prevent an 'over-the-head' deal between Washington and Pyongyang.[17] Seoul's difficulty, however, is that if Washington and Tokyo get too close to Pyongyang in reaction to its *Nordpolitik*, it may become harder to keep a delicate balance between anti-communism and pan-Koreanism. The sensitive diplomatic reaction by the Roh government in early October 1990 to the suddenly upgraded Japanese–North Korean political contacts provides good evidence. As the *Nordpolitik* further progresses, the new conservative government in South Korea will have to face this issue more seriously.

Conclusion

Entering the 1990s, three of the four parties in South Korea have cast their political dice for a common stake. The result, however, has yet to be revealed. It became more evident in the local autonomy elections in 1991, which constituted a quasi-referendum on the new conservative alliance. It became clearer in 1992. It will finally reveal itself in early 1993 when a new prime minister is designated to lead the government, although if the current presidential system survives, the next presidential elections will determine everything.

---

16 This refers to the Roh government's shift to a hard-line anti-communist stance after the unauthorised trips to North Korea by dissident clergyman, Rev. Moon Ik Hwan, and a female student activist, Lim Su Kyong, in 1989. More importantly, the 'parliamentary espionage incident' in which a PPD parliamentary member, Suh Kyong Won, was arrested for having visited the North and met Kim Il Sung in secret, further changed the political landscape of South Korea into that of strict 'Red-bashing'. Kim Dae Jung himself was indicted in August on charges tied to Suh's illegal visit to Pyongyang.

17 According to reports, US–North Korean contacts in Beijing have already reached the ambassadorial level, and the Japanese government is pursuing its intention to have an official dialogue with North Korea. See *Chosun Ilbo*, 14 January 1990, and also *Nihon Keizai Shimbun*, 9 January 1990.

The quadri-polarised South Korean political structure will become stabilised by the formation of the new conservative alliance. Above all, the tripartisan integration reflects the ideological symbiosis of the Japanese '1955 system' in terms of institutionalising the conservative dominance. At the same time, however, it contains the strategic expediency of the French '1986 system' in terms of cohabitation experiment between the contending political forces. Moreover, the socio-political basis for the 'progressive' forces in South Korea is also insufficient to encourage a constructive ideological competition exemplified by the class-based politics of British democracy. Until the final picture of the post-Roh power structure is in sight, therefore, South Korean politics will not be free from uncertainty.

The new conservative alliance government in South Korea faces complex domestic and foreign challenges in the 1990s. First, the regime transformation from a military-influenced authoritarian polity to a civic-conscious liberal democracy should be carried on. Second the democratic balance between industrial growth and social welfare should be set. Third, a stable confidence-building mechanism should be institutionalised between the two Koreas. Fourth, an adequate level of national security should be maintained under a decreasing US military presence. Fifth, the *Nordpolitik* should be pursued without straining the existing ties with the West. Whether these multiple challenges can be handled effectively in favour of long-term national interests depends on the political stability of the country under the conservative alliance.

10 New Political Development With a Vision

KIM HAK-JOON

The Beginning of an 'Honourable Political Revolution'

In 1990, South Korean politics saw a cataclysmic event that began a reshaping of the nation's political landscape. On 22 January, President Roh Tae-woo, the leader of the Democratic Justice Party (DJP), flanked by Kim Young-sam, the head of the Reunification Democratic Party (RDP), and Kim Jong-pil, the head of the New Democratic Republican Party (NDRP), announced a dramatic agreement to merge the three parties.

In a joint convention held on 9 February, the ruling DJP and the nation's second and third largest opposition parties, the RDP and NDRP, were formally merged to inaugurate a new party named the Democratic Liberal Party (DLP). The convention adopted the new party's platform setting forth its ideals, and policy guidelines. The party registered its inauguration with the Central Election Management Committee, as required by law. In its inaugural convention in April, the party established the basic framework for its leadership system and secretariat.

The three-party merger, attained not by coercion but totally through peaceful and democratic procedures, was the first of its kind in South Korea's constitutional history. More significantly, it is unprecedented in South Korean politics for a ruling party, with no immediate and obvious threat to its continued existence, to decide to dissolve itself and form a new party in conjunction with parties in the opposition camp, on an equal basis. The merger in no way appeared to be an attempt by the DJP to stay in power by winning the next election. On the contrary, the merger in fact enhanced the RDP's and NDRP's opportunity to come into power, thus paving the road for a serene and peaceful transfer of power. From this perspective, the new party's statements that 'an Honourable political revolution or a politically Honourable revolution has begun in South Korea'[1] were apparently not entirely an exercise in self-praise. The emergence of the new political party through the merger and the new political development it brings would, indeed, not only contribute greatly to democracy, but also help accelerate economic development. Furthermore, North Korea could be more strongly persuaded to enter into serious, sincere dialogue with South Korea—dialogue that should ultimately improve relations between them.

Expectations about the new political scene resulting from the three-party merger were high among many South Koreans. One indication of this was the result of a public opinion poll conducted by the *Joong-ang Ilbo*, a middle-of-the-road vernacular newspaper published in Seoul. In the poll conducted on 22 January 1990, a randomly sampled total of 982 adults aged twenty or more were interviewed by telephone. Of those interviewed, 68.8 per cent approved the merger. Another indication was seen in an opinion survey undertaken by Korea Survey (Gallup) Polls Ltd., from 29 January through 4 February. The survey, conducted in the form of interviews, covered 1,500 persons aged twenty or more across the country (except Cheju-do, the island province off the southern coast).[2] Of the respondents, 49.1 per cent expressed the view that the merger was a good move that should help improve South Korean politics. Excepting those in the Cholla provinces, more than 50 per cent of the pollees voiced a positive response in one way or another.

What led to the merger of the three political parties? What motivated these parties—one of them in the ruling camp and the other two in the opposition camp—to come together to create a new party, the Democratic Liberal Party, transcending their political differences? What are the DLP's ideals and policy priorities? In what way was South Korean politics expected to evolve after the launching of the DLP? What progress would there be in the push for democracy? What effect did the people expect the DLP's emergence to have on South Korea's economy and on its relations with North Korea? This chapter attempts to explore answers to these important questions.

---

[1] *Korea Herald*, 23 January 1990.

[2] An unpublished opinion survey report on current political issues of South Korea conducted by Korea Survey (Gallup) Polls Ltd. (in Korean), 10 February 1990.

Problems Encountered in the Conduct of State Affairs under the Four-Party System during the Sixth Republic

To examine the circumstances that led to the merger of the three parties, it is necessary to analyse the four-party system that resulted from the general elections for the 13th National Assembly held on 26 April 1988. This, in turn, must be preceded by an analysis of the 13th presidential election held on 16 December 1987.

South Korea's recent move away from authoritarian rule and toward democracy began with the 29 June 1987 Declaration of Democratic Reforms made by Roh Tae-woo, then chairman of the Democratic Justice Party. The declaration came amid massive protests against then President Chun's 13 April decision which virtually ignored the popular demand for presidential elections by direct vote—a decision that was widely viewed as an attempt to prolong the authoritarian regime of the Fifth Republic. Roh's declaration which fully accommodated popular demands, heralded a *de facto* end to the long tradition of authoritarian government. In short, it marked the beginning of the process of democratisation.

Subsequently, the declaration led to a constitutional amendment that laid the foundation for a democratic government. On 16 December 1987, the 13th presidential election was held—by direct vote. Prior to the election, however, the Reunification Democratic Party, which represented the main opposition forces, split into two parties, as Kim Dae-jung bolted from the RDP led by Kim Young-sam and organised a separate party, the Party for Peace and Democracy (PPD). The split did not result from a major difference in ideals and policies. Rather, it was apparently because of the two Kims' unyielding ambition to run in the presidential race, each of them counting heavily on his personal connections and regional ties.

More specifically the RDP came to rely on Pusan and Kyongsangnam-do, Kim Young-sam's stronghold, for its primary political backing, and the PPD on the Cholla provinces, Kim Dae-jung's home base. In addition to the RDP and the PPD, a third opposition party, the New Democratic Republican Party, emerged and fielded Kim Jong-pil, a former prime minister, as its presidential candidate. Led by Kim Jong-pil, the *de facto* No. 2 leader under the late President Park Chung-hee, and the followers of the late president, the NDRP derived its primary political support from the Ch'ungch'ong provinces. Given this background, it may well be said that the three opposition parties were more the product of the personal ambition of the three presidential aspirants who needed organisational support for their presidential campaigns than they were the product of popular wishes. This is the reason why many regarded the three opposition parties as little more than cliquish, 'private' parties formed around specific leaders and based predominantly on regional ties rather than as broadly-based national parties.

Under the circumstances, the ruling Democratic Justice Party had little choice but to seek its primary political support in Taegu and Kyongsangbuk-do, the home town of the DJP's standard-bearer, Roh Tae-woo. The 16 December 1987 presidential elections thus pitted the governing party against the three opposition parties, all heavily dependent on personal connections and regional ties. In the elections, Roh not only received overwhelming support in Taegu and Kyongsangbuk-do, but also won a fairly comfortable lead in other localities except for some limited areas where he did not fare so well. Winning the race with a comfortable plurality, Roh was sworn in as the President of the nation on 25 February 1988, and with his inauguration began the Sixth Republic. Two months later, on 26 April, the general elections for the 13th National Assembly were held.

It should be noted that a new electoral district system under which each district elected one candidate only, instead of two, was adopted for the election as desired by the public. The two-winners-in-one-electoral-district system, as had been practised under the Yushin (Revitalising Reform) Constitution of 1972, had created public aversion. In response to popular desires, the proportional representation system also was revised.

The regional confrontation that strongly characterised the 13th presidential elections was repeated in the subsequent parliamentary elections. This is shown clearly by the results of the general elections. The DJP's candidates won in twenty-five of twenty-nine electoral districts in Taegu and Kyongsangbuk-do, the PPD in all thirty-two districts in Chollanam-do and Chollabuk-do, the RDP in twenty-three of thirty-seven districts in Pusan and Kyongsangnam-do, and the NDRP in eleven of twenty-three districts in Ch'ungch'ongnam-do and Ch'ungch'ongbuk-do. The number of successful candidates in electoral districts across the country amounted to ninety-one from the DJP, fifty-five from the PPD, forty-seven from the RDP, and twenty-seven from the NDRP. Thus, Taegu and Kyongsangbuk-do accounted for about 32 per cent of the DJP's successful candidates in the nation's electoral districts, Chollanam-do and Chollabuk-do 56 per cent of the PPD's, Pusan and Kyongsangnam-do 49 per cent of the RDP's, and Ch'ungch'ongnam-do and Ch'ungch'ongbuk-do 41 per cent of the NDRP's. This clearly indicates that the three opposition parties were predominantly regionally based. Regionalism was particularly pronounced in the case of the PPD.

As the winner of the largest number of electoral districts, the DJP gained thirty-eight of the total of seventy-five proportional representation seats in the parliament, bringing its total number of National Assembly seats to 129. Of the remaining proportional representation seats, sixteen went to the PPD, thirteen to the RDP, and eight to the NDRP. Altogether, the PPD won seventy-one parliamentary seats, the RDP sixty, and the NDRP thirty-five. Four other seats in the 299-seat unicameral legislature went to independents. Thus there emerged in South Korean politics a four-party setup as a result of regional confrontation in the presidential and National Assembly elections, with the opposition parties having been hastily organised by presidential aspirants.

As such, the four-party structure tended to intensify regional conflict and antagonism, which has long plagued South Korean society. Consequently, many became seriously concerned that if the four-party confrontation based on regionalism continued through the elections for members of the local council and chiefs of local autonomous bodies scheduled for 1990–91, and the 1992 National Assembly and presidential elections, it would further deepen regional antagonism, perhaps to such an extent that the divisions would be impossible to heal.

The Gallup poll cited previously attested to the grave concern of the South Korean people about the negative impact of the four-party setup. Of the respondents to the polls, 80.8 per cent said 'yes' to the proposition, 'the current four-party setup is a bad political structure that provokes regional divisiveness, confrontation and antagonism among Kyongsang, Cholla and Ch'ungch'ong provinces'.

Intensification of regional conflict and antagonism goes squarely against democratic reform, to which the Sixth Republic was committed in response to the call of the times. Generally speaking, an authoritarian regime is one that is run by those who keep themselves in power with the support of certain favoured segments of society, groups and regions to the exclusion of many other social segments, groups and regions. Democratisation can be said to be a move to eliminate such 'exclusivism'.

Because of the tendency toward parochialism and exclusivism, regional conflict and antagonism run counter to democracy. Regional confrontation was itself an unfortunate and undesirable phenomenon. Deepening regional antagonism fuelled national divisiveness which in turn would have undermined the foundation for national cohesion and national development, and diminished the potential for achieving the unification of the Korean Peninsula. Clearly, the need to halt any further drift toward regional confrontation was acute.

Another major problem posed by the four-party structure was the emergence of a National Assembly dominated by the opposition parties— a situation often described as the large opposition camp pitted against the small ruling party. The DJP failed in 1988 to gain a majority of National Assembly seats, although it won more legislative seats than any other political party. However, the three opposition parties together garnered more than enough seats to control the National Assembly whenever they decided to act jointly. More often than not the opposition parties, through their joint strategy, restrained and frustrated the government in the conduct of the affairs of state.

The opposition-dominated National Assembly, the first such legislature ever to be formed in South Korea's parliamentary history, did have a positive effect, too. It helped the parliament rid itself of an inglorious image of being 'the handmaiden of the government'.

Indeed, the National Assembly became much more self-assertive and independent of the executive branch, as it should be in a democracy. On the other hand, the opposition's control of the National Assembly had negative results. It greatly curbed the powers of the president and of the government which were already much reduced under the present Constitution.

Quite obviously, any government is bound to face tremendous challenges and tribulations during a period of transition from an authoritarian regime to a democratic one. There is bound to arise an explosion of pent-up demands, creating an atmosphere almost like a revolution.

In South Korea the pressure of demands for liberalisation and democratisation grew very strong. Here, democratisation meant not only political but also economic and social democratisation—in other words, 'all-inclusive, or comprehensive, democratisation'. The government, of course, had to effectively meet these popular demands. Yet, successful implementation of political—and economic—democratisation required sustained economic growth.

However, the outburst of various demands and social conflicts in a period of transition to full democracy often dampens new investment and aggravates labour unrest, making it difficult for the economy to grow substantially. This, in turn, leads to an increase in unemployment and a higher rate of inflation, causing social instability, which threatens the process of political democratisation. South Korea was already experiencing some of these adverse developments. In fact, some people assert that the South Korean economy was facing a crisis. In order to prevent a further deterioration of the South Korean economy, the government needed to secure workable democratic leadership, which could only be assured by stable, broad-based support in the parliament.

It should also be noted that demands on the government were coming not only from the forces seeking gradual reforms, but also from the forces calling for radical changes—for revolution. The latter forces included leftist activists who, advocating liberation of South Korea in terms of the Marxist–Leninist theory of class struggle and Kim Il-sung's 'juche' (self-reliance) ideology, wanted to topple the government and act accordingly in defiance of the established law and order. Although not large in number, these radicals could bring trouble to the government and society in no small way, because their activities were potentially dangerous.

Nevertheless, the opposition parties in the past gave encouragement to the radical forces and even denounced the government's attempt to contain radical activities as an 'act of repression', simply for the reason that these forces were opposed to the government although these radicals did not necessarily support the opposition camp. At best, the opposition parties did nothing to help check the anti-government activities of the radical forces.

Needless to say, in times of transition to full democracy, the government needs the capacity to deal resolutely and effectively with numerous issues inherent in such a period. However, the opposition-dominated National Assembly, combined with the present Constitution, which had already reduced the powers of the president and of the administration, limited the room for the government of the Sixth Republic to act effectively. At a time when the state was called upon to work aggressively, the government instead found itself to be a 'limited government'.

With its hands virtually tied, there was not much that the government could do to meet the desires and expectations of the people. Dismayed by the situation, some people even became sceptical of the leadership of the president. Eventually, many politicians came to recognise a growing popular feeling, especially among intellectuals, that 'under the four-party setup, the government cannot properly carry out its work. The four-party structure must therefore be changed'.

The Background to Three-Party Merger

The nature of the four-party structure, the legacy of the 1987 presidential race that heightened regional confrontation, was such that it proved to be inconsistent with what the nation needed to do to meet the call of the times. Moving along the great path to democracy, South Korean society had come to a point where it was impossible to turn the clock back to authoritarian rule. Steady progress has been made in democratisation since the 29 June 1987 Declaration of Democratic Reforms and more recently since the birth of the Sixth Republic, although some may not have been satisfied with the speed of such progress.

As I have already pointed out in another paper, I believe that South Korea now has established political institutions that are quite adequate for implementing democracy.[3] And South Korea's democratic infrastructure will become more complete when additional democratisation measures are carried out as projected. These measures include implementing local autonomy and amending the National Security Act and the law governing the Agency for National Security Planning to better guarantee the basic

---

3   Hak-joon Kim, *Democratization under the Sixth Republic* (Seoul: Korean Overseas Information Service, 1989), pp. 23–5.

rights of the people. All this implies that in Korea, democracy will continue to develop now and in the future not because any leader or any political force wants it to, but because democracy has come to have its own built-up momentum.

Fortunately, the four political parties reached an accord on the controversial issue of liquidating the negative legacies of the Fifth Republic, an issue that had been a heated subject of national debate. The accord, which followed a meeting between President Roh and the leaders of the three opposition parties on 15 December 1989, was implemented as agreed upon. This was greeted by a popular comment that 'it was a tolerable solution' of the issue. The press commentaries generally agreed that 'although the solution of the liquidation issue was not really satisfactory, the nation now should put the past behind it and start working for the future'.[4]

Overall, 1990 brought to South Korea brighter prospects for democratisation. Today's South Korea has become distinctly different from what it was prior to the December 1987 presidential election. In those days, the political slogan of 'fighting for democracy' against an anti-democratic regime of dictatorial rule did have popular appeal. At that time, there were people who, depending on their views, might well have branded the Democratic Justice Party as dictatorial or anti-democratic, and hoped that those who advocated an end to its rule would be able to lead the nation to democracy. However, the situation has changed.

Today, South Korea's democratic infrastructure has been bolstered to such an extent that there can be no reversion to authoritarianism. Perhaps one of the stronger indications of this positive change is an official letter that the Republic of Korea Army chief of staff recently wrote to his subordinate army commanders. The official letter, written on 3 February 1990, emphasised that the military should reflect deeply on their past conduct, which had led to criticism that the military was 'the mother and supporter' of authoritarian regimes. The letter vowed that the military 'will faithfully keep themselves to their proper duties only'.[5] This is evidence that in today's South Korean society there is no logical justification for dividing South Korean political forces into two categories, democratic and anti-democratic, i.e., the dichotomy that prevailed in the old days of authoritarian government.

In the meantime, the world has witnessed a wave of revolutionary changes sweep over Europe, including the creation by the European Community in 1992 of a single market. This makes it more likely than ever before that the EC will also attain a political union to establish what may well be described as 'the United States of Europe' by the early 2000s.

---

4   *Korea Times*, 16 December 1989.
5   Ibid., 4 February 1990.

Along with the disintegration of the Communist bloc in Eastern Europe and the dissolution of the Soviet Union, the Communist party has lost its monopoly of power in one Eastern European country after another. Such events were unthinkable only a few years ago. The exodus of hordes of East Germans into West Germany led to the dismantling of the Berlin Wall, a fact that eloquently testifies to the fragility of the ideological barriers of the old era.

All these stunning developments convinced the South Korean people that it was time South Korea rose above the debilitating confrontation between the ruling and the opposition parties and cooperated with each other to address impending national issues in a forward-looking manner based on 'new thinking'.

That conviction has grown stronger with the increased possibility that a major change will also take place in North Korea that will bring a substantive shift in relations between South and North Korea. Some argue that it is hard to expect democratic reforms similar to those in Eastern Europe to occur in North Korea because the situation in North Korea differs from that in Eastern Europe. This argument may not be entirely mistaken. However, it is quite apparent that North Korea cannot long remain impervious to the tide of historic upheavals that has gripped the former Soviet bloc and Europe, since it is obviously the wave of the time.

In fact, North Korea will most likely experience major upheavals by the mid-1990s at the latest, by which time Kim Il-sung who was eighty years old in 1992 will probably be gone or have become too senile to wield power. Even if that does not happen, relations between South and North Korea are expected to undergo a substantial change sooner or later. In view of this likely change, which will bear importantly on the fortunes of all Koreans in the South and the North, South Korean political leaders have become increasingly convinced that the confrontational structure of South Korean politics must be reformed and improved to prepare for future developments.

The Political Nature of the Three-Party Merger

The shared recognition of the acute need to realign the domestic political structure culminated in the merger of the ruling party and two opposition parties, a truly remarkable political feat. Prior to this three-party merger, there had been large-scale political realignments on three different occasions in South Korea's constitutional history. The first was the political realignment resulting in the inauguration of the Democratic Republican Party, which followed the military *coup d'état* of 16 May 1961. The second was a political realignment brought about by the authoritarian Yushin (Revitalisation) Reforms of October 1972, and the third realignment came with the emergence in May 1980, following the assassination of President Park Chung-hee, of an authoritarian government dominated by ex-military officers.

These political realignments have several similarities. They all were carried out by those in power and by virtual coercion in order to inaugurate or reshape the ruling party. In doing so, the ruling camp absorbed part of the opposition. But the absorption was on an individual basis, not on a party-to-party basis. Furthermore, in each of these political realignments, the Constitution was rewritten under martial law to back up the newly organised ruling party.

Then what similarities or differences are there between these earlier political realignments and that of 1990? Some may argue that the recent realignment, too, was led by the ruling camp. However, it had some distinct features that make it different from the earlier ones. First, it was undertaken not by the ruling camp alone but jointly by the ruling party and the two opposition parties after several months of consultations. Perhaps more importantly, the three parties decided to merge on an equal footing, despite the difference in the number of parliamentary seats each then had. Second, the merger involved no coercion at all. It was carried out voluntarily by the three parties and the individual politicians involved. Third, almost all National Assembly members of the two opposition parties joined the new ruling party formed through the merger, with many of them serving in important posts. Significantly, they included the president of the RDP, Kim Young-sam, a longtime champion of democracy and opponent of dictatorial rule, and other leading members of the RDP, who had been in the opposition camp all along.

The fourth feature that distinguishes the recent political realignment from the previous ones is that the three-party merger was preceded by the voluntary dissolution of the ruling DJP. The fact that the head of the government dissolved his ruling party, despite the absence of any immediate and present threat to the continued existence of the party, is virtually unprecedented in the world. In the past, and even today, the DJP has been frequently denounced by the opposing forces as the principal arm of authoritarian rule. If this argument is to be taken as correct, then it follows that the three-party merger signified the disbanding of that arm. The inauguration of the new party created through the dissolution of the DJP and joined by former members of the RDP, traditionally an opposition party, must be regarded as a move away from authoritarian government and a major step toward civilian rule. This is well noted by the *Christian Science Monitor* which, in its 7 February, 1990 edition, commented that the emergence of the new party in South Korea marked a 'rapid shift away from authoritarian government'.[6]

---

6 *Christian Science Monitor*, 7 February 1990.

Indeed, it may well be said that the three-party merger was a significant move to civilian, democratic government, made through peaceful dissolution of the ruling party. The merger also firmly paved the way for a peaceful transfer of power. At the same time, the merger was the fulfilment of President Roh's election campaign pledge made in 1987 that he would play the role of a stepping stone in establishing democratic civilian government.[7]

It is further to be noted that unlike the earlier political realignments when the Constitution was altered in advance to favour the ruling camp, the new ruling party was created without modifying the present basic law. Thus, the nation's political future was left up to the people to decide.

Of course, there were some criticisms of the three-party merger. First, there was the criticism that the merger was worked out undemocratically, because it was arranged in secrecy by only a few leaders of the parties involved. The second criticism was that by switching sides, the National Assembly members of the opposition parties who joined the newly inaugurated ruling party committed an act of betrayal against those who had voted for them in the parliamentary elections. The third criticism was that by isolating the opposition Party for Peace and Democracy, whose main support comes from the Cholla provinces and from relatively low-income people, the merger aggravated regional antagonism and would be likely to intensify political confrontation. Fourth, there was concern that the new ruling party might attempt to perpetuate its ruling position by taking advantage of its overwhelmingly large number of parliamentary seats and that the ruling camp had become too large and too powerful to check.[8] I think these were reasonable criticisms.

Regarding these apprehensions, I have the following views. First, ideally speaking, it would have been desirable to have the three-party merger worked out openly. However, given the crucial nature of the matter, would it have been realistically possible for the three parties to merge if the negotiations had been conducted openly? I don't think it would have. On the other hand, it should be recalled that immediately following the merger accord, each of the three parties took appropriate steps for approval by its decision-making bodies before the merger was actually implemented.

Second, a National Assembly member, representing not only one's own constituency but also the whole nation, is entitled to make an independent decision as to what should or should not be done. Whether the decision is right or not is a matter to be judged by the electorate in the next

---

7   Roh Tae-woo, *The Great Era of Ordinary People* (in Korean) (Seoul: Eul Yoo Publishing Co., 1987), p. 20.

8   On the criticisms, refer to a column by Professor Han Sung-joo in *Newsweek*, 5 February 1990.

elections. In this regard, perhaps it is worth noting that in the Gallup poll cited earlier, only 9.8 per cent of the respondents who disapproved of the three-party merger cited 'slighting the electorate' as the reason for disapproval.

Third, the three-party merger, rather than isolating the PPD, actually provided the PPD with an increased opportunity to gain greater clout as the primary opposition party, depending upon how it managed its affairs. In South Korea, popular support of the opposition camp has been traditionally deep-rooted, with a large number of the electorate almost always voting for opposition party candidates unconditionally. This being the case, the Party for Peace and Democracy, 'the only opposition party' as it describes itself, has been given a great opportunity to develop itself as a genuine national party, removing the image of being a 'regional' party. This enhanced the chances for building a sound political structure, in which the ruling and opposition camps compete with each other on the basis of constructive and innovative policies and contest for the reins of government through elections. In short, it helped to establish an ideal two-party political system. The three-party merger, meanwhile, should contribute to alleviating regional antagonisms at least among those constituencies where popular support of the three parties is strongest.

Given these prospects, there seems to be little ground for the pessimistic prediction that the three-party merger will lead to an abrasive and extreme confrontation between the governing and the opposition parties. Again, the results of the Gallup poll seem to largely reject such pessimism. As much as 52.9 per cent of those respondents who approved of the three-party merger said that they expected the merger would help minimise partisan bickering and establish a political climate of compromise and harmony. Another 14.3 per cent said they approved the merger because it would be conducive to political stability. In contrast, of the pollees who disapproved of the merger, only 5.0 per cent said the merger would stir up regional antagonisms, and a mere 4.3 per cent said the merger would isolate the PPD.

The concern about the possibility that the merger would make it easier for the ruling party to keep itself in power and that the merger would reduce the checks on the administration did not seem to be groundless. The Gallup poll found that 25.4 per cent of those respondents disapproving of the three-party merger cited 'the possibility of the ruling party continually remaining in power' as the reason for their negative view of the merger. Another 23.9 per cent of them cited 'the possible weakening of checks on the administration' as the reason for their disapproval of the merger.

In view of these concerns, the ruling Democratic Liberal Party should exert special efforts to avoid becoming a rubber-stamp party serving the administration. While legislative support is essential to help the government resolve national issues, the National Assembly should fully exercise a check on the administration, when appropriate for the sake of the people at large. In handling a bill in the National Assembly, the ruling DLP should not resort too much to the strength of its majority of parliamentary seats.

However, there is good reason to believe that unlike the ruling parties of the past the new ruling party will not be a rubber-stamp for the government. Since the merger brought diverse political forces into the new ruling party, intra-party coordination of policies and actions will be very complicated and elaborate, and the party will have to be very responsive to public views and opinion. Politicians are all keenly aware that no party can expect to remain in power for long without duly responding to what the people want. It is important to note that the new ruling party's constitution grants greatly increased powers to the party's caucus, thus enhancing the democratic process and mechanism within the party. By all indications, the DLP is expected to push further for intra-party democratisation.

On the other hand, it would not contravene the principles of democracy if the ruling party, by virtue of its good policies, succeeded in remaining in power by beating the opposition camp in free and fair elections. By the same token, the opposition party will always have a chance to unseat the incumbent ruling party if its policies draw wide public support. In any case, the verdict will ultimately come from the people.

Ideals and Policies of the New Ruling Party and Popular Expectations

What are the ideals and policies of the Democratic Liberal Party? According to its official inaugural statement, the DLP will 'strive to implement democratisation, attain national prosperity and achieve national reunification'. To do so, the party pledged to pursue the following four primary policy goals:

First, South Korea's per capita income will triple to US$15,000 in the year 2000 through continued rapid economic development. Increased efforts will be made to accelerate the balanced development of all segments of society, sectors of industry, and geographical regions in order to help the nation achieve the status of an advanced country by the year 2000.

Second, the DLP will strive to foster mature democracy. The party will help build a democratic society full of vitality—a society which guarantees freedoms, autonomy, and the rights of individuals as well as those of various segments of society; encourages creativity and provides equal opportunities.

Third, the party will endeavour to build a society guaranteeing public welfare. It will do its utmost to resolve conflicts between different income brackets, between different geographical regions, and between generations to achieve national harmony. At the same time the party will work to ensure an equitable distribution of the fruits of national development and assure a stable livelihood for all citizens.

Fourth, the party will strengthen the foundation for national reunification. In response to the rapidly changing international order and world situation, the party will try to strengthen South Korea's political preparedness to step up efforts to improve relations with North Korea in order to hasten the day of national reunification.[9]

To achieve these objectives, the DLP further vowed to work to:

Unceasingly implement reform as called for by the people and as dictated by the times to ensure the political, economic, and social stability needed to pursue sustained national development; reform undemocratic systems and practices and continue to carry out other measures of democratisation; and boldly undertake policy measures aimed at rectifying all kinds of imbalances in Korean society.[10]

All this suggests that the DLP will emphasise both the importance of stability and the pursuit of democratic reform, because they are mutually complementary and inseparable.

As revealed by the Gallup poll, public expectations of the DLP in 1990 were quite high. To the poll's question 'Do you think that the merger of the three parties will help the nation's political development or do you think that the merger will work against political development?' 48.3 per cent of the respondents gave a positive answer, while 14.1 per cent said 'it's hard to tell yet' and 34.2 per cent were negative. (The remaining portion belonged to the 'don't know' category.)

To the question 'Do you think that the three-party merger will help resolve the nation's economic problems or do you think that it won't?' 62.9 per cent of the pollees were positive, with 15.8 per cent of them saying that 'the merger will greatly contribute to resolving the economic problems'. By contrast, those who were negative accounted for 25.5 per cent of the pollees, with only 5.1 per cent saying that 'the merger will not help resolve the economic problems at all'.

The poll's question 'Do you think that the three-party merger will promote dialogue between South and North Korea or do you think it will dampen such dialogue?' drew a positive response from 50.4 per cent of the pollees, while 14.3 per cent showed a 'wait-and-see' attitude and 25.3 per cent gave a negative response. (The remainder said 'don't know'.) Finally, to the question 'Do you think that the three-party merger will in general contribute to attaining national reunification or do you think that it

---

9   *Korea Herald*, 9 February 1990.

10   *Korea Times*, 9 February 1990.

will not?' 50.6 per cent said 'it will', while 31.4 per cent said 'it will not' and 10.3 per cent said 'it remains to be seen'. (A 'don't know' response accounted for 7.6 per cent.)

The *Dong-a Ilbo*, a traditionally outspoken vernacular daily newspaper, remarked that the Democratic Liberal Party was drawing the attention and raising the expectations of the people.[11] In an editorial carried in its 10 February 1990 edition, the paper commented on the DLP's inauguration by saying: 'We cannot help but place high expectations on the Democratic Liberal Party's pronounced resolve to pursue stability and reform. We will be paying close attention to what the new party will do to achieve its goals—democracy, prosperity, and national reunification. We call upon the new governing party to do its best to measure up to the expectations of the people'.

The three-party merger and the birth of the DLP also drew generally favourable comments from abroad. The *Economist*, a British weekly news magazine, in its 27 January 1990 issue, described President Roh Tae-woo as 'Super Roh', in apparent reference to his initiative in attaining the three-party merger.[12] Meanwhile, the *Christian Science Monitor* of the United States, in its 25 January 1990 editorial, commented: 'In fact, the (three-party) merger (in South Korea) may prove a tonic to democracy', adding that 'if the (South Korean) government were to remain unable to act on the nation's problems, it would create the risk of popular unrest— and, eventually, the possibility of a return to military rule. If this development fosters stability and gives the government the power to govern, South Koreans and the world will approve'.[13] The *Christian Science Monitor*, in its 7 February editorial, further remarked: 'The evolution of larger parties (in South Korea), embracing a national instead of a regional constituency, may prove a step toward more effective government...And the country may have an enhanced opportunity to deal with such difficult issues as trade relations with the U.S. and fraternal relations with the north'.[14]

Conclusions: Democratic Reform through Compromise to Achieve National Prosperity

I do not mean to assert that the Democratic Liberal Party itself has no problems at all, that the DLP can provide a cure-all for the problems of

---

11 *Dong-a Ilbo*, 10 February 1990.

12 *Economist*, 27 January 1990.

13 *Christian Science Monitor*, 25 January 1990.

14 Ibid., 7 February 1990.

South Korean society, or that the future of the DLP will be all bright. The party, being an amalgam of heterogeneous factors, may not be as cohesive as it wants to be. Now that the party holds a majority of National Assembly seats it may become arrogant. And it may be tempted to perpetuate its power and become overly protective of vested interests. The party may allow itself to develop special ties with the business community, especially conglomerates, and slip into the morass of 'money politics'. The party may also become fettered by intra-party factionalism based on personal connections and regional ties and thus become more a cliquish private party than a national party, as was common for party politics in the past.

Traditionally, the South Korean people have tended to be distrustful of political parties, especially of the ruling party. The DLP cannot be an exception. It is therefore crucial for the DLP to try to gain public trust. How to develop its relations with the opposition PPD and how to lessen the Cholla provinces' sense of alienation are among the other challenges facing the DLP. Furthermore, it is important for the DLP to narrow the distance between the party and young people who are unfriendly to it and between the party and the emerging progressive forces.

Fortunately, many DLP leaders are fully aware of these challenges and seem determined to deal with them positively. Moreover, I expect that the new ruling party will take best advantage of being a 'late-comer'; it will learn from the mistakes made by others in the past. Democratic reform is a key to resolving the challenges facing the party and the nation. The DLP should acknowledge the problems of our society and tackle them in earnest. Bearing in mind the axiom, 'reform or perish', the DLP must humbly listen to pleas being made by those who have been calling for reform and must try, in a forward-looking manner, to accommodate demands that are reasonable and justifiable.

In this regard, a comment made in the *Dong-a Ilbo* editorial cited earlier is instructive. It said: 'If the colossal ruling party fails to make genuine reform in its values and attitudes and if it fails to show a new way of thinking and a new perspective, the future of Korean politics will be only bleak. Without a positive shift to mature politics and without a positive change in political behavior, there can be no responsible politics. The responsible members of the Democratic Liberal Party are called upon to demonstrate a new awakening for the sake of the future of the party and of South Korean politics'.

Democratic reform can best be implemented through constructive compromise within the ruling party itself, between the ruling and the opposition parties, and between the ruling camp and various groups in Korean society. It was the spirit of compromise that made it possible to create the DLP—a discarding of the old habit of confrontation and of seeing everything in 'black and white' and a willingness to accept second best, if not the very best. This spirit of compromise, which has been long absent in South Korean politics, should take root in the soil of the nation's political culture and serve to attain gradual and steady democratisation and other reforms.

For its part, the opposition party should no longer dwell on the problems of the past and, instead, deal with the present with flexibility and from a future-oriented point of view. The days of a democratic vs antidemocratic confrontation are gone. As Kim Young-sam, co-representative of the newly-created ruling Democratic Liberal Party, asserted in his address to Kwanhun Club[15] members on 12 February 1990[16], the attitude of confrontation must give way to an attitude of harmony, negative thinking to creative thinking; and the habit of simply raising issues to a willingness to resolve issues. This shift is essential if constructive and productive relations between the opposition and the ruling party are to be fostered in order to address difficult challenges confronting the nation's economy and society, as well as to prepare the nation for an expected positive change in its relations with North Korea.

In the meantime, the DLP is expected to make special efforts to find ways for the economy to regain its momentum and achieve 'another economic miracle'. At the same time, however, the DLP should also strive to promote greater equity in the distribution of wealth and spur the balanced development of different geographical regions, and thus build a national consensus on the need both to ensure stability and to pursue democratic reform. When the DLP succeeds in these endeavours, it will become more firmly established as a vigorous and competitive national party with broad-based popular support.

---

[15] A fraternity of senior journalists in South Korea.
[16] *Korea Times*, 12 February 1990.

11 Regionalism in Electoral Politics

BAE SUN-KWANG AND JAMES COTTON

Since the end of the 1980's, the South Korean political system has undergone a process of democratic transition. Authoritarian restrictions on political competition have been lifted, and new rules of political competition have been set up. In December 1987, direct presidential elections were restored after sixteen years' suspension, and this resulted in the first peaceful transfer of power in South Korea.

One of the most distinctive characteristics of Korean electoral politics in the present phase of democratisation is regionalism. For example, in the 1987 presidential election, a majority of Korean voters cast their votes according to the regional attachment of candidates. The four major candidates performed exclusively well in their home provinces: Roh Tae-woo in Taegu and North Kyongsang; Kim Young-sam in Pusan and South Kyongsang; Kim Dae-jung in Kwangju, North Cholla and South Cholla; and Kim Jong-pil in South Chungchong (see Table 11.1). In the 1988 National Assembly election, regional differences in party support were also apparent. Each party fared exclusively well in its party leader's home provinces. Roh Tae-woo's Democratic Justice Party (DJP) did well in Roh's strongholds, Kim Young-sam's Reunification Democratic Party (RDP) in his home provinces, Kim Dae-jung's Party for Peace and Democracy (PPD) in Cholla provinces, and Kim Jong-pil's New Democratic Republican Party (NDRP) in Chungchong provinces.

In the 1992 National Assembly election, the Democratic Liberal Party (DLP), which was formed by a sudden merger of the DJP, the RDP and the NDRP in 1990, performed well in Pusan and Kyongsang provinces, and held its ground in Seoul and Kyongki/Inchon. The Democratic Party (DP), which was a coalition of the PPD and the former RDP members who did not join the ruling coalition, did well in Kwangju and Cholla

Table 11.1 Presidential and National Assembly Election Results by Special Cities and Provinces (%): Deviations from the National Mean are in Brackets

	1987				1988				1992		
	Roh	YS	DJ	JP	DJP	RDP	PPD	NDRP	DLP	DP	UNP
Seoul	30.0(-6.6)	29.2(+1.2)	32.7(+5.7)	8.2(+0.1)	26.2(-7.8)	23.4(-0.4)	27.0(+7.7)	16.1(+0.5)	34.8(-3.7)	37.3(+8.0)	19.4(+2.0)
Pusan	32.2(-4.4)	56.1(+28.1)	9.2(-17.8)	2.6(-5.5)	32.1(-1.9)	54.3(+30.5)	2.0(-17.3)	6.8(-8.8)	51.6(+13.1)	19.5(-9.8)	10.3(-7.1)
Taegu	70.9(+34.3)	24.4(-3.6)	2.6(-24.4)	2.1(-6.0)	48.2(+14.2)	28.4(+4.6)	0.7(-18.6)	13.2(-2.4)	46.9(+8.4)	11.8(-17.5)	29.0(+11.6)
Inchon	39.4(+2.8)	30.0(+2.0)	21.3(-5.7)	9.2(+1.1)	37.6(+3.6)	28.3(+4.5)	14.1(-5.2)	15.5(-0.1)	34.5(-4.0)	30.8(+1.5)	20.6(+3.2)
Kwangju	4.8(-31.8)	0.5(-27.5)	94.4(+67.4)	0.2(-7.9)	9.7(-24.3)	0.4(-23.4)	88.6(+69.3)	0.6(-15.0)	9.1(-29.4)	76.3(+47.0)	3.9(-13.5)
Kyongki	41.5(+4.9)	27.6(-0.4)	22.3(-4.7)	8.5(+0.4)	36.1(+2.1)	22.9(-0.9)	15.9(-3.4)	18.2(+2.6)	37.2(-1.3)	31.9(+2.6)	19.7(+2.0)
Kangwon	59.5(+22.9)	26.2(-1.8)	8.9(-18.1)	5.4(-2.7)	43.6(+9.6)	21.6(-2.2)	4.0(-15.3)	20.2(+4.6)	38.7(+0.3)	11.7(-17.6)	32.0(+14.6)
Chungchong North	47.1(+10.5)	28.3(+0.3)	11.0(-16.0)	13.6(+5.5)	43.7(+9.7)	16.0(-7.8)	1.4(-17.9)	33.3(+17.7)	44.3(+5.3)	23.7(-5.6)	21.8(+4.4)
Chungchong South	26.3(-10.3)	16.1(-11.9)	12.5(-14.5)	45.2(+37.1)	30.2(-3.8)	15.0(-8.8)	3.8(-15.5)	46.5(+30.9)	37.9(-0.6)	22.0(-7.3)	17.6(+0.2)
North Cholla	14.2(-22.4)	1.5(-26.5)	83.6(+56.6)	0.8(-7.3)	28.8(-5.2)	1.3(-22.5)	61.5(+42.2)	2.5(-13.1)	32.1(-6.4)	54.8(+25.5)	4.8(-12.6)
South Cholla	8.2(-28.4)	1.2(-26.8)	90.3(+63.3)	0.3(-7.8)	23.3(-10.7)	0.8(-23.0)	67.9(+48.6)	1.3(-14.3)	25.1(-13.4)	61.6(+32.3)	5.1(-12.3)
Kyongsang North	66.7(+30.1)	28.3(+0.3)	2.4(-24.6)	2.6(-5.5)	51.0(+17.0)	24.5(+0.7)	0.9(-18.4)	16.0(+0.4)	49.0(+10.5)	8.4(-20.9)	16.1(-1.3)
Kyongsang South	41.3(+4.7)	51.5(+23.5)	4.5(-22.5)	2.7(-5.4)	40.2(+6.2)	36.9(+13.1)	1.0(-18.3)	10.3(-5.3)	45.7(+7.2)	8.9(-20.4)	20.1(+2.7)
Cheju	49.9(+13.3)	26.9(-1.1)	18.7(-8.3)	4.5(-3.6)	36.0(+2.0)	27.1(+3.3)	6.0(-13.3)	3.4(-12.2)	34.1(-4.4)	19.9(-9.4)	0.0(-17.4)
Mean	36.6(16.2)	28.0(11.1)	27.0(25.0)	8.1(6.9)	34.0(8.4)	23.8(10.4)	19.3(22.2)	15.6(9.1)	38.5(7.7)	29.3(16.1)	17.4(7.5)

Note: 1. Roh is the Roh Tae-woo vote in 1987; YS is the Kim Young-sam vote in 1987; DJ is the Kim Dae-jung vote in 1987; and JP is the Kim Jong-pil vote in 1987.
DJP is the Democratic Justice Party vote in 1988; RDP is the Reunification Democratic Party vote in 1988; PPD is the Party for Peace and Democracy vote in 1988; and NDRP is the New Democratic Republic Party vote in 1988.
DLP is the Democratic Liberal Party vote in 1992; DP is the Democratic Party vote in 1992; and UNP is the Unification National Party vote in 1992.
2. When the means of deviations were calculated, the signs were ignored.

provinces, and also in Seoul. Chung Ju-yung's Unification National Party (UNP) fared well in Kangwon (which is considered as Chung's home province) and Taegu. The change of leadership to Kim Young-sam within the DLP may have resulted in some defections, especially in Taegu and Chungchong provinces, but these defections may have been limited. The votes of such defectors seemed not to have gone to the main opposition DP: they rather went to the UNP or Independents. Indeed, the pattern of regional voting for the DP is similar to that of 1987 and 1988.

There is little dispute about the substantial impact of regionalism on voting during this period, as election returns showed apparent regional differences as illustrated in Table 11.1. In a country where there are no class oriented political parties of salience, or no parties on the ideological dimension, regionalism may have played an important role in a voter's choice. This may be particularly so in the period of democratic transition, where the past pattern of political competition—that is, the electoral competition between governing party and opposition party which has been centred on the issue of democratisation of the authoritarian political system—has little or no relevance in providing a cue for the voters when they make voting decisions.

However, there are several question which must be put forward to refine this analysis. First, given that Korea is a homogeneous society in terms of its race, language and culture, it is surprising that the subtle variance of regional attributes has been susceptible to partisan political mobilisation. In other words, why regionalism rather than other factors appeared to be the most important factor in electoral competition during this period needs to be determined. Furthermore, what are the causes of the observed regional differences in political support?

Second, to what extent has regionalism exerted an impact on a voter's choice needs to be tested in relation to other electoral cleavages. More fundamentally, what have become the main electoral cleavages in Korean society, or are there changes in the structure of electoral alignment in this period compared to that of the past? These questions need to be explained by empirical research. In addition to this, other variables, which may have an impact on voting choice such as the individual's interest in relation to social structure or the voter's value orientation, need to be controlled in order to measure or isolate effects of regionalism on voting choice.

Finally, the notion widely held that regionalism hinders democratic transition of the political system in Korea needs to be discussed with reference to empirical work. If such important national agenda items as electoral competition for example, become increasingly viewed along regional lines, democratisation of the political system would merely be a formal and empty process, especially under the circumstances that one region is virtually alienated in the process of political power succession. It would be unfortunate if the deliberate manipulation of an essentially emotional regional factor ran counter to the rational electoral decisions of voters. However, to vote on the basis of the regional origins of political leaders may well be more than a purely expressive act. For example, voters may make a rational calculation of their interest, since political leaders do in fact disproportionately direct resources and appointments to their home provinces.

Regional differences in political support, understood in this respect, may be the reflection of a calculated and rational act on the part of voters. Thus, whether regionalism in Korean electoral politics is a merely emotional factor or whether it is a rational act, and its implications for political development in Korea, need to be discussed with reference to empirical evidence.

Political Process and the Rise of Regionalism

Regionalism is by no means a new phenomenon in Korean electoral politics. The regional nature of voting, i.e., voters' support of candidates from their region, continued to be a significant factor, particularly in direct presidential elections between 1963 and 1971.[1] With the candidacy of Park in 1963, voters in Kyongsang provinces along with those in the adjacent rural areas of Cholla provinces strongly favoured him, while provinces around Seoul voted for Yun Bo-son, the major opposition candidate. Replacing Yun as the opposition candidate in 1971, Kim Dae-jung drew his support heavily from his home Cholla provinces (see Table 11.2).

In a dozen National Assembly elections before the recent ones, however, regionalism was not as significant a factor as it has been in the direct presidential elections. Indeed, the difference in party preference between the urban and rural inhabitants, the so-called *yochon yado* (government rural, opposition urban) phenomenon, has been one of the most important variables in explaining the pattern of party support in parliamentary elections.[2] Regionalism by then may have been merely a tendency toward voters favouring their native political leaders, and its influence may have been limited to presidential elections: its degree may also have been

---

1   See Kim Jae-on and B.C. Koh, 'Electoral Behaviour and Social Development in South Korea: An Aggregate Data Analysis of Presidential Elections', *Journal of Politics*, vol. 34, no. 3 (1972), pp. 825–59. Also see Kim, C.I. Eugene, 'The Meaning of the 1971 Korean Election: A Pattern of Political Development', *Asian Survey*, vol. 12, no. 3 (1972), pp. 213–24.

2   See Kim Hong-nack and Sun-ki Choe, 'Urbanization and Changing Voting Patterns in South Korean Parliamentary Elections', *Journal of Northeast Asian Studies*, vol. 6, no. 3 (1987), pp. 31–50.

Table 11.2   The 1963, 1967, and 1971 Presidential Election, and the 1985 National Assembly Election Results by Special Cities and Provinces (%): Deviations from the National Mean are in Brackets

	1963		1967		1971		1985		
	Park	Yun	Park	Yun	Park	DJ	DJP	NKDP	DKP
Seoul	30.2(-16.5)	65.1(+20.0)	45.2(-6.2)	51.3(+10.4)	40.0(-13.2)	59.4(+14.1)	27.3(-8.0)	43.3(+14.1)	19.8(+0.3)
Pusan	48.2(+1.5)	47.5(+2.4)	64.2(+12.8)	27.7(-13.2)	55.7(+2.5)	43.6(-1.7)	27.9(-7.4)	36.9(+7.7)	23.6(+4.1)
Taegu	-	-	-	-	-	-	28.3(-7.0)	29.7(+0.5)	18.5(-1.0)
Inchon	-	-	-	-	-	-	37.1(+1.8)	37.4(+8.2)	22.0(+2.5)
Kyongki	33.1(-13.6)	56.9(+11.8)	41.0(-10.4)	52.6(+11.7)	48.9(-4.3)	49.5(+4.2)	34.6(-0.7)	27.8(-1.4)	20.4(+0.9)
Kangwon	39.6(-7.1)	49.1(+4.0)	51.3(-0.1)	41.7(+0.8)	59.9(+6.7)	38.8(-6.5)	46.2(+11.3)	11.3(-17.9)	17.8(-1.7)
Chungchong North	39.8(-6.9)	48.9(+3.8)	46.6(-4.8)	43.6(+2.7)	57.3(+4.1)	40.7(-4.6)	56.7(+21.4)	18.3(-10.9)	15.8(-3.7)
Chungchong South	40.8(-5.9)	49.4(+4.3)	45.4(-6.0)	46.8(+5.9)	53.5(+0.3)	44.4(-0.9)	39.5(+4.2)	21.7(-7.5)	20.8(+1.3)
North Cholla	49.4(+2.7)	41.5(-3.6)	42.3(-9.1)	48.8(+7.9)	35.5(-17.7)	61.5(+16.2)	36.8(+1.5)	26.4(-2.8)	18.8(-0.7)
South Cholla	57.2(+10.5)	35.9(-9.2)	44.6(-6.8)	46.6(+5.7)	34.4(-18.8)	62.8(+17.5)	35.7(+0.4)	25.4(-3.8)	18.0(-1.5)
North Kyongsang	55.7(+9.0)	36.1(-9.0)	64.0(+12.6)	26.4(-14.5)	75.6(+22.4)	23.3(-22.0)	44.7(+9.4)	15.7(-13.5)	16.9(-2.6)
South Kyongsang	61.7(+15.0)	29.9(-15.2)	68.6(+17.2)	23.0(-17.9)	73.4(+20.2)	25.6(-19.5)	40.3(+5.0)	23.4(-5.8)	19.4(-0.1)
Cheju	69.9(+23.2)	22.3(-22.8)	56.5(+5.1)	32.1(-8.8)	56.9(+3.7)	41.4(-3.9)	31.8(-3.5)	5.9(-23.3)	17.1(-2.4)
Mean	46.7(10.2)	45.1(9.6)	51.4(8.3)	40.9(9.0)	53.2(10.3)	45.3(10.1)	35.3(6.3)	29.2(9.0)	19.5(1.8)

Note: Park—Park Jung-hee, Yun—Yun Bo-son, DJ—Kim Dae-jung; DJP—Democratic Justice Party, NKDP—New Korean Democratic Party, DKP—Democratic Korean Party.
When the means of deviations were calculated, the sings were ignored.

limited as the *yochon yado* phenomenon was also embedded in an alignment pattern that was influenced by regionalism.

What made regional differences in political support not only so profound, but also so consistent an influence in the elections during this democratic transition period? The political process during this period may have been one of the most important factors for the rise of regionalism in electoral politics. This is the process by which subtle differences in regional attributes have been the subject of a regional political alignment. Before looking at this particular political process during this period, it is necessary to review those social, political, and economic factors that may have stimulated regionalism in electoral politics.

A review of regionalism in the Korean context should start with the issue of those relative disadvantages that the Cholla region has experienced in the last decade or so. Regional economic disparity has become an important issue as a result of the geographically skewed pattern of economic development under the Park regime (1961–1979). Economic growth tended to follow a Seoul–Pusan axis, favouring the capital area and the Kyongsang provinces in the southeast, and neglecting the Cholla provinces of the southwest. This uneven economic development resulted in regional disparities in industry, income, and infrastructure. Strong regional economic disparities may have contributed to the sharpening of that regionalism that already existed in the form of regional identity based on the variance of regional attributes such as speaking with a different accent.

There have also been regional disparities in the recruitment of ruling élites. Obviously, there exists no explicit institutional discrimination against one particular region, but there has been evidence that the Cholla region has been disproportionately underrepresented in the recruitment of ruling élites. According to a study by Kim Kwang-su, élites in the spheres of politics, economy, religion, and jurisdiction were mostly dominated by those from the Kyongsang region, and élites in the other spheres of science, culture and arts were dominated by those from Seoul.[3] Indeed, three out of the four Presidents (Park, Chun and Roh) Korea has had so far were from the Kyongsang region. Especially in the authoritarian *Yushin* regime, as dictatorial one-man rule was consolidated, the recruitment of ruling élites may have been exclusively from those who had personal connections in the élite structure. It may also be fair to say that this pattern of political recruitment continued in the Fifth Republic under Chun's presidency (1981–1987). In a society where social mobility should be open and fair, at least in principle, the virtual discrimination by regional attachment, especially in favour of the region the ruling élites were from, may have

---

3   See Kim Kwang-su, 'Cholla-do in Korean Politics' (in Korean), *Korean Political Science Review*, vol. 20, no. 1 (1986), pp. 85–108.

contributed to the regionalism that found its fatal culmination in the Kwangju incident.

It seems likely that the political orientation of those of the Cholla region has been in favour of the opposition because of the disadvantages they have had to withstand. Their political orientation toward the opposition first appeared in the 1967 presidential election. Voters in the Cholla region favoured the opposition candidate Yun, dropping the support they had shown for Park in the previous 1963 presidential election. They supported Park in 1963, as he had promised to implement plans for development of rural and fishing areas in his election campaign, but in 1967, by which time uneven economic development had emerged as a result of the first five-year economic development plan (1962–1967), their support turned to Yun. In the 1971 presidential election, the last direct presidential election until a popularly elected presidency was restored in 1987, voters in the Cholla region strongly favoured Kim Dae-jung, a native son of their region, and Park further mobilised voters in the Kyongsang region. In short, regionalism, perhaps regional antagonism between Cholla and Kyongsang regions, can best be put as a confrontation between the Cholla voters' dissatisfaction or perceived disadvantages and the Kyongsang voters' consciousness of preserving benefits from the status quo.

The impact of regionalism in electoral politics was reproduced on an expanded scale in the 1987 presidential election. The elected president, Roh Tae-woo, did extremely well in his native areas of Taegu and North Kyongsang, but he won only about 5 per cent of the vote in Kwangju and did very poorly in Cholla provinces (see Table 11.1). Kim Young-sam did well only in his native areas of Pusan and South Kyongsang, and Kim Dae-jung fared very well in his native areas of Kwangju and Cholla. Kim Jong-pil fared relatively well only in his native South Chungchong province.

In the 1987 presidential election, the combined opposition forces had a chance to win for the first time since the 1960s. Given the unpopularity and the illegitimacy of the Chun regime, Roh, a successor hand picked by the outgoing president, was never believed to have had a chance to win without resorting to fraud. The failure of the two Kims to agree on a single opposition presidential candidate was one of the main reasons for Roh's victory. The main issue of the election campaign was easily diverted from 'democratisation of the political system' to 'vote for our native son' because both the two Kims, who maintained a strong popularity in their native regions, ran for presidency. During the election campaign, all of the four main presidential candidates exploited regionalism by emphasising their own regional attachment or denigrating the other candidates' regional attachments. The anticipation that other voters in other regions would vote for their native sons may have been high among the voters, and this was realised in the actual voting pattern. This again may have consolidated regionalism to an expanded degree.

In the 13th National Assembly election in April 1988, the pattern of regional voting was repeated virtually intact. This election showed that all four parties, led by the same four presidential candidates of December 1987, had become regional parties: Kim Dae-jung's PPD in Cholla, Roh's DJP in Taegu, Kim Young-sam's RDP in Pusan, and Kim Jong-pil's NDRP in Chungchong. The PPD won every seat in Cholla provinces, but was decimated in other provinces except in Seoul. The DJP won every seat in Taegu and obtained about 80 per cent of the seats in North Kyongsang province. The RDP won all but one seat in Pusan. The NDRP won thirteen out of eighteen seats in South Chungchong province. The overall results were, however, surprising to all: the ruling party lost a majority for the first time in the history of Korean politics.

The results were totally unexpected. Even a few weeks before the election, the political fortunes of the two Kims and their parties were thought to be nearly ended, because their failure to unite had been considered to be the main cause of the opposition's defeat in 1987. This time the pattern of regional voting resulted in the ruling party's loss of legislative majority. The 13th Assembly election deviates from the preceding ones in that the region–party alliance looms large. In the past National Assembly elections, regional party alliance hardly appeared as a dominant factor, as most legislative candidates had in any case been closely tied to their districts by birth or other connections. The very substantial impact of regionalism in this election has been shown by Park in his district-level analysis.[4] In determining the vote, according to his analysis, regionalism showed a much stronger influence than did the urban–rural division, which had been a main dimension in differentiating partisan support in previous parliamentary elections.[5]

However, what Koreans call the *yoso yadae* phenomenon (large opposition and small government party) did not last for long. On 22 January 1990, the DJP, the RDP and the NDRP merged into a new governing coalition of the Democratic Liberal Party (DLP), thus leaving the largest opposition PPD, led by Kim Dae-jung, in isolation. This decision to create a conservative coalition in the National Assembly election seemed not to be well received by the voters. In the three subsequent parliamentary by-

---

4   See Park Chan-wook, 'The 1988 National Assembly Election in South Korea: the Ruling Party's Loss of Legislative Majority', *Journal of Northeast Asian Studies*, vol. 7, no. 3 (1988), pp. 59–76.

5   See Kim and Choe, 'Urbanization and Changing Voting Patterns'. Also see Lee Jin-wuk, 'Geographical Analysis of Voting Behaviour: the 8th, the 10th, and the 11th National Assembly Elections in South Korea' (in Korean), unpublished MA thesis, Ehwa Women's University, 1986.

elections, the two DLP candidates were defeated, and only one candidate won with a slight margin. In the local legislative elections held in June 1991, however, the DLP alliance yielded a landslide victory, giving Kim Dae-jung's PPD control over only the Cholla provinces. For the upcoming elections, the PPD merged with the Democratic Party, composed of former RDP members who refused to join the ruling coalition, and formed a new united opposition, the Democratic Party (DP). This merger undoubtedly helped Kim Dae-jung to overcome the public image that his party was a regional party limited to the Cholla region, and therefore the DP could be projected as a united opposition which could offer an alternative choice against the DLP.

In the 14th National Assembly election of 24 March 1992, the Korean voters delivered a protest vote, instead of the easy victory for the DLP that was surely expected. The DLP won only 116 of the 237 constituencies by gaining 38.5 per cent of the vote. Awarded the thirty-three additional proportional representation seats (out of total 62), the DLP was one short of a simple majority in parliament, and it was able to maintain a simple majority only by recruiting some of the independents who altogether won in twenty-one constituencies. The DP won 29.2 per cent of the vote, seventy-five constituencies, and twenty-two proportional representation seats, giving it a total of ninety-seven seats. Perhaps the biggest winner of this election was the Unification National Party (UNP), which was formed by the former chairman of the Hyundai conglomerate, Chung Ju-yung, a few months before the election. The UNP received 17.4 per cent of the vote, and a total of thirty-one seats (24 in contested constituencies), giving it enough seats to form an influential negotiating bloc in the assembly.

The pattern of regional voting was also maintained in the 1992 National Assembly election, even though there had been a rearrangement in the party system. The DLP led by Kim Young-sam did best in Pusan, and did well in Taegu, North Kyongsang and South Kyongsang (see Table 11.1). The DLP did relatively well in North Chungchong but not in Kim Jong-pil's stronghold, South Chungchong. Kangwon voters, who used to be ruling party supporters, also defected from the DLP. The DLP performed poorly in Cholla. The DP performed very well in Kwangju and Cholla provinces, and did well in Seoul and Kyongki, but did poorly in the other regions, especially in the Kyongsang provinces. The UNP did relatively well in the central regions of Seoul, Kyongki, Kangwon, and Chungchong. The UNP also did well in Taegu and South Kyongsang. The regional voting pattern for the DP in 1992 was almost identical to those in 1987 and in 1988. The defecting voters in Taegu and Chungchong seemed not to go to the DP, instead they supported the UNP or the independents.

The regional factor in electoral politics, which first appeared as the single most important variable in the 1987 presidential election, continued to shape the voters' choices in the 1988 and the 1992 National Assembly elections. Regionalism in this period is perhaps beyond that regional identity or regional sentiment that the voters might be expected to possess. It may be rather a regional antagonism that operates exclusively among the voter in different regions. Regional disparities in political, economic or social spheres may have contributed to the formation of regionalism that subsequently has been actively exploited by politicians.

Regionalism and Social Structure

This section explores the influence of regionalism on individual voters' choices compared to the socio-economic characteristics of the voters, by using sample survey data collected in November 1991.[6] The main objective of this section is to measure effects of regionalism over time—i.e., the pattern of party support in the 1992 elections will be compared to those in the 1987 and 1988 elections—along with possible changes in the social bases of partisan support. That is, it is aimed to explore the voters' responses to the DLP merger and the subsequent DP merger, with reference to regional and socio-economic characteristics.

Multiple regression analyses were performed with dependent variables of voting choices in 1987 and 1988, and voting intentions in 1992 (parliamentary and presidential elections), and with independent variables of social structure and residential region. The ordinary least square (OLS) partial regression coefficients for the independent variables are reported in Tables 11.3, 11.4, and 11.5 ('b' is an unstandardised regression coefficient, which can be interpreted as a percentage probability of attributing to voting choice net of other things, and 'beta' is a standardised regression coefficient, which indicates the relative strength of the variables since the unit of measure is standardised). Let us briefly look at the Tables in turn.

Table 11.3, which reports the effects of independent variables on voting choices in the 1987 presidential election, shows that the variables of education and residential region exert significant effects on the voting choices for the three main candidates. For Kim Young-sam, income also appears to have a significant effect: the higher a household's income the

---

6   The survey was designed by James Cotton and the fieldwork was carried out by the Korea Survey (Gallup) Polls Ltd, during the period of 1 November to 10 November 1991. The data, using a multi-stage stratified random sampling method, was collected by person to person interview with the population aged twenty and over, and resulted in a total sample size of 1250. The data in this analysis is weighted by age and sex to reflect the 1990 Provincial Population Projection published by the National Statistical Office. Cases are also weighted so that they correspond to the official election results.

more support for Kim Young-sam. Table 11.3 also supports the conventional wisdom in Korean electoral politics: the more a person is educated, the more he/she tends to be critical of government affairs, and thus less likely to support a governing party candidate. Education may have been the single most important variable in differentiating partisan support under the authoritarian regimes of the Park and Chun era.

Table 11.3 The OLS Partial Multiple Regression Coefficients for the Social Structural Variables on the 1987 Votes

	Roh		YS		DJ	
	b	beta	b	beta	b	beta
HEAD OF HOUSEHOLD'S JOB (Self-employed Trading)						
Blue Collar Work	-.077	-.067	.054	.051	.054	.051
White Collar Work	-.011	-.010	.039	.041	.005	.005
Self-employed Farming	.019	.016	-.002	-.001	-.020	-.040
Self-assessed Status	.011	.020	.008	.017	-.020	-.040
Education	-.107**	-.232**	.072**	.168**	.033*	.078*
Monthly Income	-.0004	-.056	.0005**	.092**	-.0001	-.025
RESIDENTIAL AREAS (Seoul)						
Pusan/South Kyongsang	-.048	-.039	.307**	.266**	-.225**	-.197**
Taegu/North Kyongsang	.257**	.175**	.051	.037	-.275**	-.203**
Inchon/Kyungki	.042	.032	-.005	-.004	-.032	-.027
Kwangju/Cholla	-.405**	-.268**	-.169**	-.120**	.662**	.475**
Chungchong	-.051	-.032	.057	.038	-.207**	-.141**
Kangwon	.087	.035	.054	.023	-.100	-.044
Constant	.694		-.059		.264	
R-Squares	.166		.167		.362	

Note: 1. *,p<.05; **, p<.01. F-test probability scores are always below .0000.
2. The variables of head of household's job are dummy variables: the reference variable is self-employed trading. Self-assessed Status and Education are coded the low, 1, to the high, 4. The unit for income is 10,000 won. The variables of residential areas are dummy variables: the reference category is Seoul.
3. Dependent variables are votes for candidates coded 1 for yes, and 0 for no. Non-voters are excluded.
4. The 'b' is the unstandardised regression coefficient, and the 'beta' is the standardised regression coefficient.

Table 11.4 The OLS Partial Multiple Regression Coefficients for the Social Structural Variables on the 1988 Votes

	DJP		RDP		PPD	
	b	beta	b	beta	b	beta
HEAD OF HOUSEHOLD'S JOB (Self-employed Trading)						
Blue Collar Work	-.028	-.025	-.058	-.058	.007	.008
White Collar Work	.017	.018	-.046	-.052	-.060*	-.074*
Self-employed Farming	.114*	.100*	-.078	-.075	-.085	-.089*
Self-assessed Status	.023	.045	.009	.016	-.024	-.054
Education	-.076**	-.169**	.064**	.157**	.016	.042
Monthly Income	-.0008**	-.122**	.0003	.046	-.0001	-.014
RESIDENTIAL AREAS (Seoul)						
Pusan/South Kyongsang	-.083	-.068	.253**	.230**	-.185**	-.182**
Taegu/North Kyongsang	.116*	.083*	.019	.015	-.186**	-.161**
Inchon/Kyungki	.008	.006	-.065	-.057	-.006	-.005
Kwangju/Cholla	-.412**	-.257**	-.169**	-.117**	.657**	.492**
Chungchong	-.225**	-.156**	.003	.002	-.166**	-.138**
Kangwon	.007	.003	.058	.028	-.161**	-.084**
Constant	.599		.049		.271	
R-Squares	.137		.141		.359	

Note: 1. *,p<.05, **,p<.01. F-test probability scores are always below .0000.
2. The variables of head of household's job are dummy variables: the reference variable is self-employed trading. Self-assessed Status and Education are coded the low, 1, to the high, 4. The unit for income is 10,000 won. The variables of residential areas are dummy variables: the reference category is Seoul.
3. Dependent variables are votes for candidates coded 1 for yes, and 0 for no. Non-voters are excluded.
4. The 'b' is the unstandardised regression coefficient, and the 'beta' is the standardised regression coefficient.

The regional residence variables were also important in shaping voting choice. For example, voters who lived in the Taegu/North Kyongsang area were far more likely to vote for Roh compared to those in Seoul, after controlling individuals' socio-economic characteristics, and they were also far less likely to vote for Kim Dae-jung. Voters living in the Pusan/South Kyongsang area were far more likely to vote for Kim Young-sam compared to those in Seoul, and far less likely to vote for Kim Dae-jung, net ofother things. Voters in Cholla were 66.2 per cent more likely to vote for Kim Dae-jung, 40.5 per cent less likely to vote for Roh Tae-woo, and 16.9

per cent less likely to vote for Kim Young-sam than voters in Seoul. Indeed, regarding the vote for Kim Dae-jung, regionalism played the most important role: except for voters in Cholla all the voters in the other regions were far less favourably inclined toward him than those in Seoul.

Table 11.4 reports the OLS regression coefficients for the votes of the three main parties in the 1988 National Assembly election. The coefficients show a similar pattern to the 1987 votes. Of the socio-economic variables, education, income and occupational variables appeared to have statistically significant impacts for the DJP vote. For the RDP, education appeared to be significant, and for the PPD occupation appeared to have statistical significance. Residential area also appeared as a significant variable showing a similar pattern to the coefficients of Table 11.3. Worth noting is the fact that voters in Chungchong in this election were far less likely to vote for Roh's DJP than those in Seoul: at Table 11.3 the coefficient of the Chungchong variable did not appear to be significant. Perhaps at least for Chungchong voters regionalism became more important than it had been in 1987.

Table 11.5 shows the pattern of political support after the DJP, Kim Young-sam's RDP, and Kim Jong-pil's party merged into the ruling DLP. The dependent variables in Table 11.5 are voting intentions for the DLP and the DP in the 1992 National Assembly election, and voting intentions for Kim Young-sam against Kim Dae-jung. Generally speaking the conclusion to be drawn from Table 11.5 is that the DLP merger was successful only in that the party broadened its political support geographically, but it failed to shift its social basis of support as compared to that of the DJP. As 'b' of education indicates, the DLP may have failed to embrace the well-educated voters, among whom Kim Young-sam had strong support. The coefficient of Taegu/North Kyongsang, the DJP's stronghold, is not significant in determining the DLP vote. Voters in the Taegu/North Kyongsang area seemed not to support the DLP as they had the DJP, but their support seemed not to go to the DP either as 'b' for the DP indicates. But when the voters were asked to choose the alternative of Kim Young-sam or Kim Dae-jung, those in Taegu/North Kyongsang were far more likely to vote for Kim Young-sam against Kim Dae-jung (see the coefficients at the third column of Table 11.5). Perhaps the nature of regionalism in Korean electoral politics is a process of mass mobilisation against Kim Dae-jung and his followers. Indeed, the pattern of DP support is almost identical to that in 1987 and 1988. The support for the DP is virtually limited to the Kwangju/Cholla area, although the well-educated voters tend to favour the DP and Kim Dae-jung, though to a limited degree.

Obviously, for a more complete explanation of voting choice there are more variances to be explained by variables other than those included in

Table 11.5 The OLS Partial Multiple Regression Coefficients for the Social Structural Variables on the Voting Intention for the DLP and DP, and for Kim Young-sam against Kim Dae-jung

	DLP		DP		YS vs DJ	
	b	beta	b	beta	b	beta
HEAD OF HOUSEHOLD'S JOB (Self-employed Trading)						
Blue Collar Work	-.066	-.057	.054	.045	-.056	-.047
White Collar Work	.100*	.093*	-.064	-.060	-.009	-.009
Self-employed Farming	-.040	-.034	.024	.020	-.035	-.029
Self-assessed Status	.039	.071	-.023	-.041	.038	.069
Education	-.101**	-.216**	.052*	.108*	-.041*	-.084*
Monthly Income	-.000	-.053	.000	.046	-.000	-.020
RESIDENTIAL AREAS (Seoul)						
Pusan/South Kyongsang	.201**	.158**	-.169**	-.129**	.352**	.271**
Taegu/North Kyongsang	.012	.008	-.196**	-.131**	.413**	.278**
Inchon/Kyungki	.018	.014	-.031	-.024	.144*	.110**
Kwangju/Cholla	-.391**	-.270**	.473**	.317**	-.509**	-.344**
Chungchong	.128*	.078*	-.108	-.064	.203**	.122**
Kangwon	.159	.064	-.192*	-.074*	.130	.051
Constant	.572		.384		.527	
R-Squares	.152		.170		.304	

Note: 1. *, p<.05; **,p<.01. F-test probability scores are always below .0000.

this study. So far, education and place of residence were found to exert significant influences on voting choice. The influence of education on voting choice found in this study perhaps is a proxy variable for the influence of socialisation or differences in the value orientation of the voters. Education may also be a factor that negates the emotional basis of regionalism. Regional differences in voting choice, which may have been the single most important factor during this period, need also to be explored further: there has been evidence that the regional nature of voting does not merely result from regional sentiment which may nevertheless be deeply seated among Korean voters.

Conclusion

This preliminary survey indicates that regionalism has remained an important characteristic of Korean voting behaviour throughout Roh Tae-woo's tenure of office. The forces which compel regional sentiment are deep seated, though they can be negated at least with some individuals by the influence of education. A number of the policies of the Roh administration can be interpreted as an attempt to mitigate the operation of this sentiment, for if politics is dominated by such perceptions to the exclusion of other factors the political system will be unable to develop a credible and broadly based opposition or indeed any political movement with national ties to the ordinary citizenry. Government decisions to upgrade the infrastructure of the western coast to permit that region to take advantage of its proximity with China (trade with China growing rapidly to almost $9 billion in 1992) can be seen as an attempt to spread economic advantage to the Cholla provinces. If the perception of disadvantage is at the root of regionalism, alleviating regional inequities should change that perception. Dealing with regionalism may also be seen as the reason for the party merger of 1990. On the one hand, the DLP widened its base of support across traditional antagonistic regions. On the other hand, this merger posed a challenge to the opposition to act similarly to widen its appeal, a challenge which was responded to in the form of the merger that created the Democratic Party later in the same year. However, as this analysis demonstrates, despite such policies regional consciousness will remain an influence in politics for some time to come.

PART III

NORTHERN POLICY AND INTER-KOREAN RELTIONS

12 The Strategic Equilibrium on the Korean Peninsula in the 1990s

PERRY WOOD

Background: The Crossroads of Northeast Asia

Korea is located at a strategic crossroads, both continental and maritime, where the interests of four major powers—the United States, the Soviet Union/Russia, China, and Japan—intersect. Historically, when one power has dominated the Korean Peninsula, it has also dominated Northeast Asia. The arrangements at the end of World War II left the peninsula divided. Stalin's gamble at grabbing all of Korea, of course, led to war, and when it looked as if the United States would take the entire country, China entered the conflict. In the end, the peninsula remained divided. The partition of Korea has created a point of enormous military tension but also a source of regional stability.

Both the Republic of Korea (ROK) and the Democratic People's Republic of Korea (DPRK) have long sought to overcome the existing division. The end of the Cold War, political realignment in Europe, and a new Russian policy toward East Asia make that goal less of a distant future aspiration and more of a feasible goal than at any time in the past four decades.

The strategies of both Koreas are changing dramatically toward one another and in some regards toward the four major regional powers. Yet both countries' ties with their traditional allies remain significant constraints on their room for manoeuvre. Because the unification of Korea would portend major new strategic alignments, the central focus of analysis will be on its prospects.

The Republic of Korea: Growing World Role

Introduction: a new self-confidence

South Korea has emerged as a significant independent actor on the international scene. It is a significant military power, and its economic strength has won international recognition and bestowed upon it growing regional influence. Economists have predicted that the South Korean economy will rival the major West European economies by early in the twenty-first century.[1] The South Korean economy has become a model for other Third World nations envious of the giant, efficient Korean *chaebol* business conglomerates which export and operate all over the world. South Korean foreign investment has become an important factor in the national economies of Southeast and South Asia, which are increasingly looking to Korea as an alternative source of technology and know-how. The growing economic and military power of South Korea is an unprecedented development which will have a critical impact on Northeast Asian security in the next decade.

South Koreans relish their newfound influence. There is a growing sense of self-confidence and aggressive nationalism in South Korea. This new feeling has been stimulated by a number of developments including South Korea's impressive economic growth, its successful, peaceful transition from authoritarian to democratic government, the international recognition won by hosting the 24th Summer Olympiad in 1988, the obvious political–economic decline of the South's rival in the north, the new policies of the Gorbachev government, and the great diplomatic successes of President Roh's *Nordpolitik* policies and the hopes they offer for Korean national reunification. Koreans have never been a shy people, and these developments have heightened their self-assurance enormously.

A brief overview of foreign policy during the authoritarian era

The new Korean assertiveness shocks Americans and Japanese because they have yet to adjust to the rapid transformation of Korea from a war-shattered, poverty-stricken nation into an economic giant. Surveys indicate that the American public's perception of Korea is largely identical with the image portrayed on the popular television show M*A*S*H: a poor, dirty, violent land. Even better-informed policy-makers and opinion shapers remain influenced by their memories of the Korean war and their old postwar relationships.

---

[1]   Robert L. Pfaltzgraff, Jr, 'Korea's Emerging Role in World Politics', *Korea and World Affairs*, vol. 11, no. 1 (Spring 1987), p. 18.

In the 1950s, the nation was a virtual dependent of the United States. The country was among the world's poorest nations, dependent on American economic aid for its survival. South Korea's tie with the United States was not only its most important external relationship, it was virtually its only one. Formal diplomatic relations with Japan were not established until 1965. Given these facts, Syngman Rhee, South Korea's first postwar leader, pragmatically restrained his strong nationalism and accepted a virtual client relationship with the United States (although he was a prickly client).

The primary foreign policy goals of the Syngman Rhee regime were national security (secured via the 1954 defence pact with the United States and the maintenance of the close US–ROK security relationship) and international legitimacy. The Rhee government engaged the communist regime in Pyongyang in an unrelenting competition to secure international recognition over their archrival. South Korea adhered to the principle established in the Hallstein Doctrine, first enunciated by the Federal Republic of Germany to guide its competition with the communist German Democratic Republic. According to this doctrine, Seoul, like Bonn, refused to recognise any nation which established relations with North Korea (and broke relations with any nation that already had recognised the ROK).

The Park Chung-hee government brought some major changes to South Korea's international posture. Park came to power through a *coup d'état* which overthrew Chang Myon and South Korea's first democratic government. The United States, although not enamoured of Chang's government, supported the idea of a democratic South Korea and was embarrassed by Park's coup. Park reacted by asserting his independence from the United States, at least with regard to domestic policy. That was to prove characteristic of his regime.

Throughout his long rule, Park was an advocate of *chuch'e* (self-reliance), a concept which Kim Il Sung has elevated into an all-pervasive ideology in the north (*chuch'e sasang*). For Park the concept was more restricted and pragmatic, but still central to Korean national identity.[2] It lay at the core of his economic development programme, by which he laid the foundation of South Korea's future international influence. It also lay behind his determination to normalise relations with Japan despite widespread popular opposition within South Korea. He recognised that

---

2 Park made frequent references to the concept of *chuch'e* and even used it to justify his effort to institutionalise his dictatorship via the 'October Revitalising Reforms' *(Siwol Yusin),* which was inspired by the *Meiji Ishin* or Meiji Restoration period in Japanese history and which Park reportedly greatly admired. See Byung Chul Koh, *The Foreign Policy Systems of North and South Korea* (Berkeley: University of California Press, 1984), p. 17ff.

Japanese foreign investment and technology were indispensable to his economic development programme and that the establishment of bilateral relations would reduce South Korea's dependence on the United States. Of course, Park was careful to restore good relations with the United States as soon as possible after his coup and maintain them thereafter. Park's policies typically displayed a very pragmatic approach to self-reliance— guaranteeing South Korea's immediate security by relying on the United States, while laying the groundwork for its future independent role.

North and South Korea share a commitment to the idea of *chuch'e*. The enduring appeal of *chuch'e* in both nations stems from the fervid nationalism of the Korean people. As Byung Chul Koh has written, 'The single most important ideological dimension for both Koreas is nationalism—the burning desire on the part of leaders and citizens alike to assert their national identity, to determine their own destiny, and to enhance their national prestige abroad in every conceivable way. The much-vaunted *chuch'e* idea is but a manifestation of this desire'.[3]

Dr Koh traces this fierce nationalism to the historical experiences of the Korean people—their long history of foreign invasion, domination, and Japanese colonial rule. Their experiences have also left the Korean people somewhat distrustful of foreigners and wary of excessive dependence on allied states. This latter characteristic is most evident in North Korea's relations with its communist allies, the USSR and the PRC, neither of whom appears to be seen as truly reliable by the North Koreans. Indeed, Dr Koh argues that Kim Il Sung's constant emphasis on *chuch'e* imparts the image of a 'siege mentality' to the North Korean leadership.[4]

In the case of South Korea, this characteristic seems more restrained, although South Koreans clearly possess a deeply ingrained distrust of their old colonial subjugator, Japan. Until recently, the United States was an exception to this norm. The Korean War forged a unique bond between the two nations. As the war era fades into the past, South Koreans' growing doubts about the strength of the American commitment and suspicions regarding the motivations for American policy are now beginning to complicate the relationship. Even during the Park era, the president himself was very cautious in his dealings with the United States and the other great powers, however much he might have relied on their assistance. In the 1970s, for example, he wrote:

> A multipolar world is certainly not a simple international environment. Unlike the Cold War days when dependence on the power of an ally was possible, we now carefully watch the moves of the United States, Japan, China, the Soviet Union and many other countries as well. This requires a high level of adaptability and creativeness.

---

3   Ibid., p. 235.
4   Ibid., p. 91.

Park went on to caution against the hazards of 'the games that Big Powers play', in which 'yesterday's friend can be abandoned without consideration, yesterday's adversary can be today's friend, and today's enemy can become tomorrow's negotiating partner'. The principal lesson, according to Park, was that 'we have only our own power to safeguard security and independence. Help is offered only when one helps oneself... Our allies will begin to help us only after they are convinced that we, and not the North Korean communists, are overwhelmingly superior'.[5]

Despite Park's strong anti-communism, his commitment to Korean nationalism and his foreign policy pragmatism led him to establish the groundwork for President Roh's much-heralded 'Northern policies'. Throughout the 1960s, North Korea made considerable gains against the South in their mutual battle for international recognition, receiving the support of the Third World 'Non-Aligned' bloc. As a fervid nationalist determined to expand South Korean international relations, Park could not accept any deterioration in South Korea's international position.[6] Accordingly, in January 1971, Park abandoned the nation's fervent anti-communist stance, scrapping the Hallstein Doctrine and announcing that his government would be willing to improve relations with 'non-hostile' communist states.

Park then initiated a series of secret negotiations with Pyongyang, which resulted in the Joint Communiqué of 4 July 1972, urging the gradual reduction of tension between the two Koreas through a series of confidence-building measures. Park followed this success with his 'Special Foreign Policy Statement Regarding Peace and Unification' on 23 June 1973. In this, speech, Park stated that Seoul would no longer oppose Pyongyang's participation in international organisations, including the United Nations, and indeed proposed separate UN memberships for the ROK and the DPRK. He also extended his earlier opening to communist states by stating that the ROK would 'open its door to all the nations of the world on the basis of the principles of reciprocity and equality'.[7] Park's offer was immediately spurned by the North Koreans, but it set the future basis for South Korean policy toward its rival.

---

5   Park Chung Hee, *Korea Reborn: A Model for Development* (Englewood Cliffs, NJ: Prentice Hall, 1979), pp. 128–9, 132. Quoted in Koh, *The Foreign Policy Systems of North and South Korea*, p. 99.

6   His actions were also undoubtedly influenced by the prevailing international trends of the time, which were embodied by the beginning of the American withdrawal from Vietnam, Sino–American rapprochement, and Soviet–American *détente*.

7   Quoted in B.C. Koh, 'Seoul's "Northern Policy" and Korean Security', *The Korean Journal of Defense Analysis*, vol. 1, no. 1 (Summer 1989), p. 129.

Park's domestic and foreign policies were interrelated, and were guided by his own fervent nationalistic ideals. His policies were directed at augmenting South Korean security, gaining international recognition and influence, and ultimately enabling South Korea to follow an independent path. The Chun Doo-hwan regime continued the basic trends of Park's foreign and domestic policies. Because the non-aligned movement had rejected the ROK's application for membership in 1973, the Chun government focused on strengthening South Korea's ties with Western Europe and attempting to develop economic and political relations with the Eastern bloc and, eventually, the Soviet Union and China. These policies built upon Park's initial efforts, and set the stage for President Roh's spectacularly successful efforts to improve South Korea's relations with the communist world. Indeed, it was Yi Pom-sok, Chun's foreign minister, who invented the term *pukbang chongch'aek* ('northern policy') in a speech at the National Defense Graduate School in June 1983.[8]

The Roh era: democracy and foreign policy activism

Despite his foreign policy innovations and his notable achievements in directing the South Korean economy, Chun suffered from weak legitimacy throughout his tenure. Almost from the moment he took office, Chun faced strong opposition which grew steadily. The era of military government was passing in South Korea. The collapse of Park's government had basically marked the end of the public's ready acceptance of military rule in the interests of economic development and national security.

By the end of Chun's term, massive public protests, American pressure, and the example of President Marcos' February 1986 overthrow in the Philippines convinced Roh Tae-woo, Chun's old Korean Military Academy classmate and chosen successor, of the political necessity of compromise. Roh announced that he would recommend that Chun accept a direct presidential election and adopt a series of other 'democratisation' measures. Roh asserted that if Chun rejected these recommendations he would withdraw as a candidate and resign from public office. That action won Roh a public following, international stature, and a reputation for daring political initiative. It also led to the decision to implement direct presidential elections in December 1987, which Roh won.[9]

Koh's successful election as the first president of a democratic South Korean government was followed rapidly by major advances in South Korea's relations with the communist nations. The catalyst for these gains

---

8   See Koh, 'Seoul's "Northern Policy"', p. 130.

9   The South Korean transition to democracy is discussed in greater detail in Perry L. Wood, 'South Korea: Towards Stable Democratic Government'. HI-4048-P (Indianapolis, IN: Hudson Institute, December 1988).

was the 1988 Summer Olympics held in Seoul. The USSR, PRC, and Eastern European countries sent large contingents of athletes to the Games, along with trade and cultural delegations. Talks on trade, investment, and other forms of relations flowered. In the aftermath of the Games, Hungary became the first communist state to open diplomatic relations with the ROK, on 1 February 1989. Others quickly followed. In June 1990, Roh met with Gorbachev in San Francisco, which set the stage for Roh's ultimate achievement—the establishment of diplomatic relations between Moscow and Seoul on 30 September 1990. These stunning developments presaged Roh Tae-woo's historic three-day visit to Moscow for a meeting with Gorbachev and Gorbachev's own visit to the ROK on 20 April 1991, during which he offered a public endorsement of South Korea's recent decision to apply for UN membership.

Roh's successes can be traced to a combination of factors, including the new foreign policy pragmatism initiated by Gorbachev, Roh's own status as the head of a new, democratic South Korea, the economic problems in the communist world and the ROK's economic power, problems in USSR–Japan relations, and, of course, Roh's continued efforts to improve ROK–DPRK dialogue and Seoul's ties to the communist world. Before the opening of the Olympic Games, Roh made a special declaration (7 July 1988) in which he pledged to abandon the traditional South Korean efforts to isolate the DPRK, announcing that Seoul would no longer oppose trade and other contacts between its allies and Pyongyang.

Roh's *Nordpolitik* policies[10] were based on the work of his predecessors but also reflected the impact of democratisation on foreign policy. Improving relations with the communist world and reducing tensions with the North—while appearing to be forthcoming on the reunification question—strengthened Roh politically. Roh derived multiple benefits from these policies: he undercut student radicals' attempts to appeal to the middle-class on the reunification issue; he reduced the security threat faced by the ROK; he gained expanded economic markets for South Korean products in a time of growing world protectionism; and he increased the ROK's world stature and legitimacy, undercut the position

---

10 *Nordpolitik* is similar to the *Ostpolitik* popularised by Willy Brandt in the 1970s with reference to West Germany's relations with East Germany and its communist allies. The term has been used in South Korean academia to describe the ROK's policies toward the North and its communist allies since the Park era. Koh's *Nordpolitik* policy is defined by one South Korean academic '…as a diplomatic strategy to normalize relations with China, the Soviet Union and East Europe and through it to establish a mechanism for peaceful coexistence between South and North Korea'. See Sang-Seek Park, 'Northern Diplomacy and Inter-Korean Relations', *Korea and World Affairs*, vol. 12, no. 4 (Winter 1988), p. 707.

of North Korea, demonstrated to the Korean people his commitment to national reunification, and increased his own international reputation and domestic popularity.

The impact of democratisation on South Korean foreign policy has already created tensions with South Korea's old allies. As one analyst has written, 'this is a heady period for South Korea. National pride and confidence are palpable. The country is feeling its oats'.[11] These feelings are reflected in national policy. Roh's basic foreign policy goals remained the promotion of the ROK's international legitimacy, preservation of the ROK's national security, and preservation and acceleration of the ROK's economic accomplishments. Roh, however, pursued these goals in a bolder, more independent fashion than his predecessors. His *Nordpolitik* policies were undertaken at his own initiative, and, contrary to the expectation of many American policy-makers, led to impressive diplomatic coups for his government. Regionally, Roh's ROK has become one of the strongest proponents of the idea of Asia–Pacific economic cooperation embodied in the new Asia–Pacific Economic Council (APEC). South Korea's arrival on the world scene was truly heralded by the Roh government's successful application for UN membership.

Roh was actively attempting to carve out for his nation an independent international role commensurate with its rising economic and political prominence. While Roh attempted to improve ties with the ROK's old adversaries, he was also attempting to establish a more equal relationship with the United States and Japan. South Koreans believe that they have their own destiny to fulfil, and no longer wish to assume the compliant sidekick role traditionally accorded them by American and Japanese leaders. Many Americans and Japanese are uncertain as to how to respond to the ROK's transformation from a rabidly anti-communist 'little buddy' into an independent-minded nation willing to open relations with every state. Inevitably, the growing assertiveness of the Koreans is leading to misunderstandings and generating tension with Korea's old friends. Managing these tensions is a major challenge for the government in Seoul. Roh wanted an independent role for the ROK in world affairs, but he sought to preserve strong links to his old allies at the same time. The United States and Japan remain critical to South Korea's economic, political, and security interests. In particular, Seoul needs to maintain secure and friendly relations between the ROK and the US.

---

[11] Edward A. Olsen, 'U.S.–ROK Relations: Common Issues and Uncommon Perceptions', *Korea and World Affairs*, vol. 13, no. 1 (Spring 1989), p. 43.

Korea and the Great Powers

The United States

The ROK–US relationship remains South Korea's most important external relationship. Despite the ROK's recent successes at expanding and diversifying its foreign export markets, the United States remains its most important market and also an important source of foreign investment and technology. Roh also requires American support for his international initiatives. The ROK application for UN membership is a good example. Reportedly, the ROK depended heavily on American and Japanese support for its efforts to sway China and the Third World nations to support its application. Roh also needed the United States to assist his initiatives toward North Korea by coordinating with the ROK its own policies toward Kim Il Sung's regime. Unilateral American policies toward the DPRK could still have a deleterious effect on the Korean peoples' hopes for national reunification.

The United States remains the ultimate guarantor of South Korean security. Currently, the United States maintains about 40,000 troops in Korea (7,000 of which are scheduled to be removed over the next three years), including approximately 29,000 assigned to the Eighth US Army (including the Second Infantry Division) and the 314th air division, which operates bases in Kunsan, Osan, Suwon, and Taegu. In conjunction with US planes based in Japan and Okinawa, the 314th air division provides tactical support to both US and ROK ground forces. The United States currently maintains no naval support facilities in South Korea because it has access to nearby Japanese facilities. South Korea has been mentioned, however, as an alternative to the US naval and air bases in the Philippines.

Although the ROK military is becoming increasingly capable of defending the nation against its northern rival (see the section on the military balance later in this chapter), the US security guarantee remains essential for three reasons. First, in the short- to medium-term, the threat of a DPRK attack remains high because of the DPRK's internal political dynamics and its declining military capabilities *vis-à-vis* the ROK.

Second, the US security guarantee is a deterrent which the ROK military cannot match, ever. Although the ROK's military capabilities are rising, the balance between North and South will probably always remain tenuous. Accordingly, the DPRK leaders, given the political incentive or necessity, could always decide to risk an attack. Any attack, even if the ROK successfully blunted it, would devastate South Korea and destroy the economic and political achievements of the past three decades. The South Koreans believe that only the preservation of a strong US security commitment to defend the ROK offers an adequate deterrence to potential North Korean adventurism.

Finally, in the long term, South Korean policy-makers recognise that their nation remains surrounded by powerful, potentially hostile states: Japan, China, and the USSR. South Korea will never possess the economic, political, or military clout of these nations. A security link to a powerful, friendly, but distant state with vital interests in the region—such as the United States—enhances South Korea's strategic position significantly.

The preservation of close US–ROK ties, however, will not be easy. Tensions clearly exist in US–ROK relations today—the inevitable consequence of the need to restructure the relationship on a more equal basis. The US–ROK economic relationship, for example, has become extremely conflictual—a source of tension which could sour general bilateral relations. Despite considerable Korean progress in opening up their economy in recent years, the United States continues to suffer large trade deficits in its bilateral trade account with Korea. American pressure on trade issues often creates deep resentment among the Korean populace, which perceives the United States as a rich bully in these matters. Such pressure fuels the rise of anti-Americanism. As a result, public American pressures are often counterproductive—making it more difficult for the ROK government to compromise on economic issues, while damaging overall bilateral relations. Trade issues will be on the front burner of US–ROK relations for some time.

US relations with North Korea are also likely to introduce considerable tension into the US–ROK relationship. Although South Korea has eagerly sought to expand relations with its rival's communist allies, it has been wary of efforts by the United States and Japan to establish links with the North (despite Roh's recent policy statement indicating that he would no longer oppose such ties).

For these reasons, the South Koreans want the United States and Japan to consult fully with them on any changes in their policies toward the North. Ideally, the ROK would like to have the three allies pursue a coordinated policy toward the North, to avoid mutual misunderstandings and unforeseen complications for South Korean security and reunification goals.

To date, American policy has been supportive of South Korean concerns in its dealings with the North. The United States has taken four steps to initiate contact with the DPRK. First, the United States has increased diplomatic contact with North Korea, arranging eleven meetings between embassy political counsellors in Beijing (from 1989 to July 1990). Second, the US government has encouraged North Korean private citizens to visit the United States. Third, the US allowed travel to the North by private Americans in January 1989. Fourth, the United States has allowed the limited export of American food and medical products to North Korea to 'meet basic human needs'. In 1989, these exports were valued at $8.4 million. At the same time, the Bush administration has called upon North Korea to achieve 'real progress' in North–South talks on confidence-building measures; to accept inspection of its nuclear plants and research facilities by international atomic energy agencies; officially to abandon its support of international terrorism; and to return the remains of Americans killed in the Korean War.[12]

The most troubling problem in ROK–US relations is the visible increase in anti-Americanism in South Korea in recent years. Their recent emergence on the world scene has made the Koreans very proud. At the same time, their historical legacy of dependence on the United States and subjugation by foreign powers has created within many Koreans a feeling of insecurity. As one senior diplomat has stated: 'The Koreans have come too far, too fast. They are still trying to catch up with themselves'.[13] The combination of pride and insecurity can easily be mistaken for arrogance. It also accounts for the extreme importance attached to minor incidents. To the South Koreans, such incidents indicate a lack of respect for them and their nation by the United States and Americans. Fundamentally, South Koreans are now demanding that their old patron treat them with respect and as an equal. This attitude was exemplified by the comments of one young South Korean who was fulfilling his Korean military service as a *Katusa* (an acronym for Koreans serving in the US army) on the US army base in Seoul. He said, 'Most of us Katusas are better educated than the GIs. It isn't the 1950s anymore. It's time for a change in our relations. It's time we had a Korean, not an American, in charge'.[14]

Korean nationalism does not necessarily mean anti-Americanism. The assertion of Korean independence and national identity is not incompatible with Korea's friendship with the United States. Roh's initiatives demonstrated that an assertive South Korea is not necessarily harmful to US

---

12 More than 8,000 Americans are still listed as missing in action in Korea. See Daryl M. Plunk, 'For the U.S.A. New Policy for Korean Reunification', *Asian Studies Center Backgrounder*, no. 107 (The Heritage Foundation: 19 September 1990), p. 12.

13 Quoted in John McBeth, 'Still a Hermit on the World Scene', *Far Eastern Economic Review*, 8 December 1988, p. 24.

14 Quoted in Susan Moffat, 'Koreans See Need to Cut U.S. Military', *Asian Wall Street Journal*, 5 October 1988.

interests.[15] There is no fundamental conflict between the two nations. Indeed, the United States and South Korea continue to share critical strategic, economic, and political interests. Assuming Korean and American leaders manage the evolution of the new relationship constructively, anti-Americanism will fade over time, as Koreans become more confident of their new role and assume greater responsibility for their own defence, and as the influence of the United States over internal Korean affairs declines and the presence and visibility of US forces on the peninsula are reduced. On the other hand, if the relationship is allowed to deteriorate, it will be difficult to preserve close US–ROK ties once the immediate threat from the DPRK declines.

Koreans see coordination in US–ROK decision-making as vital. South Koreans will not respond well to American calls for increased burden-sharing, trade liberalisation, or other reforms unless such proposals entail a willingness to practise increased 'decision-sharing' as well.[16]

Japan

Japan has always regarded Korea as critical to its own security; it fought two wars, with China and Russia, to secure control over the peninsula in the early years of this century. The Koreans have not appreciated Japan's interest in their land. The era of Japanese colonial domination left deep-seated bitterness toward their colonial oppressor within the hearts of many Koreans. Today, South Korea and Japan are bound together by geography, economics, and mutual ties to the United States. Japanese trade, investment, and technology are vital to the South Korean economy. In turn, US forces based in Japan are critical to South Korean security. But Japan and Korea remain uneasy associates rather than true allies.

Public opinion polls in both nations consistently indicate their peoples' mutual dislike. Koreans rank Japan as one of the countries they like least, second only to North Korea; while Japanese rank South Korea third on their list of most-disliked nations, behind only the Soviet Union and North Korea. Koreans believe that the Japanese look down upon the Korean people and their culture, citing Japanese treatment of their own ethnic Korean population. Many Koreans are uncomfortable with their close economic links to Japan—fearing Japanese exploitation and manipulation.

---

15 An assertive South Korea could become harmful to US interests if it led to a serious, potentially destabilising conflict between the ROK and Japan. But such a conflict is hardly inevitable. Indeed, the preservation of good US relations with both nations will help to prevent any such eventuality. This is one argument for preserving the US–ROK security tie once the immediate threat from the DPRK is past.

16 The term is from Byung-Joon Ahn. See his 'Decision-Sharing in Korea-U.S. Relations', *Korea and World Affairs*, vol. 14, no. 1 (Spring 1990), pp. 5–15.

They are also ambivalent about US demands that Japan assume a larger security role in Northeast Asia. Although many Koreans have echoed American complaints regarding Japan's 'free ride', they fear that any Japanese defence buildup will acquire its own momentum, transforming 'pacifist' Japan and leading it once again to begin throwing its weight around the neighbourhood.[17] For example, Japanese Prime Minister Kaifu's recent decision to placate the United States by sending minesweepers to the Persian Gulf prompted a firestorm of alarmism in the South Korean press, although the government adopted a measured, uncritical response.[18]

On the other hand, many Japanese perceive South Korea as more nationalistic and militaristic than Japan.[19] It would appear logical for some Japanese to be concerned that an increasingly powerful Korea could become something of a neighbourhood bully itself. Such concerns are echoed by the views of one rising school of opinion in Japan, which sees Korea as an emergent economic competitor.

The depth of the two nations' mutual suspicions is easy for Americans to underestimate. Many Americans have argued for increased Korean and Japanese security cooperation. Because there is a clear interdependence between the US–Japan security relationship and US–ROK security ties, it would appear, on the surface, that increased bilateral defence cooperation between Japan and Korea—or even a trilateral defence arrangement involving Korea, Japan, and the United States—would offer an effective means of securing all three nations' interests.[20] In reality, however, such an arrangement is politically impractical.

The security interests of Korea and Japan are not identical. South Korea is primarily concerned with the threat posed by the North. South Koreans do not see Russia as a direct threat, but only as a secondary adversary (and now perhaps not even that)—an ally of their enemy. Indeed, in the absence of a threat from the north, it is more likely that

---

17 Chong Whi Kim, 'Korea–Japan Relations and Japan's Security', in Dora Alves (ed.), *Pacific Security Toward the Year 2000,* The 1987 Pacific Symposium (Washington, DC: National Defense University Press, 1988), p. 135ff.

18 The morning daily *Choson Ilbo* asked, 'Why Japan? Why should Japan clear mines when it did not even fight during the Gulf War? Japan is an ex-convict...It makes us uncomfortable to see an ex-convict pick up the sword again, even if it is allegedly for peaceful purposes'. See 'Media Sound "Shrill" Warning', FBIS-EAS-91-081, 26 April 1991, p. 29.

19 Masashi Nishihara, 'Japan's Gradual Defense Buildup and Korean Security', *The Korean Journal of Defense Analysis,* vol. 1, no. 1 (Summer 1989), p. 105.

20 See, for example, Edward A. Olsen, *U.S. Policy and the Two Koreas* (Boulder, CO: Westview Press, 1988).

Korean security concerns would focus on Japan rather than the Soviet Union, or now Russia. Japan, on the other hand, perceives the USSR, and probably its successor, Russia, as its primary direct threat. North Korea is not seen as a realistic independent threat to Japan.

South Korean strategy toward Japan is simple. The ROK government would like to continue to develop economic and political ties with Japan but avoid any security link. The ROK and Japan share many economic interests. Indeed, the two countries have cooperated in their efforts to promote enhanced Asia–Pacific economic cooperation. On the other hand, the ROK supports American efforts to pressure Japan to open its market to foreign goods. After all, it is likely that Korea would seize a larger share of the Japanese market than the United States would. At the same time, however, Koreans are disturbed by growing Japanese military power.

Japanese overtures to North Korea are an especially sensitive issue for South Koreans. They fear that Japan wishes to keep the peninsula divided. Indeed, South Koreans felt considerable consternation over the 28 September 1990 joint declaration signed by the representatives of Japan's leading political parties—the Liberal Democratic Party (LDP) and the Japan Socialist Party (JSP)—and the Korean Workers' Party (KWP) in Pyongyang, which urged the Japanese government to commence official negotiations to normalise Japan–DPRK relations.

South Korean concern focused on five issues. First, many South Koreans were disturbed by Japan's willingness to normalise relations with the DPRK without any preconditions, as well as by the 'excessive speed' involved in the Japan–DPRK rapprochement. Second, South Koreans doubt the wisdom of Japan's efforts to normalise relations with the North at such a critical stage in North–South relations. Japanese normalisation and economic assistance to the North could undermine the Roh government's efforts to pressure the DPRK to compromise in its negotiations with the South. Third, many Korean officials were also concerned by a provision in the joint declaration which begins with the phrase 'Korea is one...'. Since this is the basic premise of the North's reunification policies, that statement could be interpreted as indicating Japan's acquiescence to Pyongyang's unification policies. It also fails to recognise the existence of South Korea, which is North Korea's official position but certainly not Japan's. And it appears to contradict the 1965 ROK–Japan Basic Treaty, which clearly indicated that the ROK was 'the only lawful' government of Korea according to the UN General Assembly resolution 195 (III) of 1948.

Fourth, the question of Japanese compensation to North Korea touched a sore nerve. When Park normalised relations with Japan in 1965, Tokyo agreed to pay compensation only for the period of Japanese colonial rule in Korea, not for the twenty years of abnormal relations between the two nations from 1945–1965. In contrast, the joint Japan–DPRK declaration indicated that Japanese compensation would also cover the 'losses inflicted upon the Korean people in the ensuing 45 years after the war'. Japanese compensation money could provide Kim Il Sung with the ability to postpone reforms. Finally, South Koreans were also disturbed by Prime Minister Kaifu's apology to Kim Il Sung for Japan's colonial rule in Korea. Originally, Japan had promised the Roh government that Kaifu would apologise to Kim simply as the LDP president, not in his official capacity as Prime Minister, since Japan still did not recognise the DPRK. As it happened, however, Kaifu used the phrase 'he, as Prime Minister...' in his remarks.[21]

Roh firmly expressed the ROK's position to Kanemaru Shin, the LDP representative at the talks with Kim Il Sung, in a meeting on 8 October 1990. While he reiterated the official ROK position that it does not oppose the establishment of Japan–DPRK relations, Roh stressed that such changes should not threaten 'meaningful progress' in North–South relations, and requested that Japan consider the following five principles in negotiating with North Korea:

1. Japan should consult with Seoul before starting government-to-government talks with Pyongyang on normalising bilateral ties.

2. Japan should urge North Korea to sign the nuclear safety agreement with the International Atomic Energy Agency (IAEA).

3. Japan should pay adequate attention to the state of North–South Korean dialogue.

4. Japan should withhold compensation or economic assistance to North Korea until formal diplomatic ties are established between the two countries, and it should ensure that any funds provided by Japan would not be used for upgrading North Korea's military capability.

5. Japan should take steps to prompt Pyongyang to move toward openness and reforms.[22]

These South Korean concerns were reportedly supported by the United States, which made similar requests to Japan in early October 1990.[23]

In Japan, by contrast, there appears to be emerging an attitude which favours 'rescuing' Kim economically in the interests of preserving stability on the peninsula. The argument rests on the assumption that continued economic decline, coupled with international isolation, will lead Kim Il

---

21 Hong Nack Kim, 'The Normalization of North Korean–Japanese Diplomatic Relations: Problems and Prospects', *Korea and World Affairs*, vol. 14, no. 4 (Winter 1990), pp. 664–6.

22 Ibid., p. 667.

23 Ibid.

Sung to lash out at his old enemies while he still can. The common analogy is to a cornered rat. Wataru Kubo, a JSP MP involved in preparing the Kanemaru visit, argues, 'Unless Japan normalizes relations, North Korea will feel threatened by a strong chain linking South Korea with Japan and the U.S.'. Not surprisingly, South Koreans see this Japanese argument as self-serving. The popular view in the south is that Japan wants to keep the peninsula divided to retard Korea's emergence as an economic rival, and for that reason is attempting to prop up Kim's 'doomed' regime.[24]

The South Koreans were reported to be concerned that Japan, in deference to North Korea, would not support its current effort to enter the United Nations. The Japanese, however, have indicated publicly that they will support the ROK bid, and are reported to be working with the United States and South Korea to increase support among the non-aligned countries and convince China to abstain on the question. Japan's diplomatic efforts in this area should improve the atmosphere of ROK–Japan relations, but the future outlook for ROK–Japan relations suggests that continued bouts of tension are more likely than closer cooperation.

South Korea's ability to pursue successfully its strategy toward Japan depends heavily on the United States. Only US cooperation can ensure that Japan does not shore up the DPRK and block eventual Korean unification on Seoul's terms.

The Soviet Union/Russia

Gorbachev's new policies toward the Asia–Pacific Region permitted South Korea to reverse its longstanding strategy of opposing Soviet influence in any form whatsoever. Although the Soviet Union had always been a secondary strategic concern for the ROK—behind North Korea— Moscow has suddenly become a primary means for weakening North Korea.

The Russians, like the Japanese and Chinese, have long sought to exert their influence over the Korean Peninsula. In the postwar era, Soviet–Korean relations have until very recently meant Soviet–North Korean relations. The USSR and the ROK had no diplomatic relations before last year. USSR–DPRK relations have tended to fluctuate, because Kim Il Sung has attempted to maximise his bargaining position by shifting between the Soviets and the Chinese.

Generally, Kim has been closer to the Chinese politically, but always turned to the Soviets when he needed economic or technological infusions or military equipment which the Chinese could not supply. Soviet–North Korean relations, like Soviet–Vietnamese relations, have never been a

---

24 Shim Jae Hoon, 'Pyongyang Paradox', *Far Eastern Economic Review*, 29 November 1990, p. 28.

love match. Mutual distrust has always coloured the relationship. The Soviets resented what they saw as Korean ingratitude, and worried over Kim Il Sung's adventurist tendencies. The North Koreans were always convinced of the Soviets' desire to dominate and exploit them, and never truly believed that Moscow was a reliable ally.

From 1984 to 1989, Soviet–North Korean relations were on the upswing. Kim Il Sung visited Moscow in 1984, his first visit in seventeen years, which was followed by yet another visit in 1986. During these years, Soviet–North Korean security ties grew much closer. Moscow helped Kim modernise his air force, providing him with Mig-23 and Su25 Frogfoot aircraft, as well as Mig-25s and SA-3 and SA-5 SAMs later. In October 1986, the two nations conducted their first joint military exercise, which subsequently became an annual event.[25] During the same period, USSR–DPRK economic ties grew significantly. In 1988, for example, the Soviet Union accounted for over 50 per cent of North Korea's foreign trade (although trade with the DPRK accounted for only about 1 per cent of Soviet trade). The Soviets also provided North Korea with large amounts of technological assistance during this period, building seventy industrial projects producing approximately one-quarter of the DPRK's gross output. The growing military–economic relationship between the DPRK and the USSR greatly increased North Korean dependence on the Soviet Union during these years.[26]

Kim's increasing dependence on the Soviet Union was probably caused by his inability to obtain the economic aid and civilian and military technology he required from the Chinese. In addition, Deng's reform efforts would also have served to complicate PRC–DPRK relations during this period. In any case, it was a brief honeymoon. Soviet–North Korean relations began to suffer immediately after the Soviets began to develop ties with South Korea.

Gorbachev appears to have desired initially to limit Soviet–South Korean links to the economic sphere, while preserving Soviet–North Korean political and military links and using Soviet influence to pressure the North to undertake its own *perestroika*. Nevertheless, to gain South Korean economic support, Gorbachev was ultimately forced to cast aside his concern for North Korean opinion. In June 1990, President Roh met Gorbachev in San Francisco. Although Gorbachev implied at that time that full diplomatic relations were still very distant[27], in fact, Moscow

---

25 Robert A. Manning, *Asian Policy: The New Soviet Challenge in the Pacific* (New York: Priority Press Publications, 1988), pp. 61–2.

26 Byung-Joon Ahn, 'South Korean–Soviet Relations: Issues and Prospects', *Korea and World Affairs*, vol. 14, no. 4 (Winter 1990), pp. 675–6.

27 Gorbachev stated only that diplomatic relations 'may arise as bilateral ties develop and in the context of the general improvement of the political situation

established relations with Seoul on 30 September 1990—only three months later. Not surprisingly, the decision did not please the North Koreans.

When Soviet Foreign Minister Shevardnadze visited Pyongyang to inform Kim that the USSR would normalise relations with South Korea, Kim reportedly refused to meet with him. Following normalisation, North Korea published an editorial entitled 'Diplomatic Relations Bargained for Dollars', in which it characterised the Soviet decision as an act of betrayal, accusing the Soviets of having sold the dignity and honour of a Socialist state and the interests and faith of its loyal ally for South Korean economic aid. The North Koreans also stated that they had come to believe that the USSR had joined with the United States to isolate North Korea and perpetuate the division of the peninsula.[28] Gorbachev's decision to support publicly the ROK's bid for UN membership was the ultimate insult to Kim Il Sung, and undoubtedly confirmed Kim's belief that Gorbachev had committed his government to supporting the continued division of the peninsula.

Gorbachev's decision to accelerate the development of USSR–ROK ties can be traced to South Korea's refusal to provide significant economic aid and investment to the Soviet Union until Moscow normalised diplomatic relations, the Soviet Union's inability to gain significant Japanese aid, and the USSR's increasingly dire economic situation. Four months after normalisation, on 22 January 1991, South Korea agreed to provide the Soviet Union with a financial cooperation package valued at $US3 billion over the next three years (including $1.5 billion in loans for purchasing Korean consumer products, $0.5 billion in trade credits for Korean capital goods, and $1 billion in commercial syndicate loans by Korean banks).[29]

South Korean interest in the Soviet Union—now Russia—has been primarily political, not economic. The ROK government wants to establish relations with Moscow for several reasons: to enhance its international legitimacy, to reduce the security threat posed by the DPRK by alienating it from its most important source of military support, and ultimately to promote Korean national reunification by weakening the DPRK and forcing it to negotiate on the ROK's terms. The Soviet Union's successor

---

in the region and on the Korean peninsula'. See Sheldon W. Simon, 'Security and Uncertainty in the North Pacific', *The Korean Journal of Defense Analysis*, vol. 2, no. 2 (Winter 1990), p. 89.

28 Dae-Sook Suh, 'Changes in North Korea and Inter-Korean Relations', *Korea and World Affairs*, vol. 14, no. 4 (Winter 1990), p. 616.

29 'Korea's Economic Cooperation with the U.S.S.R.', Republic of Korea Ministry of Finance, *MOF Bulletin,* no. 90 (January 1991), p. 10.

states also offer a new, potentially significant market for Korean exports and investment, but such benefits are less certain and of less importance. The South Koreans surprised many Americans by their apparently warm feelings toward the Soviet Union. In part, Soviet–ROK normalisation reflected the fact that South Korea did not perceive the USSR to be a direct threat. In part, it reflected pride in being courted by a superpower. It also reflected a belief that the Soviet Union's new policies were helping the cause of Korean national reunification.

As long as the Soviet Union existed, it was unrealistic to expect South Korean–Soviet relations to blossom into a close relationship, at least in the near future. As Roh made clear to Gorbachev at their April 1991 meeting, South Korea remains wary of Moscow's collective-security schemes for Asia.[30] Furthermore, many outstanding tensions remain between the two countries. The shooting down of KAL 007 is one example. The March 1991 publication of the first photos of the undersea wreckage of the airplane (one of which showed a severed arm on the seabed) sent shock waves through Korea. Likewise, earlier reports from the USSR that the pilot responsible for shooting down the plane was aware that he had fired on a civilian aircraft did not do much for the Soviet image. The families of the deceased have renewed pressure on the ROK Foreign Ministry to provide information on the incident and obtain the remains of those slain.[31]

Improvement in Russian–ROK relations seems likely to continue, especially after President Yeltsin's November 1992 visit to Seoul and the initialling of a new treaty on basic relations. South Korea's main benefit is in its competition with the DPRK. Aside from enhancing its leverage on the DPRK, Russia has little to offer the ROK, compared to the United States. Both countries could offer potential counters to Japan and China, but the US is economically and militarily stronger, with closer historical and personal ties with the Korean leadership and people, and is much more distant geographically and therefore less threatening. Furthermore, close Russian–ROK ties would aggravate ROK–Japan relations and might encourage Japanese rearmament, while preservation of US–ROK security bonds would not.

Russian–DPRK ties seem likely to continue to decline. Moscow's decision to put the two nations' bilateral trade on a hard-currency basis effective January 1991 has inevitably led to a decline in economic exchanges between them. For their part, the DPRK leadership will probably loathe Boris Yeltsin's Russian political and diplomatic policies more than it did Gorbachev's. Still, Kim Il Sung's distaste for the Russian leadership will probably be checked by his real economic dependence on

---

30 Ibid.

31 'Photographs of KAL 007 wreck shock South Korea', *Far Eastern Economic Review*, 11 April 1991, p. 14.

Russia for oil and military supplies. The Chinese can offer only political aid and limited economic support. Unless Kim can open economic relations with Japan or other Western nations, he will have to suffer Russia's humiliations in order to gain whatever economic benefits he still can from the Moscow relationship. While Yeltsin's policies are not yet clear, they are likely, even in the best case for the DPRK, to be far less accommodating than the changed Soviet policies.

China

South Korea's strategy toward China has also changed considerably, and for the same reason as the change toward the USSR and Russia—opportunities to isolate the DPRK. Initially, however, Seoul had less success with Beijing. The ROK offered economic ties in exchange for political help against North Korea, but failed until August 1992 to get China to deal openly and normalise relations. The reasons are to be found in China's very different view of the Korean Peninsula, and also in China's better access to the market economies on the Asian rimland.

Korea possesses greater strategic significance for the Chinese than for the Russians. The peninsula is adjacent to Manchuria—China's industrial heartland—which makes it a vital buffer between China and any outside power. For centuries, Chinese policy has been to prevent Korea from being dominated by any outside power. Since the end of the Korean War, the Chinese have carefully cultivated their relationship with North Korea, and have generally enjoyed better overall relations with the Kim Il Sung regime than have the Russians. Kim Il Sung appears to value his ties with China, as a source of both international political support and leverage on Moscow. Although the Chinese cannot match Moscow's military, economic, or technological gifts, Kim appears to trust the Chinese more than the Soviets, certainly more than the Russians. The Chinese, of course, have possessed cultural, historical, and personal advantages over the Soviets in their competition for influence in Pyongyang. The assistance of Chinese troops during the Korean War created a bond between the Chinese and North Korean leadership comparable to that between South Koreans and the United States and quite unlike the Soviet–North Korean relationship, which has always been based purely upon economic and military aid. In addition, the long historical and cultural ties between Korea and China make Koreans more comfortable with the Chinese than with the Russians. Finally, both leaderships share important experiences and perspectives: both experienced the often crushing embrace of the Soviet Union, both are divided nations, and both country's leaders still come from the revolutionary generation.

Nonetheless, Chinese–North Korean relations have still suffered from considerable tension from time to time. Difficulties have stemmed from a variety of factors, including the DPRK's tendency in the past to turn to Moscow for economic and military aid which China could not provide; Kim's refusal to spurn the USSR and side entirely with China during the Sino–Soviet split; Chinese rapprochement with the United States and Japan, North Korea's chief enemies; and, of course, China's growing ties to South Korea.

Despite Chinese intervention during the Korean War, South Korea does not appear to have significant security concerns regarding China at this time. The South Korean perception of China contrasts sharply with popular views of Japan, and may be partially due to cultural links between the two nations and China's relative backwardness. Since the mid-1980s, China has maintained an extensive trade relationship with South Korea; it has grown significantly over the years. In 1990, the two nations agreed to establish trade liaison offices in Seoul and Beijing. Nevertheless, official political contact between Seoul and Beijing remained strictly limited until late 1992.

Chinese–North Korean relations have grown closer since 1989 because of both nations' defensive reactions to the collapse of communist power in Eastern Europe and the Soviet rapprochement with South Korea. Given Chinese strategic concerns, it seems unlikely that China will willingly risk reducing its ties to Kim's regime. On the other hand, China has little to offer Kim in economic and military assistance with which to prop up his regime. Personal contacts and shared political perspectives appear to constitute the main basis for the relationship. Overall, DPRK–PRC relations will probably remain fairly static while the two nations' conservative, geriatric leaders still live. Meanwhile, ROK–PRC relations have continued to improve, despite DPRK objections.

In the long term, Chinese–Korean relations could become tense. Korean unification would insure it. China has traditionally preferred to have weak, divided states on its borders—states over which it could expect to exercise considerable influence and from which it could expect to exclude undesirable foreign influences. Chinese policy in Indochina is a classic example of this strategy. Ideally, the Chinese would prefer to perpetuate the present arrangement, in which Korea is kept divided and weak and China exercises considerable influence over Korean affairs through its ties to Pyongyang. Although an independent, unified Korea is better than a unified Korea under foreign influence (e.g., that of the US, Japan, or Russia), it is decidedly a second-best outcome for the Chinese.

At the same time, a unified Korean state is likely to feel more threatened by China than South Korea does today. A unified Korea could expect to face a significant Chinese military deployment on its borders. The recent rapid development of the Chinese Navy would also pose a challenge to Korean security planners who sit across the Yellow Sea from the Chinese North Sea Fleet.

North–South Relations in the 1990s

Overview

Since the 1970s, the two Koreas have engaged in an intermittent dialogue concerning confidence-building measures and unification. The principal motivations for South Korea to engage in this dialogue are to reduce the level of tension on the peninsula and the risk of war, to satisfy its American ally, to prevent the DPRK from gaining the diplomatic advantage it would if Seoul were to appear to be intransigent in the face of DPRK reasonableness, and, more recently, to take advantage of the favourable international environment to press for national unification on its own terms and increase domestic popular support for the government. The Roh government pressed hard recently on inter-Korean relations, not only because of domestic political reasons and the new developments in the international environment but also because of a perception that compromise arrangements may be more feasible while Kim Il Sung is alive. There is concern that a Kim Jong Il regime (Kim's son and chosen successor) would be less able to compromise, because the younger Kim would be in a weaker political position.

Kim Il Sung's reasons for talking with his southern rivals are subject only to speculation. But they appear to include efforts to gain international advantage from the talks, to use the talks to undermine domestic popular support for the ROK government, to split the ROK–US alliance and instigate the withdrawal of US troops, and, of course, ultimately to promote reunification on North Korean terms.

Distrust has been the major characteristic of the talks, with the two sides typically talking past each other to a wider Korean and international audience. South Korea's basic position has been to recognise the reality of two existing regimes on the Korean Peninsula and then work toward developing relations between the two regimes, leading ultimately to peaceful reunification. Since the 1970s, South Korea has maintained that cross-recognition of the two Koreas and simultaneous admission to the United Nations (similar to the German approach) should form the basis for peace on the peninsula. The North, however, has vigorously rejected this approach.

The North Koreans argue that simultaneous establishment of diplomatic relations and simultaneous admission to the UN would merely perpetuate the division between the two Koreas. They claim that the main obstacle to peace and reunification is the US military presence on the peninsula. They maintain that if the US military left the peninsula, a political federation between North and South Korea could be established and guarantee peace and eventual reunification. Despite much rhetoric, these two divergent positions have not changed significantly.

In reality, North–South relations are a diplomatic game in which each side attempts to gain the advantage of the other. Both sides are trying to use the negotiations to gain reunification on their own terms. Their respective approaches to the negotiations reflect their assessment of their relative strengths and weaknesses.[32]

South Korea, an open society with a strong economy and considerable international sophistication, believes that if it forces North Korea to open its closed, monolithic society, the North Korean people will learn the truth about their society and switch their allegiance to the ROK government, as the best hope for all Koreans. For this reason the South Korean strategy emphasises societal integration prior to political unification. Most importantly, the South wants to avoid any action that could weaken the US–ROK security alliance, which it believes deters North Korea from attacking. The South believes it has the advantage in the long-term political competition between the two Koreas, but remains at risk in the short-term.

North Korea's strengths, by contrast, are its highly regimented party organisation, its military power, and its propaganda apparatus. Kim's starting assumption appears to be that the ROK government is unpopular, and that, if he forces the United States to withdraw its troops, the weakened ROK government will be unable to suppress the activities of dissidents in the south. With his federation already in place, Kim can use a 'United Front' strategy to disarm the ROK government, gain control of the federal government, and use its authority to order local authorities in the south to ease control over pro-DPRK forces there. These will then agitate for complete national reunification under Pyongyang's central authority. Above all, Kim wants to avoid opening North Korean society to outside influences as Seoul desires, because this threatens his personal political rule of the North itself. Events leading to the unification of Germany have probably strengthened his determination in this regard.

North Korea: domestic decline and the risk of international isolation

North Korea is trapped in an economic vice which threatens the long-term survival of its political order. In 1989, North Korean GNP was estimated at $21.1 billion, and per capita GNP was $987. From 1987 to 1989, the country's economic growth averaged less than 3 per cent per year.[33] Future growth is currently predicted at around 2 per cent annually; some

---

[32] This analysis of South and North Korean strategies in their unification policies is derived from Rhee Sang-Woo, 'North Korea in 1990: Lonesome Struggle to Keep *Chuch'e*', *Asian Survey*, vol. 31, no. 1 (January 1991), p. 77.

[33] Ibid., p. 72.

estimates maintain the economy is actually shrinking. Poor agricultural harvests have forced the government to reduce the already meagre food rations. Nevertheless, military spending continues to absorb an estimated 24 per cent of national GNP.[34]

South Korea, by contrast, continues to grow rapidly. In 1990, South Korean GNP grew by 9 per cent, and by 7 per cent in 1991.[35] According to projections made by South Korean and Japanese analysts, the South Korean economy is projected to become at least seven times the size of that of the North by the mid-1990s.[36] North Korean economic decline *vis-à-vis* the South not only poses serious problems for North Korea's military capabilities (to be discussed later), but also threatens the fundamental legitimacy of Kim Il Sung's government. The declining living standard undercuts Kim's claims that his *chuch'e* socialist system is superior to other systems, especially the South Korean capitalist system.

Evidence suggests that the economic decline has stimulated popular discontent. There have been reports of wall posters critical of the government's economic policies, of opposition slogans being painted on a Pyongyang railway station, of scattered industrial strikes, and even of some incidents of sabotage. Frequent visitors indicate that they now hear open criticisms of communist party cadres.[37] It would be a mistake to believe that these isolated incidents indicate that Kim Il Sung's rule is becoming tenuous, but they do indicate a radical change from the complete control his regime previously enjoyed.

To offset the economic decline, Kim launched a frantic 'work-harder campaign' in 1990. No amount of hard work, however, can compensate for outmoded technology, inefficient plants, declining capital investment, and the limitations imposed by a small, overprotected, and uncompetitive domestic economy. North Korea needs to undertake radical economic reforms and open its economy to the outside world. Limited efforts in this direction have been made, but these changes amount to half-hearted gestures. Serious economic reform would fundamentally threaten the basis of the Kim regime, and significant reforms are extremely unlikely while he remains in power.

Still, the increasing impatience of Pyongyang's communist allies with North Korea's inefficiencies and boondoggles may ultimately leave the leadership with no choice. Despite his incessant harping upon *chuch'e*, or

[34]   Mark Clifford and Sophie Quinn-Judge, 'Caught in a Vice', *Far Eastern Economic Review*, 29 November 1990, p. 30.

[35]   Damon Darlin, 'Korean Economy Shows New Resilience', *Asian Wall Street Journal*, 11 April 1991, p. 1.

[36]   Pfaltzgraff, Jr, 'Korea's Emerging Role in World Politics', p. 26.

[37]   Norman D. Levin, 'Global Detente and North Korea's Strategic Relations', *The Korean Journal of Defense Analysis*, vol. 2, no. 1 (Summer 1990), p. 37.

self-reliance, economic and military support from Moscow and Beijing have been indispensable to Kim's government. Without Russian and Chinese support Kim will be unable to sustain his economy and his high levels of military expenditure. Such assistance is costly for Kim's allies, however, and they no longer appear willing or able to sustain it. As indicated earlier, the Soviet Union placed its trade with North Korea on a hard-currency basis in January 1991. Trade between Pyongyang and its communist allies dropped by approximately 10 per cent in 1989. The bottom line is that North Korea has little to sell and little with which to buy other nations' goods.[38]

Its deteriorating economic situation and declining support from its traditional allies account for the DPRK's decision to seek normalised relations with its old arch-enemy, Japan. 'Anti-Japanism' has been one of the major themes of North Korean propaganda for more than forty-five years. Park's move to normalise ROK–Japan relations was a target of venomous DPRK propaganda at the time. Kim's sudden decision to respond to Japanese overtures is a blatant effort to gain Japanese economic assistance for his dying economy. Japanese economic aid could allow him to put off significant economic and political reforms and preserve, at least temporarily, his political system. Successfully opening relations with Japan is essential to Kim's efforts to revive his economy. It is also an essential first step toward breaking out of North Korea's growing international isolation.

If North Korea fails to normalise relations with Japan and the United States, it will be increasingly isolated in the international arena. On the other hand, for North Korea to establish relations with South Korea's allies it will probably have to accept the South Korean unification formula of cross-recognition and confidence-building measures. Such an acceptance would also, however, constitute a long-term threat to the stability of the Kim Il Sung government. It would be starting down the road taken by East Germany. Ultimately, there may be no way for the DPRK to avoid this path, however. Unless the Japanese are willing to antagonise the United States and South Korea by following an independent path (which their support for the ROK's UN membership indicates is highly unlikely), North Korea will probably have to come to terms with the South to obtain significant economic support.

Therefore, the position of Kim Il Sung's regime is precarious. While it faces no immediate threat of revolt or collapse, its future looks increasingly bleak. The growing pressures on North Korea to undertake radical internal reforms and new foreign policy initiatives have important implications for the succession to Kim Il Sung and the future security environment on the Korean Peninsula.

---

[38] Clifford and Quinn-Judge, 'Caught in a Vice', pp. 31–2.

North Korean political dynamics and the prospects for Korean national reunification

It would be wrong to draw a strong analogy between the political fragility that helped engender a rapid collapse of the regimes in East Europe, especially East Germany, and that of North Korea. The DPRK enjoys more legitimacy among the population, and it has no foreign troops on its soil to symbolise dependence. Although North Koreans may be unhappy with current economic conditions, they recognise Kim's success in raising the standard of living over that of the old days, and they appear to accept his nationalist credentials and the 'myth' of his liberation of Korea.

They also have no reliable means of judging the regime's assertions. Unlike the Eastern European regimes, through its monopoly of the media the DPRK has been able to control virtually all access to information. North Koreans don't have shortwave radio receivers with which to listen to the BBC, the Voice of America, et al. Moreover, unlike the citizenries of most of the Eastern European nations, North Koreans have no close links to neighbouring countries undergoing radical reforms.

Soviet political pressure could have stimulated North Korean reform as it did in Eastern Europe, but, unlike the Europeans, the DPRK could turn to the conservative Chinese to offset Soviet political pressure. Since Pyongyang believes that its *chuch'e* philosophy has transcended Marxism–Leninism at least as far back as the Sino–Soviet split in 1960, neither Eastern European nor Soviet ideological debates have had much impact on the North Koreans. The collapse of the Soviet Union, of course, merely vindicates Pyongyang's judgement that reform is a deadly path to be avoided.

The German model of unification is also unlikely to have any *immediate* relevance to North–South relations. Although North and South Korea began to negotiate in the early 1970s (the two German states signed their accord in 1972), their relations have not followed the German model. There are no communications, mail, media, personnel, or economic exchanges between the two states. North Koreans know very little about their neighbours to the south. The DPRK has deliberately rejected the East German approach, in the belief that it would undermine the communist political order. Indeed, it appears that they were right. The German example, as indicated earlier, will reinforce their determination to prevent significant social and economic interaction between the two nations prior to political unification.

The recent changes in Eastern Europe, therefore, have only indirect relevance to future events in North Korea. Change in North Korea will probably follow the post-Mao Chinese model, rather than the Eastern European model. As in China, the main stimulants for change will probably be deteriorating economic conditions, a relative decline in the nation's international power position (in this case declining military capability *vis-à-vis* the South), factionalism within the leadership, rising popular political discontent amenable to manipulation by the competing leadership élites, and the nation's first leadership succession.

Significant change will have to wait until after Kim Il Sung leaves the scene. Kim will not undertake major reforms himself. Under Kim, reform efforts will be limited to tactical steps intended to offset the DPRK's decline, rather than initiatives that introduce fundamental changes to correct the inefficiencies in the North Korean economy and political system. Any such changes would undermine the basis for Kim's rule, so closely tied as it is to his *chuch'e* ideology and the current structure of North Korean society. Change is Kim's greatest enemy. Moreover, if Kim does not support reform, no other figure will be able to force through significant changes while he remains alive. He still dominates the system.

The most likely moment for change, therefore, is when Kim steps down and hands power to his chosen successor, his son, Kim Jong Il.[39] (Rumours indicate that Kim may step down next year in favour of his son; but, if he did, he would continue to wield real power behind the scenes. Real change will come only when he can no longer exercise power—that is, when he is dead or incapacitated.) Kim Jong Il (50 years old) is widely believed to lack his father's popular charisma, political skills, and carefully cultivated personal connections within the military, government, and party bureaucracies.

Kim Jong Il's only significant political asset is his legacy as the son and heir of the great leader, Kim Il Sung. The mantles of previous great communist leaders, however, have not proven particularly advantageous to their inheritors in other communist systems. Furthermore, Kim Jong Il's status as Kim Il Sung's son and successor generates potential opposition not only among opponents of his father's policies, but also among supporters of his father who do not want to establish an hereditary, dynastic mode of succession. This assumption is supported by the fact that although Kim Il Sung announced his succession plans at the fifth Central Committee meeting in 1974, he did not manage to obtain Kim Jong Il's formal appointment to senior Party status until 1980—six years which he apparently spent overcoming opposition to his son's succession.

---

39 Of course, if conditions deteriorate past minimally acceptable levels before Kim dies (he is presently 80 years old), it is remotely possible that he could be removed from office by a coup. Given Kim's political dominance, his wily political acumen, and highly developed Party in-fighting skills, such a development must be classified as very unlikely. These are major incentives for opponents to avoid taking risks and postpone any action until the old man is dead or incapacitated.

There is strong evidence that various factions continue to contend for influence in North Korean politics and that not everyone supports Kim Jong Il's succession. Consistent reports indicate that there is opposition to the younger Kim within the military, the technocrats (educated in the USSR and Eastern Europe), alienated leaders within the Party establishment, and even within Kim Il Sung's own family.[40] The DPRK government announced recently (7 February 1991) that it had crushed a plot by 'anti-revolutionary elements' opposed to Kim Jong Il's succession; this suggests that opposition has not dissipated. Although it is unlikely that such a plot actually existed, the government clearly intended the announcement as a warning to any who harboured such ideas—a clear indication that the government believes that such opposition exists and is concerned about it as a threat to the stability of the succession.[41] Also, recent statements by South Korean officials have indicated their belief that there is within the North Korean leadership a moderate faction urging the government to undertake reform and openness in economics and technology.[42] Although these moderate factions are not necessarily identical with any groups opposed to Kim Jong Il, one can certainly assume (given the younger Kim's power base) that they do not support him.

As noted earlier, Kim Jong Il has not been associated with the tentative economic reforms of the last few years. A Kim Jong Il regime would not be in a position to implement wholesale changes in the DPRK's political–economic system. As his father's heir, Kim would have to preserve his legacy or undercut his own greatest source of legitimacy. Consequently, Kim Jong Il is not likely to instigate the much-needed reform of North Korean society.

Indeed, it is unlikely that a Kim Jong Il regime would be stable. He would probably face intensified economic problems with a weaker political base than his father. Assuming that he was able to consolidate his position immediately after his father's death (a very big assumption), it is highly likely that he would fall from power or become the powerless (and temporary) figurehead of a collective leadership shortly thereafter. In other words, he would probably face immediate arrest (the 'Gang of Four' model) or medium-term political humiliation (like Hua Guofeng).

The danger is that the younger Kim's technique for retaining his hold on power, and strengthening his weak base of support within the military,

---

[40] There are reports of conflict between Kim Jong Il and his stepmother, Kim Song-ae, and his uncle, Kim Young-ju (Kim Il Sung's younger brother). See Suk-Ryul Yu, 'Political Succession and Policy Change in North Korea', *Korea and World Affairs*, vol. 10, no. 1 (Spring 1986), p. 38.

[41] 'Coup Talk in the Hermit Kingdom', *Asiaweek*, 22 February 1991, p. 39.

[42] '"Moderate Faction" Reportedly Exists in North', FBIS-EAD-91075, 18 April 1991, p. 33.

might be by following a path of military adventurism. He could use the DPRK's still-potent military power to attack the South and attempt to reverse the decline of North Korean fortunes on the battlefield.[43] The Japanese fear this possibility.

South Koreans are quite aware of the risks of continued North Korean isolation and decline. There is currently a debate within South Korean academic and political circles on this very question. Many Koreans worry that Roh's *Nordpolitik*, by isolating and destabilising the DPRK regime, may actually undermine the goal of national reunification and risk a military attack.[44] Yang Sung Chol, a Kyunghee University professor, has made the point very simply: 'A lean tiger is a mean tiger'.[45] Therefore, some South Koreans—including opposition figure Kim Dae Jung—argue that the government should not try to pressure the DPRK but rather adopt a patient waiting game and allow the situation in the north to work itself out.[46]

The Roh government, however, clearly believed that progress on national reunification would be impossible without further pressure on the DPRK government. This remains a delicate path. The key is to preserve the US security deterrent, which will make it absolutely clear to the North Korean military that an attack could not possibly succeed. For this reason, the Roh government placed the highest premium on maintaining the US–ROK security relationship.

Assuming, then, that the United States does not withdraw from the peninsula, the more likely outcome is the overthrow or eclipse of the Kim Jong Il regime by a coalition North Korean government consisting of a mixture of military officers, Soviet-trained technocrats, and disaffected leaders of the Party apparatus. The resulting regime would resemble the initial post-Maoist coalition of military officers and technocrats which coalesced around Deng Xiaoping and began the process of reform in China in the late 1970s and early 1980s. Like the early Dengist coalition, this new DPRK government would be a mixture of conservatives, concerned over the decay of internal political order and national power, and

---

43   The senior Kim would not be likely to undertake such an adventure. Since his personal political position would probably not be seriously challenged, such a dangerous action would not be worth the extreme risk entailed; and in any case, he has grown more cautious as he has grown older

44   See, for example, Sang-Seek Park, 'Northern Diplomacy and Inter-Korea Relations', *Korea and World Affairs*, vol. 12, no. 4 (Winter 1988), pp. 729–36.

45   Quoted in Shim Jae Hoon, 'Pyongyang Paradox', *Far Eastern Economic Review*, 29 November 1990, p. 28.

46   Shim Jae Hoon, 'Pyongyang Paradox', p. 28.

moderates dedicated to economic development. (Contrary to popular perception, so-called 'liberal' forces did not become a significant factor in the Dengist government until the mid-1980s.)

This regime would begin the difficult process of economic reform and international initiatives. It would have to accept the ROK formula on unification. It would also have to develop economic and political relations not just with the United States and Japan but also South Korea. As reform proceeded, the new regime would be trapped in a time-compressed version of the East German experience. The East German regime remained stable for two decades after beginning to develop its relations with the West German government. A post-Kim Il Sung DPRK government would not enjoy such a long life. Expanding relations with the South would rapidly destabilise the government. The regime's claim to an independent identity would be undermined by the inevitable abandonment of Kim Il Sungism and *chuch'e*. The commitment of both North and South Koreans to a single national identity—coupled with the repudiation of Kim Il Sungism—would leave a reformist DPRK regime with little prospect of stability. Once the reform and opening process began, the political and economic dynamics would engender the inevitable absorption of the DPRK regime by the ROK. The main challenge would be to minimise the political and economic destabilisation.

In the long term, the reunification of the Korean Peninsula appears highly probable. While the old dictator should be able to preserve his *chuch'e* state as long as he lives, his successors will be forced to preside over the termination of the DPRK. Kim Il Sung's regime is caught in a dead end. Once he is gone, his successors will have to accept the necessity of reform. If they fail to do so, the DPRK will probably collapse within five years of Kim's death. If they attempt reform, they will be caught in the same process of political dissolution that eventually overcame the East German government, and they will thus face political absorption by the ROK within ten years of Kim's death.

This positive long-term prognosis, however, does not mean that the DPRK will disappear tomorrow, nor does it mean that the North Korean threat can be dismissed. Kim Il Sung should be able to maintain his government as long as he is able to function effectively, and his successors will not willingly abdicate their power to their hated rival in the south. Furthermore, in the short term, the risk of instability on the peninsula will grow—particularly in the immediate aftermath of Kim Il Sung's death or incapacitation. South Korea and its allies cannot afford to let down their guard.

Korean unification will have a revolutionary impact on the balance of power in Northeast Asia. The unification of Korea will create, for the first time in history, a powerful, united Korea capable of an independent role in Asian international affairs. Moreover, the stable diplomatic equilibrium that has existed since the end of the Korean War—with each rival power bloc possessing its own ally on that half of the peninsula most strategically vital to their concerns—will be terminated. As a result, the unification of Korea will also set the four great powers scrambling to compete for influence with the single, remaining Korean regime. The trend toward increasing multi-polarity in the world and in Asia will intensify this competition. The United States, Japan, Russia, and China may all pursue their own policies toward Korea in varying degrees of competition with each other.[47] The situation will probably bear a closer resemblance to North Korean relations with its two communist allies than to traditional South Korean foreign policy, with its extremely close association with the United States. Nevertheless, if US–ROK relations are managed effectively in the next decade, it seems likely that the US will be the favoured external power on the Korean Peninsula.

---

[47] The degree of US–Japan competition will, of course, depend on the degree of divergence that begins to occur between US and Japanese foreign policy in the 1990s and beyond as Japan begins to assume a greater international role. US and Japanese policies toward Korea could continue to be coordinated very closely, could diverge in limited areas, or could diverge significantly and compete directly.

13 Northern Diplomacy and Inter-Korean Relations

PARK SANG-SEEK

Introduction[*]

The term 'northern policy' or 'northern diplomacy' has been used in academia since the early 1970s. It is analogous to the *Ostpolitik* popularised by Willy Brandt in the 1970s. The Korean government used the term for the first time in 1983 when then Foreign Minister Lee Bum-Suk gave a speech at the National Defense University. He defined northern policy as follows:

> Our most important foreign policy goal in the 1980s is to prevent the recurrence of war on the Korean peninsula, and our most important diplomatic task is to pursue the northern policy successfully which aims at normalizing relations with the Soviet Union and China.[1]

According to this definition, 'northern policy' refers to the nation's policy toward China and the Soviet Union.

President Roh defines northern diplomacy as follows: 'I will approach the communist bloc more vigorously in order to realize peaceful coexistence between South and North Korea and ultimately peaceful unification'.[2]

According to this definition, northern diplomacy is synonymous to the policy toward the Communist bloc including China, the Soviet Union and East Europe. In other words, northern policy of diplomacy is a rhetorical

---

[*] The views expressed in this article are my personal ones and do not represent those of the Foreign Ministry.

[1] Lee Bum-Suk, *Sonjin Choguk Changjo reul wihan Oegyo* (Diplomacy for the Creation of the Advanced Fatherland), a speech delivered at the National Defense University, 29 June 1983. The translation is mine.

[2] Roh Tae-woo, *Widae han Botong Saram eu Sidae* (Era of the Great Common Man) (Seoul: Eulyu Munhwasa, 1987), p. 229. The translation is mine.

expression of the policy toward China and the Soviet Union or the policy toward the Communist bloc.

However, it should be noted that the two definitions relate the objective of northern diplomacy and inter-Korean relations. Lee Bum-Suk defines the objective of northern diplomacy as follows:

> The Soviet Union and China...(are) countries that maintain a military alliance and intervened in the Korean War. Therefore, we have to establish good-neighbourly relations with these countries for the maintenance of peace on the Korean peninsula. It is true that northern policy will be successful if inter-Korean relations are normalized. It is also true that northern policy is successful, inter-Korean relations will improve.[3]

Both definitions maintain that the foremost objective of northern diplomacy is to preserve peace and security on the Korean Peninsula. I integrate both definitions and define northern diplomacy as a diplomatic strategy to normalise relations with China, the Soviet Union and East Europe and through it to establish a mechanism for peaceful coexistence between South and North Korea. In other words, the establishment of a peace mechanism is the primary goal and the normalisation of relations with the communist countries is the secondary one. However, the former is a dependent variable, while the latter is an independent variable.

To the present, the Korean government has tried to improve relations with North Korea through dialogue. However, dialogue has not made any breakthrough. Now, the Korean government attempts to approach North Korea through China and the Soviet Union. It hopes that these two North Korean allies will influence North Korea to improve relations with South Korea. As Foreign Minister Lee said, there is a close relationship between the nation's policy toward China and the Soviet Union and inter-Korean relations. If South Korea's relations with China and the Soviet Union improve, inter-Korean relations are likely to improve, and vice versa.

Objectives of Northern Diplomacy

Korea has pursued four foreign policy goals since its inception. They are national security, economic prosperity, peaceful reunification and national prestige. Regimes have changed but these four foreign policy goals have not.[4]

In pursuit of these goals the Korean government has resorted to a strategy of supremacy. To be specific, it has conducted foreign policy in the

---

[3] Lee Bum-suk, *Sonjin Choguk Changjo reul wihan Oegyo*.

[4] Park Sang-Seek, 'Determinants of Korean Foreign Policy', *Korea and World Affairs*, vol. 10, no. 3 (Fall 1986), pp. 457–83.

conviction that the only way to make North Korea abandon its policy to communise South Korea by all means and seek peaceful coexistence is to make South Korea's economic and military capabilities and its diplomatic position irrevocably superior to North Korea's.

However, recently South Korea has begun to question the desirability and practicability of this strategy of supremacy.

First, if South Korea continues to expand its defence system by strengthening the Korea–US security system and the bonds with its traditional friends, would North Korea not feel more threatened and expand its military capabilities and strengthen its military alliances with China and the Soviet Union? Would this not, in turn, intensify tensions on the Korean Peninsula instead of realising peaceful coexistence between South and North Korea?

Secondly, would the policy of isolating North Korea internationally not make North Korea more militant toward South Korea? South Korea has made every effort to prevent North Korea from establishing diplomatic relations with pro-South Korean countries, from expanding trade and economic cooperation with them, and from participating in international organisations.

Third, if South Korea continues to make rapid economic progress, while obstructing North Korea's trade and economic cooperation with Western countries, would it not increase the economic gap between the two Koreas and consequently impoverish North Korea? Should the South Korean people enjoy the suffering of the North Korean people who are their brethren? Would the increasing economic gap not make the prospect of Korean reunification more remote?

Fourth, can a structure of peaceful coexistence be established and peaceful reunification be realised without the cooperation of the Soviet Union and China? So far, South Korea has tried to build a peace mechanism through the South–North dialogue. However, both sides' approaches to peaceful reunification are so different that they have failed to reach any agreement on substantive issues. Each side believes that the other side's proposal is disguised because its ulterior objective is to unify Korea on its own terms. For example, when North Korea proposed a 'Koryo federation', South Korea rejected it, believing that its ulterior objective is to communise South Korea through a united front strategy.[5] On the other hand, when South Korea proposed a national conciliation and democratic unification formula, North Korea rejected it, believing that its ulterior

---

5   Kim Il-sung proposed the Koryo Democratic Republic Formula at the Sixth Congress of the Labor Party on 10 October 1980. For the full text, see *Rodong Shinmun*, 11 October 1980. The South Korean side of the South–North Co-ordinating Committee rejected it and called for the resumption of the committee on 15 October 1988.

motive is to remove the communists from North Korea and to unify Korea under 'capitalism'.[6]

The northern policy is to discard the traditional strategy of supremacy and to remedy the above-mentioned contradictions. Let me examine the northern policy in terms of the four foreign policy goals of South Korea.

First, Korea has attempted to deter North Korean aggression through two means since the Korean War: its own military forces and the Korea–US security system.

Since US President Nixon declared the Nixon Doctrine in 1969, Korea has pursued a forces modernisation programme to possess a self-sufficient defence capability. The United States has encouraged and supported the programme in accordance with its plan to reduce military commitments to its allies in Asia.

North Korea has responded to the forces modernisation programme by expanding its own military forces and by receiving more modern weapons and technologies from the Soviet Union. The Soviet Union in return, has gained the right to use North Korean ports and to overfly North Korean territory. Consequently, the Soviet–North Korean military alliance has been reinforced.

Northern diplomacy is an attempt to stop this kind of vicious circle. Specifically, the Korean government seeks to deter North Korean aggression by maintaining friendly relations with the Soviet Union and China. Seoul can make it known that, if they guarantee that North Korea will give up its militant policy, it is willing to negotiate with North Korea on the withdrawal of US troops in South Korea and disarmament. Through them South Korea can persuade North Korea to abandon its militant policy. The South Korean government argues that North Korea's unilateral declaration of non-aggression is not sufficient to ensure peace and security on the Korean Peninsula. At the same time, it is aware that North Korea might have the same feeling toward South Korea. Therefore, it can assure North Korea that the United States and Japan will guarantee that South Korea will never use force first against North Korea. This is why President Roh in his address at the United Nations General Assembly on 18 October 1988, proposed a six-power consultative conference on peace and prosperity in Northeast Asia.[7]

North Korea might fear possible attempts by South Korea to undermine the Soviet–North Korean alliance and the Chinese–North Korean

---

6 President Chun Doo Hwan proposed the formula in his 'state of the nation' address on 22 January 1982. Kim Il-sung, chairman of the Committee for the Peaceful Unification of the Fatherland, rejected it on 26 January 1982.

7 The full text of Roh's UN speech can be found in *Korea Times*, 19 October 1988, p. 10. The text in Korean is available in *Seoul Shinmun*, 19 October 1988, p. 3.

alliance through northern diplomacy while maintaining its own alliance. In order to dissipate such a fear President Roh and President Reagan hinted that as South–North Korean relations improve, the US troops in Korea will be reduced.[8]

Second, if South Korea succeeds in establishing diplomatic relations with China, the United States and Eastern Europe, its diplomatic horizon will widen and its international status will be enhanced. Moreover, if South Korea improves relations with the communist countries, it will become easier for South Korea to improve relations with radical Third World countries.

This does not necessarily mean that North Korea will become more isolated. As will be examined later, the July 4th Declaration and the subsequent guidelines issued by the Foreign Ministry state that South Korea will not oppose North Korea's improving relations with the United States, Japan and other Western countries, its participation in international organisations and conferences, and its trading with Western countries, provided North Korea reciprocates South Korea's policy. Therefore, the expansion of South Korea's diplomatic horizon does not entail the shrinking of North Korea's diplomatic horizon. However, if North Korea refuses to pursue a similar policy toward the Western countries, it will become more isolated diplomatically.

Third, if South Korea's trade and economic cooperation with the Soviet Union, China and Eastern Europe expand, its economy will become more prosperous. South Korea needs more international markets for further economic growth in the face of the growing protectionist trends in the West and the Third World.

While Korea–China trade is complementary, the trade between Korea and the Soviet Union and East Europe is complementary as well as competitive. However, at present it is more complementary than competitive.[9]

The July 7th Declaration and the guidelines for trade with North Korea issued by the Economic Planning Board state that South Korea would welcome trade between North Korea and Western countries. This means that South Korea does not seek to increase the economic gap between South and North Korea by unilaterally benefiting from trade with communist countries.[10]

---

8 *Dong-a Ilbo*, 22 October, 1988.

9 Lee Ki-Young, 'The Roles of the United States and Japan in Trade between South Korea and the Communist Block', *Kukjejongchi Nonchong (Journal of International Politics)*, vol. 22, no. 2 (1988), pp. 225–8 and 235–40.

10 For the guidelines for trade, see *Dong-a Ilbo*, 7 October 1988. The guidelines include:

   1. Permit South Korean private companies to trade with North Korea directly or through their countries;

Fourth, if South Korea does improve relations with the Soviet Union and China, it can ask them to persuade North Korea to work toward establishing a peace mechanism for the Korean Peninsula. It believes that North Korea is likely to give up its militant policy and resume the dialogue with South Korea if its allies press it to do so or if they decide not to support North Korea's unification policy.

South Korea has made it clear that it would not impose its own unification formula on North Korea and is willing to accommodate some ideas embodied in North Korea's unification formula.[11]

Background

Both domestic and external environments are favourable to the northern diplomacy.

First, domestically, South Korea's economic capability and international status have far surpassed North Korea's. After the 1988 Seoul Olympics this trend will be accelerated. Only in the military field is South Korea still inferior to North Korea. However, even in this field a balance between South and North Korea will be obtained when South Korea's forces modernisation programme is completed. The US forces in South Korea make up for the military imbalance, and the four powers restrain North Korea from provoking South Korea. Therefore, North Korea is not likely to launch a military attack on South Korea.

As the democratisation process accelerates, the aspiration of the people in the South to recover national identity with the people in the North will intensify. Thus, the security environment of the Korean Peninsula makes northern diplomacy possible, while the popular aspiration for national reunion makes it necessary.

---

2. Permit mutual contacts and visits between South and North Korean businessmen;
3. Permit South Korean overseas travellers to bring North Korean goods into South Korean ports;
4. Permit the use of North Korean trademarks for North Korean goods;
5. Guarantee the safe conduct of merchant ships into and out from South Korean ports;
6. Waive all levies including duties on imported North Korean goods.

[11] President Roh's 'state of the nation' address at the National Assembly, 30 May, 1988. For the full text of the address, see *Korea and World Affairs*, vol. 12, no. 2 (Summer 1988), pp. 425–31.

Second, North Korea is now at the crossroads where it should examine whether it is wise to continue to keep itself closed and preserve its centrally planned economy or open itself up to the outside world and pursue open door and reform policies as the Soviet Union and China are doing.

North Korea is likely to maintain its closed system for fear that if North Korean society is opened up, its one-man dictatorship will collapse. This is the reason why Pyongyang cannot abandon its militant policy. As Stalin used the theory of capitalist encirclement to justify his totalitarian rule, Kim Il-sung uses the threat from South Korea to justify his totalitarian rule, and reunification to legitimise the communist regime in North Korea. The North Korean leaders believe that reunification is a national liberation struggle and therefore the use of violence is justified.

The South Korean government maintains that, in view of the nature of the North Korean political system, the best way to make the North Korean leadership more realistic and pragmatic is to destroy the one-man dictatorship and open up the closed system. The South Korean government holds that its northern policy is to bring North Korean society into the international community for this purpose.

Third, the security environment in Northeast Asia is favourable to northern diplomacy. For the first time since World War II, the United States, the Soviet Union, and China seek rapprochement with one another. In the first half of the 1980s the Soviet Union and China sought rapprochement, while the United States and the Soviet Union were hostile to each other. Under such circumstances, the United States will seek to maintain and strengthen the US–China strategic coalition to contain the Soviet Union. At the same time the United States and the Soviet Union are likely to strengthen security cooperation with their respective allies, South and North Korea. However, when the United States, China and the Soviet Union pursue rapprochement with one another simultaneously, they will desire strongly a peaceful environment on the Korean Peninsula and refrain from providing military assistance to their respective allies.

On the other hand, the Soviet Union and China both will try to restrain North Korea's provocations against South Korea. In such a situation it will be difficult for North Korea to demand that both powers support its militant policy toward South Korea. If both powers desire, therefore, they can ignore North Korea's opposition and expand relations with South Korea and support South Korea's unification policy. Since they seek rapprochement and desire peace and stability on the Korean Peninsula, they are likely to coordinate their policies toward North Korea and consult with each other on the Korean question.

This is the reason why the South Korean government considers its northern policy timely.

Fourth, China, the Soviet Union and Eastern European countries desire to expand trade and economic cooperation with South Korea, because they now put top priority on economic development. China, in pursuit of its reform policy, has increased the number of special economic zones and has formulated a programme for the development of its West Coast. This has increased the chance for Korea and China to expand economic relations. The Soviet Union also, in pursuit of its open door and reform policies, is making greater efforts to expand economic relations with Asia–Pacific nations while accelerating its Siberian development programme.[12] In this connection the Soviet Union has formally proposed economic exchanges with South Korea.[13] Eastern European countries also are following suit. They are particularly interested in expanding economic relations with newly industrialised countries like South Korea.

The pragmatic policy of the communist countries makes South Korea's approach to them easier.

Recent Developments

Relations with China

South Korea had almost no contact with China in the 1970s despite the June 23rd Declaration, which enunciated an open-door policy toward the communist countries. Under the programme for the reunion of separated families that began in 1978 a few Chinese of Korean descent visited Korea during the period. Indirect trade between South Korea and China also began in 1978. However, the volume of trade in that year was only $40,000.

The highjacking of a Chinese airliner in May 1983 and the Rangoon bomb incident in October of the same year changed the Chinese attitude toward South Korea. The Rangoon bomb incident made China fear the possibility of a North Korean military attack on South Korea.

Since 1983 China has permitted more Koreans and Chinese to participate in multilateral international conferences held in China and South Korea

---

12 See 'CPSU General Secretary Mikhail S. Gorbachev's Speech in Vladivostok', on 28 July 1986, in *American and Soviet Studies*, Annual (Seoul: Center for American and Soviet Studies, Danuk University, 1986), pp. 221–47. The text of Gorbachev's Speech can be also found in *Korean Unification: Source Materials with an Introduction*, Vol. III (1979–86) (Seoul: Research Center for Peace and Unification of Korea, 1986), pp. 542–7.

13 See 'Excerpts from CPSU General Secretary Mikhail S. Gorbachev's Speech to Workers: The Seven Points in the Asian Plan, in Krasnoyarsk, Siberia, 16 September 1988', in 'Source Material' section of *Korea and World Affairs*, vol. 12, no. 3 (Fall 1988), pp. 652–7.

Table 13.1   Trade Between South Korea and China (in thousand US dollars)

	1978	1979	1980	1981	1982	1983	1984	1985	1986	1987
Export	–	3,960	114,980	204,952	48,006	51,264	229,027	682,765	667,702	813,172
Import	40	14,829	72,926	147,778	80,816	82,602	232,631	608,999	615,423	673,440
Total	40	18,789	187,906	352,730	128,822	133,866	461,658	1,291,764	1,283,125	1,486,612

Source: Korean Customs Office for 1978 data; KOTRA for 1979–85 data; *Korea Times*, 1 November 1988, p. 17 for 1986–87 data.

respectively. It has also allowed mutual visits of separated families of Korean descent in increasing numbers. Trade between China and South Korea has increased tremendously since 1984.

As the trade has expanded, the number of businessmen visiting between the two countries has also increased. It should be noted that as the opening day for the 1988 Seoul Olympics drew closer, the economic and cultural exchanges between the two countries accelerated. This suggests that the Seoul Olympics had become a watershed in Korean-Chinese relations. All indications show that China is speeding up its relations with South Korea in all non-political fields.

Unless and until inter-Korean relations improve substantially, China is likely to limit its relations with South Korea to non-political fields. However, China is likely to permit bilateral exchanges in the cultural, academic and sports fields and direct trade in the economic field. The pace of growth of relations between South Korea and China has been slow as the relations have moved from indirect to more direct ones. For instance, trade was conducted through a third party at first but is now involving direct negotiation and direct shipping.

In order to establish political contact with South Korea, China would more actively urge North Korea to improve relations with the United States and Japan, while coordinating its policy toward the Korean Peninsula with the Soviet Union.

Northern policy is compatible with its Korea policy because China has actually pursued a *de facto* two-Korea policy, although it has officially denied it. Therefore, China will pursue an increasing number of policies compatible with northern policy in the future.[14]

---

14 For developments in South Korea–China relations, see the following: *Dong-a Ilbo*, 3 March 1988 (Chinese support of South Korea's programme for the development of the Hwang-hae coast); *Choongang Ilbo*, 10 March 1988 (possibility of direct trade between South Korea and China); *Dong-a Ilbo*, 12 April 1988 (trade with China); *Choong-ang Ilbo*, 3 May 1988 (Chinese relaxation of restrictions on visas to Korean businessmen); *Choongang Ilbo*, 18 May 1988 (direct trade between South Korea and China); *Korea Herald*, 21 May 1988 (joint ventures between South Korea and China); *Dong-a Ilbo*, 25 May 1988 (Korean investments in China); *Korea Herald*, 2 July 1988 (improvement of South Korean–Chinese relations; *Korea Herald*, 30 August 1988 (Chinese support of the July 7th Declaration); *Dong-a Ilbo*, 7 September 1988 (opening of three cities to Korean businesses); *Chosun Ilbo*, 6 October 1988 (joint ventures between South Korea and China); *Dong-a Ilbo*, 12 October 1988 (direct export of Korean fertilisers to China); *Dong-a Ilbo*, 5 November 1988 (possibility of exchanging trade offices between South Korea and China).

Relations with the Soviet Union and Eastern Europe

Exchanges between South Korea on the one hand and the Soviet Union and Eastern Europe on the other have grown considerably. They are usually of a multilateral kind; but in the cases of Hungary, Yugoslavia and some other Eastern European countries bilateral exchanges have gradually increased.

Table 13.2 Trade Between South Korea and the Soviet Union and Eastern Europe (in thousand US dollars)

		1984	1985	1986	1987
Soviet Union	Ex.	26,194	59,675	49,895	67,231
	Im.	31,052	62,328	63,884	97,002
	Tot.	57,246	122,003	113,779	164,233
Yugoslavia	Ex.	4.115	50,851	9,668	15,982
	Im.	5,698	40,306	210	176
	Tot.	9,813	91,157	9,878	16,158
East Germany	Ex.	13,401	23,437	21,235	37,566
	Im.	1,531	4,042	377	4,049
	Tot.	14,932	27,479	21,612	41,615
Poland	Ex.	17,580	20,419	18,986	20,898
	Im.	7,241	8,756	5,581	1,924
	Tot.	24,821	29,175	24,567	22,822
Czechoslovakia	Ex.	2,873	3,663	7,090	8,556
	Im.	4,342	3,791	1,577	2,528
	Tot.	7,215	7,454	8,667	11,104
Hungary	Ex.	1,110	7,027	7,316	14,985
	Im.	5,387	3,970	1,375	3,154
	Tot.	6,497	10,997	8,691	18,139
Romania	Ex.	1,894	1,600	2,252	3,084
	Im.	2,510	16,944	-	16,848
	Tot.	4,404	18,544	2,252	19,932
Bulgaria	Ex.	2,155	767	1,092	1,281
	Im.	1,977	1,141	632	218
	Tot.	4,132	1,903	1,724	1,499
Albania	Ex.	52	19	-	-
	Im.	-	-	-	
	Tot.	52	19	-	-

Source: KOTRA.

Trade between South Korea and the Soviet Union and Eastern Europe has also increased very rapidly since 1987. Although South Korea's trade with them is indirect, direct trade with some countries like Hungary and Yugoslavia recently started. South Korea has exchanged a permanent mission with Hungary and a trade mission with Yugoslavia. Some Korean companies have established their branch offices in East Germany and Poland, while a Polish–Japanese joint venture company based in Tokyo (AGKOPOL) has established its branches in Seoul.

As economic exchanges grow, mutual visits of businessmen, consultations for joint investments, and participation in trade fairs held in each other's territories have also increased. Also, the Soviet Union and Eastern European countries and South Korea have exchanged journalists, while South Korea and some Eastern European countries also have started academic and cultural exchanges.

With the exception of Albania, all Eastern European countries and the Soviet Union participated in the 1988 Seoul Olympics. After the Olympics they have shown greater interest in cultural, sports and academic exchanges as well as trade. However, they would restrict their relations with South Korea to non-political fields in fear of North Korea's opposition. On the other hand, they are likely to urge North Korea to expand relations with Western countries, particularly the United States and Japan.

In the future, exchanges between South Korea on the one hand and the Soviet Union and Eastern Europe on the other are likely to accelerate. Indirect trade will be replaced by direct trade, and bilateral cultural, sports and academic exchanges will increase.

All this shows that the Soviet Union and Eastern European countries tacitly support the northern policy as China does. It is not surprising because the northern policy is in harmony with their policy toward the Korean Peninsula, which is a *de facto* two-Korea policy.[15]

---

15 For developments in economic relations between South Korea on the one hand the Soviet Union and Eastern Europe on the other, *Kyunghyang Shinmun*, 6 April 1988 (exchange of trade missions between South Korea and Yugoslavia); *Dong-a Ilbo*, 12 April 1988 (trade with the Soviet Union); *Dong-a Ilbo*, 6 May 1988 (Soviet desire to have economic exchanges between South Korea and the Soviet Union and Eastern Europe); *Kyunghyang Shinmun*, 20 May 1988 (Soviet desire to exchange trade offices with South Korea); *Dong-a Ilbo*, 23 May 1988 (Korean trade fair and joint ventures in the Soviet Union); ibid. (technical exchanges between South Korea and Eastern European countries); ibid., 25 May 1988 (economic exchanges between South Korea and the Soviet Union and Eastern Europe); ibid., 17 September 1988 (Gorbachev's seven-point proposal for peace in the Asia–Pacific region); ibid., 20 September 1988 (Prospect of direct trade between South Korea and the Soviet Union); *Dong-a Ilbo*, 5 October 1988 (exchange of trade offices with Bulgaria and Poland); *Korea Herald*, 13 October 1988 (Soviet recognition of the existence

Relations with North Korea

Since the primary purpose of northern diplomacy is to improve relations with North Korea, South Korea has made efforts to do so as it has made efforts to expand relations with other communist countries. Let me review the developments in inter-Korean relations from the inception of the Sixth Republic to the end of 1988.

• In his inaugural address on 25 February 1988, President Roh urged North Korea to resume the inter-Korean dialogue, and welcomed the intermediation of any country seeking a solution for the Korean question.[16] Until that time, South Korea had rejected North Korea's proposals for a political–military conference, a multi-national disarmament conference, and a joint conference of government authorities from South and North Korea, political parties and social organisations, and had made counter-proposals. The bombing of a Korean airliner in November 1987 froze South–North relations. However, President Roh in his interview with the NHK-TV of Japan on 15 February 1988, after his election as president expressed a readiness to resume the dialogue regardless of the KAL incident.[17] He seemed to envisage a multilateral conference on the Korean question when he welcomed the intermediary participation of other countries.

• North Korea rejected President Roh's order and insisted on a joint conference of the government authorities of South and North Korea, political parties and social organisations (28 February 1988).[18]

---

of the two Koreas); ibid., 16 October 1988 (business cooperation accord between KOTRA and the Soviet Chamber of Commerce); *Dong-a Ilbo*, 18 October 1988 (exchange of trade office between South Korea and the Soviet Union); *Korea Times*, 1 November 1988 (trade with the Soviet Union and Eastern European countries); *Dong-a Ilbo*, 4 November 1988 (prospect of South Korea's participation in the Siberian development project.

For the exchange of permanent missions between South Korea and Hungary, *Dong-a Ilbo*, 13 September 1988; *Kyunghyang Shinmun*, 27 October 1988; *Korea Herald*, 29 October 1988.

16 For the full text of the inaugural address in English, *Korea and World Affairs*, vol. 12, no. 1 (Spring 1988), pp. 175–80, and in Korean, *Choongang Ilbo*, 25 February 1988.

17 National Unification Board, *Nambukhan Tongil Daehwa Jeeui Bigyo* (Comparison of South and North Korea's Proposals for Unification and Dialogue) (Seoul: National Unification Board, 1988), p. 522.

18 Editorial of *Rodong Shinmun* (Nodong News), 28 February 1988.

- On the occasion of the anniversary of the March First Independence Movement, President Roh urged North Korea to participate in the 1988 Seoul Olympic Games.[19]

- North Korea condemned President Roh's remarks as 'not worth a penny', and maintained that the question of joint hosting of the Olympics could be discussed at the North–South joint conference.[20]

- On 29 March 1988, Kim Jung-ki, a candidate for the Student Council of Seoul National University, issued an open letter to the students of Kim Il-sung University. In the letter he proposed (1) a cross-country march of college students of South and North Korea from 1–14 August and a festival for national unity at Panmunjom, (2) all athletic competition between South and North Korean students at Seoul National University or Kim Il-sung University from 15–17 September and (3) a preparatory meeting at Panmunjom or Geneva on 10 June.[21]

- On 4 April 1988, the Student Committee of Kim Il-sung University issued a letter to the Student Council of Seoul National University. In the letter it accepted the proposal and offered Panmunjom as the venue for the preparatory talks.[22]

- On 21 April 1988, President Roh at his press conference emphasised that the most effective way to improve South–North relations is a South–North summit conference and stated that his term of office will be devoted to pursuing peaceful reunification through South–North cooperation.[23]

- On 14 May 1988, the National Coordinating Council of University Student Representatives of South Korea adopted the agenda for the preparatory talks to be held on 10 June. The agenda included: (1) a cross-country march and an athletic competition, (2) mutual visits of separated families, (3) student exchanges between South and North Korea, and (4) staging of the 1988 Olympic Games for the promotion of national harmony (i.e., joint hosting of the Olympics).[24]

---

19 *Nambukhan Tong-il Daehwa Jeeui Bigyo*, p. 526.

20 Editorial of *Rodong Shinmun*, 3 March 1988.

21 Research Institute of Ideological Issues, *Nambuk Haksaeng Hwoedam Kwalyeon Jaryo* (Materials on South–North Korean Student Conference) (Seoul: Research Institute of Ideological Issues, 1988), pp. 5–6.

22 *Nambukhan Tong-il Daehwa Jeeui Bigyo*, p. 533.

23 Ibid., p. 534.

24 Ibid., p. 534; *Nambuk Haksaeng...*, pp. 9–11.

- On 17 May 1988, the National Confederation of University Student Committees of North Korea issued a letter to all university students of South Korea and accepted the proposal by the South Korean side.[25]

- On 2 June 1988, the Minister of Cultural Affairs and Information of South Korea announced the government position on the unification issue as follows:

    1. Public debate on the unification issue will be encouraged, and the publications of and on North Korea and other communist countries, which have been banned, gradually will be made available to the public.

    2. The government will retain the sole authority to negotiation with North Korea and to make proposals for unification.

    3. The government will make sincere efforts to promote personnel and economic exchanges between South and North Korea.

    He made it clear that the government would not allow private persons or organisations to negotiate with North Korea and make proposals for unification to North Korea. In other words, private persons and organisations may discuss but may not formulate policy on unification.[26]

- On 3 June 1988, Prime Minister Lee Hyun-Jae of South Korea proposed a conference of high-level government officials, to comprise a cabinet member and four lower officials from each side. The agenda will include: (1) joint participation in the 1988 Seoul Olympics, (2) personnel exchanges, (3) the resumption of the existing inter-Korea conferences, such as the Red Cross talks, the economic talks and the inter-parliamentary talks, (4) and other matters of mutual concern.[27]

    The proposal was made through the radio, because the North Korean side refused to receive the letter containing the proposal through the usual channel at Panmunjom. The North Korean side said that if the South Korean side replied to North Korea's letters proposing the joint conference of government authorities, political parties and social organisations, and transmitted the letter of the North Korean university student representatives to their South Korean counterparts, then it would receive the letter.[28]

- A few days later, North Korea changed its mind and expressed a willingness to consider South Korea's proposal for a high-level authorities meeting. On 6 June 1988, the Preparatory Committee for the Joint

---

25 Ibid., p. 537.
26 Ibid., p. 542.
27 Ibid., p. 542.
28 Ibid., p. 543.

Conference of North Korea issued a statement maintaining that if the joint conference were held, personnel exchanges could be realised and the existing talks could be resumed and that the high-level conference could be held to prepare for the joint conference.[29]

- On 6 June 1988, Lee Hong-Koo, minister of the Unification Board of South Korea, announced that the question of the exchange of South and North Korean students could be discussed at the high-level conference proposed by South Korea. This was in response to the declaration of the Preparatory Committee for the North–South Korean Students' Meeting of North Korea demanding that the South Korean authorities should permit the student conference if they really desired dialogue.[30]

- On 10 June 1988, Foreign Minister Choi Kwang-Soo of South Korea in his address at the Third Special Conference of the UN General Assembly on Disarmament offered a three-stage disarmament process for the Korean Peninsula. He said that in the first stage South and North Korea should establish confidence-building measures through dialogue, contact and cooperation; in the second stage they should conclude a non-aggression pact as an institutional means to prevent the recurrence of hostile acts; and in the third stage they could negotiate on armed forces reduction. He called upon North Korea to accept Prime Minister Lee Hyun-Jae's proposal for cabinet-level talks.[31]

- On 11 June 1988, nine student organisations including the National Coordinating Council of University Student Committees held a rally for the South and North Korean Student Conference and joint hosting of the 1988 Olympics, and proposed the South and North Korean Student Conference for 15 August 1988, a cross-country march of South and North Koreans including Korean residents abroad on 8–14 August and a grand debate and festival on unification on 14 August. They also decided to establish a joint struggle committee for the co-hosting of the 1988 Olympics in South and North Korea, and in foreign countries.[32]

- On 13 June 1988, the National Coordinating Council of University Student Committees of North Korea sent a letter to South Korean students supporting the above proposal. The Red Cross Society of North Korea tried to transmit the letter to its South Korean counterpart at Panmunjom. However, the Red Cross Society of South Korea refused to receive it, claiming that student exchanges between South and North

---

29 Ibid., p. 545.
30 Ibid., p. 546.
31 Ibid., p. 548.
32 Ibid., p. 550.

Korea should be arranged by South and North Korean government authorities.[33]

* President Roh announced a special declaration on national pride and unification and prosperity on 7 July 1988 (known as the July 7th Declaration). In the declaration he put forward the following six principals:

1. Promotion of personnel exchanges in various fields between South and North Korea and permission of visits to South and North Korea by Korean residents abroad;

2. Encouragement of exchanges of correspondence and mutual visits for separated families;

3. Promotion of trade between South and North Korea and treatment of South–North trade as internal trade;

4. Promotion of balanced economic development between South and North Korea, and permission of trade between countries friendly to South Korea and North Korea, provided it does not involve goods for military use;

5. Ending of counter-productive diplomatic competition with North Korea and permission of contact between South and North Korean representatives at international forums: and

6. Support of North Korea's improvement of relations with the United States, Japan and other countries friendly to South Korea and pursuit of improved relations with the Soviet Union, China and other socialist countries.[34]

This declaration embodies the most important changes in South Korean foreign policy since the June 23rd Declaration, which adopted an open-door policy toward communist countries and proposed the joint entry of South and North Korea into the UN.

The first three principles mainly deal with inter-Korean relations and the second three principles with international relations. This shows that the South Korean government wants to pursue the dialogue with North Korea and its northern policy simultaneously. It recognises that the success of the former depends on the success of the latter, and vice versa.

The declaration also emphasises a parallel relationship between South Korea's relations with communist countries and North Korea's relations with Western countries. In other words, it makes it clear that it will not oppose North Korea's improvement of relations with Western countries as long as North Korea does not oppose South Korea's

---

33 Ibid., p. 551–3.

34 For the full text, *Korea and World Affairs*, vol. 12, no. 3 (Fall 1988), pp. 627–30.

improvement of relations with communist countries. The declaration officially renounces the policy of supremacy.

- On 9 July 1988, the National Assembly of South Korea adopted a resolution calling for North Korea's participation in the 1988 Seoul Olympics, and personnel exchanges at various levels and in various fields, taking advantage of the Olympics.[35]

- North Korea, through a declaration by the Committee for the Peaceful Unification of the Fatherland, condemned the July 7th Declaration as a cosmetic revision of the Proposal for National Harmony and Democratic Unification of 22 January 1982, and demanded that the South Korean government agree to the South and North Korean Student Conference and the joint hosting of the 1988 Olympics if it truly desires unification and the establishment of a national community (11 July 1988).[36]

- The Red Cross Society of South Korea indirectly rejected North Korea's demand by way of urging the resumption of the Red Cross talks (13 July 1988).[37]

- Education Minister Kim Young-sik of South Korea proposed a meeting of the education authorities of both sides for the preparation of student exchanges between South and North Korea (15 July 1988).[38]

The South Korean government apparently changed its previous position on South–North student exchanges and decided to permit exchanges of a non-political character. North Korea rejected South Korea's proposal, insisting that the question of student exchanges should be decided by students themselves, not by the government authorities (17 July 1988).[39]

- On 16 July 1988, Foreign Minister Choi Kwang-Soo of South Korea announced the detailed foreign policy guidelines to implement the July 7th Declaration.

  1. Concerning trade between countries friendly to South Korea and North Korea:

     (i) No objection to trade in non-military goods.

     (ii) No objection to mutual visits of civilians for business purposes.

---

35 *Nambukhan Tong-il Daehwa Jeeui Bigyo*, p. 554.
36 Ibid., p. 557.
37 Ibid., p. 558.
38 Ibid., p. 560.
39 Ibid., p. 565.

(iii) No objection to the establishment in North Korea of branch offices for business purposes by nations friendly to South Korea.

2. Concerning the ending of counter-productive diplomatic competition:

(i) Support of North Korea's participation in the international community as a responsible member.

(ii) Ending of counter-productive diplomatic competition with North Korea and no objection to North Korea's normalisation of relations with non-aligned and Third World countries.

(iii) Cooperation for North Korea's entry into the United Nations and inter-governmental organisations for regional cooperation and development.

(iv) Request for North Korea's self-restraint concerning slander and defamation against South Korea at international forums.

(v) Call for contacts and dialogue between South and North Korean diplomats in the countries where both Koreas maintain resident missions.

(vi) Support of North Korea's participation in all cultural, academic and sports events wherever they are held.

3. Concerning contact between South and North Korean representatives in international fora:

(i) Call for contacts and dialogue between South and North Korean representatives in all international conferences and other cultural, academic and sports events.

(ii) Call for contacts and dialogue between South and North Korean diplomats in the countries where both have resident missions.

4. Concerning North Korea's relations with Western countries:

(i) No objection to exchanges in non-political fields between North Korea and Western countries and no objection to contacts and dialogue between South and North Korean diplomats in third countries of neutral settings.

(ii) Call for North Korea's reciprocal act.[40]

---

[40] For the full text, *Korea and World Affairs*, vol. 12, no. 3 (Fall 1988), pp. 632–5.

- On 19 July 1988, Foreign Minister Choi called for a conference of the South and North Korean authorities concerned to discuss the safe conduct of Korean residents abroad visiting South and North Korea.[41]

- Ignoring South Korea's call for the education authorities' talks and the foreign policy authorities' talks, North Korea proposed inter-parliamentary talks to discuss the non-aggression issue. It wanted to include the declaration of non-aggression and other matters South Korea deems necessary for the reduction of tension and the maintenance of peace in the agenda. It also presented a draft declaration of non-aggression. The draft declaration included items identical to those suggested in Kim Il-sung's address at the Supreme People's Assembly on 30 December 1986. The most important items are the phased reduction of the armed forces of both Koreas and the corresponding withdrawal of foreign troops, and the establishment of a neutral nations' supervisory force to patrol the demilitarised zone.[42]

North Korea suggested that political parties, social organisations and other important figures from both sides could participate in the joint inter-parliamentary conference. Previously, it had repeatedly called for a joint conference of government authorities, political parties and social organisations. Now, it retreated from this position. In other words, it still contended but did not insist that political parties and social organisations should participate in the conference.

- Five days later, North Korea proposed that the inter-parliamentary talks could discuss the question of co-hosting the 1988 Olympics also.[43]

- South Korea decided to accept North Korea's proposal. Accordingly, the South and North Korean legislative representatives held preliminary talks at Panmunjom on 19–22 August 1988. But they failed to reach an agreement on the number of participants. The North insisted that the entire membership of the legislative bodies of both Koreas should participate in the conference, while the South insisted that the number of participants should be limited to thirty each.[44] If all legislators of both sides were to participate, the Southern side would be outnumbered by the Northern side 655–299.

---

41 *Nambukhan Tong-il Daehwa Jeeui Bigyo*, p. 566; for the full text, Bureau of Information and Culture, Ministry of Foreign Affairs, ROK.

42 Ibid., p. 569–73.

43 Ibid., p. 573.

44 *Korea Herald*, 20 and 22 August 1988; *Chosun Ilbo*, 20 August 1988; *Dong-a Ilbo*, 19, 20 and 22 August 1988.

- They met again to resolve differences on 13 October 1988, and agreed that the main conference would be attended by a selected number from the legislative bodies of both sides but that the opening and closing sessions would involve all members. Thus, both sides made some concessions.

The above review reveals the following:

First, the Sixth Republic has made greater efforts to resume the inter-Korean dialogue than had the Fifth Republic. The July 7th Declaration provided a turning point in the history of inter-Korean relations. I have already examined the background for this policy change. Therefore, it has made considerable concessions to reopen the dialogue. In contrast, North Korea has not made corresponding concessions. North Korea's motive for the change seems to be different from South Korea's. In the case of North Korea it wanted to improve its international image tarnished by the bombing of the Korean airliner by North Korean agents, as it had to do after the Rangoon bomb incident in 1983. Historically, North Korea has made peace initiatives immediately before and after making militant moves. Another reason for North Korea's policy change seems to be related to the changes in the security environment in Northeast Asia. The Soviet Union and China might have urged North Korea to become more conciliatory and to resume the dialogue.

Second, although South and North Korea have made concessions, they have never relaxed their guards and have been no less suspicious of the motives of each other's proposals. This indicates that unless they accept each other's proposals at face value, they cannot get into a serious dialogue.

Third, South Korea, since the Sixth Republic came into being, has made conscious efforts to link the inter-Korean dialogue and northern diplomacy. This effort was particularly manifested in the July 7th Declaration, which provides three principles for inter-Korean relations and three principles for northern policy.

Problems and Prospects

The success of northern diplomacy should be judged by three criteria: the degree to which South Korea improves its relations with the Soviet Union, China and Eastern European countries; the degree to which North Korea improves its relations with the United States, Japan and Western European countries; and the degree to which South and North Korea improve relations with each other. The rationale is that the primary purpose of northern diplomacy is to improve relations with North Korea through improving relations with the Soviet Union, China and Eastern European countries and bringing North Korea into the international community.

What will happen if North Korea refuses to seek 'a southern diplomacy'? In other words, if South Korea's relations with the communist countries grow greatly, while North Korea becomes more isolated, would North Korea not become more militant and would not tensions on the Korean Peninsula intensify? If North Korea's relations with the Western countries do not improve as much as South Korea's relations with the communist countries, the following situations might occur:

From the perspective of security, the Korea–US security system might be undermined. More specifically, the Soviet Union might attempt to drive a wedge between South Korea and the United States by offering attractive economic cooperation projects, by stopping military assistance to North Korea, by supporting South Korea's unification policy, or by establishing diplomatic relations with South Korea.

The South Korean government would not be misled by such Soviet manoeuvres; however, the people of South Korea might. Some South Koreans might judge that the Soviet Union is more reliable than the United States or as reliable as the United States and that therefore South Korea should maintain an equidistance policy toward them. Some others might argue that the United States is a declining power and is reducing its defence commitments to its allies and that therefore South Korea should maintain close relations with its neighbouring big powers. Still others might think that the United States directs South Korea and that therefore South Korea should check the United States by balancing the Soviet Union against the United States. All these people would argue that the South Korean government should use northern policy to become more independent of the United States.

Such a view would stir up anti-Americanism, which has already grown to dangerous proportions. In such a situation the United States, which has been considering reducing its military forces stationed in foreign countries, might misjudge the situation in South Korea and withdraw its forces from South Korea. A premature withdrawal of US troops would tip the balance of power in Northeast Asia in favour of the Soviet Union and North Korea and disturb peace and security on the Korean peninsula.

Therefore, in order to prevent the United States from misjudging the true purpose of northern diplomacy, South Korea should maintain closer consultation with the United States. Northern diplomacy is not intended to change South Korea's basic security strategy, which is to deter North Korean aggression through the Korea–US security system and its good neighbour relations with Japan. Northern policy aims at supplementing this basic strategy, not replacing it. This strategy is in accord with the American and Japanese security strategies in Northeast Asia. West Germany pursues a similar strategy. It maintains friendly relations with the Soviet Union while participating in NATO, whose primary objective is to deter Soviet aggression. In this regard, the security interests of West

Germany and the United States are closer than those of South Korea and the United States because the adversaries of West Germany and the United States in Europe are identical, while those of South Korea and the United States in Northeast Asia are not. It is generally known that a military alliance tends to be stronger when the interests of member nations are identical than when they are not. Therefore, South Korea should make more efforts to preserve its alliance with the United States than does West Germany. It should be pointed out that although the adversaries of South Korea and the United States are not identical, their security interests are closely linked because by deterring North Korea, South Korea's adversary, the United States can contain Soviet expansionism and protect Japan, its key ally in Asia. It also should be pointed out that the United States considers South Korea as a forward military base against the Soviet Union and potentially against China.

From the perspective of national prestige, South Korea's international status will immensely be enhanced while North Korea will become more isolated than ever before, because South Korea will be able to expand relations with communist countries and with radical non-aligned countries.

This will defeat one of the important purposes of northern diplomacy: the opening of North Korea. North Korea seems to face a dilemma. If it improves relations with the United States, Japan and Western European countries, this will be interpreted by them as an indication that North Korea has agreed to the cross-recognition proposal. Even if it denies that its improvement of relations with the West does not necessarily mean its acceptance of cross-recognition, this will provide a favourable environment for cross-recognition. On the other hand, if it refuses to improve relations with the West, it will become more isolated and its relations with the East also will likely sour.

The United States and Japan have shown interest in improving relations with North Korea, but North Korea has reacted to their overtures negatively.[45] On the other hand, North Korea strongly protested when Hungary decided to exchange a permanent mission with South Korea, threatening the severance of diplomatic relations with Hungary. Hungary

---

[45] The United States lifted some restrictions on North Korea which were imposed after the KAL bombing incident in November 1987 and asked North Korea to respond positively. See *Korea Herald*, 2 November 1988. However, North Korea condemned the US measures as a ploy to keep South Korea as a permanent colony. See *Rodong Shinmun*, 4 November 1988. Japan also made a conciliatory move, but North Korea has not responded to it. See *Chosun Ilbo*, 29 November 1988. Prime Minister Takeshida said in the Diet that Japan wishes to normalise relations with North Korea. See *Hankook Ilbo*, 27 October 1988.

ignored the North Korean threat by saying 'They (North Koreans) have to understand that Hungary is a sovereign country'.[46]

It should be remembered that until now North Korea has made every effort to expand diplomatic relations with Western countries, particularly the United States and Japan. This seemingly self-contradictory behaviour indicates that North Korea wants to expand relations with the West in order to isolate South Korea and has no intention of establishing diplomatic relations with it at the sacrifice of the East.

In relation to the Third World, North Korea seems to seek continued diplomatic expansion. This is revealed by the fact that it has established diplomatic relations with Columbia and has sought to upgrade its trade mission[47] after South Korea issued the July 7th Declaration.

Judging from North Korea's behaviour North Korea seems to believe that the simultaneous establishment of diplomatic relations with Western and communist countries by South and North Korea is likely to perpetuate the division of the Korean Peninsula, while the simultaneous establishment of diplomatic relations with Third World countries by both Koreas does not.

Under the circumstances, South Korea should urge its Western friends, particularly the United States and Japan, to approach North Korea more actively and ask North Korea's friends, particularly the Soviet Union and China, to persuade North Korea to establish relations with Western nations. In his speech at the United Nations General Assembly, President Roh Tae-woo indicated that South Korea would do it.

From an economic perspective, South Korea might make more rapid economic progress if its economic relations with the Soviet Union, China and Eastern European countries expand, while North Korea's economy might continue to stagnate. Experts believe that unless North Korea reforms its Stalinist economic system and expands economic relations with Western countries, it will not be able to make economic progress.

As pointed out earlier, however, North Korea is faced with a dilemma: it cannot have economic reforms and its totalitarian political system simultaneously. Therefore, highly delicate diplomatic skill is required to induce North Korea to opt for a reform and open-door policy.

The South Korean government has decided to make efforts to reduce the economic gap between South and North Korea. It has proposed direct trade with North Korea and has urged foreign nations, Western and communist, to increase economic exchanges with North Korea.

From the perspective of peaceful reunification, northern policy might entail the following problems:

---

[46] *Korea Herald*, 29 October 1988.

[47] *Kyunghyang Shinmun*, 27 October 1988.

If South Korea's relations with the Soviet Union and China rapidly improve, while North Korea's relations with the United States and Japan do not due to North Korea's objection, tensions between the two Koreas might increase, and consequently inter-Korean dialogue would become more difficult.

On the other hand, if South Korea's relations with the Soviet Union and China and North Korea's relations with the United States and Japan improve simultaneously, North Korea is more likely to accept cross-recognition and simultaneous admission into the United Nations. In such a situation the four powers might be more interested in the perpetual division of Korea than in Korean reunification.

The South Korean government rejects both arguments. It maintains that cross-recognition and simultaneous admission are not meant to perpetuate the division of Korea but to establish a peace mechanism in Korea, and that the peace mechanism jointly established by South and North Korea and the four powers facilitates reunification. North Korea rejects this view and contends that such a peace mechanism can guarantee neither peace on the Korean Peninsula nor reunification.

Whose view is more realistic?

North Korea's approach to peace and reunification is based on two assumptions. One is that the main obstacle to peace and reunification is the US military presence in South Korea. The other is that a political federation between South and North Korea guarantees peace.

North Korea proposes a tripartite conference among South and North Korea and the United States to discuss the question of US troop withdrawal, and a bilateral conference between South and North Korea to discuss the political federation. Two questions can be raised about North Korea's approach. Is the US troop presence the main obstacle to peace and reunification? Can the political federation proposed by North Korea guarantee peace and prevent the permanent division of Korea?

North Korea contends that if South and North Korea adopt a declaration of non-aggression and reduce their respective armed forces to equal numbers after the withdrawal of US troops, peace and security on the Korean Peninsula can be maintained. North Korea further argues that if South and North Korea join the United Nation together and establish diplomatic relations with the four powers, reunification is impossible.

I will dispute this view by way of comparing the German and Korean cases. South Korea's approach to reunification is similar to West Germany's in terms of means but not in terms of objectives. South Korea's proposal for cross-recognition by the four powers and a joint admission of both Koreas into the United Nations are means to build a peace mechanism for the Korean Peninsula, not an alternative to reunification. Considering the power configuration in Northeast Asia, a simple declaration of non-aggression and disarmament cannot ensure peace and security on the Korean Peninsula without guarantee by the big powers concerned. Cross-recognition is a sure way to the four-power guarantee. This was the reason why President Roh proposed a six-nation conference. Cross-recognition may not be necessary if the four powers can establish a structure to ensure peace and stability on the Korean Peninsula without recognising both Koreas.

In the case of Germany the two Germanies have given up reunification: East Germany officially and West Germany practically. Both Germanies maintain that their armed forces are primarily there to defend themselves against outside forces and secondarily against each other. The foreign troops stationed in the two Germanies also are there primarily to defend Eastern and Western Europe respectively. This means that the two Germanies do not feel threatened by each other. Therefore, they need neither a non-aggression treaty nor bilateral disarmament. Nor do they need a big power guarantee. Consequently, the recognition of the two Germanies by Eastern and Western powers and the simultaneous entry of the two Germanies can be considered devices to ensure the perpetual division of Germany.

In the case of Korea the opposite is true. First, the two Koreas consider reunification as sacred mission. In fact, reunification is the most important basis of their legitimacy. Secondly, they feel threatened by each other. Therefore, they maintain armed forces primarily to defend themselves against each other. They also maintain alliances with big powers to reinforce their own military forces. The United States stations its troops in South Korea primarily to defend South Korea against North Korea. Therefore, we can see why the United States maintains its military forces as a member of a bilateral collective self-defence system in Korea and as a member of a multilateral collective self-defence system in West Germany. Therefore, the two sides need not only a non-aggression pact and bilateral disarmament but also a big power guarantee.

Since South Korea keeps American troops to deter the North Korean threat, it can request the United States to withdraw its troops if the above three conditions are met. North Korea would have no excuse to refuse the resumption of a serious dialogue with South Korea after the withdrawal of the US troops.

Third, cross-recognition and joint entry do not necessarily perpetuate the division of Korea. In the case of Germany, not only the two Germanies themselves but also all neighbouring powers desire a divided Germany. However, in the case of Korea not only do the two Koreas desire reunification but also the four powers do not actively oppose it. Therefore, even if the four powers cross-recognise the two Koreas and the two Koreas enter the United Nations jointly, the two Koreas will not give up reunification and the four powers will not promote a divided Korea. However, the four powers will not promote reunification either.

Under the circumstances, South and North Korea should cooperate with each other on two fronts for the maintenance of peace and security between themselves and for the realisation of unification. On the one hand, they should meet together to devise confidence-building measures. On the other hand, they should meet with the four powers for the guarantee of peace and unification. Theoretically, these two meetings can be held simultaneously and combined. However, it will be more practical to hold the bilateral meeting first and the multilateral meeting later.

More importantly, if the bilateral conference is successful, the above-mentioned four problems—the erosion of the Korea–US security system, the isolation of North Korea, an increase in the economic gap between South and North Korea, and the delay of reunification—can be avoided.

There is a correlation between inter-Korean dialogue and northern diplomacy. If inter-Korean dialogue is successful, South Korea can expand relations with the Soviet Union, China and Eastern European countries more rapidly, and vice versa.

14 The Republic of Korea's Northern Policy: Origin, Development, and Prospects*

KIM HAK-JOON

At the same time that a wave of political reform is sweeping across many of the world's communist or formerly communist countries, the Republic of Korea is making great progress with its 'Northern Policy', the principal South Korean strategy for approaching those countries, and has established diplomatic ties with many of them. On 4 June 1990, South Korean President Roh Tae-woo and Soviet President Mikhail Gorbachev held an unprecedented summit meeting in San Francisco. The encounter was regarded as a historic event heralding a thaw in the cold war in the Far East. On 30 September of that year South Korea and the Soviet Union established diplomatic relations, an event underscored by President Roh's four-day state visit to Moscow in December.

With respect to the People's Republic of China, South Korea normalised relations with her on 24 August 1992 and President Roh visited China on 28 September for a tête-à-tête with Chinese President Yang Shangkun.

These developments bear great significance not only for South Korean diplomacy but also for relations between South and North Korea and for the overall political situation in Northeast Asia. Accordingly, the Northern Policy is drawing increasing attention both at home and abroad. My intent in this chapter is to review the circumstances that have affected the policy thus far and to consider its prospects.

Before I take up the main theme, two explanatory points are in order. First the various developments that pertain to the Northern Policy are divided into three periods for the purpose of this discussion: the period prior

* This chapter is slightly revised from the version which appeared in *The Japan Review of International Affairs*, special issue, vol. 5 (1991).

to the 1970s, before the policy's formulation; the period from the 1970s to the establishment of the Sixth Republic in 1988, during which the policy was conceived; and the period since 1988, in which the Sixth Republic has actively pursued the policy. Second, the 'northern countries' that the policy is designed to address primarily consist of North Korea, the Soviet Union, the East European countries, China, and Mongolia. In this discussion, however, North Korea's role will be excluded from consideration for the most part. In view of the North's great significance for South Korea, it deserves separate treatment in another paper.

Before the 1970s: In the Absence of a Northern Policy

The Republic of Korea had yet to formulate its Northern Policy during the period between the republic's establishment on 15 August 1948, and the end of the 1960s. Firmly adhering to the bipolarism of the cold war, the government in Seoul denied the existence of any middle ground between the Western free world led by the United States and the Eastern communist bloc headed by the Soviet Union. South Korea utterly rejected the notion of rapprochement with the northern socialist countries. Claiming to be the sole representative of the Korean people, Seoul insisted that no country that had already recognised or was willing to recognise it should establish relations with North Korea. The South portrayed itself as the only legitimate state on the Korean Peninsula, and the North was characterised as an illegal, anti-state organisation.

Let us begin with a review of the events that occurred during South Korea's First Republic, from 1948 to 1960.[1] Established with the full support of the United States and in the face of opposition from the Soviet Union, South Korea declared itself from the beginning to be anticommunist, and it regarded the Soviet Union, China, and the East European countries as its enemies. From Seoul's viewpoint, the communist countries were demons to be exorcised in holy wars waged by western crusaders. For the most part, the communist countries expressed their enmity toward South Korea, entering into formal affiliations with North Korea and rejecting the pursuit of relations with the South. Because no dealings with the northern countries were permitted under the thinking that prevailed in Seoul, no positive northern diplomacy could take place.

---

[1]   Hakjoon Kim, 'The Soviet Union in American–Korean Relations', in Youngnok Koo and Daesook Suh (eds), *Korea and the United States: A Century of Cooperation* (Honolulu: University of Hawaii Press, 1984), p. 203; Ilpyong J. Kim, 'Policies Toward China and the Soviet Union', in Youngnok Koo and Sung-joo Han (eds), *The Foreign Policy of the Republic of Korea* (New York: Columbia University Press, 1985), pp. 198–218.

South Korea intensified its anticommunist stance following the outbreak of the Korean War on 25 June 1950. The South's antagonism toward the northern countries was reinforced by its belief that the North Korean invasion had its origins in a Soviet–Chinese conspiracy. As the war continued, the Soviet Union, China, and Eastern Europe showed open hostility toward South Korea, causing the situation to decline further.[2] Claiming that the war was the work of a conspiracy of American imperialists operating in league with South Korea, communist countries harshly denounced the government in Seoul.

Even after the conclusion of the armistice agreement in July 1953, which effectively ended the Korean War, the mutual animosity failed to subside. South Korean President Syngman Rhee continued to faithfully follow the anti-Soviet, anti-China policies of the United States, expressing ardent hostility toward all communist countries. In Eastern Europe, Yugoslavia had at that time become a leader in the nonaligned movement and was attempting to free itself from Soviet influence. For Rhee, however, no differences existed among communist countries. He viewed the communist bloc as a monolithic entity under the domination of Moscow.

Washington and Moscow began to seek ways to reduce tensions in the late 1950s. In related developments, an ideological conflict broke out between the Soviet Union and China, and anti-Soviet movements were launched on a limited scale in some East European countries. These developments helped to change the conventional Western conception of the communist bloc, a view based on the presumption that Moscow was manipulating all the communist countries uniformly for the purpose of communising the entire world. There was no change, however, in President Rhee's attitude. He continued to believe that the Soviet Union was irrevocably committed to communising the entire world and that peaceful coexistence between East and West was an impossibility. In Rhee's view, the moves to ease the tensions between the United States and the Soviet Union were undesirable.[3]

The First Republic collapsed in April 1960, and Rhee was replaced by Prime Minister Chang Myon (John M. Chang). For the brief duration of the Second Republic, relations with the northern countries continued to be characterised by mutual hostility and the preclusion of contacts. Certain so-called progressives criticised South Korea's 'excessive dependence on

---

2   B.C. Koh, *The Foreign Policy Systems of North and South Korea* (Berkeley: University of California Press, 1984), p. 80.

3   Hakjoon Kim, *Unification Policies of South and North Korea, 1945–1985: A Comparative Study*, rev. ed. (Seoul: Seoul National University Press, 1986), pp. 191–2.

the United States' and demanded steps to improve relations with the communist bloc, but such critics were few in number.[4]

The *coup d'état* that took place in May 1961 put an end to the Second Republic and led to military rule, establishing a government that maintained the pro-American and anticommunist policies of the past and continued to rule out dealings with any nation in the communist bloc. This military government went a step further by enacting the draconian Anticommunist Law, which strictly banned all contact with North Korea and the other communist states. In a departure from the policy upheld by the First and Second Republics, however, the military government sought to make friends among the nonaligned countries. This policy shift was prompted by the need to overcome the diplomatic edge North Korea had gained through its relations with nonaligned states. Nevertheless, Seoul remained hostile toward the Soviet Union, China, and Eastern Europe, which, for their part, continued to show animosity toward South Korea.

The military regime was succeeded by the Third Republic, which lasted from December 1963 to December 1972. The early years of the Third Republic saw no change in the status quo with regard to the northern countries, and the government maintained especially close ties with the United States. American influence was responsible in part for Seoul's decision to normalise relations with Tokyo by signing the Treaty of Basic Relations Between Japan and the Republic of Korea in July 1965. Encouragement from Washington also provided motivation for South Korea's participation in the Vietnam War, which began around the same time and which strengthened South Korea's image as a country in the vanguard of anticommunism in Asia. Cooperation between the South Korean government and the United States also played a major part in the creation of a regional organisation known as the Asian and Pacific Council. ASPAC was envisioned as a kind of anticommunist regional military alliance.[5]

In the meantime, the communist countries were intensifying their criticism of South Korea. The Soviet Union, for example, charged that the treaty with Japan would provide a foundation for a Northeast Asian version of the US-led North Atlantic Treaty Organization. When Soviet Premier Aleksei Kosygin visited Pyongyang in February 1965, he and North Korean leader Kim Il Sung issued a joint statement that set forth

---

4   Sung-joo Han, *The Failure of Democracy in South Korea* (Berkeley: University of California Press, 1974), p. 201.

5   Hakjoon Kim, *Korea in Soviet East Asian Policy* (Seoul: Kyunghee University Press, 1986), pp. 19–21.

this view.[6] Moscow had equally harsh words for the decision to send troops to Vietnam and denounced the formation of ASPAC as well.

Outside of the political realm, however, the South was beginning to make a noteworthy attempt to open ties with the Soviet Union and Eastern Europe. Aware of the worldwide reduction in tensions, Seoul felt that it should free itself from the undesirable diplomatic consequences of excessive dependence on the United States. As a means of improving relations on a very limited scale, as well as to check North Korea diplomatically, the government sought to secure the participation of South Korean citizens in international academic conferences, art festivals, and athletic competitions held in communist countries. Despite this effort, few South Koreans were granted entry visas. In the late 1960s, though, limited commercial exchanges began to take place between South Korea and Yugoslavia, and small numbers of South Koreans were permitted entry to East European countries.[7]

From the 1970s to 1988: The Policy's Conception

South Korea's relationship with the northern countries began to change in the 1970s, and the Northern Policy gradually took shape. A review of that era's international political developments and Seoul's response to them should be sufficient to reveal how this came about.

Following the inauguration of US President Richard Nixon in January 1969, Washington's principal global policies were revised, causing a shift in relations among the world's major powers. The most prominent change was the advent of *détente* between the United States and the Soviet Union, which set the stage for a curtailment of American obligations in East Asia, in accordance with the 'Nixon Doctrine'. For South Korea, the application of this doctrine meant the withdrawal in 1971 of one-third of the US troops stationed there. But as Washington slowly reduced its role as Seoul's patrol, the South Korean people began to lose faith in the United States.[8]

This erosion of confidence in the United States was accelerated when, in July 1971, Nixon announced his plan to visit China. In the absence of

---

6   Ki-shik Hao, 'The Soviet Far Eastern Policy and the Reunification of Korea', *Journal of Asiatic Studies*, vol. 8, no. 4 (December 1970), pp. 130, 134.

7   Sung-joo Han, 'South Korean Policy Toward the Soviet Union', in Sung-joo Han (ed.), *Soviet Policy in Asia: Expansion or Accommodation?*, (Seoul: Panmun Book Co., 1980), pp. 316–19.

8   Bernard K. Gordon, 'U.S. Policy Toward Korea', in Young C. Kim (ed.), *Major Powers and Korea*, (Silver Spring, Md.: Research Institute on Korean Affairs, 1973), p. 49.

prior notification of the agreement between Washington and Beijing, the Seoul government was shocked to hear that Nixon would visit a country that had fought against both South Korea and the United States in the Korean War. Seoul was further perplexed by pressure from Washington to open a direct dialogue with Pyongyang and to seek joint admission to the United Nations. For the Republic of Korea, whose refusal to recognise North Korea was based on the conviction that its own government was the only legitimate one on the Korean Peninsula, this shift in American policy was an alarming development.[9]

What did the US administration seek to achieve on the Korean Peninsula through this policy adjustment? The answer may be found in a paper written by Morton Abramowitz, who was in charge of the Korea desk at the US Department of State during this period.[10] Arguing that in order to resolve the Korean situation it would first be necessary to ease the military confrontation between the South and the North, Abramowitz advised Seoul to recognise North Korea, which would bring relations on the peninsula into line with the relationship between East and West Germany. He stressed that Seoul needed a *Nordpolitik*, making what was, at least in published records, the first clear reference to a northern policy. Apart from recommending that the two Koreas recognise each other, Abramowitz urged Seoul to make diplomatic overtures to the Soviet Union, China, and the East European countries.

Given the changing political environment and the new US policy toward East Asia and the Korean Peninsula, Seoul needed to revise its foreign policies, particularly its anticommunist line. The emergence of a new attitude became evident in the government's amendment of trade legislation in January 1971. The Soviet Union, China, and the East European nations were classified as non-hostile countries under the revised trade law, and exchanges of commodities with them were permitted. The government began seeking ways to make friends in the communist bloc. In a statement before the National Assembly in August 1971, then Foreign Minister Kim Yong-shik said, 'If the Soviet Union and China do not take hostile action against the Republic of Korea, we could positively consider establishing diplomatic relations with them'.[11] Then, for the first time since the republic's establishment, the government sent a trade delegation to Yugoslavia and began receiving visitors from communist countries. Perhaps most importantly, the South Korean government entered into talks

---

9   For my analysis of the United States' Korean policy in this period, see my *Unification Policies* (fn. 3 above), pp. 325–34.

10 'Moving the Glacier: The Two Koreas and the Powers', *Adelphi Papers*, no. 80 (London: International Institute for Strategic Studies, 1971).

11 *New York Times*, 8 August 1971.

with North Korea at a conference sponsored by the Red Cross in August 1971.

President Nixon visited China in February 1972 and issued a joint statement with Premier Zhou Enlai in Shanghai. Contained within this crucial document were passages spelling out new policies, both American and Chinese, toward the Korean Peninsula. Both countries voiced their support for efforts to expand communications between the South and the North. Instead of advocating the resolution of the Korean question through the good offices of the United Nations—the position taken until then by South Korea, the United States, and their supporters—Washington and Beijing called for the arrangement of a settlement through an inter-Korean dialogue.[12] Though this was not an unexpected development, it pointed up all the more acutely Seoul's need to revise its North Korean policy and its stance toward the northern countries in general.

Against this backdrop, South Korean President Park Chung-hee expressed his willingness to improve relations with communist countries. In a statement made on 16 May 1972, he said 'If they do not take hostile action against us, we will seek cooperation with them, though they are different from us in social systems'.[13] At the time Seoul was negotiating with the North through a secret exchange of envoys, the upshot of which was the South–North Joint Communiqué issued on 4 July 1972. This historic document, which established reunification as a goal, marked a critical turning point in inter-Korean relations and in South Korea's relationship with the communist world. From Seoul's standpoint, the statement was a pledge to resolve the Korean conflict through the principles of self-reliance, peace, and grand national unity. The underlying premise was that the South would consent to *de facto*, if not *de jure*, recognition of the North.

The communiqué raised expectations at home and abroad that progress toward reunification would soon be forthcoming, and it also helped North Korea attain official recognition from some of the countries that had previously shunned it. But the northern countries would not retreat from their refusal to recognise South Korea, and the inter-Korean dialogue quickly broke down despite the initial hopes for it.[14]

To break the impasse, on 23 June 1973, South Korea issued a special presidential declaration stating that it would open its doors to all countries 'that differ from it in ideology and political systems' and calling on those

---

12 Xinhua News Agency, 27 February 1972; Foreign Broadcast Information Service (FBIS), *Daily Report* (China), 28 February 1972.

13 FBIS, *Daily Report* (Korea), 17 May 1972.

14 Hakjoon Kim, *Unification Policies*, pp. 340–3.

countries to reciprocate.[15] This declaration amounted to a virtual withdrawal of the South Korean government's claim to be the sole representative of the Korean people. Even so, North Korea rejected the 23 June declaration. China, one of Pyongyang's closest allies, also responded negatively, but the reaction from the Soviet Union was fairly positive. According to Professor Kim Youn-soo, the Soviets began to pursue 'open policies' of rapprochement with South Korea around this time.[16]

As it turned out, 1973 saw a number of momentous events in the relationship between Seoul and Moscow. That year, for the first time, South Korean citizens were granted visas to enter the Soviet Union when a South Korean theatrical director was permitted to participate in an international meeting in Moscow and thirty-eight South Korean athletes were welcomed to the Moscow Universiade. In November Kim Dong-jo, then Seoul's ambassador to the United States, met with his Soviet counterpart, Anatoly Dobrynin, at the headquarters of the United Nations in New York to exchange views on the Korean question, and at the end of the year the Soviet Union sent a representative to Tokyo to attend an academic seminar organised by the Korean institute for the purpose of discussing Moscow's policy toward Northeast Asia.[17] Moscow is also said to have helped India establish diplomatic ties with both South Korea and North Korea in December 1973.

Relations between Seoul and Moscow continued to thaw in 1974. Trade contacts were established between the two countries for the first time, albeit unofficially, and the South Korean media played up the possibility of an expanding exchange of products. In May there were discussions between officials of the South Korean Embassy in Washington and those of the Soviet consulate general in San Francisco on the Korea question, and in October the first official exchange between South Korea and the Soviet Union took place when the National Assembly Library in Seoul traded books with the Lenin State Library in Moscow.[18]

Faced with strong protests from North Korea and China, which warned that these developments would only perpetuate the territorial division of the peninsula, Moscow could do little more in the way of openly approaching Seoul, but it continued to pursue secret contacts. It has been reported, for instance, that in January 1975 a Soviet official from the

---

[15] Pyong-choon Hahm, 'The Initiative for Korean Unification', *Korea Journal*, vol. 11, no. 11 (November 1981), p. 11.

[16] Youn-soo Kim, 'Towards the Opening of New Relations Between Korea and East European Countries: The Soviet Union as the Key Actor', *Korea and World Affairs*, vol. 1, no. 2 (Summer 1977), p. 181.

[17] Tai-hwan Kwak, 'Recent Soviet Policy Toward the Two Koreas: Trends and Prospects', *Korea and World Affairs*, vol. 4, no. 2 (Summer 1980), pp. 202–3.

[18] Ibid., p. 187.

Academy of Social Sciences met with the chief of the South Korea Trade Promotion Corporation in New York to discuss the opening of bilateral trade ties.[19]

In addition, in spite of objections from Pyongyang, Moscow continued to extend visas permitting South Koreans to participate in conferences and sports events held in the Soviet Union. South Korean athletes participated, for example, in the September 1975 World Amateur Wrestling Championships held in Moscow. Two months later Han Pyo-wook, then South Korea's ambassador to London, went to Moscow for a conference sponsored by the United Nations Children's Fund (UNICEF), becoming the first South Korean diplomat to be granted a visa to enter the Soviet Union.[20]

Other important political contacts followed in 1978. In May a Korean Air Lines passenger plane that had violated Soviet air space made an emergency landing in Murmansk. The Soviet government handled the incident swiftly, calmly, and in a friendly manner, and the South Korean government issued a presidential statement expressing its appreciation.[21] Also that year, Moscow allowed a South Korean delegation led by then Minister of Health and Social Affairs Shin Hyun-hwak to attend a meeting held in Alma-Ata, the capital of Kazakhstan, which was jointly sponsored by the World Health Organization and UNICEF; this was the first official trip to the Soviet Union by a cabinet member of the South Korean government. Entry visas were also granted to South Korean journalists who requested permission to cover the meeting. When a volleyball team from Seoul participated in an international competition in Moscow, the *Kazakhstan Pravda* referred to South Korea using its official name: the Republic of Korea. In May 1979 the Soviet government again permitted the entry of two South Korean reporters. Other noteworthy developments during this period include the participation by South Korean athletes in an international athletic competition in Moscow, the opening of telephone lines between Seoul and Moscow via London, and the participation of South Korean political scientists in an international seminar held in Moscow.[22]

These developments were interpreted as signs that relations between Seoul and Moscow were improving, and they gave rise to speculation that the Kremlin was about to make a formal diplomatic overture to Seoul and,

19 Youn-Soo Kim, 'Opening of New Relations', p. 187.

20 Kwak, 'Recent Soviet Policy Toward the Two Koreas', p. 203.

21 Han, 'South Korean Policy Toward the Soviet Union', p. 327.

22 Hakjoon Kim, *Korea in Soviet East Asian Policy*, pp. 58–60.

as Washington had done, initiate a two-Koreas policy.[23] Indeed, South Korea and the Soviet Union were edging closer together in the 1970s; as many scholars and analysts agree, the earnestness of Moscow's intention to make friends with South Korea should not be underestimated. The Soviets may well have been unhappy to have so little contact with a country whose economy was growing so rapidly that it was expected to become a 'little Japan' within a decade or two. The Soviets may also have seen South Korea's scientific, technological, and economic competence as a potential source of assistance for their development projects, especially those in Siberia.[24]

In the end, though, in spite of its increasingly flexible attitude the Kremlin made no move to recognise Seoul. Moscow rejected as unrealistic North Korea's claims that it was the only legitimate state on the peninsula and that South Korea was an American colony, and the Soviets also seemed to acknowledge that the territorial division of the peninsula was a *fait accompli* and would persist for years to come. But when it came to Seoul's desire for formal diplomatic relations, Moscow was not sympathetic.[25] The Kremlin's unwillingness was motivated by strong resistance from North Korea and China to South Korea's aspirations. Moscow could not afford to disregard protests from Pyongyang, since it did not want to weaken its ties with North Korea's leadership, and the Soviets also had to stand up to Beijing, which accused them of betraying the North by edging closer to the South.

The partial thaw that had come about between Seoul and Moscow appeared to undergo a reversal late in 1978. Three-way cooperative ties among the United States, Japan, and China were taking shape at that time, and the Soviet Union and North Korea reacted to what they perceived as an anti-Soviet development by strengthening their ties to one another. Within this context the Soviet Union declared in a 12 October *Pravda* commentary that it considered North Korea to be the sole legitimate state on the Korean Peninsula. The commentary also criticised Seoul's call for joint recognition of the South and the North.[26]

---

23 Manwoo Lee, 'The Prospects for Normalization of Relations Between Moscow and Seoul', *Korea and World Affairs*, vol. 4, no. 1 (Spring, 1980), p. 130.

24 Donald Zagoria, 'Soviet Policy Dilemmas in East Asia', *Asian Perspective*, vol. 2, no. 2 (Autumn 1978), p. 167.

25 Young C. Kim, 'Soviet Policy Toward Korea', *Sahoekwahak kwa Chongch'alkyonku* (Social Sciences and Policy Research), vol. 2, no. 2 (December 1980), p. 95.

26 Donald Zagoria, 'North Korea's Soviet and China Policy', in Korean Association for Communist Studies, *North Korea: Today and Tomorrow*, (Seoul: Peopmoonsa, 1982), p. 366 (in Korean).

As the foregoing demonstrates, the Northern Policy employed by the South Korean government in the 1970s produced no substantial results. One reason for the policy's failure was the fact that Seoul, acting within the framework of the cold war, responded passively to changes in the international political situation. More than that, the South had yet to free itself from security-oriented, defensive thinking and persisted in viewing inter-Korean relations in terms of confrontation and competition. As a result, Seoul was unable to forcefully pursue a realistic unification policy.[27]

Factors like these continued to restrict Seoul's northern diplomacy in the 1980s, although the South Korean government began to assume a more positive attitude toward the communist camp following the inauguration of the Fifth Republic in October 1980. In a speech in June 1983 at the National Defense College, then Foreign Minister, Lee Bum-suk made the first use of the term 'Northern Policy' by a ranking government official. Lee stated that he would give the highest priority to pursuing the Northern Policy in order to normalise relations with the Soviet Union and China.[28] Underlying this statement, however, was a desire to hold North Korea in check diplomatically, made evident by a further remark: 'Pushing the Northern Policy is necessary to prevent the recurrence of war on the peninsula'. As envisaged by Lee, the policy was a vehicle designed only to serve national security interests. At the time the Northern Policy was based on the concept of North–South confrontation, as is apparent from another remark made by Lee: 'We will selectively block or allow North Korea's advance into the international community, though so far we have tolerated Pyongyang's moves in most cases, in accordance with the declaration of June 23, 1973'.[29]

A more comprehensive analysis of the Northern Policy at that time has been presented by Park Chul-un, a National Assembly member who, as a personal aide to President Roh, is one of the chief architects of the Sixth Republic's Northern Policy.[30] According to Park, in the past the policy had limited aims—preventing another war and forcing North Korea to endorse Seoul's unification strategy by improving South Korea's relations with China and the Soviet Union and thereby weakening Pyongyang's principal alliances. Such grand tasks as resolving the Korean question and

---

27 Daljoong Kim, 'The Northern Policy and the Meaning of the Improvement in the South Korean–East European Relationship', *Minjokjiseong*, August 1989, p. 32 (in Korean).

28 *Kyunghyang Daily News*, 29 June 1983 (in Korean).

29 Daljoong Kim, 'The Northern Policy', p. 68.

30 Chul-un Park, 'Korea's Future and Its Northern Policy', *Minjokjiseong*, April 1989, pp. 190–1 (in Korean).

realising national self-esteem were not considered to be among the policy's primary goals. Yet the strategy of weakening North Korea's relationships with its chief allies in order to achieve political superiority only generated suspicion in North Korea, China, and the Soviet Union. Under such conditions, the progress of the Northern Policy came to a standstill.

As others have pointed out, the policy in those days was not linked to unification, and in the context of the cold war no progress could be made with it. Relations between Seoul and Moscow took a sharp turn for the worse in September 1983, when a Soviet fighter plane shot down Korean Air Lines Flight 007. The relationship between Seoul and Beijing, by contrast, improved some four months later, when a Chinese airliner made an emergency landing in South Korea, prompting direct diplomatic talks between the two countries.[31]

The Policy's Development in the Sixth Republic

With the inauguration of the Sixth Republic on 25 February 1988, the status of the Northern Policy was upgraded from that of a highly restricted strategy of nominal importance to a position at the centre of South Korea diplomacy. One of the many factors underlying this transformation was a change in the international political situation. Ever since his rise to power in March 1985, Soviet leader Gorbachev had been working vigorously to reduce international tensions and carry out drastic reforms at home. In a speech delivered in Vladivostok in June 1986 and another given in Krasnoyarsk in September 1988, Gorbachev announced his intention to seek cooperation and friendship with the Pacific nations. These speeches helped to transform the perception of the Soviet Union that prevailed in the Asia–Pacific region.[32] Ideological barriers between East and West began to come down in the new atmosphere, and the East European countries made conspicuous moves to rid themselves of communist doctrine and Soviet influence. Such developments created circumstances favourable to the active and effective promotion of the Northern Policy.

The successful staging of the 1988 Seoul Olympics held great importance for the *Nordpolitik*. The event enabled the northern countries to see South Korea in an entirely new light, one that revealed neither a colony of the 'American imperialists' nor a nation economically dependent on 'international capitalism'. Visitors could confirm firsthand that South

---

[31] Hakjoon Kim, *Unification Policies*, p. 409.

[32] Byung-joon Ahn, 'Soviet Policy Toward Korea', in Tokyo Club Foundation for Global Studies, *Political and Economic Prospects for the Asian Pacific Region: The Views of the Asian Experts*, (Tokyo: Tokyo Club Foundation for Global Studies, 1990), pp. 63–70.

Korea was a prospering nation well on the way to becoming a democracy. The games also provided South Korean businesses with opportunities to initiate trade with northern countries, and their efforts met with favourable reactions. Thus, the Seoul Olympics helped to create an atmosphere conducive to the implementation of the Northern Policy.[33]

Another important factor for the policy was the enhancement of a sense of national self-esteem among the South Korean people, who gained new confidence in themselves as a result of their achievements in many fields. This confidence and the pride that goes with it have given the South Koreans a sense of mission, a desire to advance into the international community and to make the reunification of Korea a reality. The renewed national spirit has been a driving force behind South Korea's endeavours to succeed with its Northern Policy.

In his 1987 campaign pledges and his 1988 inaugural address, President Roh Tae-woo made it clear that 'northward diplomacy' would be a key policy of the Sixth Republic. Adopting the slogan 'creating a vibrant era of national self-esteem', Roh proclaimed a new beginning, 'an era of hope, which will see Korea, once a peripheral country in East Asia, take a central position in the international community'.[34] He declared that he would devote his efforts to realising peace on the peninsula and reuniting the divided nation, and he promised to advance the Northern Policy aggressively.

Particularly noteworthy is the fact that Roh linked this policy closely to the goal of reunification, introducing a concept of linkage that was absent in the policies of the Fifth Republic. Addressing this subject in his inaugural address, Roh said: 'We will broaden the channel of international cooperation with the continental countries with which we have had no exchanges, with the aim of pursuing a vigorous northern diplomacy. Improved relations with countries with ideologies and social systems different from ours will contribute to stability, peace, and common prosperity in East Asia. Such a northward diplomacy should also lead to the gateway of unification'.[35] The president reiterated this position in a speech on 1 March 1988:

> I am willing to meet anyone as part of my efforts to pave the way for national reunification, whatever the difficulties and hardships. I will push for improved relations with the northern countries with which we

---

33 Ibid., pp. 66–8. For a presentation of Soviet viewpoints, see Alexander Fedorovsky, 'South Korea as a New Economic Power', in Vladimir Ivanov (ed.), *USSR and the Pacific Region in the 21st Century*, (New Delhi: Allied Publishers Ltd., 1989), pp. 94–102.

34 The Presidential Secretariat of the Republic of Korea, ed. *Korea: A Nation Transformed* (Seoul: Donghwa Publishing Company, 1990), pp. 57–64.

35 Ibid., p. 10.

have no diplomatic ties. In this new era we will open broad ways for contact with those countries, which I believe will help us make progress in our endeavors to achieve unification.[36]

The broad guidelines laid down by Roh have been explained in detail in a paper written by his aide Park Chul-un, who offers three reasons for the Sixth Republic's great emphasis on the Northern Policy.[37] First, the opportunity to resolve the question of national reunification is expected to arise in the course of the policy's execution. Second, the policy is expected to help South Korea move beyond its peripheral status in East Asia and take a prominent role on the centre stage of world history. Third, the northern diplomacy should also help the nation economically.[38] Park summarised his observations by saying,

> The Northern Policy is designed to advance the date of realizing peace and unification, which is the solemn task of our era. It is also aimed at establishing national self-esteem, building a prosperous future, and making the twenty-first century ours.[39]

To provide specific guidelines for the policy, on 7 July 1988, Roh issued a 'Special Declaration in the Interest of National Self-esteem, Unification, and Prosperity'. This declaration proclaims that South Korea will seek common prosperity with the North based on the concept of a single national community and, while helping the North improve relations with friendly noncommunist nations, will try to normalise its own relations with China, the Soviet Union, and other communist countries. The declaration was intended, in other words, to clear the way for unification while seeking prosperity for both nations through cooperation in the international community. In this regard the declaration marked a major turning point for Seoul's policies toward inter-Korean relations and unification.

Having reviewed the ideological background of the Northern Policy as formulated by the Sixth Republic, let us turn our attention to the basic principles applied in the policy's execution.[40] The first principle is to refrain from actions that would isolate North Korea. This means that even after forging diplomatic ties with communist countries friendly to Pyongyang, the South will encourage them to maintain amicable relations with the North. By so doing, Seoul hopes to contribute to the opening of the North and to the realisation of a reconciliation on the peninsula.

The second principle, mentioned above, is to link the Northern Policy to unification. The third is to pursue political and non-political exchanges

---

[36] Ibid., p. 39.

[37] Chul-un Park, 'Korea's Future', pp. 188–9.

[38] Ibid., p. 189.

[39] Ibid.

[40] Ibid.

simultaneously. Communist countries have tended to put their economic interests first and to postpone the normalisation of bilateral ties in order to keep their political and economic affairs separate. Seoul maintains that in the absence of normal political relations, full-fledged economic cooperation is impossible. In spite of the fact that it understands why communist countries try to separate politics and economics, the South Korean government still insists the two be linked.

The fourth principle is to pursue northern diplomacy in accordance with a national consensus. This makes the government responsible for fostering an awareness among the people of the great importance of the Northern Policy. To this end, the Sixth Republic has established inter-ministerial organisations to provide policy coordination and consultation in every field. The chief organs are (1) the Coordination and Consultation Committee on the Northern Policy, composed of fourteen cabinet-level ministers, which hammers out policies and guidelines; (2) the External Economic Cooperation Committee, which is presided over by the deputy prime minister and the economic planning minister and which deals with economic exchanges with the northern countries; (3) the Private Economic Council of Korea, which includes four major business organisations among its members and which serves as a private-sector channel for economic exchanges with the northern countries; (4) a conference of ministers in posts related to national security, which is chaired by the national unification minister and which handles questions concerning inter-Korean relations; and (5) the Committee for the Promotion of the Northern Policy, which is led by the prime minister and which provides comprehensive support for the policy. In June 1989 Kim Young-sam, then president of the opposition Reunification Democratic Party and now one of the leaders of the ruling Democratic Liberal Party, led a delegation from his party to the Soviet Union; this mission was widely seen as a sign of suprapartisan support for the Northern Policy.

The final principle is to pursue the Northern Policy while continuing to cooperate with South Korea's traditional allies, notably the United States. For Seoul, maintaining close ties with its established allies is crucial to national security, trade, and economic cooperation; such relationships constitute a prerequisite for the Northern Policy's success. In this light, Washington's repeated statements in support of the policy carry great weight. When US President George Bush visited Seoul and addressed the National Assembly on 27 February 1989, for instance, he announced his support for the policy. On 17 October of that year, during a summit with President Roh in Washington, Bush again praised the Northern Policy, describing it as complementary to American policies.

Having examined the principles of its execution as well as its ideological background, let us review what the Northern Policy has accomplished, proceeding in roughly chronological order.[41] The policy's first major achievement was the opening of diplomatic relations with Hungary. Back in 1985, Yonsei University's Institute of East and West Studies began conducting academic exchanges with Hungary, a development that was followed by the opening of a Hungarian trade office in Seoul on 25 March 1988. On 13 September of that year, South Korea and Hungary agreed to exchange permanent ambassadorial missions, which were set up in Seoul and Budapest on 1 December. Finally, on 1 February 1989, the two countries established full diplomatic ties and opened resident embassies. Bilateral exchanges have since taken place at a brisk pace in many fields. President Roh made an official trip to Hungary on 22 November 1989, becoming the first South Korean head of state to visit an East European nation, and Hungarian President Arpad Goncz reciprocated with a visit to Seoul in November 1990. These visits served to accelerate the development of ties between Seoul and Budapest.

The second accomplishment was the establishment of formal relations between South Korea and Poland. Having exchanged trade offices in April and May of 1989, the two countries agreed on 1 November 1989, to establish full diplomatic relations and open resident embassies. Seoul opened its embassy in Warsaw on 27 November and Poland opened an embassy in Seoul on 17 January 1990.

The policy's third achievement was the normalisation of relations between South Korea and the Soviet Union. In April 1989 the Trade Promotion Corporation opened a trade office in Moscow, and at the same time the Soviet Chamber of Commerce set up an office in Seoul; on 8 December of that year the two countries agreed to establish *de facto* consular ties, and they exchanged consular offices in March 1990. That same month Kim Young-sam and Park Chul-un visited Moscow, and it was agreed in a meeting between Kim and Gorbachev that relations would be normalised at an early date. On 2 August 1990, a government delegation led by Kim Choung-in, senior secretary for economic affairs to President Roh, and Kim Chong-hui senior assistant for diplomacy and national

---

41 For reference, see the six articles in the special issue on the Northern Policy in *Korea and World Affairs*, vol. 12, no. 4 (Autumn 1988). See also Hong-nack Kim, 'Sino-Soviet Rapprochement and Its Implications for South Korea's Northern Policy', and Andras Hernadi, 'The South Korean–Hungarian Relationship: An International Perspective', *Korea and World Affairs*, vol. 13, no. 2 (Summer 1989); and Jung Ha Lee, 'South Korea's Policy Toward Socialist Countries: Its Impact on Inter-Korean Relations', and Byung-Chul Seo, 'Nordpolitik of Korea and Eastern Europe', *Korea and World Affairs*, vol. 13, no. 4 (Autumn 1989). For official statements of the South Korean government, see Korean Overseas Information Service, Ministry of Culture and Information, *Backgrounder*, vol. 49 (2 March 1989), and *Northern Diplomacy*, vol. 16, no. 2 (February 1990).

defence to the president, visited Moscow for talks on economic cooperation and the establishment of diplomatic ties. On 14 September the two countries signed provisional aviation and trade treaties. Finally, on 30 September, South Korea and the Soviet Union normalised relations, eighty-six years after Russia and Korea's Yi dynasty had severed all ties under pressure from Japan. The Korean Embassy in Moscow opened on 30 October, and on that day the first South Korean ambassador to the Soviet Union began work. Such was the background to Roh's trip to Moscow on 13–17 December, the first state visit to the Soviet Union ever made by a South Korean leader. In return, on 19 April 1991 Gorbachev went to Cheju-do, the southern island of Korea, for a summit meeting the next day.

Exchanges with the Soviet Union were promoted in a variety of fields. These exchanges continued with the Russian Republic from 1991. Private-level contacts, we should note, have been going on ever since Gorbachev's Krasnoyarsk speech in 1988. In November of that year Moscow finalised a plan for direct trade with Seoul, and it has since pursued exchanges in other fields. The Soviet Union has made specific proposals, some of which have been adopted, in the following areas: (1) establishing a bilateral economic cooperation council and inviting South Korean economic missions; (2) building a trade centre in Nakhodka with loans from Seoul; (3) approving the construction of a timber-processing plant in Siberia by South Korean businesses, in return for which South Korea will be provided with timber; (4) selling enriched uranium to Seoul; (5) opening air routes; and (6) negotiating directly over the question of the Korean residents on Sakhalin. This new climate of friendly relations has led to a sharp rise in the number of people travelling between the two countries—from seventy-two in 1986 to 19,229 in 1991—and in the value of bilateral commercial transactions, which swelled from $200 million in 1987 to $992 million in 1991. In the academic sphere, Yonsei University and Moscow State University agreed in early 1990 to exchange students and teachers.

The fourth major accomplishment of the Northern Policy is the improvement of South Korea's relations with other East European countries, such as Yugoslavia. The South Korea Trade Promotion Corporation set up a trade centre in Ljubljana, Slovenia, in June 1988, and the Slovenia Chamber of Commerce opened an office in Seoul four months later. In February 1989 this office was granted the status of a trade mission representing the Yugoslavian Federal Chamber of Commerce. At the end of that year, on 18 December, the two countries announced the establishment of formal diplomatic ties; Seoul's embassy in Belgrade opened on 7 February 1990, and Yugoslavia's embassy in Seoul will be opening soon. On 7 November 1990, Yugoslav President Borisav Jovic became the first leader of an East European country to make a state visit to South

Korea. In a magazine interview Jovic commented that 'even in the short period of less than a year since diplomatic relations were established between our two countries, they have expanded at an unprecedented pace'.[42]

Bulgaria opened a trade office in Seoul in July 1989, three months after South Korea set up an office of its own in Sofia. On 23 March 1990, during a visit to Sofia, Foreign Minister Choi Ho-joong signed an agreement with the Bulgarian government to establish ambassadorial-level diplomatic relations. Just one day before that, on 22 March, South Korea and Czechoslovakia had agreed to normalise relations. Jiri Dienstbier, Czechoslovakia's foreign minister, visited Seoul on 26 October of that year and signed accords on aviation, trade, and economic cooperation. In addition, on 30 March 1990, South Korea and Romania established full diplomatic ties.

Relations with East Germany have, naturally, come to a different conclusion. The Daewoo industrial group opened a branch office in East Berlin in January 1988; the Samsung group followed a year later. On 2 April 1990, the governments of the two countries signed an agreement to exchange trade offices, but even though East Germany expressed a desire to normalise relations, South Korea chose to await the outcome of the German reunification process that was then in motion. Since Germany was eventually reunified on 3 October 1990, the question of normalising relations became irrelevant. Albania, on the other hand, is not yet eager to mend fences with Seoul. When the waves of reform washing over Eastern Europe eventually reach Albania, however, changes can be expected in the country's domestic and foreign policies that should lead to friendship with South Korea.

The Northern Policy's fifth achievement is the improvement of relations with China. Beijing, which had initially permitted only private-level exchanges, eventually gave its approval to contacts between Seoul and China's provincial governments; such relationships have been established with both Shandong and Liaoning. Since April 1988 the two countries have exchanged various missions and have promoted, among other things, mutual participation in trade expositions. Bilateral trade grew from $1.2 billion in 1985 to $3.2 billion in 1989, a year in which as many as 23,000 people travelled between China and South Korea. Another sign of an improving relationship was Seoul's participation in the 1990 Beijing Asian Games, which involved dispatching a consular mission to look after the interests of the South Korean athletes.

On 20 October 1990, Seoul and Beijing signed an agreement to exchange trade offices, a step that was subsequently to lead to the establishment of official ties. Under the accord, the offices were staffed by fewer than twenty persons, including government officials from the

---

[42] *Diplomacy*, vol. 16, no. 11 (November 1990), p. 9.

respective foreign and trade ministries, and performed such consular services as entrusted to it, including the issuing of visas. President Roh appointed Roh Jae-won, a former vice foreign minister, to head the office in Beijing. While acknowledging that Beijing's close relationship with Pyongyang limited its ties with Seoul, Roh Jae-won believed that the decision to exchange trade offices with Seoul was indicative of a change in China's policy.[43] Admittedly, China has intensified its efforts to solidify its system of government and has strengthened its ideological bonds with North Korea in the period since the June 1989 suppression of the democracy movement of Tiananmen Square. Even so, the opening of the trade offices was expected to offer opportunities for Seoul and Beijing to normalise their relations. In fact, the two countries set up diplomatic relations on 24 August 1992, and subsequently President Roh visited Beijing on 28 September that year for summit talks with Chinese President Yang Shangkun.

The sixth and final major accomplishment of the policy is the establishment, for the first time, of full diplomatic relations between Seoul and an Asian communist country. South Korea and Mongolia officially recognised each other on 26 March 1990. This breakthrough should favourably affect Seoul's relations with Vietnam, which have been steadily improving, especially in the field of economic cooperation. On 2 April 1992 South Korea and Vietnam agreed on opening liaison offices. Accordingly, on 17 August 1992, Korea set up a liaison office in Vietnam and Vietnam is expected to open its liaison office before the end of November of the same year. In the meantime, on 15 January 1990, Seoul established diplomatic relations with Algeria, which is not among the northern countries, but which has a socialist government.

Summary and Prospects

As the foregoing demonstrates, the push to promote Seoul's Northern Policy has produced remarkable progress since the founding of the Sixth Republic in 1988. Over the next few years, several factors should pave the way for further advances. These include an international political situation marked by reduced tensions and the virtual elimination of ideological barriers; the winds of democratisation and reform that are sweeping through the former Soviet Union and Eastern Europe, where campaigns are underway to achieve 'socialism with a human face'; the eagerness of the communist and formerly communist countries to expand economic cooperation with South Korea; and the keen interest of the people in the success of the Northern Policy.

---

[43] *Korean Herald*, 5 December 1990.

By means of this policy, Seoul has brought to life what had been a diplomatic 'dead area'. It has succeeded thus far in normalising its relations with many northern countries. In the next stage South Korea will focus its efforts on expanding its cooperative ties in cultural, academic, and scientific fields and, above all, on economic cooperation.

In the beginning North Korea strongly protested the rapprochement between South Korea and the members of the communist bloc. Pyongyang argued that the establishment of diplomatic ties between the East European countries and South Korea was an endorsement of the Western view that there are two states on the Korean Peninsula and an act in support of a plot to perpetuate the territorial division. But the East European nations, along with the rest of the international community, have ignored North Korea's allegations, and Pyongyang is beginning to accept the normalised relations as a *fait accompli*.

The normalisation process should help to ease the North Korean government's rigid attitudes. In a written interview with the Soviet *Far Eastern Journal* just before his visit to Moscow, President Roh stated that 'the normalization of our relations will contribute greatly not only to increased understanding and cooperation between our two nations [South Korea and the Soviet Union] but also to the relaxation of tension and a durable peace on the Korean Peninsula'. Mikhail Kapitsa, director of the Institute of Oriental Studies in Moscow, has offered this view:

> Progressively developing its relations with South Korea, the Soviet Union proceeds from the belief that this will contribute to normalization of the situation of the Korean Peninsula to a peaceful dialogue between Pyongyang and Seoul.[44]

It is now quite clear that the final objective of Seoul's northern diplomacy is to establish a peaceful relationship between South and North Korea and to reunify the Korean Peninsula. Consider, for instance, this passage from a recent speech by ex-foreign Minister Choi Ho-joong:

> In the future, we must first consider the inter-Korean aspect of our Northern Policy. To date, the rapprochement between the South and the North has been overshadowed to an extent by the improvement of relations between South Korea and the socialist countries.

> In this connection, I wish to stress the priority we have set for inter-Korean dialogue. I would say that any agreement on rapprochement in the political-military area between Seoul and Pyongyang is not worth the paper it is written on as long as it is not made on the basis of mutual trust.

---

[44] 'Yalta System and After: Stability and Change in Northeast Asia' (paper prepared for the nineteenth international conference sponsored by the Korean Institute of International Studies, held in Seoul on 2–4 September 1990), *Diplomacy*, vol. 16, no. 9 (September 1990), p. 30.

A unification-for-unification's sake approach is frequently exploited by North Korea for propaganda purposes, having a counterproductive effect.

At the other extreme, there exists strong skepticism that the North Korean regime will never change; thus, some believe, all dialogue is futile.

But it is hard to believe that North Korea will remain immune to the global trend of reforms and openness for good. The success of German unification reminds us of the necessity to watch changes in North Korea with cool-headed reason, free from illusion or skepticism, and to cope with them with wisdom.[45]

In the meantime, Japan, the United States, and other Western countries can be expected to improve their relations with the North, and this should also enhance Pyongyang's flexibility. On 24 September 1990, a group of fifteen Japanese politicians arrived in North Korea on a visit that Japan hopes will help to thaw the icy relations between the two Asian neighbours. Japan and North Korea have agreed to further negotiations on normalising their relations, and Pyongyang has asked to be compensated economically for losses sustained during Japan's occupation of its territory from 1910 to 1945. Although it will take more than a matter of months for North Korea and Japan to normalise their relations, clearly they will maintain their formal contacts.

Several recent developments in the relationship between the North and the South deserve mention here. As a follow-up step to Roh's declaration of 7 July 1988, then Deputy Prime Minister Rha Woong-bae unveiled a package of measures on 7 October 1988, aimed at expanding economic exchanges with the North. This opened the way for a January 1989 visit to the North by Chung Ju-yung, founder and honorary chairman of the Hyundai group, who discussed with North Korean officials the prospects for jointly developing Mount Kumgang and for arranging economic cooperation in other fields, such as shipbuilding and ship maintenance.

A series of secret visits to Pyongyang by South Korean dissidents in the spring and summer of 1989 strained inter-Korean relations, however, and matters were only made worse by the disclosure of a secret trip to the North in 1988 by Suh Kyung-won, a representative of the opposition Party for Peace and Democracy. Moreover, Pyongyang became extremely concerned about the repercussions of the democratic revolutions taking place in Eastern Europe in the fall of that year, and it has since taken a negative attitude toward relations with the South.

---

45 'Northern Policy and Korean Reunification' (speech delivered at the International Seminar on Comparative Analysis of German Reunification and the Korea Case, in Seoul, 5 November 1990), *Korea Update*, vol. 1, no. 7 (9 November 1990), p. 5.

In the face of international pressure, however, including pressure from the Soviet Union, and the continuing success of South Korea's *Nordpolitik*, North Korea has been unable to dismiss entirely the worldwide trend toward reconciliation. The first high-level talks between South and North Korea took place when the prime ministers of the two countries met in Seoul from 4–7 September 1990. In a separate development, soccer matches have been played in Pyongyang and Seoul between the South Korean national team and North Korea's team, marking the first inter-Korean athletic exchanges in forty-five years. Events like these represent small triumphs for the Northern Policy, but while they send hopeful signals regarding inter-Korean relations, it is too much to expect Pyongyang to overhaul the principles of its foreign policy at any time soon.

In this transitional period, the South and the North must each try to respect and accommodate the other's positions and demands. Through its 7 July declaration, South Korea has already signalled its willingness to shift its policies toward mutual reconciliation. If the North Korean government can change its attitudes correspondingly, the two Koreas should be able to achieve peaceful coexistence by 1995, when they mark their fiftieth year as separate nations. On the basis of their capacity to coexist in peace, the two sides could then go through an interim integration stage in the late 1990s, eventually achieving reunification. At that point the Sixth Republic's unification formula for bringing about a single national community by first creating a 'South–North community' will have borne fruit.

15 Inter-Korean Relations Oriented Toward Reconciliation and Cooperation

LIM DONG-WON

Introduction

South and North Korea put into effect the Agreement on Reconciliation, Non-Aggression and Exchanges and Cooperation between the South and the North (hereinafter referred to as the 'Basic South–North Agreement') on 19 February 1992 during the sixth round of South–North High-Level Talks.

Two other significant inter-Korean documents also took effect on that date. One was the Joint Declaration of the Denuclearization of the Korean Peninsula, and the other was the Agreement on the Formation of Sub-committees of the South–North High-Level Talks.

The South and the North were thus able to overcome their state of mutual confrontation and distrust with their own efforts for the first time in the half-century history of national division. Thereby, they are moving toward a new stage of reconciliation and cooperation aimed at durable peace and unification.

However, a written pledge alone does not necessarily bring about reconciliation and cooperation. This can be brought about only through faithful implementation of what has been agreed on. This is why the process of future follow-up implementation is of the utmost importance.

Key to Resolution of the Korean Question

The shared opinion of experts was that if the Korean question were to be resolved peacefully, the following four issues have to be settled first:

- First, the South and the North should recognise each other and establish a mechanism of peaceful coexistence.
- Second, the South and the North should be able to function as responsible members of the international community. To this end, the two should jointly enter world organisations, in particular the United Nations.
- Third, the four major powers with a stake in the Korean Peninsula should cross-recognise South and North Korea.
- Fourth, military tensions on the Korean Peninsula should be eased, and the issue of foreign troops resolved.

As recently as a few years ago, it appeared almost impossible to resolve these four questions. Surprisingly, however, a clue has recently been found to their resolution.

The foundation was laid for the settlement of the first question as South and North Korea adopted and effectuated the Basic South–North Agreement through their own efforts.

The second task was resolved when the two sides joined the United Nations simultaneously in September 1991.

The third question of cross-recognition, too, is nearing resolution. South Korea normalised relations with the former Soviet Union, and then with China. The North's effort to normalise relations with Japan and seek rapprochement with the United States has become only a matter of time.

The fourth issue of foreign troops, also, is in the process of being resolved. A plan on the phased reduction of US forces in Korea was agreed on between Seoul and Washington in early 1990. In the initial stage, 7,000 American troops were to be withdrawn in the first of a series of phased reductions. And, as President Roh Tae-woo declared in December 1991, not a single nuclear weapon exists on South Korean soil.

These changes have occurred in the past two years, ushering in a historic turning point on the Korean Peninsula.

Process of South–North High-Level Talks

The South–North High-Level Talks were first suggested by Prime Minister Kang Young-hoon on 28 December 1988. In a message to his North Korean counterpart Premier Yon Hyong-muk, Prime Minister Kang proposed that South–North High-Level Talks be held. On 16 January 1989, Premier Yon agreed to hold the 'South–North High-Level Political and Military Talks'.

After the agenda topics of the high-level talks—the elimination of the state of political and military confrontation and the promotion of multi-faceted exchanges and cooperation between the South and the North—

were adopted through eight preliminary meetings between the two sides, the first round of South–North High-Level Talks was held in Seoul on 4 September 1990. Thereafter, five more rounds were held until February 1992.

South Korea's strategic goals for the high-level talks are to: (1) improve inter-Korean relations, end an age of hostility and confrontation, and open a new age of reconciliation and cooperation; (2) induce North Korea to open itself and reform, and; (3) lay the groundwork for peaceful unification.

Through more than thirty meetings—six rounds of high-level talks and twenty-five delegate contacts—the South and the North managed to produce the Basic South–North Agreement and the Joint Declaration of Denuclearization. In addition, subcommittees have begun to function to discuss the tangible implementation of the accords envisaged in these documents.

Characteristics of the Basic South–North Agreement

In a sense the adoption of the Basic South–North Agreement meant that the two sides neared a perceptional accord on a considerable part of the method of approach between South and North Korea.

First, the two sides substantially shared the conception that unification would be regarded as a process. Second, they agreed that therefore, an interim stage is needed in the unification process; and third, they understood that in this interim stage various factors detrimental to unification should be eliminated.

In other words, the two sides, while observing that unification cannot be achieved outright, made a pledge to recognise each other's system, coexist peacefully without resorting to war, and cooperate while travelling back and forth between the two zones, preparing for unification independently.

Therefore, effectuation of the Basic South–North Agreement was an epochal event forming a watershed in the history of national division, since it constituted the legal enactment of a document the two sides adopted to lay the groundwork for the actual institution of a 'mechanism of peaceful coexistence' in a process toward unification.

By referring to the character of the Basic South–North Agreement at some length, the stage of 'peaceful coexistence' deemed indispensable to the process of unification could be classified into: (1) a stage of pre-'South–North Commonwealth'—a stage of reconciliation and co-operation—and; (2) an institutional stage of 'South–North Commonwealth'. Thus, the Basic Agreement may be regarded as a treaty governing the pre-'South–North Commonwealth' stage.

Accordingly, the Basic Agreement is not a pledge of unification itself, but rather a time-limit agreement applicable only to the 'stage of reconciliation and cooperation'.

Although another feature of the Basic Agreement envisages the nature of a 'Peace Agreement', it could be said in a strict sense that, a 'Peace Agreement' and an 'Armistice Agreement' should coexist and complement each other until the question of the Armistice Agreement has been resolved.

In fact, there still remains the issue of how to dispose of the Armistice Agreement. If and when a South–North Commonwealth is institutionalised, a National Community Charter (or a South–North Commonwealth Peace Charter) that incorporates both the Armistice Agreement and the Basic Agreement could be adopted. After going through this stage, the South and the North could adopt a Unified Constitution to accomplish the final stage of unification.

Therefore, if unification can be likened to building a house on a sunny side of a hill, then the Basic South–North Agreement could be a plan for building a road of access to the construction site rather than the blueprint of the house itself.

Process of and Disputes in Adoption of the Basic Agreement

The Basic South–North Agreement consists of three chapters—'reconciliation' governing political relations, 'non-aggression' related to the elimination of military confrontation, and 'exchanges and cooperation'. In what follows, an attempt will be made to briefly discuss the contents of the agreement as well as the items disputed during the meetings.

The Basic South–North Agreement regulates the legal nature of inter-Korean relations, 'recognizing that their relations, not being a relationship between states, constitute a special interim relationship stemming from the process towards unification'.

It cannot be overlooked that many difficulties were encountered in the course of reaching the Basic Agreement. For instance, the South, while strongly urging the North to abandon its 'revolutionary policy against the South', emphasised the need for a clause that 'The two sides shall not attempt any actions of sabotage and subversion against each other'. The North, however, opposed this point initially, asserting, 'We have no intent, ability or policy whatsoever to foment a revolution or sabotage or overthrow the other side' (Article 4).

Another clause the North persistently opposed almost to the end was Article 5, 'The two sides shall endeavor together to transform the present state of armistice into a solid state of peace between the South and the North and shall abide by the present Military Armistice Agreement until such a state of peace has been realized'.

The North also opposed this point initially because it was synonymous with the 'principle of resolution between direct parties involved'. The North's final acceptance of it could be viewed as a sign of change in its longstanding logic calling for conclusion of a 'peace agreement' with the United States. Also, the North's 'One Korea' policy, which brands the South a 'colony of the United States', and its attitude toward the South as a 'target of liberation' appear to have faded away.

The North further rejected the idea (Article 7) of establishing permanent liaison offices in Seoul and Pyongyang. The two sides compromised and agreed to establish the liaison offices at Panmunjom instead.

Regarding the issue of 'guaranteeing the implementation of non-aggression' (Article 12), the South originally wanted a separate article on measures to promote military confidence building, but since the North rejected the idea, a compromise plan was adopted for a South–North Joint Military Commission to take up the question. On the other hand, despite the North's opposition, the South pushed through a five-point list of items— the mutual notification and control of major movements of military units and major military exercises, the peaceful utilisation of the Demilitarized Zone, exchanges of military personnel and information, phased reductions in armaments including the elimination of weapons of mass destruction and offensive capabilities, and verification thereof— related to confidence building and arms reduction in connection with the implementation and guarantee of non-aggression.

In the area of exchanges and cooperation (Chapter 3), the issue of dispersed families was reflected. However, as the North was negative toward the 'mutual opening and exchanges of newspapers, radio and television programs, and publications' in their apparent fear of unification realised with the North being absorbed into the South, Seoul conceded the words 'mutual opening' and instead used the phrase, '...shall carry out exchanges and cooperation in various fields such as...publishing and journalism including newspapers, radio and television broadcasts and publications' (Article 16).

The South also went ahead with a plan to establish implementation bodies for exchanges and cooperation as the two sides agreed on the establishment of a Joint Economic Exchanges and Cooperation Commission and other sectoral joint commissions within three months of the effectuation of the Basic Agreement.

Moreover, Seoul proposed and worked to adopt and effectuate the joint Declaration of Denuclearization of the Korean Peninsula as a means of keeping the North from developing nuclear weapons to threaten peace or

refusing to undergo nuclear inspections despite their agreement on non-aggression.

Factors Behind Conclusion of the Basic Accord

The following three parallel factors were instrumental in ensuring the conclusion of the Basic South–North Agreement.

First, the international environment was moving in a direction favourable to such an outcome. With the collapse of Communism and the disintegration of the Soviet Union, the Cold War mechanism that reigned over the international order for some forty years after World War II had been transformed into an age of reconciliation and cooperation. The East–West polarisation thus collapsed.

North Korea's military alliance system was weakened and its diplomatic dilemma deepened, obliging Pyongyang to accept simultaneous entry with the South into the United Nations, an entry which the North had firmly resisted earlier. The containment policy of the United States directed against the Soviet Union, too, came to an end. And, accordingly, the strategic standing of the US forces in Korea has changed. These changes in the international situation served to facilitate new changes in the Cold War system of the Korean Peninsula.

Second, it should be recognised that the adoption of the Basic Accord was also the result of the South's solid and incessant efforts. The 'Northern Policy' based on President Roh Tae-woo's July 7 Declaration, could have been a 'strategy of indirect approach' meaning that a route via Moscow and Beijing could be a shortcut to Pyongyang. The 'Northern Policy', on which the government placed exceptional emphasis, was a resounding success.

Moreover, Seoul offered the Korean National Community Unification Formula as a 'strategy of direct approach', and took the initiative in holding the South–North High-Level Talks to prompt the North to open up, even if only partially. One point that should be made here is that in this process, internal liberalisation and democratisation efforts in the South contributed much to cultivating the unification capability. As radical forces in the South declined, Seoul was in a better position to negotiate with the North.

Third, North Korea responded affirmatively. In other words, the North showed flexibility of a kind unseen in the past. It is believed that the North had no choice but to accept Seoul's proposal in their 'strategy for survival' in view of their isolation from the rest of the world, lingering economic difficulties, and the susceptibility of a transitional period for instituting hereditary power succession.

The North may have feared that, if no agreement were worked out at the fifth round of the high-level talks, the '92 Team Spirit military exercise would be staged, leading to the suspension of the South–North dialogue and the subsequent deadlock of inter-Korean relations following the birth of a new government through elections in the South.

The North may have judged that, if the South–North dialogue were to break up, they would have no chance to normalise relations with Japan, face greater international pressure for nuclear inspections, and experience deeper isolation from the world community—a development which, they feared, would only serve to aggravate their economic difficulties and accelerate a threat to their political system.

When did North Korea begin to show signs of a change in its policy? In retrospect, until as recently as the third round of high-level talks, the North used the inter-Korean dialogue only as a means of 'softening' their external image while feigning to be interested in the dialogue.

Their first turnaround was displayed in May 1991 when Pyongyang publicly announced its intention of joining the United Nations and partially moderated its policy toward the South. It is assumed that advice from China was in the backdrop of such moderation. And it appeared that Kim Il-sung's visit to China in October 1991 was a significant event that had a substantial effect on the North's policy change.

However, what should be noted here is that the signs of the North's policy change were not for a change that would alter their political–social system but rather for a change that would further cement their totalitarian system. This stand was well displayed in Kim Jong-il's 3 January 1992 statement, 'Historical Lesson of Socialist Construction and the General Policy of Our Party'. The North was asserting that if their existing system were to be consolidated, the need would arise to reconstruct their economy, readjust their external relations and improve inter-Korean relations.

In short, the conclusion we can draw is that the Basic South–North Agreement was a feat South Korea attained by making full use of various opportune factors like the needs of North Korea and the flow of the international situation in a favourable direction.

Future Problems

Today, unification is an approaching reality, not a mere dream. South and North Korea have now entered a stage where they discuss and implement solutions to concrete issues one by one, rather than engaging in emotional and fruitless debate.

The immediate task is how to translate the Basic Agreement into practice. Haste is not advisable. Still, what is important is the wisdom to make full use of various favourable factors in the international environment.

Currently, political, military, and exchanges and cooperation subcommittees, as well as a Joint Nuclear Control Commission, are in operation. However, we should not be overly optimistic about their future. Overnight change can hardly be expected in Pyongyang's basic stance simply because of the effectuation of the Basic Agreement. Both sides, which have gone through an age of confrontation and distrust over a long period of time, should patiently cope with problems, being aware that rough paths inevitably lie ahead.

Some sectors of South Korean society question whether North Korea can be trusted, or if anything after all can genuinely be put into practice between the two sides of Korea. But, we have to work to 'create' improved inter-Korean relations and favourable conditions for unification, though they could in some way 'arise' in and of themselves. Even if the North had some ulterior intent, we must take initiatives and lead the North, telling them, 'Now that we have agreed, let us translate it into action'.

As for implementation of the Basic South–North Agreement, it appears that there are some areas where accords could be implemented earlier and others where implementation could be delayed. Matters like material exchanges and economic cooperation could progress quickly. Projects related to dispersed families, such as the creation of a meeting centre at Panmunjom and the postal exchanges, could also be carried out immediately if North Korea would agree.

One area where implementation is unlikely to be carried out is in the sector of free personnel exchanges. Since North Korea would not tolerate such winds of freedom to blow through its closed society, personnel exchanges would be limited to controlled numbers only. They would try to stave off any inflow of information. Similarly it would take quite a long time before the two sides are able to resolve military issues and expect satisfactory progress on the issue of arms reduction.

Seoul expects North Korea to adopt a policy of peaceful coexistence along the lines of the "86 Budapest Appeal', switch its military strategy to a 'defensive defence strategy', and realise arms reduction of its own accord under the principle of reasonable sufficiency.

North Korea is also expected to be more positive on the question of South–North economic cooperation. The goal of inter-Korean economic exchanges and cooperation may well be to improve the North's economy to a certain level, thereby to realise balanced economic development between the South and the North, and to form a National Economic Community provided for unification. In the course of inter-Korean economic exchanges, we must therefore help the North Korean economy transform itself in an orderly manner into a more efficient economic system where creativity can be respected.

The fact that the cost of East and West German unification was in the range of 750 billion dollars and that Germany now suffers much from unification after affects such as rising unemployment, inflationary trend and socio-cultural frictions (so-called crises of homogeneity, reliability and public peace), suggests much to us.

Some studies estimate Korean unification cost would require $200 billion to $400 billion. However, I believe that if South Korea and advanced nations like Japan and the United States were to help North Korea rebuild its economy, as well as to open itself to foreign capital and technology, a sound unification approach could be achieved whereby the costs could be reduced to a minimum and also the after affects of unification could be minimised.

Conclusion

The Korean National Community Unification Formula is a method whereby a national community is to be constructed along with the North as a partner, and then unification could be achieved by itself after differences in living standards or in the ways of thinking are reduced in due course.

Lately, North Korea seems to pursue practical interests rather than ideology in response to events on the international scene. Pragmatists, too, are increasingly likely to emerge. Policy-makers appear to be trying to copy the 'Chinese model' of economic construction without harm to the political system. North Korea's signing of the Basic South–North Agreement and the Joint Declaration of Denuclearization may well be affirmatively taken as its recognition of the need for change or a declaration of the beginning of change.

Since the North faces the dilemma of maintaining its political system while overcoming economic difficulties and international isolation, the South must wisely induce the North to implement smooth and steady change.

The Korean Peninsula is now in the stage of historical transition. The features of a transitional period involve a blending of both past and future and both function and inverse function, as well as the appearance of opportunities and challenges. If a person is concerned only with danger, he may plunge into conservatism. If he thinks only about opportunities, he may expose himself to dangers. Koreans must challenge problems wisely with new thinking. In the sense that we ourselves are the master of history and destiny, we must seize and use given opportunities tactfully.

The inter-Korean question is an issue on which all citizens of the South and the North should agree on and carry out. In this new environment, Koreans find themselves at a stage where there is an acute need for nationwide determination to resolve the national issue independently with 'new thinking'.

The date of unification, a wish of the nation, is now within visible range. The South and the North should overcome the forty-seven-year-long bitter history of mutual distrust and confrontation and forge a new historical chapter of reconciliation and cooperation, advancing the day of peaceful unification.

16 Korean Reunification: A Seoul Perspective

KIM HAK-JOON

Introduction

As the 'revolution' of Eastern Europe in 1989–90 ushered in a new era in East–West relations concomitant with the rapid realisation of the peaceful unification of the two Germanies as well as the two Yemens, the Korean problem has become the focus of increasing attention. Coming on the heels of significant changes in South Korea's relationship with the Soviet Union as evinced by the San Francisco summit meeting between President Roh Tae-woo and President Mikhail Gorbachev in June 1990, and the subsequent establishment of diplomatic relations between Seoul and Moscow in September 1990, Seoul's 'Northern Policy' has introduced a new phase of cooperation with its former antagonists. At the same time, recent press reports have suggested that both Moscow and Beijing have begun to 'pressure' North Korea to enact at least some reforms and to also expedite progress in the on-and-off South–North dialogue.[1] But the process of peaceful and incremental integration between the two Koreas has been stifled by mutual hostility and the lack of any wide-ranging confidence-building mechanisms.

Whatever the prospects may be for unification between the two Koreas in the 1990s, it is important to note also the changes in South Korea since the 1980s which have influenced the entire spectrum of the domestic unification debate. For example, after the enunciation of the June 29 Declaration on Democratization in 1987 by President Roh (then Chairman of the ruling Democratic Justice Party which was reconstituted in February 1990

---

[1] *Korea Times*, 19 June 1990.

as the Democratic Liberal Party together with the former Reunification and Democratic Party and the New Democratic Republican Party)[2] the unification issue has been a source of major debate within South Korea across the political spectrum, but particularly amongst the student movement and the more radical political organisations. In addition, a series of developments, including the visit to North Korea by a number of prominent South Korean dissidents in 1989, have resulted in a growing demand for a more effective unification policy on the part of the South Korean government. At the same time, the increasingly pluralised and at times polarised debate within South Korea on the unification issue has meant that the government no longer has a monopoly on the conduct of relations with North Korea. Therefore, as the domestic and international environment becomes increasingly complex, South Korea's policy towards North Korea in the 1990s will warrant a more complete and effective posture than ever before. At this crucial juncture, this paper seeks to examine some formulae, e.g., the Korean National Community Formula, the Unified South–North Systems Formula, and the Korean National Community Unification Formula, proposed by the South Korean government in 1989 in relation to various concepts of the unification of multi-system nations.

Some Reflections on the Methods for the Unification of the Two Koreas

In the course of comparing South and North Korea's unification policies over the years, it has been perceived that North Korea from the earlier period has placed greater emphasis on a single structure under which the two Koreas can be unified, while the South has only in the recent period come up with a similar proposal. For instance, since 1960 North Korea has consistently called for a confederation between the two Koreas, and since 1980 it has articulated the so-called Democratic Confederate Republic of Koryo Proposal which upholds the principle of confederacy for a unified state with the official state name of Koryo. In South Korea's case, however, it was only in 1982 that it first proposed a future prospect for a unified state under the National Reconciliation and Democratic Unification Proposal which stressed the creation of a unified and a democratic state built on the principles of nationalism, democracy, independence, and wel-

---

2   Hakjoon Kim, 'New Political Development with a Vision for the 1990s and Beyond', *Korea and World Affairs*, vol. 14, no. 1 (Spring 1990), pp. 34–53.

fare.[3] Whilst this was an improvement it still did not include, for example, the official name of the yet-to-be-unified state.

Therefore, it is necessary for the South Korean government to develop a more realistic unification proposal which takes into account how to develop a single systematic framework for the South and the North, or to put it more simply, how to create a single roof or a hat over the South and the North. Such a state of events ushered in calls from the opposition political parties, as well as the opposition at large, including the 'Confederation of the Republics Proposal' (the Kim Dae Jung proposal), 'Confederation' (proposed by Rev Moon Ik Hwan) or the 'Korean National Confederation Proposal' which was called for by the Reunification and Democracy Party, which has been merged into the ruling Democratic Liberal Party.[4]

Seen from these perspectives, it was imperative for the South Korean government to come up with a unification policy which included some form of systematic integration of the two Koreas, and that is probably why the National Unification Board formulated in early 1989 the Korean National Community and the Unified South–North Systems Formulae. Specifically, then Minister of National Unification Lee Hong-koo announced on 5 January 1989 that the government was considering a confederation based on a 'One Nation, Two Systems' framework which would eventually lead towards the creation of a one nation, one state system.[5] In September, 1990, the South Korean government finally announced the Korean National Community Unification Formula.

Then, why has the South been so tardy? To answer this question, it is important to recall the legal basis of the conduct of the South Korean government's unification policy.

From the First Republic until the current Sixth Republic, the constitution of the Republic of Korea has stipulated that its territory consists of the whole Korean Peninsula and its adjacent islands, and the current constitution of the Sixth Republic (Article 3) maintains a similar clause. The basic

---

3   For a comparison of the two proposals, see Hakjoon Kim, *Unification Policies of South and North Korea, 1945–1985: A Comparative Study* (Seoul: Seoul National University Press, 1986), pp. 400–6

4   For other references, refer to Ho-Jin Kim, 'The Opposition and Students' Unification Discussion and Unification Policy Posture', in Research Department of the Dong-a Ilbo (eds), *How to Achieve Unification: A Symposium on South–North Unification Proposals* (Seoul: The Dong-a Ilbo, 1988). In addition, see Jung Tae-Yoon, 'The Progressive Alliance's Unification Policy', *Minjok Jiseong*, April 1988, pp. 161–6; Park Kwan-Yong, 'The Korean National Community Unification Proposal', ibid., April 1988, pp. 142–7. (All three works are in Korean).

5   *Korea Herald*, 1 January 1989.

spirit of this clause is legislated in the more specific form in the former anti-communist law and the present national security law which stipulates that the Democratic People's Republic of Korea is an anti-state organisation which illegally occupies a part of the territory of the Republic of Korea. As a result, the basic posture of the South Korean government has rested in the allegation that the citizens of North Korea should be free from such an illegal occupation and that it is the legal duty of the South Korean government to dissolve the anti-state organisation in the North and to also retake the territorial area which was illegally occupied. Such a position was based also on South Korea's own interpretation of a resolution by the third United Nations General Assembly in 1948. Although it stipulated that the government of the Republic of Korea, which was formed on the basis of an election observed by the United Nations, was the only legitimate government in the areas where that election was held, the South Korean government used this resolution to solidify its position that it was the only legitimate government in the Korean peninsula. This basic posture was reflected in the adoption of the South Korean version of the Hallstein Doctrine which was in effect until the early 1970s, i.e., given that South Korea was the only legal government in the Korean Peninsula, the South Korean government broke off relations with those states which recognised North Korea since that would legitimise an anti-state organisation as a state.

The South Korean government's position was widely accepted throughout the 1950s in the international community, but after the 1960s, particularly with the rise of the Non-Aligned Movement, a growing trend was visible which articulated that North Korea should also be recognised by the international community. As a result, the basic quandary confronting the South Korean government was that if it accepted the international community's acceptance of the two Koreas, such a move would in fact prove to be contradictory of South Korea's basic position which held that the Democratic People's Republic of Korea was an anti-state organisation. Therefore, in order to reduce the South Korean government's quandary, succeeding constitutions which were adopted after 1972 have included provisions calling for the peaceful unification of the Korean Peninsula, implying that the South recognises the North at least as an independent political entity. On 7 July 1988, the South went one step forward by declaring that the North is the South's partner in pursuing national reconciliation and unification.

A brief overview of the German example, for instance, reveals a different approach towards unification. As is well known, following the partitioning of Germany after World War II and the creation of the German Democratic Republic in the east and the Federal Republic of Germany in the west, East Germany officially advocated the two-German-states theory, arguing that there existed the two equal German states. From this perspective, it called for the eventual creation of a confederated German state on the principle of equality. West Germany also recognised, albeit tacitly, the existence of two German states. Although, until the enunciation of *Ostpolitik* by Chancellor Willy Brandt in the late 1960s, West Germany continued to apply the Hallstein Doctrine advocating West Germany's sole representation claim over the whole Germany, West Germany's territorial jurisdiction only applied within its own border. In other words, the provisions of the Basic Law of West Germany were only applicable to the territory under the jurisdiction of West Germany. Therefore, West Germany from the onset accepted the existence of two German states as a *fait accompli*. Such a position enabled West Germany to conclude the Basic Treaty with East Germany in 1972 which allowed for the two Germanies to enter the United Nations.[6] Nevertheless, it should be pointed out that under Article 23 of the West German Basic Law, the provinces comprising East Germany could opt to enter the West German federal structure.

As for the Chinese example, both the People's Republic of China (mainland) and the Republic of China (Taiwan) have maintained their own legitimacy, but since the late 1970s the PRC has maintained the so-called 'One Nation, Two Systems' approach which means that while there is only one China, there are two different systems. In contrast, some scholars in Taiwan, as well as Chinese scholars in the United States with ties to Taiwan, have called for the so-called 'One Nation, Multi-system State'.[7] Therefore, the Chinese approach stresses that although there is only one Chinese nation there are also two systems.

Given these contrasting positions, is it feasible to call for a similar approach to the Korean problem? In light of the strong nationalistic tradition in both South and North Korea, it is difficult to imagine that a 'Two Koreas' policy could be officially accepted by either of the two sides as in the German case. But seen from this perspective, it could be asserted that the current situation in the Korean Peninsula has moved perhaps closer to the Chinese model for the following reasons: (1) assuming the adoption of the 'One Nation, Two Systems' approach; (2) considering also that neither side gives up on the notion that it retains unique representative powers but nevertheless recognises each other not as a state but as a system; and (3)

6   John H. Herz, 'Germany' in Gregory Henderson et al., *Divided Nations in a Divided World* (New York: David Mckay, 1974), pp. 9–10.

7   Yung Wei, 'The Unification and Division of Multi-system Nations: A Comparative Analysis of Basic Concepts, Issues, and Approaches', in Hungdah Chiu and Robert Downen (eds), *Multi-System Nations and International Law: The International Status of Germany, Korea and China* (Baltimore: School of Law, University of Maryland, 1981), p. 62.

understanding that both sides move towards the formation of a common-wealth or a union.

Nevertheless, as has been noted above, any such rapprochement between the two Koreas may prove to be difficult for a number of reasons. To begin with, in the event of North Korea's acceptance of a 'Two Koreas' policy, the Kim Il Sung regime will certainly face serious reper-cussions domestically since North Korea has consistently called for the 'liberation' of South Korea. As for South Korea, should it revise its con-stitution which limits its territorial jurisdiction to the area under its realis-tic control in order to enhance the basis for the peaceful coexistence between the two Koreas, it will confront domestic opposition. More specifically, were the South Korean government to undertake such a move as a measure to seek a more rational and peaceful solution towards unifi-cation by temporarily stabilising the state of partition, the South Korean government would be accused of being anti-unification by some of the more strident opposition groups within South Korea. Therefore, it seems prudent to suggest that the South Korean government should place a greater emphasis on decreasing incrementally such uncertainties as it seeks to advocate a more realistic and implementable unification policy although it remains uncertain as to how much public support such a move will receive.

Based on the reflections noted in this study thus far, what are some of the steps which could be taken in the formulation of a unification proposal based on some type of systematic framework? The key question is whether it is possible to formulate a realistic unification proposal which takes into account the existence of the North Korean government while maintaining at its minimum the principles of the Republic of Korea. The answer may be found in the principle of equality between South and North Korea. Specifically, efforts to solve a number of issues should be imple-mented after recognising the equality of the two Koreas. For instance, as based on the affirmation of the principle of equality in the July 4 1972 Joint Communiqué, systematic efforts to realise peaceful unification would be facilitated if both sides are willing to reorder their respective domestic laws and systems. If this proves to be the case, it means that both sides must resolutely discard the notion of absorbing each other's system. This means that each side must recognise each other as they are in an effort to peacefully resolve their differences.

Nevertheless, it is difficult to imagine at the present time that the two Koreas are likely to discard the so-called sole representation claim since it would prove to be untenable domestically for a number of reasons. For South Korea it is difficult to imagine that it would readily give up its cur-rent position when North Korea insists on unifying the peninsula under its own terms. Therefore, it seems realistic to assert that for the time being both sides will continue to maintain their respective positions, while striving to reach some form of *modus vivendi* on the basis of the principle of equality.

A Review of the Korean National Community Proposal

Based on the points which have been assessed thus far, it is fitting to analyse more specifically the basis of the Korean National Community concept. This particular phrase can be said to refer to two central themes. First, it entails a general reference to the homogeneity of the Korean people who have enjoyed a common heritage which embodies such themes as a common cultural, social, and economic community which could eventually lead towards the formation of a common political community. Second, it can be seen specifically as a counter-proposal to North Korea's own confederation proposal.

One of the first South Korean scholars to stress the Korean national community approach was Lee Hong-koo. In 1976, Lee, then a professor of political science at Seoul National University, stressed that the uniqueness of this proposal was based on the fact that the initiative for unification should not be led by the government or the political leadership but rather by the people at large, and that the first priority should be placed on the welfare of the people as the initial step towards reconciliation.[8]

Another example can be cited as the so-called 'National Co-Prosperity' proposal by five leading political scientists. In 1984, they stipulated that bilateral South–North cooperation must be emphasised in order to achieve peaceful unification. Moreover, they argued that through political negotiation and national reconciliation South and North Korea should exchange missions and also hold summit meetings between their respective leaders.[9]

Still another proposal, the Korean National Community Formula which was put forth by the Reunification and Democratic Party in 1988, consisted of achieving unification on the basis of independence, reconciliation, incremental progress, peace, and mass participation. This proposal also included steps towards undertaking democratic reforms within South Korea and to also push for democratic reforms in North Korea followed by gradual exchange across all fronts, including the strengthening of non-

---

[8] Hongkoo Lee, 'The Korean Commonwealth and the Asian Community', a paper presented at the 30th International Congress of Human Sciences in Asia and North Africa, Mexico City, Mexico, 3–8 August 1976.

[9] Kim Deok, Ahn Byung-Joon, Rhee Sang-Woo, Lee Hongkoo, and Han Sung-Joo, *National Coprosperity Unification Proposal*, a project report submitted to the South–North Dialogue Bureau, National Unification Board, 1984 (in Korean).

political cooperation followed by cooperation in the political and diplomatic arenas which would lead ultimately towards the objective of developing a 'One Nation, One System' structure.[10]

The final example can be cited as the unification proposal put forth by the opposition figure Kim Rak-Joong, the so-called 'Unified Koryo Commonwealth'. In this proposal, Kim argued that, on the basis of the conclusion of a basic treaty between South and North Korea, a Koryo National Federal Assembly should be created which would strive to achieve peaceful unification. He also stipulated that the youth of South and North Korea would incrementally assume the authority to charter the course for a united Koryo state which would adhere to the principle of non-aligned neutrality.[11]

In a more recent vein, then Minister of National Unification Lee Hongkoo announced on 5 January 1989 that the Korean National Community and the Korean Commonwealth Proposal was made in order to foster the creation of an interim national commonwealth based on cooperation. He further noted that based on the principle of 'One Nation, Two Systems', a commonwealth could be created which would promote all aspects of exchange. Specifically, both South and North Korea on the basis of accepting each other's system would create a national commonwealth so that in all areas, excluding diplomatic and military fields, material and people exchanges would be promoted so that confidence would be restored, and on that foundation a system unification would be formed on the basis of a 'One Nation, Two States' process.[12] Minister Lee's usage of the term 'Korean National Commonwealth' is referred to here not as a specific measure to counter North Korea's confederacy proposal but as a reflection of a broader term used by President Roh on the occasion of announcing his Special Statement on Unification on 7 July 1988 which called for the eventual creation of a 'One Nation, One State' system.

Seen from this perspective, the fostering of a Korean National Community concept would be affected by a series of events during the course of development of a system unification. In other words, consistent with the winds of reform in the socialist bloc, it is not difficult to imagine that in the not-too-distant future, North Korea would also be influenced by South

---

[10] For additional details, see Jang Myung-Bong, 'A New Unification Proposal: "Commonwealth" or "Confederation"', *Shin Dong-a* (February 1989), pp. 156–7 (in Korean).

[11] Kim Rak-Joong, 'Korean National Community Unification Proposal: Its Problems and Limits', *Minjok Jiseong* (November 1989), pp. 37–43 (in Korean).

[12] Hongkoo Lee, 'Unification through a Korean Commonwealth: Blueprint for a National Community', *Korea and World Affairs*, vol. 13, no. 4 (Winter 1989), pp. 635–46.

Korea in the event that exchange and cooperation become formalised between the two Koreas. In such an instance, one could also expect that a movement towards liberalisation would also take place within North Korea which could embody the acceptance of the principles of liberal democracy and a market economy. In such circumstances, the Korean National Community concept would encompass aspects of a welfare and ideological community.

Some Reflections on the 'Unified South–North Systems' Concept

Among the points cited in the Korean National Community proposal, the key element of obfuscation lies in the concept of a unification of South–North Systems scheme. To begin with, the concept of a confederation can be examined which means the integration of states, i.e., the integration of sovereign territorial nation-states. Moreover, under this process a central federal government is created with circumscribed powers based on the representatives of the integrated states but which does not supersede the nationals nor the governments of the respective member states. Also, since each state retains sovereignty it can opt to remove itself from the confederation should it choose to exercise that option. While there are exceptions, the concept of a commonwealth which is the point of focus here differs from the concept of confederacy noted above. Two cases of a state which moved from a confederated structure to that of a commonwealth can be cited as the American example, from 1781 until 1789 when the American Confederation was existent, and the example of Switzerland until it formed a commonwealth constitution in 1848 when it was organised as a Swiss Confederation though continued to retain that title even after it was changed to a commonwealth system.

To reiterate, a confederated state structure recognises the sovereignty of the member states and is a conference system based on the membership of sovereign states.[13] A current example can be cited as the United Nations. Based on such a perspective, it could be argued that as the first step towards mutual and institutional recognition towards the process of peaceful unification, South and North Korea could form a confederation as an interim measure towards a more formal integration. Nevertheless, whereas the creation of confederations can be found in states with different nationalities, languages, histories, and cultures, the creation of a confederation among a homogeneous nationality such as two Koreas cannot

---

13 Ivo D . Duchacek, *Power Maps: Comparative Politics of Constitutions* (Santa Barbara, Calif.: American Bibliographical Center–Clio Press, 1973), pp. 143–4.

be found. Moreover, such a concept—even as an interim measure—could be criticised for prolonging the 'One Nation, Two States' system.

A contrasting scheme, however, can be found in the concept of a federation. In this example, those members who seek to join a federation give up their respective sovereignty and as a result, sovereignty is exercised by the newly formed federal government. As a result, a practical outcome of this scheme is that once a federation has been made, it can be said that a unified state has been created. However, if this approach is applied to the Korean context, it is difficult to imagine that a federal government would be able to exercise sovereign powers or for that matter, that both South and North Korea would completely renounce their respective sovereignties. In other words, owing to the fact that both Koreas are reluctant to renounce their sovereign powers it can be assumed that national discord would follow in the event that a united and federal state is formed.

As a result, an intermediary stage between confederation and federation can be seen in the concept of a systems commonwealth. If the concept of a confederation is said to retain the principle of 'One Nation, Two States' and a federation retains the principle of 'One Nation, Two Provincial Governments', the concept of a systems commonwealth is based on the principle of 'One Nation, Two Systems'. In other words, while South and North Korea would both retain their respective sovereign rights in the conduct of international relations, both sides would maintain bilateral relations on the basis of a national commonwealth in order to overcome outstanding differences. In summary, it can be said that the systems commonwealth proposal has the potential to satisfy the conditions which realistically divide the two Koreas, while at the same time striving for the common goal of unification. In turn, it can be said that while the basis for unification is strong under the terms of a federation, the realistic problems confronting South and North Korea exclude this option, whereas the basis for unification by a confederate structure is weak.

What is the likely response to the systems commonwealth approach? To begin with, this proposal would go a long way towards reducing the tension between the two Koreas since it would seek to promote national cooperation and reconciliation on the basis of recognising each other's system. Therefore, the major positive attribute of the Korean National Community proposal lies in the fact that it seeks to recognise the existence of two different systems in the Korean Peninsula, the Republic of Korea and the Democratic People's Republic of Korea, and that further it seeks to improve bilateral relations on the basis of exchange and cooperation which would lay the foundation for peaceful unification.

The Korean National Community Unification Proposal

With regard to the Korean National Community proposal which has been assessed above, it is instructive to note that President Roh on 11 September 1989, announced the Korean National Community Unification Proposal, and as an interim step this proposal called for the creation of a Korean Commonwealth.[14] The overall content of this proposal does not differ from the national community concept which has been described in previous sections.

According to Ahn Byung-Joon, it is important to bear in mind that the term National Commonwealth refers to the sum total of efforts which must be made in order to achieve peaceful unification based on the principles of peace and cooperation, that by referring to this process as one of a 'National Commonwealth' one can overcome the realistic difficulty of referring to a particular system or political entity, and that the preservation of mutual interests is ensured under the tenets of this proposal.[15] Based on this interim step and without discarding one's sovereignty, a process of reconciliation and cooperation can be built towards the ultimate objective of creating a unified democratic republic. This proposal also warrants attention given that it seeks to overcome the weaknesses in previous unification proposals put forth by the South Korean government, and by stating the willingness to accept the existence of a contending system in the Korean Peninsula, it is a realistic proposal which would go a long way towards reducing tension between the two Koreas.

At its core, the formula's implementation is based on the following three major steps. First, to build mutual confidence on the basis of a South–North dialogue and to hold a South–North summit meeting, including the adoption of a Korean National Community Charter. Second, the creation of a Korean Commonwealth, being a common sphere of national life to promote common prosperity and to restore national homogeneity. And third, the creation of a unified assembly and government based on national elections as stipulated in a unified constitution so that a unified and democratic republic can be formed.

From a structural viewpoint, a Council of Ministers would be co-chaired by the Prime Ministers of the South and the North and would comprise around ten cabinet-level officials from each side, and a number of standing committees could be created to deal with diplomatic, political, and military issues. Such bodies could then specifically discuss ways to

---

14 National Unification Board, *To Build National Community through the Korean Commonwealth — A Blue Print for Korean Unification* (Seoul: National Unification Board, 1989).

15 Ahn Byung-Joon, 'In Search of a New Unification Proposal', *Minjok Jiseong*, September 1988, pp. 189–90 (in Korean).

accelerate political dialogues, agree on military confidence-building measures, the transformation of the current Armistice Agreement into a peace treaty and changing the demilitarisation zone into a Peace Zone.

The Korean Commonwealth would have a Council of Presidents as the highest decision-making organ, the already-mentioned Council of Ministers, and a Council of Representatives to be composed of equal numbers of members of the legislatures in both the South and the North. The Council of Representatives would draft a constitution for a unified republic and develop methods and procedures to bring about unification. With agreement on a draft of the constitution, the next step would be to promulgate it through democratic methods and procedures including the holding of a general election under the unified constitution, which would then lead to the formulation of a unified legislature and a unified government. Thus, a unified and democratic republic would be created.

What changes, then, did this formula introduce in Seoul's unification policy? Most importantly, for the first time Seoul has spelled out in explicit terms the principal structural components of an interim stage on the road to unity. Second, the new formula differs from its predecessors in delineating the contours of a unified Korea, which shall have a bicameral parliament, shall be a democratic republic, and shall gear its policies toward the goals of promoting the welfare of all members of the national community, safeguarding the permanent security of the nation, and maintaining friendly relations with other countries. Third, the manner in which the Korean National Community Unification Formula was prepared marks a notable departure from previous practice. Whereas the 1982 formula was prepared without any appreciable input from the public, the 1989 formula is the product of the most extensive consultation between the government and the people in the ROK's history. Finally, the new formula is said to have accommodated some elements of the North Korean proposals on unification. All the organs that will make up the Korean Commonwealth will thus embody the principle of absolute equality between the two Koreas.[16]

Concluding Remarks

With the revolutionary change of the international political order which made possible the reunification of two Germanies, discussions on the reunification of South and North Korea has become more lively than ever. Koreans, however, admit that the unification of the Korean Peninsula does not seem possible in the near future. Koreans all know that there are significant differences between the cases of Germany and Korea.

---

[16] Byung Chul Koh, 'Seoul's New Unification Formula', *Korea and World Affairs*, vol. 13, no. 4 (Winter 1989), pp. 662–4.

Many proposals and ideas on the unification methods of multi-system nations have been presented. Even though I think an institutional approach is very important in talking about the unification of South and North Korea, the present stage of inter-Korean relationship, however, asks for more lively discussions on methods to build confidence between the two systems and to realise free exchanges of people, materials and communication between two Koreas. No matter how desirable an idea on the unification of multi-system nations South or North Korea suggests, a system which does not incorporate trust in the other's real intention will never be accepted.

Obviously, the Korean National Community Unification proposal will not be readily accepted by North Korea, nor is it feasible to expect that any real progress can be made in the foreseeable future. Nevertheless, as the events in Eastern Europe have shown, hitherto unexpected political change can happen in North Korea, although there exist differences between North Korea and Eastern Europe. Moreover, with the relaxation of tensions between the East and West as evinced by the new phase of co-operation between Washington and Moscow, it may not be entirely unrealistic to assume that inter-Korean relations may also improve to the extent that the Korean National Community Unification proposal would become a solid basis for inter-Korean negotiations in the 1990s.

17 The Two Koreas and Rapprochement: Foundations for Progress?

JAMES COTTON

In 1971 and again in 1984 the two Korean states initiated a series of contacts which were both ostensibly aimed at achieving reconciliation and the first steps to an eventual unification. On both occasions documents were signed and pledges given, but the processes then foundered in an atmosphere of mutual acrimony.

The reasons for the failure of these early attempts at reconciliation are complex. The division of Korea since 1948 had created powerful interests, military and political, the *raison d'être* of which was the maintenance of antagonistic division. The most important factor was the inability of North Korea to accept without equivocation South Korea as a legitimate authority and dialogue partner. Although engaging in negotiations with Seoul, Pyongyang never ceased to represent the government of South Korea as a creature of the United States, and always attempted at some stage to involve other groups (typically, those critical of their own government) in these negotiations. For their part the authorities in Seoul emphasised the need to move first to a recognition of the status quo, which tactic was open to the interpretation that they did not really wish to realise unification.

The third round of the North–South contacts which began in earnest with the meeting in September 1990 between the prime ministers of the two states, at first repeated many of the steps taken in the previous rounds. Differing positions were stated but there seemed little prospect of their reconciliation. The North wished the two sides to adopt a non-aggression declaration which would commit the South to severing its military alliance with the United States. By contrast, the South wished to proceed by implementing a series of political and military confidence building measures in order to ensure that any comprehensive agreement between the two governments (such as that signed with much fanfare but no result in 1972) would be erected on a real foundation.

As the contacts developed—stalling in early 1991 but reviving later in the year—the issue of North Korea's nuclear ambitions came to have a prominent place.[1] Contradictory statements from Pyongyang as to its intentions on this issue increased apprehension in Seoul and (with the example of Iraq in mind) elsewhere in the international community.

Pyongyang had avoided assenting to the International Atomic Energy Agency (IAEA) system of nuclear safeguards after having signed the Nuclear Non-Proliferation Treaty (NPT) in 1985. North Korea sought consistently to link its acceptance of these safeguards to a withdrawal of American nuclear weapons from South Korea. An announcement that North Korea was to accept the IAEA regime was rescinded and then restated, conveying the impression that there were important differences of view within the policy-making circle in Pyongyang. Finally South Korea and the United States announced that a programme of American troop reductions already being implemented would be halted until the position was clarified.

The 1991 Agreements

In December 1991, however, the two sides made public the text of an agreement covering both reconciliation and provisions for realising mutual non-aggression as well as various types of exchanges and contacts. The twenty-five articles of the agreement (subsequently to be ratified in each of the states) are extremely comprehensive, but the ease and speed with which they were composed suggest that there has been some rethinking by the parties of the issues involved.

It is clear from the format and content of the agreement, and from a comparison of the document with the negotiating drafts circulated by the delegations at successive prime ministerial negotiations, that both sides have been prepared to modify their positions, with North Korea demonstrating unusual flexibility. From the point of view of North Korea, though the agreement incorporates six articles concerned with measures to promote non-aggression (a long-standing North Korean aim), none could be taken specifically to require South Korea to abandon the American alliance. From the point of view of South Korea, though a number of social and economic confidence building measures are adopted in the document (in keeping with the South Korean insistence that such would be

---

1   Larry A. Niksch, 'North Korea's Nuclear Weapons Program', CRS Issue Brief IB91141 (Washington: Congressional Research Service, 1991).

the foundation of any lasting accord), all the various measures are incorporated in a single declaration of grand principles.

From the perspective of the past history of North–South Korean exchange, it is noteworthy that the concrete measures to be realised are defined in very general language, and in the most difficult area of all, military confidence building measures, the actual steps to be taken have been left to a Military Committee to decide. Both sides commit themselves to exchanges in diverse fields, freedom for their residents to visit the other state, and the resumption of every kind of communications and economic intercourse. However, again, no specific steps are stated.

The process moved a stage further when, at the end of December, an agreement was announced which appeared to resolve that issue which had become by 1991 the key to the Korean confrontation, the problem of nuclear weapons on the peninsula. Both sides declared that they would not store or possess such weapons, nor the means to produce them. They also stated their commitment to establishing an inspectorate to verify by mutual observation the absence of such weapons and facilities.

Again the concessions are noteworthy. North Korea had always linked the nuclear issue with the alliance between Seoul and Washington. Latterly the North Korean position had been that a withdrawal from Korean territory of American nuclear weapons would only be sufficient if accompanied by a declaration or 'guarantee' that such weapons would not be used against it. Such a guarantee has not of course been forthcoming. For their part the South Koreans have assented to a significant limitation upon their military relationship with the United States, since this text commits them in addition to refusing to 'accept' nuclear weapons, a phraseology which could be interpreted as implying a prohibition upon visitations by (potentially) nuclear armed naval vessels.

It was widely reported that unwritten mutual concessions helped provide the foundation for the agreement. North Korea undertook to sign and implement the IAEA safeguards agreement while South Korea promised to cancel the annual 'Team Spirit' joint military exercises with the United States.[2]

So far it seems that progress in this round of North–South contacts has been remarkable. While concrete measures are still lacking it would be premature to regard these developments as the beginning of a qualitatively new stage. When a South Korean team has been permitted to inspect the alleged nuclear reprocessing facility at Yongbyon, and a North Korean team has visited the hangars of the American air-base at Kunsan, then we could be sure that real progress had been achieved. However, even to have come this far some conditions must have led to the adopting of a new perspective by the policy-makers involved, especially in North Korea. In

---

[2]   *Far Eastern Economic Review*, 9 January 1992, p. 10.

brief, what circumstances have changed by comparison with the early 1970s and the mid-1980s?

South Korean Policy

In South Korea it is clear that the democratisation achieved in 1987 has imposed new requirements upon the political process including in the area of unification policy. Public apprehension at the prospect of a nuclear armed North Korea required new efforts to seek rapprochement, both to placate the citizenry as well as to remove any excuse some elements of the military might have to take pre-emptive action (in the manner of Israel's raid upon Iraq's Osirak reactor in 1981). Government estimates of the time it would take for North Korea to possess a nuclear weapon imposed a two year deadline upon the negotiations.

Another more immediate deadline also loomed for Seoul's policy-makers. Elections for the National Assembly were due to be held in March 1992, and the ruling party had also to confront the difficult task of selecting a candidate for the presidential elections scheduled for the end of the year which would choose a successor to President Roh Tae-woo. Facing a revivified opposition the party, somewhat tarnished by charges of corruption and mismanagement, needed to associate itself with policy success. If well managed such success might also serve to keep the deeply factionalised party from dissolving into its constituent groups in the process of selecting Roh's successor.

After the heady successes of *Nordpolitik* and the openings to the Soviet Union and Eastern Europe, the manner of the collapse and death throes of East European socialism had led some more thoughtful members of the governing élite to reassess their approach to Pyongyang. Instead of promoting the isolation and then collapse of the North Korean system as the prelude to unification on terms made in Seoul, they began to see the need to cushion that system from crisis and thus to an extent prolong its life. For one thing the German case illustrated the costs of unification were likely to be ruinous. For another, it could be seen from Romania (where the Ceaucescu cult was modelled directly upon the Kim Il-sung prototype) and elsewhere that the rapid demise of socialism would breed dislocation and discontent which could trigger dangerous disorder. With a million armed troops and weapons widely dispersed in North Korea, the potential for bloodshed and misery was considerable.

Finally, a particular policy choice by South Korea greatly facilitated the framing of the two agreements. Although in part a response to developments in the Soviet Union, President Bush's August 1991 announcement that the United States would withdraw and scrap all theatre nuclear weapons met a long-standing North Korean concern. Although their presence was never officially confirmed, it was widely held that the United States had stationed such weapons in Korea since the 1960s. Subsequently, President Roh was able to declare in December that the territory of South Korea was nuclear free.

North Korean Policy

Evidences for a preoccupation with timetables and deadlines can also be seen in North Korea's policy choices.

The most significant impetus to change for Pyongyang has come from the regime's loss of external patronage. While revolutionary ties still figure in the relations between Kim Il-sung and Deng Xiaoping, China's interest in North Korea has waned. Beijing cannot provide the aid necessary to keep the present model in operation, and in any case is now developing a fruitful economic relationship with South Korea. Thus China in 1991 finally signalled its intention not to block Seoul's application to join the United Nations, a move which forced Pyongyang to reverse one of the stated fundamentals of its policy and seek entry also. Only the continuing influence of Deng Xiaoping and his generation prevented Beijing from opening full diplomatic recognition of Seoul until August 1992.

If China's now only lukewarm attitude has forced readjustments in North Korea's approach, the collapse of the USSR has had an impact upon the foundations of North Korea's world strategy which can only be described as cataclysmic.[3] Already Moscow's recognition of South Korea and Gorbachev's visit, taken together with Soviet insistence that future trade with North Korea be conducted in hard currency, portended the end of the economic, political, and military alliance that had existed since 1948. Until 1990 around 60 per cent of North Korea's trade was conducted with the Soviet Union (to whom it owed a sizeable debt), the Soviet Union continued up to that year to provide significant aid, and was also the source of all high technology armaments (apart from those acquired through the clandestine world arms trade). Even into 1991 the North Korean leadership still appeared to hope that something at least could be retrieved of their ties with Moscow, and their spokesmen were quick to report the coup against Gorbachev whom they had previously condemned for selling the prestige of socialism for Seoul's aid. Now the ending of the USSR's seventy-four year history and the repudiation of

---

3   Eugene Bazhanov and Natasha Bazhanov, 'Soviet Views on North Korea: The Domestic Scene and Foreign Policy', *Asian Survey*, vol. 31 (1991), pp. 1123–38.

- On the occasion of the anniversary of the March First Independence Movement, President Roh urged North Korea to participate in the 1988 Seoul Olympic Games.[19]

- North Korea condemned President Roh's remarks as 'not worth a penny', and maintained that the question of joint hosting of the Olympics could be discussed at the North–South joint conference.[20]

- On 29 March 1988, Kim Jung-ki, a candidate for the Student Council of Seoul National University, issued an open letter to the students of Kim Il-sung University. In the letter he proposed (1) a cross-country march of college students of South and North Korea from 1–14 August and a festival for national unity at Panmunjom, (2) all athletic competition between South and North Korean students at Seoul National University or Kim Il-sung University from 15–17 September and (3) a preparatory meeting at Panmunjom or Geneva on 10 June.[21]

- On 4 April 1988, the Student Committee of Kim Il-sung University issued a letter to the Student Council of Seoul National University. In the letter it accepted the proposal and offered Panmunjom as the venue for the preparatory talks.[22]

- On 21 April 1988, President Roh at his press conference emphasised that the most effective way to improve South–North relations is a South–North summit conference and stated that his term of office will be devoted to pursuing peaceful reunification through South–North cooperation.[23]

- On 14 May 1988, the National Coordinating Council of University Student Representatives of South Korea adopted the agenda for the preparatory talks to be held on 10 June. The agenda included: (1) a cross-country march and an athletic competition, (2) mutual visits of separated families, (3) student exchanges between South and North Korea, and (4) staging of the 1988 Olympic Games for the promotion of national harmony (i.e., joint hosting of the Olympics).[24]

---

19 *Nambukhan Tong-il Daehwa Jeeui Bigyo*, p. 526.

20 Editorial of *Rodong Shinmun*, 3 March 1988.

21 Research Institute of Ideological Issues, *Nambuk Haksaeng Hwoedam Kwalyeon Jaryo* (Materials on South–North Korean Student Conference) (Seoul: Research Institute of Ideological Issues, 1988), pp. 5–6.

22 *Nambukhan Tong-il Daehwa Jeeui Bigyo*, p. 533.

23 Ibid., p. 534.

24 Ibid., p. 534; *Nambuk Haksaeng...*, pp. 9–11.

- On 17 May 1988, the National Confederation of University Student Committees of North Korea issued a letter to all university students of South Korea and accepted the proposal by the South Korean side.[25]

- On 2 June 1988, the Minister of Cultural Affairs and Information of South Korea announced the government position on the unification issue as follows:

  1. Public debate on the unification issue will be encouraged, and the publications of and on North Korea and other communist countries, which have been banned, gradually will be made available to the public.

  2. The government will retain the sole authority to negotiation with North Korea and to make proposals for unification.

  3. The government will make sincere efforts to promote personnel and economic exchanges between South and North Korea.

  He made it clear that the government would not allow private persons or organisations to negotiate with North Korea and make proposals for unification to North Korea. In other words, private persons and organisations may discuss but may not formulate policy on unification.[26]

- On 3 June 1988, Prime Minister Lee Hyun-Jae of South Korea proposed a conference of high-level government officials, to comprise a cabinet member and four lower officials from each side. The agenda will include: (1) joint participation in the 1988 Seoul Olympics, (2) personnel exchanges, (3) the resumption of the existing inter-Korea conferences, such as the Red Cross talks, the economic talks and the inter-parliamentary talks, (4) and other matters of mutual concern.[27]

  The proposal was made through the radio, because the North Korean side refused to receive the letter containing the proposal through the usual channel at Panmunjom. The North Korean side said that if the South Korean side replied to North Korea's letters proposing the joint conference of government authorities, political parties and social organisations, and transmitted the letter of the North Korean university student representatives to their South Korean counterparts, then it would receive the letter.[28]

- A few days later, North Korea changed its mind and expressed a willingness to consider South Korea's proposal for a high-level authorities meeting. On 6 June 1988, the Preparatory Committee for the Joint

---

25 Ibid., p. 537.
26 Ibid., p. 542.
27 Ibid., p. 542.
28 Ibid., p. 543.

socialism has forced in Pyongyang a new approach to political and economic fundamentals.[4]

The forced nature of North Korea's policy innovations should be particularly stressed. From recent (elliptical but still intelligible) statements on the state of the economy, the country faces a severe energy shortage undoubtedly as a result of the fact that Soviet supplies of oil (the Soviet Union being formerly the chief source of this energy input) have all but dried up. Perennial shortages of food and consumer commodities have grown worse, and without an infusion of capital and technological assistance economic crisis looms.

North Korea's need for capital and for trade diversification lies behind the attempt, initiated in 1990, to advance contacts with Japan. However, obstacles emerged in the negotiations undertaken in 1991. North Korea sought reparations not merely for the colonial period, but also for the years from 1965 during which Tokyo recognised Seoul but not Pyongyang. For their part Japan's negotiators did not wish to achieve too much progress in the absence of Seoul–Pyongyang exchanges and while the nuclear issue remained unresolved. North Korea's increasing willingness to treat with South Korea in the latter half of 1991 may be traced to Pyongyang's awareness that this was the key to opening direct and official relations with Japan. A similar calculus has been applied to relations with the United States, with whom Pyongyang had been holding exploratory contacts through diplomats in Beijing, contacts which are now being further pursued in New York.

Although these recent developments are an indication that North Korea's long-standing unification policy has been finally proved unsuccessful, this has been clear for many years though not perhaps to all the members of the North Korean leadership. It may be conjectured that for Pyongyang the 1991 agreements mark not so much an abandonment of previous policy as an attempt to use even the present vicissitudes to the advantage of the leadership's political priorities.

From the early 1970s Kim Il-sung has been committed to handing power on to his eldest son, Kim Jong-il. Much of the inflexibility of North Korean policy in the last decade may be interpreted as a consequence of that strategy. Even amidst the present scramble to frame a viable instrument for reconciliation with Seoul, or perhaps because of it, Kim found time to name his son as supreme commander of the armed forces. The elder Kim (always a close student of events in China) observed how ill the reputation and policy inheritance of Mao Zedong fared at the hands of his successors. The rationale for the family succession was to ensure that, unlike China, there would be no deviation from the correct revolutionary

---

4   Lee Dong-Bok, 'The Soviet Events and Inter-Korean Relations', *Korea and World Affairs*, vol. 15 (1991), pp. 626–39.

path even 'generation after generation'. If significant policy change was required, of course, the rationale for such a succession was destroyed.

Now even Kim Il-sung has been forced to acknowledge, albeit tacitly, that changes must be made. His reasoning is likely to be that if changes have been forced, it is better to give them his personal imprimatur rather than leave them to Kim Jong-il to realise. This would open the latter to charges of 'revisionism', a failing associated with so many fallen leaders of the former socialist world.

The Limits of Policy Reform

Given what has been argued regarding the political parameters within which reform must be realised, but keeping in view the fact that the 1991 reconciliation agreement requires North Korea to implement policies to effect social and economic opening and thus reform, what scope exists for such reform? Even within the limitations imposed by the continuation of the Kim dynasty, some at least of the features of the Chinese model of economic innovation with political stasis could be adopted.

The limited measures to facilitate joint ventures and market opening which were adopted in 1984–85 and then largely shelved could be revived. North Korea could open Special Economic Zones (regulations for which have already been announced) at selected sea ports and border locations to take advantage of comparative advantage in labour costs, proximity to raw materials, and transport connections with the Russian Far East and Manchuria. The Tuman River project (involving collaboration between North Korea, China, and Russia) which was the subject of preliminary studies in 1991, and the attempt to interest the South Korean Daewoo *chaebol* in joint export production facilities at Nampo, are indicators that some elements of this option are presently being considered. North Korean Ministries have already had years of experience supplying the Russian Far East with labour while keeping the individuals concerned separate from the local population. Such an operation would be easier to manage on North Korean territory particularly if (as is the case with the Tuman River) the site concerned was remote from the major centres of population.

Domestic policy would be much harder to manage, given the rigidities and extremes associated with both agricultural and industrial practices. Some concessions to the use of private peasant plots could be the means to a modest agricultural return which might extinguish North Korea's dependence on grain imports (imports which must be paid for in scarce hard currency). Greater enterprise initiative, a measure discussed for some years but yet to be effectively implemented, could introduce a degree of economic rationality in the industrial sphere. And the overall position of

North Korea in the world trading order would be very much transformed if North Korea would accept its obligation to repay its international loans from the 1970s. It would not be beyond the capacity of the economy to do so, and with external capital then becoming available investment in internationally viable undertakings would be possible. There is some indication that the 'reparations' being sought from Japan as part of a mutual recognition package are intended for such investment.

Of course, there are many features of the 'Chinese model' that could not or would not be applied in the North Korean case. North Korea, with its limited market size and relative remoteness could never generate the same degree of interest to outside capital. In addition, the newly-industrialised countries' (NICs) route to modernisation will not be as easy to pursue in the 1990s as it was in the 1970s and 1980s. Moreover it is clear that both Chinese advice and independent North Korean study will incline the leadership to avoid the political dimensions of the Chinese reforms. Against these factors it is already evident that for political as much as for economic reasons international agencies (such as the Asia Development Bank) would be prepared to assist North Korea if the circumstances were acceptable. Multi-lateral investment involving South Korean capital is also a possibility. The Hyundai group have signalled their willingness, even under present conditions, to collaborate in improving North Korea's tourist potential.

So far none of the policies discussed would be beyond the limits of the possible for the Kim dynasty, though agreeing to accept responsibility for international debts, for example, would lead to some loss of face. What is lacking is the knowledge of external conditions necessary to choose the right policy elements, though some cautious experimentation could make good some of this deficiency. Dispensing with the two Kims, however, would open the way to a rapid adoption of such innovations as part of what would probably be a more comprehensive programme.

The Prospects for More Comprehensive Reform

This is not to suggest that a new North Korean leadership is likely to abandon the Kimist legacy except after an extended period. Nor, indeed, is it proposed that Kim Il-sung will do anything other than die while still in power if not in office (which is likely to be assumed by Kim Jong-il). There is the possibility that Kim Jong-il will be shunted aside after his father's demise, though having been now heir apparent for almost two decades and in control of much government business since about 1980 he has had every opportunity to surround himself with loyalists. This latter step is undoubtedly something contemplated by members of the Kimist court since they will be well aware that Kim Jong-il is the one leader who cannot repudiate his father's policy except at the price of undermining his own legitimacy.

If Kim Jong-il is displaced, the interests of the élite of this most highly bureaucratised and socially constrained of societies would be to retain their power and privileges while adopting economic policies which would give the system at least some chance of survival. Kimist purism (of the kind seen in Hua Guofeng's 'whateverism') is not an option and its pursuit would sooner or later provoke that upheaval from which this élite has most to lose. Such a strategy would be assisted by the inheritance of political culture, incubated by isolation and government propagated xenophobia.

In these circumstances the new leadership are bound to take a leaf from Deng Xiaoping's book, written in either a minimalist—'seek truth from facts'—or a maximalist—'four cardinal principles' style. No doubt by degrees Kim's more egregious claims for his own achievements would be deflated, and a more realistic version of the nature of the outside world (and South Korea) would become current. But the existence of a separate North Korean state with its own character and aspirations would be retained.

The scenario so far is not one which could be maintained indefinitely. Economic reforms would require some opening to the forces of the world economy. This would bring, in turn, the beginnings of social transformation. A North Korean population possessed of accurate first hand knowledge of South Korea would eventually succumb to the forces of nationalism which are amongst the most powerful factors at work in the Korean equation. In those circumstances unification, though not entirely on Seoul's terms, would be the ultimate outcome. But this would take some time. Meanwhile, the example of Vietnam shows just how far a relatively opened system much of it dependent upon the operations of free but mostly illicit market exchange can subsist along with a leadership still trapped in the verities of socialist theory. With Kim Jong-il in charge these forces would be slowed though not completely stopped; with a Deng style transition leadership these forces would encounter many fewer obstacles in their operation.

Foundations for Real Rapprochement?

Have the foundations finally been laid for Korean unification, clearing the way for some measure of reform in North Korea? While the potential for a degree of rapprochement undoubtedly exists, so far the evidence is not unambiguously encouraging. According to Kim Il-sung's New Year message—often an occasion to set the tone for the year's policies—nothing is wrong with socialism, the collapse of socialism elsewhere has been due to the pursuit of the wrong policies under the wrong leaders, and regarding progress on the unification front the efforts of the government in Seoul are not worthy of a mention.[5]

As far as the prospects for internal reform in North Korea are concerned, while some measures have been promulgated in connection with the creation of free trading areas, contradictory tendencies are also apparent. A good deal of attention was given in late 1991 to the Taean work system and the Chongsan-ri method, that is, the organisational foundations of the Kim Il-sung system in industry and agriculture respectively, both of which would have to be completely scrapped if reform was to be effected.

For their part the government in South Korea has continued in a conciliatory vein. In his new year cabinet reshuffle President Roh removed his Defence Minister, who had earlier suggested that a preemptive military raid upon North Korea's nuclear facilities was feasible. So far the generally bipartisan approach to Pyongyang taken by mainstream politicians in Seoul has been maintained.[6] The 1992 season of elections is, however, imposing extraordinary strains upon the new political process, and if Pyongyang is tempted to use the unification issue as a lever in that process (as in 1987) the spirit of conciliation may diminish.

Assessing the foundations for the progress made in 1991, therefore, as compared with the previous episodes of North–South Korean contacts, though changes in South Korea have played a part what is new are the policy reversals that have been forced on Pyongyang. Rather than embracing their brethren in a suffusion of patriotic sentiment the North Korean leadership have moved towards an accommodation with South Korea because there is nowhere else to go and because this will enhance, in the present circumstances, the prospects for the dynastic succession. In short, a positive commitment towards unification has yet to emerge.

1992: Realising the Agreements?

The proceedings of the sixth round of North–South negotiations held in February indicate that this estimate of the limits that exist to real rapprochement is accurate.

For their part the South Korean side has been insistent that progress on the nuclear question will be the indicator of how much the two agreements have really achieved. Thus they have made the suggestion that there should be a trial inspection by each side of a single military–nuclear facility in the other, and have raised the issue of the rapidity with which North

---

5   *Pyongyang Times*, 4 January 1992, pp. 1–3.

6   Kim Dae-Jung, 'The Once and Future Korea', *Foreign Policy*, no. 86 (Spring 1992), pp. 40–55.

Korea accepts its obligations under the IAEA Treaty. And they have put on hold the ambitious plans of the Daewoo group chairman to construct export manufacturing plants in a site at the port city of Nampo.

At the sixth round of the North–South negotiations in February 1992 both the agreements of the preceding year, having been ratified, were exchanged. The joint subcommittees concerned with military issues, political issues, and exchange and cooperation matters provided for in the agreements were established and their ground rules specified. But regarding the 'North–South Joint Nuclear Control Committee' which was intended as a mechanism to realise mutual inspection and regulation, agreement on its formation required repeated meetings, even though both parties were obliged to reach such an agreement within a month of ratification. Further, North Korea has adopted the tactic of pressing for international guarantees to be achieved on the denuclearisation of the peninsula before accepting mutual facility inspection. Moreover, the tone of North Korean remarks during the ceremonies which accompanied the exchange indicated that Pyongyang was reintroducing old grievances, making new demands, and refusing (despite gaining the important concession of the withdrawal of US nuclear weapons from the South) to accept the validity of Seoul's nuclear anxieties.

Apart from flatly rejecting as 'unimaginable' the possibility of North Korea ever developing or acquiring nuclear weapons, Kim Il-sung in his talk with the delegates from South Korea dwelt at length on the need for Seoul to abrogate its military alliance with the United States, remove American bases from its territory, and accept a programme of arms reductions. Any other approach would not be consistent with the 'independent' stand which both should take towards the unification issue:

> In a situation where the country is divided into the North and the South, if one side relies on foreign forces and allows foreign forces interference, this is an attitude of confrontation, not an attitude for reunification. With such an attitude of confrontation, the agreements between the North and the South cannot be smoothly implemented and responsible and reliable dialogue cannot be expected between them.[7]

North Korean Premier Yon Hyong-muk was even more forthright in drawing out the implications of taking an 'independent' stand. Not only did this mean an abandonment of military exercises and the 'withdrawal of foreign forces', it also required the South to ignore those ideological differences between the two Korean states which were the product of foreign intervention. This allowed Yon to argue that the ideologically motivated security laws of South Korea should be repudiated, and those who had been imprisoned as a result of them (notably Mun Ik-hwan and Im Su-

---

7   *Summary of World Broadcasts/Far East/*1310, A3/3, 21 February 1992.

kyong) should be released. Having criticised South Korea's legal system (a step proscribed by the 1991 agreement), Yon then plainly stated that the agreements and their anticipated outcomes would only be treated by Pyongyang as a 'package'. Seoul's attempt to treat the various issues on a 'case by case' basis, that is requiring progress first on the nuclear question, would 'delay the solution of the question'.[8] In short, taken together with the problems encountered by the joint nuclear committee, it is clear that North Korea is not in a hurry to meet South Korea's principal concerns.[9]

Under the North Korean constitution (Article 96) the president (Kim Il-sung) has the power to ratify and abrogate treaties concluded with foreign countries without the need for further consultation. The Supreme People's Assembly (SPA—the North Korean parliament) has no such role, except in so far as it is enjoined generally to establish the basic principles of foreign policy, a task which is given also to the Central People's Committee.[10] Yet the SPA Standing Committee referred the IAEA Treaty to be debated at the next SPA plenary session, which prevented ratification of the treaty until April.[11] The only interpretation of these moves is that delay was being sought.

Happy Birthday, Kim Jong-il

Meanwhile, if the North Korean media is to be taken at face value, these weighty matters have been a mere sideshow for the real issue of the day, which has been Kim Jong-il's fiftieth birthday and what is portended therein. The younger Kim's pronouncements at the beginning of the year have been adverted to, though his admission that socialism had not everywhere been successful was the only negative statement to be found in the text. As his birthday in February approached, the already overtaxed syntactical powers of Pyongyang's leader writers and ideological workers were further tested as they were called upon to produce paroxysms of hyperbole on his immortal revolutionary achievements.[12] The first volume (in what is assured to be a continuing series) of Kim Jong-il's *Selected Works* made its appearance, and some of the terms heretofore reserved exclusively for statements about his father were applied to him. It was

8 *Summary of World Broadcasts/Far East*/1311, A3/1-4, 22 February 1992.

9 *North Korea News* (Seoul) no. 617, 10 February 1992, p. 3.

10 Suh Dae-Sook 1981, *Korean Communism 1945-1980* (Honolulu: University of Hawaii Press), pp. 511–15.

11 *North Korea News*, no. 620, 2 March 1992, pp. 2–4.

12 *Summary of World Broadcasts/Far East*/1306, C1/5-7, 17 February 1992; *Far East*/1308, C1-2, 19 February, 1992.

clear that the stage was being set to have the younger genius replace the elder in at least some of his formal posts, perhaps soon after the latter's eightieth birthday.

The family succession strategy had long been planned, but from the point of view of North–South Korean relations it is significant that it has generated at this juncture a flood of words referring to the universal and timeless applicability of the most unreconstructed perennials of North Korean domestic policy. In such an atmosphere, debate on the reforms which would have to accompany a comprehensive rapprochement on the peninsula would be doubly difficult. It would be understandable if those amongst the leadership in Pyongyang who are the proponents of reform sought to keep an even lower profile in the next few months.

18 Unification Through a Korean Commonwealth: Blueprint for a National Community

LEE HONG-KOO

An Overview

We are witness today to a series of changes in the regional and global contexts symbolised by the winds of reform now sweeping the Soviet Union and much of Eastern Europe. Both the United States and the Soviet Union have entered into what many have referred to as a period of 'new *détente*', and fresh proposals on arms reductions, for instance, have appeared with increasing rapidity. The Sino–Soviet relationship has also entered into a new phase as earmarked by the Gorbachev–Deng summit of May 1989.

But nowhere has change evolved so rapidly and fundamentally as in Eastern Europe. Both Poland and Hungary have inaugurated non-communist governments for the first time since the Soviet Union established the Iron Curtain in the aftermath of World War II. East Germany—for long the economic showcase of COMECON and the USSR's most important strategic country in the East bloc—is now undergoing an upheaval without parallel in its postwar history. The yearning for democracy has also spread to Bulgaria, traditionally a bastion of Soviet support in Eastern Europe, and nationalism has emerged as a potent political force in virtually all of the nationalist republics in the Soviet Union. For all intents and purposes, therefore, the Yalta system has been broken, and with it the Cold War era can be said to have also ended.

Nevertheless, the conditions of the Cold War are still very much apparent on the Korean Peninsula, despite the prevailing trend of reconciliation. To be sure, it is difficult to conceptualise any rapid improvement in inter-Korean ties given the closed nature of North Korea, not to speak of the tenuous military balance that has been maintained by the South and the North since the end of the Korean War. Despite the best of intentions of the Republic of Korea to engage in multi-level dialogues with the North, the response has all too often been disappointing. As South Korea enters the 1990s, the key task remains unchanged: to open a new page in inter-Korean relations and to inaugurate a new foundation for the eventual unification of the two sides. This solemn task has been undertaken with great vigour and foresight by President Roh Tae-woo since the Sixth Republic was launched in February 1988.

Perhaps more clearly and stridently than ever before, national unification has become a focal point of South Korean politics, particularly since the country has moved rapidly with democratisation following the inauguration of the Sixth Republic. In the period since President Roh assumed office, democratisation and unification have emerged as the two focal points in South Korea's domestic politics. The unification issue has generated unparalleled interest within South Korea given the opening of the unification debate within and without the political institution. Moreover, the Roh administration has been firmly committed to the building of a more cooperative relationship with North Korea, beginning with the acceptance of the North as an equal partner in search for national reconciliation.

In an effort to inaugurate a new era in inter-Korean ties, President Roh gave a major policy address at the National Assembly on 11 September 1989, on the issue of national unification. Specifically, he unveiled a 'Korean National Community Unification Formula', which with a more realistic accent entails a number of significant developments in South Korea's approach to the unification issue. Some of the more salient features of this new proposal, including an assessment of recent developments in inter-Korean relations and within the Republic of Korea, will be described in this chapter in an effort to clarify the basis and objectives of the Sixth Republic's unification policy.

Emerging Domestic and International Environments

Since policy cannot be formulated without due consideration of the environment in which it is to be implemented, it is critical to note the almost breathtaking transformations that have taken place in the recent period. For the Republic of Korea, such changes have an important impact on the conduct of its foreign policy. At least three broad trends are currently discernible in the international political spectrum. First, as already mentioned, is the thawing of the Cold War as exemplified by the new US–Soviet *détente* including the already concluded INF Treaty, as well as the ongoing START and MBFR negotiations. Moreover, some of the most pronounced regional conflicts have been resolved with the direct and indirect participation of the two superpowers, such as the Soviet withdrawal from Afghanistan, the Vietnamese withdrawal from Kampuchea, the end of the Iran–Iraq War, and the settlement of Namibia. The summit meeting at Malta could inaugurate a new era in the US–Soviet relationship and thereby a new chapter in world politics.

Second, a major catalyst for change has appeared in the Soviet Union under the leadership of Mikhail Gorbachev and his twin policies of *glasnost* and *perestroika* in the Soviet Union as well as the undertaking of democratic reforms in Eastern Europe. This has resulted in an epic sea-change within the Soviet Union and the East Bloc.

Gorbachev's 'New Thinking' has prompted major Soviet initiatives in the areas of arms control, East–West relations, and wide-ranging economic and political reforms within the Soviet Union. Although the Communist Party still retains political control, a slow process of political pluralisation is evident. Gorbachev has openly acknowledged failures in the Soviet economy and history, such as the current movement within the USSR to reassess the Stalinist era. In the foreign policy domain, the Soviet Union has exhibited a new openness: Foreign Minister Eduard Shevardnadze has severely criticised the initial decision to occupy Afghanistan and has also acknowledged that the Krasnoyarsk radar was an 'open violation' of the ABM Treaty. Indeed, a Soviet Foreign Ministry spokesman, Genadiy Gerasimov, has even categorically noted the formal demise of the Brezhnev Doctrine. With respect to the Asia–Pacific region, although the Soviet Union still maintains a formidable military presence, Gorbachev has signalled the desire to expand relations with all nations of this region, including the desirability of setting up new ties with the Republic of Korea.

Third, parallel with these developments, Korea has gained increasing prominence in the international arena commensurate with its corresponding status as middle-ranking economic power in Asia. It is the world's tenth largest trading country, and has continued to register an impressive growth rate, although it is important to bear in mind that structural reforms have to be undertaken also in order to sustain a more balanced and stable growth into the 1990s.

But Korea's growing confidence has not been based solely on its economic performance. As the successful hosting of the 1988 Seoul Olympics demonstrated, Korea is fully able to undertake its share of international responsibilities. At the same time, the rapid political transition from decades of authoritarianism to democracy has ushered in a new optimism within the Korean people. It was only two years ago when the streets of Seoul as well as the other major cities in Korea were filled with demonstrators from all walks of life demanding democratic reforms. With the inauguration of the Sixth Republic, Korea has made significant gains in democratic reform, and open debate on virtually every issue has been the hall-mark of the current domestic political environment. In this regard, the unification issue is no exception.

Seen from this perspective, President Roh Tae-woo's enunciation of the 'July 7th Declaration' on South–North relations signalled an ardent desire on the part of the government to articulate a new vision for the conduct of inter-Korean relations. The existent situation on the Korean Peninsula, however, is an exception to the global and regional trend towards reform and openness. North Korea has refused to modify its orthodox and obstructionist position and remains in a state of 'angry isolation'. South Korea's improved ties with the Socialist bloc—it has already developed full diplomatic relations with Hungary and Poland—must have been a blow to North Korea's prestige in that it has lost support even from its fellow Socialist countries.

New Meaning for a National Community

In the years immediately following the division of Korea in 1945, Koreans had shown a tendency to consider the task of unification as an effort to return to an original condition on reunification. In the four decades since division, however, many Koreans have come to realise that national unification should not be a return to the past but a creation of the future. Unification means a process of building a new national community, which will not only restore continuity to the national tradition of Korea but also encompass new realities for Koreans in the last decade of the twentieth century and the beginning years of the next century. What are the more striking characteristics of those new realities?

Perhaps the most dramatic feature of the new Korean community is the gigantic migration of Koreans during the past one hundred years. Close to ten million Koreans had to leave their homes and move to other parts of Korea and more significantly to other nations of the world. Around five million Koreans fled from North Korea to South Korea crossing the 38th parallel between 1945 and 1952. If each refugee had left one member of family in the North, the total number of Koreans belonging to 'separated families' exceeds ten million. Another five million Koreans either have immigrated or have been forced to move to foreign lands during the last one hundred years, including nearly two million to China, over one million to the United States, about 700,000 to Japan, over 400,000 to the Soviet Union, and nearly 100,000 to Latin America and so on. Along the unhappy course of colonial subjugation and then national division, Koreans have become a people spread widely around the world. By unification, therefore, we now mean creation of a national community that will join not only the people of North and South Korea but also link together the nearly seventy million Koreans around the world.

In the history of the Korean people, society always had primacy over polity in the normative dimension. In the tradition of Korean national community, social, economic and cultural dimensions have had as much, if not more, importance as the political dimension. In short, national unification is not exclusively and perhaps not primarily a political task. The immediate goal at the moment for the Korean people is to build a single community in which the people could form a common living zone to share freely common experience and welfare in the social, economic, cultural and political dimensions. It is hoped that the progress of community-building will provide opportunities for political solution, which will eventually produce a single state and a complete unification.

In the blueprint for the future, the boundary of the Korean national community does not necessarily coincide with the boundary for the unified state. The geographic boundary of the unified Korean state will be the Korean Peninsula, with the Yalu and Tuman Rivers serving as demarcation lines. On the other hand, there should be no set lines defining boundaries for the Korean national community, because they will be determined by the patterns of communal communication, transaction and movement among the seventy million Koreans spread around the world. In a sense, technological innovations could make the traditional land-bound notion of community boundaries less meaningful. For example, the one and three-quarters of a million Koreans in Southern Manchuria adjacent to North Korea, who are loyal citizens of China, at the same time could become members of the Korean national community as Southern Manchuria and the Korean Peninsula will be increasingly inter-connected and eventually form a single living zone. Development of such a communal living zone encompassing Korea and Manchuria will serve the mutual interest of China and Korea in terms of economic and cultural development and will positively contribute to the historic amity between China and Korea.

The first step in building such a wide-ranging national community has to be of course to bring down the walls of confrontation between North and South Korea and to open a door for exchange and cooperation. In this respect, what has happened between East and West Germany in terms of the gradual but steady increase in communication, travel, and cooperation during the last two decades is extremely instructive. A unification formula with a high degree of normative validity and realistic feasibility has to set its focus on building a new Korean community which could furnish a ground upon which a unified state will be built. The new unification formula announced by President Roh on 11 September 1989, in fact closely follows such a prescription.

The Commonwealth as an Interim Institution

The 'Korean National Community Unification Formula' is premised on a number of constructive steps leading eventually to the creation of a unified and democratic republic. At its base, the formula's implementation is based on the following three major steps. First, to build mutual confidence on the basis of a South–North dialogue and to hold a South–North summit meeting, including an adoption of a Korean National Community Charter. Second, the creation of a Korean Commonwealth[1], being a common sphere of national life to promote common prosperity and to restore national homogeneity, thereby accelerating the development of a national community. And third, the creation of a unified assembly and government based on national elections as stipulated in a unified constitution so that a unified and democratic republic can be formed.

The three principles of unification—self-determination, peace, and democracy—are important elements in the realisation of the goals inherent in the 'Korean National Community Unification Formula'. As President Roh noted in his speech to the National Assembly on 11 September 1989, 'indisputably, unification must be achieved independently in keeping with a spirit of national self-determination and under the principles of peace, non-use of military force, and grand national unity through democratic procedures'. The basis of self-determination stems from earlier pronouncements on unification, such as the 'July 4th South–North Communiqué' issued in 1972 which underlined the need to achieve unification primarily through the efforts of the Koreans on both sides. Moreover, the spirit of self-determination extends to the need in rostering a permanent peace on the Korean Peninsula without the threat of war and to seek ways to strengthen inter-Korean cooperation as a vital development towards international peace. Moreover, under the principles outlined in the 'July 4th South–North Communiqué', individual freedom and liberty are very much a part of the spirit governing the effort for unification. Self-determination, after all, has to be executed and institutionalised through peaceful and democratic means, and for the purpose of peace and freedom.

As explicated earlier, the 'Korean National Community Unification Formula' rests on the principle that the creation of a unified republic has to be on the basis of a national community. In other words, it is imperative to set an interim stage towards unification during which both sides will

---

[1]   The notion of the Korean Commonwealth was initially presented in my paper 'The Korean Commonwealth and the Asian Community', presented at the 30th International Congress of Human Sciences in Asia and North Africa, Mexico City, Mexico, 3–8 August 1976. It received a further elaboration in my essay, 'Political Unification and Social Welfare', *Korea and World Affairs*, vol. 8, no. 1 (Spring 1984), pp. 5–16.

recognise each other and seek coexistence and co-prosperity, regardless of the existence of different political systems, and will endeavour to seek a speedy integration of the national community. Therefore, to accommodate the need for integration the interim creation of a 'Korean Commonwealth' is a critical step, and it differs from the accepted norm, of a commonwealth as based in international law. Specifically, both the South and the North under the 'Korean Commonwealth' would be sovereign states; yet, the relationship between them will not be an international relation but a special relation under an interim arrangement. For example, trade and travel between the two parts will be considered internal and not international. Given that this is an interim step towards the ultimate creation of a unified and democratic republic, it can be said that from a functional point of view the step has attributes similar to those of the European Community or the Nordic Council.

Outstanding political and military issues would also be resolved in this interim process, given the excessive resources that are currently being put into defence spending on both sides. At the same time, there is a need to implement mutual confidence-building measures in order to reduce the high level of tension persisting at the demilitarised zone. It should also be noted that the presence of US forces and the fact that the Republic of Korea is not a signatory to the Armistice Agreement have further complicated political and military issues between the South and the North. Another factor contributing to the current tension has been the North's superior military capability and the threat it has continued to pose on the security of the South. Nevertheless, consistent with the global trend towards a diminution in the role of force and the need to reduce armaments, there is a need to pay closer attention to how best to reduce the military tension on the Korean Peninsula.

On the occasion of his address to the UN General Assembly on 19 October 1988, President Roh outlined the desirability of holding a 'Six-Nation Consultative Peace Conference in Northeast Asia' so that the two Koreas, the United States, Japan, China, and the Soviet Union could jointly approach the issue of how best to maintain peace on the Korean Peninsula. At the same time, the Roh administration has consistently called for a summit meeting between the South and the North at the highest level to discuss all relevant political and military issues. The new unification formula envisages that the South and the North would conclude a mutual non-aggression treaty, which could be incorporated in the National Community Charter. Moreover, from a structural viewpoint, a Council of Ministers would be co-chaired by the Prime Ministers of the South and the North and would comprise around ten cabinet-level officials from each side, and a number of standing committees could be created to deal with diplomatic, political, and military issues. Such bodies could then specifically discuss ways to accelerate political dialogues, agree on military confidence-building measures, the transformation of the current Armistice Agreement into a peace treaty and changing the demilitarised zone into a Peace Zone.

The Korean Commonwealth would have a Council of Presidents as the highest decision-making organ, the already mentioned Council of Ministers, and a Council of Representatives to be composed of equal numbers of members of the legislatures in both the South and the North. The Council of Representatives would draft a constitution for a unified republic and develop methods and procedures to bring about the unification. With agreement on a draft of the constitution, the next step would be to promulgate it through democratic methods and procedures including the holding of a general election under the unified constitution, which would then lead to the formulation of a unified legislature and a unified government. Thus, a unified and democratic republic would be created.

As noted above, it is critical to achieve unification based on the principle of democracy. The Republic of Korea cannot cherish any vision of a unified Korea that does not conform to the principles of representative democracy, and this principle will govern its effort to facilitate the intermediate process towards unification. However, it has to be borne in mind that North Korea's concept of freedom and human rights differ widely from that of South Korea's, and its democracy is premised on the basis of class struggle and 'people's liberation'. As a result, it is all the more important to resolve these contending perceptions and definitions during the interim stage of a Korean Commonwealth.

A final important aspect of the Korean National Community Unification Formula is its openness. It is not too difficult to discern the fact that several aspects of North Korea's own unification proposal have received serious consideration in drawing up the new unification formula. For instance, North Korea's consistent calls for the resolution of political and military issues will be attended to in the Korean Commonwealth. In all of the interim institutions the South and the North would be represented on an equal basis. Above all, the Korean National Community Unification Formula seeks to undertake a flexible attitude *vis-à-vis* North Korea's unification proposals, including certain aspects of its confederation formula, while understanding that the Republic of Korea's own proposal can be revised if the conditions warrant such a change.

Challenges on the Road Towards Unification

The Korean people have withstood a number of challenges and ordeals in the twentieth century, and they are entering into a new era of prosperity and confidence unparalleled in their history. However, it also has to be borne in mind that periods of transition entail both opportunities and risks.

The fact that South Korea faces the two major tasks of democratisation and unification during this transitionary period attests to the challenges and opportunities. Nevertheless, the challenge before the Korean people does not end with these two tasks; in fact, they confront other tests such as the need to remedy structural imbalances in the economy owing to the rapid industrialisation of the last two decades. Additionally, the Korean people have to meet new obligations in the international community by undertaking a fair share of reciprocal responsibilities.

The last two years have demonstrated that South Korea is fully able to meet the new challenges, as it has overcome difficulties with strength and determination. However, it is also true that in the process of democratisation the outpouring of demands from all walks of life contributed to a sense of discord. In particular, national unification has emerged as an important political agendum as well as an all-embracing political symbol, while North Korea has sought to take advantage of the diversification of opinions within South Korea to advance its so-called united front strategy. From the viewpoint of North Korea, the process of democratisation is not necessarily a way to strengthen the political and social system of the South but possibly an opportunity for instigating a disintegration of the system. Such problems notwithstanding, the Republic of Korea is proceeding with a sense of optimism based on the judgement that the fortitude of its people and the general trend of world history in the long run will guarantee the success of its effort to build a new national community.

For the Korean National Community Unification Formula to be realistically implemented, it is essential for a number of reasons to continue the effort to bring positive results at the ongoing South–North dialogues. First, such a step would enable both sides to enter into future negotiations on the basis of mutual recognition. Second, even a minimal success at the South–North dialogue would show that both sides are able to resolve their outstanding differences on the basis of peaceful means. And third, it would demonstrate the ability of Koreans to move jointly towards unification without the involvement of third parties. Given these obvious reasons, the Republic of Korea is making an all-out effort for success at the Red Cross dialogue for uniting separated families, the sports talks to form a single team to represent Korea at the 1990 Asian Games in Beijing, the preliminary contacts to prepare an inter-parliamentary conference and most importantly preliminary meetings of the two governments to prepare for a meeting of their respective prime ministers.

The paramount importance of constructive dialogue between North and South Korea does not mean that the international community will have no role to play in the reduction of tension and the building of peace on the Korean Peninsula. Given the current state of the South–North military balance, it is essential to receive the support of the regional powers so that peace can be guaranteed on and around the Korean Peninsula. At the same time, South Korea will also endeavour to maintain its traditional relationships with the west while striving to make new inroads into its relationship with the Socialist countries. Towards such an effort, President Roh's proposal for both South and North Korea to jointly seek membership in the United Nations as well as the holding of a consultative peace conference are two important methods in which the international community can actively assist in the building of peace on the Korean Peninsula.

The road towards unification is a long and arduous one, but the Republic of Korea is determined to make steady progress towards this national goal. The twentieth century has been a century of unparalleled trial and hardship. For thirty-five years between 1910 and 1945, Korea had to suffer the ignominy of being a colony of Japan. The joy of liberation at the end of the World War II was immediately taken away by the cruel division of Korea under the unfortunate Yalta arrangement. For the next forty-five years between 1945 and 1989, the Koreas have become collective victims of the cold and hot wars as an artificially divided nation. In short, Koreans have not had a united and independent nation for the last eighty years. The Korean people are determined to close this unhappy chapter in their history before this century comes to an end and to welcome the twenty-first century as a proud and unified nation, which could carry a major share in building a better world. As the winds of reform are sweeping through much the European continent—imbued with a new spirit—it is hoped that the threshold for unity and peace can be found between South and North Korea based on a grand design for a unified national community.

PART IV

DOCUMENTS

List of Documents

1.

Grand National Harmony and Progress Towards a Great Nation; Special Declaration on June 29, 1987

My dear fellow citizens,

I have now come to a firm conviction about the future of our nation. I have anguished long and hard over the genuine mission of politicians at this historic time when deep-seated conflicts and antagonisms have so accumulated among our citizens that they have erupted into a national crisis. I have also solicited the wisdom of people from various walks of life—academicians, journalists, businessmen, religious leaders, workers, and young people, including students, and have thus ascertained the will of the people.

Today, I stand before history and the nation with an extraordinary determination to help build a great homeland in which there is love and harmony among all segments and strata of the population, in which all are proud of being citizens and in which the government can acquire wisdom, courage and genuine strength from the people.

I will hereby forthrightly present my ideas. I intend to recommend them to President Chun Doo Hwan and am resolved to translate them into concrete action with the enthusiastic support of my party colleagues and the general public.

First, the Constitution should be expeditiously amended, through agreement between the government-party and the opposition, to adopt a direct presidential election system, and presidential elections should be held under a new Constitution to realize a peaceful change of government in February 1988. This does not mean a change in my belief that a parliamentary cabinet system, under which the majority of the cabinet members are National Assemblymen directly elected by the people and under which the principles of democratic and responsible politics can be most faithfully realized through free and open dialogue and compromise, is the form of government best suited to enabling democracy to take hold in our country.

However, if the majority of the people do not want it, even the best-conceived system will alienate the public, and the government which is born under it will not be able to dream and suffer together with the people.

Accordingly, I have come to the conclusion that a presidential election system must be adopted at this juncture in order to overcome social confusion and achieve national reconciliation. The people are the masters of the country and the people's will must come before everything else.

Second, in addition to switching to a direct presidential election system through constitutional revision, I think that to carry out elections democratically, it is necessary to also revise the Presidential Election Law so that freedom of candidacy and fair competition are guaranteed and so that the genuine verdict of the people can be given. A revised election law should also ensure maximum fairness and justness in election management, from the campaigns to the casting, opening, and counting of ballots.

Even under a direct election system, there should not be groundless character smearing and demagoguery to incite hostility, confusion, disorder and regional antagonisms, thereby undermining national stability and impeding genuine democratic development. There must be a solid framework to ensure that elections are bona fide competitions in policies and ideas.

Third, antagonisms and confrontations must be resolutely eradicated not only from our political community but also from all other sectors to achieve grand national reconciliation and unity. In this connection, I believe that Mr Kim Dae-jung also should be amnestied and his civil rights restored, no matter what he has done in the past. At the same time, all those who are being detained in connection with the political situation should also be set free, except for those who have committed treason by repudiating the basic free and democratic order on which our survival and posterity hinges and for a small number of people who have shaken the national foundation by committing homicide, bodily injury, arson and vandalism. I ardently hope that all those people will thus be able to return to society as democratic citizens.

There can be no present without a past. However, I believe it is important at this point in our history to create an occasion for all to rejoice heartily. In such an event, the next presidential elections will be elevated into a national festival, and the new government thus elected with solid and broad public support will be able to work even more effectively to build a great nation.

Fourth, human dignity must be respected even more greatly and the basic rights of citizens should be promoted and protected to the maximum. I hope that the forthcoming constitutional amendments will include all the strengthened basic rights clauses being proposed by the Democratic Justice Party, including a drastic extension of habeas corpus.

The government should take utmost care not to let human rights abuses occur. The Democratic Justice Party should make greater efforts to effectively promote human rights. For example, it should hold periodic meetings with the lawyers associations and other human rights groups to promptly learn of and redress human rights violations.

Fifth, to promote the freedom of the press, the relevant systems and practices must be drastically improved. The Basic Press Law, which may have been well meant but has nonetheless been criticized by most journalists, should promptly be either extensively revised or abolished and replaced by a different law. Newspapers should again be permitted to station their correspondents in the provinces, the press card system should be abolished and newspapers should be allowed to increase the number of their pages as they see fit. These and other necessary steps must be taken to guarantee the freedom of the press to the maximum.

The government cannot control the press nor should it attempt to do so. No restrictions should be imposed on the press except when national security is at risk. It must be remembered that the press can be tried only by an independent judiciary or by individual citizens.

Sixth, freedom and self-regulation must be guaranteed to the maximum in all other sectors also, because private initiative is the driving force behind diverse and balanced social development which in turn fuels national progress. In spite of the forthcoming processes of amending the Constitution, local councils should be elected and organized without any hitch according to schedule. The establishment of municipal and provincial councils should also be studied in concrete terms and carried out soon thereafter.

Colleges and universities—the institutions of higher learning—must be made self-governing and educational autonomy in general must be expeditiously put into practice. To that end, the personnel and budgetary policies and general administration of universities and colleges should be free of outside intervention. Enrolment and graduation systems should also be improved to allow them greater autonomy. Scholarship systems should be improved with sufficient budgetary provisions made so that good students need not be frustrated by financial difficulties.

Seventh, a political climate conducive to dialogue and compromise must be created expeditiously, with healthy activities of political parties guaranteed. A political party should be a democratic organization that presents responsible demands and policies to mold and crystalize the political opinion of the people. The state should exert its utmost effort to protect and nurture political parties, so long as they engage in sound activities and do not contravene such objectives. Within such a framework, political parties should abide by the laws of the nation and exercise their political capabilities to resolve social conflicts and contradictions through dialogue and compromise in an amicable and harmonious manner to forge and maintain national coherence. As long as there exists an opposition party which is intent on pressing its unilateral demands by all means, even through violence, the governing party cannot always make concession after concession.

Eighth, bold social reforms must be carried out to build a clean and honest society. In order that all citizens can lead a secure and happy life, crime against life and property, such as hooliganism, robbery and theft, must be stamped out, and deep-seated irrationalities and improprieties that still linger in our society must be eradicated. Groundless rumors, along with regional antagonism and black-and-white attitudes, should be banished forever to build a society in which mutual trust and love prevail. In that way, we must ensure that all citizens can live an active life in a stable social environment, free of anxiety and with pride and confidence. I believe that these are the immediate tasks which must be accomplished if we are to resolve the current difficult situation and project the nation forward.

My fellow countrymen,

On the strength of your expectations that there will be continued development rather than disruptions, I dare to make this proposal today in humble veneration of history and the people. These ideas stem from my genuine patriotism, and I am confident that they will blossom with support from all the people, not only President Chun and members of the Democratic Justice Party.

When these basic ideas have been accepted, additional details can be worked out. If they fail to be accepted, however, I want to make it very clear that I will resign from all public duties including the presidential candidacy and the chairmanship of the Democratic Justice Party.

My fellow countrymen,

The shining achievements of the government of the Fifth Republic should at no time be underestimated. We have begun to root democracy deep into the soil of our nation's constitutional history by implementing a single term presidency. We have realized a trade surplus by stabilizing prices and improving our international competitiveness. We have drastically bolstered national security and obtained the right to host the Olympic Games.

Under no circumstances must we neglect to safeguard and promote the liberal democratic system. The task of peacefully changing administrations is the immediate task at hand. Furthermore, now that the Olympics are approaching, all of us are responsible for avoiding the national disgrace of dividing ourselves and thus causing the world to ridicule us.

With the sacred right to vote at hand, let us all work together to create a society where young people develop their capabilities to realize their ideas, where workers and farmers can work free of anxiety, where busi-

ideas, where workers and farmers can work free of anxiety, where businessmen exert even greater creative efforts and where politicians exercise the art of debate and compromise to work out the nation's future. I pledge my utmost efforts to help create a dynamic, developing and genuinely democratic society where law and order prevail.

This country belongs to us. It is our historic duty to both exert our efforts and exercise restraint and wisdom to more successfully develop the country which was founded and nurtured with the blood of our forefathers and the lives of the patriots, and to proudly hand it over to the next generation. I sincerely hope that national wisdom will be pooled to demonstrate to the world that the Korean people will not go backward but will go forward to make a contribution to world history.

My fellow countrymen, my party colleagues and opposition politicians, I earnestly pray that my genuinely well-meant proposal will be accepted and will solve our current problems, that it will be a breakthrough in the effort to create a great nation where all our people can live stable and happy lives.

Thank you.

2.

We Can Do It; Inaugural Address, February 25, 1988

My sixty million compatriots; President Yun Po Sun and President Choi Kyu Ha, both of whom have been so instrumental in developing constitutional government; President Chun Doo Hwan, who has set a historic precedent of a peaceful change of administration; congratulatory envoys; distinguished guests,

Today, we gather in front of this sacred hall of the people to proclaim a new beginning, an era of hope which will see Korea, once a peripheral country in East Asia, take a central position in the international community.

As I assume the presidency forty years after a democratic government was first established in this country, there is a strong wind of change blowing over the land. Nevertheless, I think we should pause to remember our ancestors, who struggled constantly to shape the nation. With an indomitable spirit of independence, they created our illustrious culture and maintained our national integrity uninterrupted, overcoming numerous foreign invasions and other ordeals. We should emulate their great spirit.

I think we should also pay tribute to those persons whose hands show the marks of hard work in the face of adversity. We grew up in a world of poverty and war, and our hands were empty. However, with our empty hands, we toiled with enthusiasm and single-minded determination to improve our lot. As a result, this country has emerged as a dynamic, newly industrializing nation. It has grown into a full-fledged democracy with the start of a tradition of peaceful changes of government.

We have thus proved to be a truly great people. Korea's extraordinary inherent capabilities are an inexhaustible source of encouragement for all of us who are endeavoring to propel the country into the ranks of the advanced democratic countries before the twentieth century is over. As I take on the challenge of leading the nation toward that goal, I am profoundly grateful to all those whose hard work has made Korea what it is today.

My fellow citizens,
The Korean people have faced numerous challenges and have triumphed over all of them with courage and tenacity. Now we have a new challenge—to create a vibrant era of national self-esteem. I hereby solemnly declare before the nation that just such an era has opened.

My fellow citizens,
We can do it, and we must.

We must successfully meet that challenge by reforming ourselves. A bird must itself break out of its egg before it can learn to fly. Now is the time for us, too, to break out of our shell of old habits and, with the creative enthusiasm that characterized the pioneers who made something out of nothing, create a unified, powerful and self-respecting nation by enabling all citizens to enjoy democratic rights and privileges, as well as prosperity. It is certainly a time for change, renovation and quantum leaps—a time for dynamic progress.

Accordingly, the time has come to put an end to excessive internal squabbling. The past can undoubtedly be put to good use as a mirror by which to examine ourselves, but it should not be a shackle to hamper indefinitely our progress toward a bright future. The great democratic choice made by the people last December eliminated the sources of strife that had built up over the past forty years. Let us here and now bury regional antagonism, partisan and factional egoism and personal resentment. If all of us yield a little in the spirit of reconciliation and forgive each other and bury the residue of hatred, our children will be able to enjoy the abundant fruit of democracy and welfare.

Fellow citizens,
From this moment on we will sail full steam ahead toward a land of hope brimming with freedom and happiness. We have a new chart of democracy and a new compass of national reconciliation that you, my fellow countrymen, examined and agreed to use when you elected me president.

With the launching of the new Republic, we will sail steadfastly toward democracy. This is not at all because democracy is the fashionable word today, but because democracy represents just values that give dignity and worth to our lives. Only a democratic society will guarantee freedom, dignity and full participation.

The day when freedom and human rights could be slighted in the name of economic growth and national security has ended. The day when repressive force and torture in secret chambers were tolerated is over. At the same time, the day when confusion was irresponsibly created on the pretext of freedom and participation must also come to an end. We will have an era of mature democracy, when human rights are inviolable and freedom with responsibility prevails, so that both economic development and national security are assured.

We are determined to create a society in which honest and hardworking people have nothing to fear and can live dignified and productive lives. We will also create a democratic body politic in which all citizens can creatively participate in national development as the true masters of the nation.

With the new Constitution incorporating the will of the people now going into effect, I declare that the new administration will be a government of the people. It will open an era of democracy in which each citizen can reach his full potential. It will help make every segment of our diversified pluralistic society free and dynamic and able to exert its inherent rights to the greatest possible extent.

The people want an honest and ethical government. I intend to give them one. All leaders, including myself, will be honest and truthful. Promises to the people will be kept without fail.

The cheers of support I heard in the recent campaign have given me strength and the criticisms have been good medicine. I will listen to the views of those who did not vote for me and will reflect them in government policies without fail. I will not disregard their criticisms. In this spirit, I earnestly appeal to the opposition parties and others who opposed me. With a shared concern for the affairs of state, let us start a dialogue; and with a spirit of co-operation, let us work together to make democracy work, to unify the nation and to bring prosperity to everyone.

Fellow citizens,

Our goal is national reconciliation. The history of development since the 1970s teaches the grim lesson that no matter how high or sustained economic growth may be, it alone cannot ensure that we will attain our ideal of a harmonious, balanced and happy society. Of course, high growth has raised our living standard and transformed the agriculture-dominated traditional Korean society into a pluralistic, industrial one.

At the same time, this has created obstacles all along our path. Growing disparities between social strata and geographical regions have bred strife and schisms, seriously undermining national cohesion. Unless this problem is effectively addressed, our endeavors to build a democracy ensuring the welfare of all may be frustrated. Accordingly, we all desire reconciliation warm enough to melt the ice of conflict and divisiveness.

The time has come for the government and all segments of society to strive in concert to achieve a just and fair distribution of income, so that every citizen can share the fruits of growth. I will ensure that no one will be disadvantaged or, on the other hand, receive unjustifiable favors because of birth, sex or political persuasion.

Individuals who have not received a fair share because of the emphasis on the development of the nation as a whole will no longer be sacrificed. Efforts will be made to see that the sick are treated and the poor and weak are given aid and support. The creative initiative of businessmen and the principle of free enterprise will be further encouraged, while the rights and interests of farmers, fishermen, workers and small and medium-sized merchants and industrialists will be promoted to the maximum extent.

Everything possible will be done to provide the young, who still shoulder the future of the nation, with the best possible education. Meticulous efforts will be made to foster the ideals and dreams of young people and to shape a progressive society that constantly reforms and renews itself. Since the new era that we are going to create will, before long, have to be turned over to the care of the next generation, their dreams and passions will be an invaluable stimulus for progress. We will energetically promote academic studies, culture, and the arts, so that there will be a cultural renaissance to match our economic miracle. Thus all citizens will have access to rich cultural experiences.

All citizens will be encouraged to make life better by trying to understand and help their neighbors. My administration will resolutely reject any form of privilege, irregularity and corruption that obstructs social justice and deepens conflict. I intend to stamp out violence, property speculation and inflation. The era of the great common man will feature a society in which unjust accumulation or concentration of wealth is done away with, and in which everyone profits by honest work and can thus plan for the future with hope. We must now open a great era for the common man through democratic reforms and national reconciliation.

However, national reconciliation cannot be achieved by government policies alone; it must grow in the heart of every citizen. Accordingly, I ask my fellow citizens not to leave the task of national reconciliation in the hands of the government alone. Let us all reflect on the issue ourselves and approach it from a realization that it must be first planted in the heart of each of us. Those who are strong must help the weak. Those who have plenty should show self-restraint and magnanimity toward those who have less.

Fellow citizens,
The Seoul Olympics, which will be a grand event for all Koreans and a festival of peace for all the five billion people on earth, are fast approaching. On this occasion, when Korea will burst on the world scene, there should be no family squabbles. Let us make joint, concerted efforts to make the Seoul Olympics long remembered by the inhabitants of the global community as the most successful.

Let me emphasize, moreover, that the greatest historic significance of the Seoul Olympics is that it will bring the day of unification closer. The sonorous chorus of reconciliation which will emanate from Seoul when East and West meet together for the first time in twelve years will be a signal to the entire world that an era of unification is finally opening on the Korean Peninsula.

In response to that great chorus, the Republic of Korea will intensify its diplomatic efforts to promote international peace and co-operation with all nations in the world. While further consolidating ties with Japan, the United States and other Western countries, we will further cultivate friendships with the Third World. We will broaden the channel of international co-operation with the continental countries with which we have hitherto had no exchanges, with the aim of pursuing a vigorous northern diplomacy. Improved relations with countries with ideologies and social systems different from ours will contribute to stability, peace and common prosperity in East Asia. Such a northward-looking diplomacy should also lead to the gateway of unification. Here I appeal to my fellow countrymen who yearn for an early end to the territorial division. Unification is a goal which we cannot forget, even in our sleep. We cannot be optimistic about attaining it but we need not be pessimistic, either. We should simply do our best to reach it. Coincidentally, our national self-esteem has grown much stronger. It is going to be the major driving force behind our endeavors to achieve unification as well as eminence in the world. We must thus nurture our democratic capability on the strength of national self-esteem, so that we can go through the gateway of unification while strengthening national security.

We must keep in mind the object lesson that opportunity comes first not to those who wait for it but to those who are well prepared to seize it. If only I can perceive a path to peace and reunification on the Korean Peninsula, I am prepared to go anywhere on earth for a sincere dialogue with anyone.

I propose to North Korea that they discard the wild dream of compelling the free citizens of this land, who have internalized democratic values, to accept their doctrinaire ideology that has been rejected even by other communist countries; and that they acknowledge that dialogue, not violence, is the most direct route to ending the division and bringing about unification.

I reaffirm that the door to dialogue will always be open. In keeping with our new national self-esteem, let us have dialogue. Let us coexist peacefully and on that basis cooperate so that spring can come to the Demilitarized Zone. In that way, let us begin to pave the way for unification together.

I would like to say this to other nations interested in Korean unification. Fundamentally, South and North Korea—the parties immediately involved—will work to resolve the Korean question peacefully through democratic means. However, we will welcome to Seoul without fear or favor any messenger of peace and unification from any place on earth.

Fellow citizens,
The twentieth century began for us with suffering and frustration, but as it comes to an end we have the wherewithal to overcome anything. The vision of a unified Korea looming just beyond the horizon of the twentieth century is beckoning us. When our soaring capabilities and self-esteem are fused into a burst of incandescent energy, Korea will certainly emerge as a brilliant young giant in the world and will be a leader in the Asia–Pacific Age. But let us not forget how many patriotic ancestors and compatriots have had to sacrifice themselves and toil so that we could have this excellent opportunity

The era of the common man has arrived. From now on, everyone, not just a single person, will have a say in what is good for the country. This will be an era during which cooperation among many people with old-fashioned common sense will be more important than the outstanding talents of a few. It will also be an era in which national development will directly translate into freedom, affluence and well-being for all individual citizens.

Fellow citizens,
Today, I stand on this grand platform at the behest of all of you, my fellow countrymen. As it was raised by you, it does not separate me from you. Bearing that fact in mind, I vow today to be a president who shares your heartbeat and thoughts.

I do not want to be a president who bullies his fellow countrymen. But I will not be one who is bullied by mobs, either. The kind of president that I truly want to be is one who rubs shoulders with his fellow citizens and shares their dreams and pains.

We are now lined up on the starting line of democracy. Having built this glorious platform together, let us all take energetic forward strides together with courage, drive and confidence in the future.

Let us march toward 'a land of hope, brimming with liberty, equality, peace and happiness'—to quote the words of a much-loved song.

My fellow citizens,
Let us march together.

3.

A Single National Community; Special Declaration in the Interest of National Self-Respect, Unification and Prosperity, July 7, 1988

My sixty million compatriots,

Today, I am going to enunciate the policy of the Sixth Republic to achieve the peaceful unification of our homeland, a long-standing goal dear to the hearts of the entire Korean people.

We have been suffering the pain of territorial division for almost half a century. This national division has inflicted numerous ordeals and hardships upon the Korean people, thus hindering national development. Dismantling the barrier separating the South and the North and building a road to a unified and prosperous homeland is a duty that history has imposed on every Korean alive today.

The South and the North, divided by different ideologies and political systems, have gone through a fratricidal war. The divided halves of the single Korean nation have distrusted, denounced and antagonized each other since the day of territorial partition, and this painful state has yet to be remedied. Though the division was not brought about by our own volition, it is our responsibility to achieve national unification through our independent capabilities.

We must all work together to open a bright era of South–North reconciliation and cooperation. The time has come for all of us to endeavor in concert to promote the well-being and prosperity of the Korean people as a whole.

Today, the world is entering an age of reconciliation and cooperation transcending ideologies and political systems. A brave new tide of openness and exchange is engulfing peoples of different historical and cultural backgrounds. I believe we have now come to a historic moment when we should be able to find a breakthrough toward lasting peace and unification on the Korean Peninsula which is still threatened with the danger of war amidst persisting tension and confrontation.

My fellow compatriots,
The fundamental reason why the tragic division has still to be overcome is that both the South and the North have been regarding each other as an adversary, rather than realizing that both halves of Korea belong to the same national community, so that inter-Korean enmity has continued to intensify. Having lived in a single ethnic community, the Korean people have shaped an illustrious history and cultural traditions, triumphing over almost ceaseless trials and challenges with pooled national strength and wisdom.

Accordingly, developing relations between the South and the North as members of a single national community to achieve common prosperity is a shortcut to realizing a prosperous and unified homeland. This is also the path to national self-esteem and integration.

Now the South and the North must tear down the barrier that divides them and implement exchanges in all fields. Positive step after positive step must be taken to restore mutual trust and strengthen our bonds as members of one nation.

With the realization that we both belong to a single community, we must also put a stop to confrontation on the international scene. I hope that North Korea will contribute to the community of nations as a responsible member and that this will accelerate the opening and development of North Korean society. South and North Korea should recognize each other's place in the international community and cooperate with each other in the best interests of the entire Korean people.

My sixty million fellow compatriots,
Today, I promise to make efforts to open a new era of national self-esteem, unification and prosperity by building a social, cultural, economic and political community in which all members of Korean society can participate on the principles of independence, peace, democracy and welfare. To that end, I declare to the nation and to the world that the following policies will be pursued:

- We will actively promote exchanges of visits between the people of South and North Korea, including politicians, businessmen, journalists, religious leaders, cultural leaders, artists, academics, sportsmen and students, and will make necessary arrangements to ensure that Koreans residing overseas can freely visit both parts of Korea.

- Even before the successful conclusion of the North–South Red Cross talks, we will promote and actively support, from a humanitarian viewpoint, all measures which can assist separated families in their efforts to find out whether their family members in the other part of the Peninsula are still alive and to trace their whereabouts, and will also promote exchanges of correspondence and visits between them.

- We will open doors for trade between South and North Korea, which will be regarded as internal trade within the national community.

- We hope to achieve a balanced development of the national economy with a view to enhancing the quality of life for all Korean people—in both the South and the North—and will not oppose nations friendly with us trading with North Korea, provided that this trade does not involve military goods.

- We hope to bring to an end counter-productive diplomacy character-ized by competition and confrontation between the South and the North, and to co-operate in ensuring that North Korea makes a positive contribution to the international community. We also hope that repre-sentatives of South and North Korea will contact each other freely in international forums and will co-operate to pursue the common inter-ests of the whole Korean nation.

- To create an atmosphere conducive to durable peace on the Korean Peninsula, we are willing to co-operate with North Korea in its efforts to improve relations with countries friendly to us, including the United States and Japan; and in tandem with this, we will continue to seek improved relations with the Soviet Union, China and other socialist countries.

I trust that North Korea will respond positively to the measures out-lined above. If the North shows a positive attitude, I should like to make it clear that even more progressive measures will be taken one after another. I hope that this declaration today will serve to open a new chapter in the development of inter-Korean relations and will lead to unification. I believe that if the entire 60 million Korean people pool their wisdom and strength, the South and the North will be integrated into a single social, cultural and economic community before this century is out. On that basis, I am confident that we will accomplish the great task of uniting in a single national entity in the not so very distant future.

4.

Declaration on General Principles of Relations Between the Republic of Korea and the Union of Soviet Socialist Republics, Moscow, December 14, 1990

President Roh Tae Woo of the Republic of Korea and President Mikhail S. Gorbachev of the Union of Soviet Socialist Republics, having met in Moscow on December 14, 1990 and having discussed the state and the prospects of the bilateral relations as well as a wide range of relevant international issues, expressing a mutual interest in the development of comprehensive cooperation between the two countries; aware of the importance of peace on the Korean Peninsula for that of Northeast Asia and the world at large; recognizing the aspiration of the Korean nation for unification and welcoming the expansion of South–North contacts, including the recent negotiations between the Prime Ministers of the Republic of Korea and of the Democratic People's Republic of Korea; being firmly committed to the building of a new, more equitable, humane, peaceful and democratic world order; declare that the Republic of Korea and the Soviet Union shall be guided in their relations by the following principles:

- Respect for each other's sovereign equality, territorial integrity and political independence, noninterference in the internal affairs of the two states, and recognition that all nations are free to choose their own way of political and socioeconomic development;

- Compliance with the standards of international law, respect for the purposes and principles of the United Nations, set forth in the UN Charter;

- Inadmissibility of the threat or use of force, of providing one's own security at the expense of other states, and of settling international controversies and regional conflicts by any means other than reaching political agreements on the basis of reasonable consent by all the parties concerned;

- Development of a broad mutually beneficial cooperation among states and nations, leading to their rapprochement and to a deeper mutual understanding;

- Joining the international community's efforts to deal, on a priority basis, with the global issues of reducing the arms race, nuclear or conventional; preventing the environmental disaster facing mankind; overcoming poverty, famine and illiteracy; narrowing the dramatic gap between the development levels of various nations;

- Establishment of a secure and equitable world which would ensure progress for mankind and a decent life for all nations in the coming millennium.

Proceeding from the above-mentioned principles and opening a new page in the history of their relations, the Republic of Korea and the Union of Soviet Socialist Republics are determined to build these relations in the spirit of good neighborhood trust and cooperation in the interests of the peoples of both countries. To these ends, the two states will conclude a variety of agreements with a view to establishing and improving links and contacts between the two countries in the political, economic, trade, cultural, scientific, humanitarian and other areas. The Republic of Korea and the USSR will ensure priority of universally recognized international legal standards in their domestic and foreign policies and will implement in good faith their treaty obligations.

The presidents support the willingness of businessmen from both countries to deepen an effective and mutually beneficial cooperation in economy, trade, industry and transport, to exchange advanced technology and scientific achievements and to develop joint entrepreneurship and new forms of cooperation, and welcome the development of and investments into mutually beneficial projects. An exchange of ideas, information, spiritual and cultural values, an expansion of human contacts in the field of culture, art, science, education, sports, media and tourism, and a reciprocal travel by citizens of their countries will be encouraged. The sides will coordinate their efforts to control international terrorism, organized crime and illicit trafficking in drugs, and to protect the environment and to that end will cooperate in international and regional organizations.

The Republic of Korea and the Union of Soviet Socialists Republics are committed to the ideas of establishing in Asia and the Pacific region equal, mutually beneficial relations based on the balance of interests and self-determination, and of making Asia and the Pacific a region of peace and constructive cooperation through a process of unilateral and multilateral consultations. The presidents reaffirm their conviction that the development of Korean–Soviet relations contributes to the strengthening of peace and security in Asia and the Pacific, is in line with the changes underway in the region, deepens the processes leading to the removal of confrontational mentality and to the elimination of 'the Cold War' in Asia, contributes to regional cooperation and facilitates the relaxation of tension and the establishment of the climate of trust for the eventual reunification on the Korean Peninsula.

The Soviet Union stands for the continuation of a productive inter-Korean dialogue for the removal of the political and military confrontation between the two Korean sides, for a just and equitable settlement of the Korean problem by peaceful, democratic means in accordance with the will of the entire Korean people.

The Republic of Korea, welcoming the global turn from the era of confrontation to reconciliation and cooperation on the basis of universal values, freedom, democracy and justice, emphasizes a success of the Soviet reform policy as a major factor of future international relations, improvement of the situation in Northeast Asia and progress in relations between the two countries.

The presidents proceed from the general understanding that the development of links and contacts between the Republic of Korea and the USSR must not in any way affect their relations with third countries or undermine obligations they assume under multilateral or bilateral treaties and agreements.

The Republic of Korea and the Union of Soviet Socialist Republics have agreed to pursue a political dialogue at the highest level, and to hold regular meetings and consultations at various other levels on matters of deepening the bilateral relations and on relevant international issues.

ROH TAE WOO

M. GORBACHEV

Moscow,
December 14, 1990

5.

Declaration of Non-nuclear Korean Peninsula Peace Initiatives, Seoul, November 8, 1991

My fellow Koreans,

This morning, I am going to announce an important decision to help build a durable structure of peace on the Korean Peninsula and in Northeast Asia.

In the process of removing the legacies of the Cold War and in efforts to build a world of peace, many courageous and previously unimagined initiatives are being taken around the world today.

Not only have the former adversaries joined hands but they vow friendship and cooperation for a better future for all mankind. What is more, epoch-making measures are being taken to reduce all weapons of mass destruction, which threaten to destroy human civilization in an instant.

Both the United States and the Soviet Union are in the process of reducing and dismantling nuclear weapons on a large scale, and inter-national negotiations are currently under way in Geneva to completely eliminate chemical weapons, which could inflict indiscriminate killing on a massive scale.

Looking at these global waves of reconciliation and cooperation, there are those who mistakenly believe that threats of confrontation have disap-peared from our own land also. Unfortunately, however, a situation that is unique in the world and is quite inconsistent with the tides of history per-sists on the Korean Peninsula.

At a time when reduction and destruction of nuclear weapons are being carried out worldwide, North Korea shows no sign of giving up its efforts to build nuclear weapons, while reneging on its professed duties as a sig-natory to the Nuclear Non-proliferation Treaty. It has been well docu-mented that North Korea also manufactures, and has a stockpile of, chemical–biological weapons.

As is well known, there has been a tragic fratricidal war in Korea and, subsequently, an intense military confrontation and arms race ensued on the Korean Peninsula for almost four decades. Under these circumstances, North Korea's development of nuclear weapons has to be a matter of grave concern, and it will escalate the Korean question into an entirely new dimension. Indeed, nuclear weapons in North Korean hands would be so dangerous and destabilizing that they would not only threaten the very survival of our nation, but could in an instant shatter the peace in Northeast Asia and the world.

It is for these reasons that the gravely worried international community joins us in our concerted efforts to deter North Korea from developing nuclear weapons.

In my address to the United Nations General Assembly last September, I made it clear that I was prepared to discuss with North Korea the nuclear issues on the Korean Peninsula as soon as North Korea would sign the nuclear safeguards agreement, renounce the development of nuclear weapons, and agree on inter-Korean military confidence-building measures.

And yet, rather than positively respond to my proposals North Korea continues to evade its international duties on account of groundless charges and excuses.

In an effort to initiate the resolution of nuclear issues on the Korean Peninsula and in my earnest desire to bring about a durable structure of peace on our land, I have come to an important decision and have determined to take steps to carry it out.

Reaffirming our commitment to the cause of peace and in order to eliminate from our land all chemical–biological weapons and to secure a non-nuclear Korean Peninsula, I declare the following to be our policy:

First, the Republic of Korea will use nuclear energy solely for peaceful purposes, and will not manufacture, possess, store, deploy or use nuclear weapons.

Second, the Republic of Korea will continue to submit to comprehensive international inspection all nuclear-related facilities and materials on its territory in compliance with the Nuclear Non-proliferation Treaty and with the nuclear safeguards agreement it has concluded with the International Atomic Energy Agency under the treaty, and will not possess nuclear fuel reprocessing and enrichment facilities.

Third, the Republic of Korea aspires for a world of peace free of nuclear weapons as well as all weapons of indiscriminate killing; and we will actively participate in international efforts toward a total elimination of chemical–biological weapons and observe all international agreements thereon.

We will faithfully carry out this non-nuclear, no chemical–biological weapons policy.

Now, there can be no reason or justification for North Korea to develop nuclear weapons or evade international inspection of its nuclear facilities.

I strongly call upon North Korean authorities to immediately take steps corresponding to my declaration today.

Just as the Republic of Korea has done, North Korea also should renounce unequivocally the possession of nuclear reprocessing and enrichment facilities.

As soon as North Korea takes these steps, beginning with the signing of the nuclear safeguards agreement, we will initiate bilateral discussions on other military–security issues, including the nuclear issue, and seek to resolve them through South–North high-level talks.

Any and all issues pertaining to the Korean Peninsula should be resolved through direct inter-Korean negotiations in a spirit of self-reliance.

Consequently, I call upon North Korea in the name of seventy million fellow Koreans to immediately abandon the attempt to develop nuclear weapons so that together we may open a new era of peace on the Korean Peninsula, having secured a land free of nuclear weapons.

My fellow Koreans,
Prior to the enunciation of our policy today, the government has very carefully examined its possible impact on the national security. My decision is based on a firm assessment that our national security will continue to remain solid.

It is sincerely hoped that North Korea will accurately evaluate current international realities and decide to join us in our common efforts to eliminate the sources of national tragedy and to achieve national harmony and peaceful unification.

6.

Agreement on Reconciliation, Non-aggression, and Exchanges and Cooperation between the South and the North (to enter into force as of February 19, 1992)

The South and the North, in keeping with the yearning of the entire Korean people for the peaceful unification of the divided land; reaffirming the principles of unification set forth in the July 4 (1972) South–North Joint Communique; determined to remove the state of political and military confrontation and achieve national reconciliation; also determined to avoid armed aggression and hostilities, reduce tension and ensure the peace; expressing the desire to realize multi-faceted exchanges and cooperation to advance common national interests and prosperity; recognizing that their relations, not being a relationship between states, constitute a special interim relationship stemming from the process towards unification; pledging to exert joint efforts to achieve peaceful unification; hereby have agreed as follows;

Chapter I South–North Reconciliation

Article 1: The South and the North shall recognize and respect each other's system.

Article 2: The two sides shall not interfere in each other's internal affairs.

Article 3: The two sides shall not slander or vilify each other.

Article 4: The two sides shall not attempt any actions of sabotages or subversion against each other.

Article 5: The two sides shall endeavor together to transform the present state of armistice into a solid state of peace between the South and the

North and shall abide by the present Military Armistice Agreement (of July 27, 1953) until such a state of peace has been realized.

Article 6: The two sides shall cease to compete with or confront each other in the international arena and shall cooperate and endeavor together to promote national prestige and interests.

Article 7: To ensure close consultations and liaison between the two sides, South–North Liaison Offices shall be established at P'anmunjom within three (3) months after the coming into force of this Agreement.

Article 8: A South–North Political Committee shall be established within the framework of the South–North High-Level Talks within one (1) month of the coming into force of this Agreement with a view to discussing concrete measures to ensure the implementation and observance of the accords on South–North reconciliation.

Chapter II South–North Non-aggression

Article 9: The two sides shall not use force against each other and shall not undertake armed aggression against each other.

Article 10: Differences of views and disputes arising between the two sides shall be resolved peacefully through dialogue and negotiation.

Article 11: The South–North demarcation line and areas for nonaggression shall be identical with the Military Demarcation Line specified in the Military Armistice Agreement of July 27, 1953 and the areas that have been under the jurisdiction of each sides until the present time.

Article 12: To implement and guarantee nonaggression, the two sides shall set up a South–North Joint Military Commission within three (3) months of the coming into force of this Agreement. In the said Commission, the two sides shall discuss and carry out steps to build military confidence and realize arms reduction, including the mutual notification and control of major movements of military units and major military exercises, the peaceful utilization of the Demilitarized Zone, exchanges of military personnel and information, phased reductions in armaments including the elimination of weapons of mass destruction and attack capabilities, and verifications thereof.

Article 13: A telephone hotline shall be installed between the military authorities of the two sides to prevent accidental armed clashes and their escalation.

Article 14: A South–North Military Committee shall be established within the framework of the South–North High-Level Talks within one (1) month of the coming into force of this Agreement in order to discuss concrete measures to ensure the implementation and observance of the accords on nonaggression and to remove military confrontation.

Chapter III South–North Exchanges And Cooperation

Article 15: To promote an integrated and balanced development of the national economy and the welfare of the entire people, the two sides shall engage in economic exchanges and cooperation, including the joint development of resources, the trade of goods as domestic commerce and joint ventures.

Article 16: The two sides shall carry out exchanges and cooperation in various fields such as science and technology, education, literature and the arts, health, sports, environment, and publishing and journalism including newspapers, radio and television broadcasts and publications.

Article 17: The two sides shall promote free intra-Korean travel and contacts for the residents of their respective areas.

Article 18: The two sides shall permit free correspondence, reunions and visits between dispersed family members and other relatives and shall promote the voluntary reunion of divided families and shall take measures to resolve other humanitarian issues.

Article 19: The two sides shall reconnect railroads and roads that have been cut off and shall open South–North sea and air transport routes.

Article 20: The two sides shall establish and link facilities needed, for South–North postal and telecommunications services and shall guarantee the confidentiality of intra-Korean mail and telecommunications.

Article 21: The two sides shall cooperate in the international arena in the economic, cultural and various other fields and carry out joint undertakings abroad.

Article 22: To implement accords on exchanges and cooperation in the economic, cultural and various other fields, the two sides shall establish joint commissions for specific sectors, including a Joint South–North Economic Exchanges and Cooperation Commission, within three (3) months of the coming into force of this Agreement.

Article 23: A South–North Exchanges and Cooperation Committee shall be established within the framework of the South–North High Level Talks within one (1) month of the coming into force of this Agreement with a view to discussing concrete measures to ensure the implementation and observance of the accords on South–North exchanges and cooperation.

Chapter IV   Amendments and Effectuation

Article 24: This Agreement may be amended or supplemented by concurrence between the two sides.

Article 25: This Agreement shall enter into force as of the day the two sides exchange appropriate instruments following the completion of their respective procedures for bringing it into effect.

December 13, 1991

Chung Won-shik Prime Minister of the Republic of Korea	Yon Hyong-muk Premier of the Administration Council of the Democratic People's Republic of Korea
Chief delegate of the South delegation to the South–North High-Level Talks	Head of the North delegation to the South–North High-Level Talks

(unofficial translation)

7.

Joint Declaration of the Denuclearization of the Korean Peninsula (to enter into force as of February 19, 1992)

The South and the North, desiring to eliminate the danger of nuclear war through denuclearization of the Korean Peninsula, and thus to create an environment and conditions favorable for peace and peaceful unification of our country and contribute to peace and security in Asia and the world, declare as follows;

1. The South and the North shall not test, manufacture, produce, receive, possess, store, deploy or use nuclear weapons.

2. The South and the North shall use nuclear energy solely for peaceful purposes.

3. The South and the North shall not possess nuclear reprocessing and uranium enrichment facilities.

4. The South and the North, in order to verify the denuclearization of the Korean Peninsula, shall conduct inspection of the objects selected by the other side and agreed upon between the two sides, in accordance with procedures and methods to be determined by the South–North Joint Nuclear Control Commission.

5. The South and the North, in order to implement this joint declaration, shall establish and operate a South–North Joint Nuclear Control Commission within one month of the effectuation of this joint declaration.

6. This joint declaration shall enter into force on the day on which the South and the North exchange notifications of completion of the formalities for the entry into force of the present declaration.

January 20, 1992

Chung Won-shik
Prime Minister of the
Republic of Korea

Yon Hyong-muk
Premier of the
Administration Council
of the Democratic People's
Republic of Korea

Chief delegate
of the South
Delegation to the
South–North
High-Level Talks

Head
of the North
Delegation to the
the South–North
High-Level Talks

(unofficial translation)

8.

Joint Press Communique on the Occasion of President Roh Tae Woo's Visit to the People's Republic of China, September 30, 1992

1. President Roh Tae Woo of the Republic paid a state visit to the People's Republic of China from September 27 to 30, 1992 at the invitation of President Yang Shangkun. President Roh Tae Woo, as the first Korean President ever to visit China, received a cordial welcome and warm hospitality from the Government and the people of the People's Republic of China.

2. During his visit, President Roh had a meeting with President Yang in an amicable atmosphere and met with General Secretary Jiang Zemin and Premier Li Peng respectively. At the meetings, the two sides explained the political and economic situations of their respective countries and exchanged their views on ways to further develop friendly and cooperative relations between the two countries. The two sides also exchanged their views extensively on the current international situation as well as on that in the Northeast Asian region.

3. The leaders of both countries highly praised the significance of the establishment of diplomatic relations between Korea and China. They further recognized that, after surmounting the abnormal relations of the past, the enhancement of friendly and cooperative relations between the two countries on the basis of 'the Joint Declaration of Establishment of Diplomatic Relation', will not only serve the interests of both peoples but will also be consistent with the current trend of international relations and have an important bearing on the peace and development of the Asian region and the world as a whole.

4. The leaders of both countries took note of the fact, with satisfaction, that the two Governments signed the Trade Agreement, the Investment Protection Agreement, the Agreement on the Establishment of the Joint Committee for Economic, Trade, and Technical Cooperation, and the Agreement on Scientific and Technological Cooperation during the visit of President Roh to China. Both sides, moreover, have decided to actively promote exchange and cooperation in such various fields as economy, trade, science and technology, transportation, culture, and sports.

5. President Roh Tae Woo explained Korea's position on the South–North dialogue and the realization of denuclearization and peaceful reunification of the Korean Peninsula. Chinese leaders highly appreciated the progress made in the South–North dialogue and expressed the hope for the early realization of the goals set forth in 'the Joint Declaration of the Denuclearization of the Korean Peninsula'. The leaders of both countries shared the common view that the relaxation of tension on the Korean Peninsula will not only serve the interest of the whole Korean people but also will be favorable for the settlement of peace and stability of the Northeast Asian region as well as of the whole of Asia. They also agreed that this trend of the relaxation of tension should be continuously developed.

6. The leaders of both countries shared the view that strengthening of economic cooperation in the Northeast Asia and Asia–Pacific region is conducive to development and common prosperity among nations in this region, and have agreed to closely cooperate in the regional institutions such as the Asia–Pacific Economic Cooperation (APEC).

7. Both Korea and China share the conviction that the successful visit of President Roh Tae Woo to China would contribute to further developing the friendly and cooperative relations between the two countries in the future.

8. President Roh Tae Woo expressed his gratitude to the Government and the people of China for their hearty welcome and hospitality, and extended an invitation to President Yang Shangkun for a visit to the Republic of Korea at a convenient date and President Yang, expressing his gratitude, accepted the invitation with pleasure.

(unofficial translation)

9.

Korean–Russian Joint Statement, November 20, 1992

1. At the invitation of H.E. Roh Tae Woo, President of the Republic of Korea, H.E. Boris Nicholayevich Yeltsin, President of the Russian Federation, paid an official visit to the Republic of Korea November 18–20, 1992.

2. The President of Russia laid a wreath at the Monument of Unknown Soldiers in the National Cemetery, delivered a speech at the National Assembly and made a tour to an industrial complex in Suwon.

3. At the summit meeting held in a cordial and friendly atmosphere, the two Presidents had frank and useful exchanges of views concerning the international situation including the situation in Northeast Asia and the Korean Peninsula as well as the Commonwealth of Independent States, and issues of expanding bilateral relations.

The two Presidents shared the view that political stability and economic prosperity of the Russian Federation and other CIS countries are essential to maintaining peace and stability of the world, and President Roh reassured the support and cooperation of the Republic of Korea for the political and economic reform of the Russian Federation.

4. H.E. Boris Yeltsin and H.E. Roh Tae Woo noted with satisfaction the consolidation of peace and stability in recent years and the transformation of the old international political structure of confrontation into a new world order based on peace and cooperation. The two Presidents shared the view that it is necessary for the two countries to cooperate with each other to maintain and further develop current international tendency towards peace and cooperation, and expressed their support for the international community's efforts to lessen the arms races, and reduce the weapons of mass destruction including nuclear weapons, and prevent their proliferation.

The two sides agreed to strive to strengthen the role of the United Nations in establishing a new world order based on the supremacy of international law, and to develop close cooperation between the two countries within the framework of the United Nations and other international organizations.

5. The two Presidents exchanged views on the situation in the Asia–Pacific region and recognized the necessity for closer cooperation among nations in the region for peace and common prosperity. In particular, President Yeltsin expressed the confidence that Russia would make its own due contribution to economic cooperation in the Asia–Pacific region.

President Yeltsin supported the idea of President Roh concerning the necessity of dialogue among interested parties in Northeast Asia for the purpose of building confidence and promoting mutual understanding and common prosperity in the region.

6. The two Presidents concurred that unification of the two Koreas should be realized in a peaceful manner through dialogues between the two parties concerned and reaffirmed that the faithful implementation of 'the South–North Agreement on Reconciliation, Non-Aggression and Exchanges and Cooperation' and 'the South–North Joint Declaration on Denuclearization of the Korean Peninsula' is essential for making meaningful progress in the South–North dialogues.

7. President Roh highly valued 'the Russian–US Joint Statement on Nuclear Non-Proliferation on the Korean Peninsula' signed by President Yeltsin and President Bush in June, 1992. President Yeltsin assured that the Government of Russia would support measures to prevent proliferation of nuclear weapons on the Korean Peninsula and supported the idea of reciprocal nuclear inspections in accordance with 'the South–North Joint Declaration on Denuclearization of the Korean Peninsula'.

8. The two Presidents signed 'the Treaty on Basic Relations between the Republic of Korea and the Russian Federation'. They shared the view that the Treaty, which reflects the will of the two countries to develop forward-looking relations as friendly countries with the guidance of their shared values of freedom, democracy, respect for human rights and market economics, would serve as a legal basis for deepening friendship and understanding between the two peoples, and furthering practical and cooperative relations between the two countries in all areas.

The two Presidents expressed satisfaction in connection with the signing of the Cultural Cooperation Agreement, the avoidance of Double Taxation Convention, and the Customs Cooperation Agreement.

9. President Yeltsin expressed deep regrets over the tragic incident involving KAL 007 in September 1983. President Roh expressed thanks for President Yeltsin's courageous and moral decision to make public documents on the KAL incident and hand them over to Korea, and welcomed the delivery of the documents as an important progress in bringing to light true facts of the incident. The two Presidents agreed that

the two sides will continue to cooperate with each other to probe all the unknown facts about the incident and also expressed the hope for cooperation with the international community for that purpose.

10. The two Presidents agreed that the question of property right to the plot of land of the former Russian mission in Seoul will be settled through negotiations between their Governments at an early date.

11. President Roh, recalling the historical fact that many ethnic Koreans were relocated and dispersed against their will from the Russian Far East to the Central Asian region during the 1930s, expressed the hope for the Russian Government's favourable consideration for restoring the deprived rights and honour of those ethnic Koreans. President Yeltsin noted that the resolution of 1937, according to which Koreans were expelled from the Russian Far East, and repressions against Koreans during the period of 1937–53 were condemned in Russia.

President Yeltsin also stressed that laws of the Russian Federation 'on Rehabilitation of Repressed Nationalities' and 'on Rehabilitation of Victims of Political Repression', enacted in recent years, provide for the Russians of Korean origin equal opportunities with other nationalities in exercising their political rights and freedom including the freedom of national development, as stipulated in the existing laws.

12. The Presidents noted with satisfaction that bilateral cooperation in the fields of economy, trade, science and technology has grown substantially since the establishment of diplomatic relations between their countries and that a basic legal framework for further cooperation has been laid down.

13. The Presidents also welcomed the signing of the Regulation on the Organization and Operation of the Korean–Russian Joint Committee on Economic, Scientific and Technological Cooperation by their respective Deputy Prime Ministers. The Joint Committee will meet on a regular basis and the first meeting will take place at the earliest date agreeable to both sides.

14. The two Presidents discussed the establishment of a Korean Industrial Complex in the Nakhodka Free Economic Zone and confirmed that Russia's speedy legislation of the relevant laws, development of infrastructure and introduction of investment incentives are essential to ensuring the success of the project. They noted that the two Governments would continue their efforts for the establishment of a Korean Industrial Complex.

15. The Presidents noted that favorable conditions exist for developing mutually beneficial cooperation in various industrial fields including general machinery, electrical, electronic, chemical, metallurgical, shipbuild-

ing, textile and aerospace industries and also stressed the necessity for small and medium sized enterprises to participate in cooperative projects.

16. The two Presidents emphasized the importance of Korea's participation in the exploration and exploitation of oil, gas and other natural resources in the territory of the Russian Federation including Siberia, the Far East and Sakhalin. They welcomed the signing of agreements between consortia of the two countries on the preparation of feasibility studies for joint development of the natural gas field in the Republic of Sakha (Yakutia) and construction of pipelines for transport of natural gas to the Republic of Korea. They agreed that the two Governments would make joint efforts for the development of several Sakhalin offshore gas fields in order to supply gas from Sakhalin to the Republic of Korea.

17. The Presidents agreed on the need for active participation of Korean firms in the exploitation of forestry resources in the Russian Far East, and to this end agreed to make concerted efforts to foster an environment conducive to cooperation in the field of forestry.

18. The two Presidents underlined the importance of bilateral scientific and technological cooperation and agreed to support the implementation of the 74 joint projects already agreed upon as well as the activities of the Science and Technology Cooperation Centers established in both countries. They further agreed on the need to explore new spheres of cooperation, to exchange information and specialists in the fields of science and technology.

19. President Yeltsin, taking into account the enormous potential of the Russian economy, requested that the Korean private sector actively invest in Russia, and President Roh said that the Korean Government would encourage the Korean business community to expand its investments in Russia and to assist with the conversion of the Russian defense industry for civilian use.

20. The two Presidents expressed satisfaction with the agreements to resume the commodity loan earmarked for 1991. Both sides anticipated that it would contribute greatly to the promotion of bilateral economic cooperation.

21. The two Presidents shared the view that the Taejon International Exhibition 1993 would greatly contribute to the advancement of science and technology and the efficient use of existing resources. President Yeltsin, confirming Russia's participation in this exhibition, expressed the hope that it would further contribute to Russian–Korean economic, trade and industry, and science and technology cooperation.

22. The two Presidents, recognizing the importance of the promotion of bilateral trade, agreed to exert concerted efforts for the removal of barriers and obstacles to trade.

The two Presidents welcomed the planned opening of the Korea Trade Center in Moscow, which will promote bilateral trade.

23. The two Presidents stressed the need to promote fisheries cooperation to the full extent within the framework of the bilateral fisheries agreement of September 16, 1991. They also agreed to strengthen further cooperation including joint ventures between their public and private sectors in the field of fishing, processing and marketing of fisheries products and modernization of facilities and equipment.

24. The two Presidents, recognizing the importance of cooperation in the field of construction, agreed to encourage the establishment of joint ventures for participation in construction projects in both countries.

25. The Presidents agreed to expand bilateral collaboration in the area of telecommunication including joint production of telecommunication equipment and the laying of optical fiber cable in the Russian Federation.

26. The two Presidents shared the view that President Yeltsin's visit to Korea greatly contributed to promoting the friendly and cooperative relations between the two countries as well as to further enhancing the mutual understanding between the two peoples.

27. President Yeltsin expressed his sincere appreciation for the warm and friendly reception and hospitalities accorded to him and his party by the Government and the people of the Republic of Korea.

Seoul, November 20 1992
(unofficial translation)

10.

Treaty on Basic Relations between the Republic of Korea and the Russian Federation, November 19, 1992

The Republic of Korea and the Russian Federation,

Desirous of strengthening the bonds of peace and friendship between the two countries and of promoting closer economic and cultural co-operation between their peoples,

Conscious of the traditional relations between their two peoples and determined to overcome the consequences of the adverse period of their common history,

Convinced that future relations between the two countries should be guided by the common values of freedom, democracy, respect for human rights and market economics,

Affirming their conviction that the development of friendly relations and cooperation between the two countries and their peoples will contribute not only to their mutual benefit but also to the peace, security and prosperity of the Asian and Pacific region and throughout the world,

Reaffirming their commitment to the purposes and principles of the Charter of the United Nations,

Recognizing that the Moscow Declaration of 14 December 1990 shall continue to govern relations between the two countries,

Have agreed as follows:

ARTICLE 1

The Republic of Korea and the Russian Federation shall develop friendly relations in accordance with the principles of sovereignty, equality, respect for territorial integrity and political independence, non-intervention in internal affairs and other generally accepted principles of international law.

ARTICLE 2

1. The Contracting Parties shall refrain in their mutual relations from the threat or use of force and shall settle all their disputes by peaceful means in accordance with the Charter of the United Nations.

2. The Contracting Parties shall use, to the maximum extent possible, United Nations mechanisms to settle international conflicts and shall co-operate and endeavour to enhance the role of the United Nations in the maintenance of the international peace and security.

ARTICLE 3

1. The Contracting Parties shall develop cooperation for the promotion of stability and prosperity in the Asian and Pacific region.

2. The Contracting Parties shall strengthen their cooperation, including exchanges of information, within the framework of international and regional organizations.

ARTICLE 4

1. The Contracting Parties shall hold consultations on a regular basis between their Heads of State, Foreign Ministers and other members of their Governments, or their representatives to discuss matters concerning bilateral relations as well as international and regional issues of mutual interest,

2. The consultations shall normally be held in the Republic of Korea and the Russian Federation alternately.

ARTICLE 5

1. The Contracting Parties shall promote the development of broad contacts and ties between their nationals and social organizations.

2. The Contracting Parties shall support contacts and exchanges between the parliaments of the two Countries.

3. The Contracting Parties shall encourage direct contacts between their regional and local governments.

ARTICLE 6

1. The nationals of either Contracting Party shall, subject to the laws and regulations relating to the entry and sojourn of aliens, be permitted to enter or leave, to travel or stay in the territory of the other Contracting Party.

2. The nationals and juridical persons of either Contracting Party shall, within the territory of the other Contracting Party, enjoy full protection and security in accordance with relevant laws and regulations.

ARTICLE 7

1. The Contracting Parties shall promote and develop extensive cooperation between the two countries in the economic, industrial, trade and other fields to their mutual benefit and on the basis of principles generally recognized in international practice.

2. The Contracting Parties shall promote and develop cooperation in the fields of, inter alia, agriculture, forestry, fisheries, energy, mining, communication, transport and construction.

3. The Contracting Parties shall also promote and develop, on the basis of their mutual interest, cooperation in the areas of protecting the environment and the rational use of natural resources.

ARTICLE 8

1. The Contracting Parties, recognizing that scientific and technological cooperation will be of great value in advancing the well-being of their peoples, shall develop broad cooperation in the fields of science and technology for peaceful purposes.

2. In the scientific and technological cooperation between the two countries, special attention shall be devoted to promoting exchanges of scientists and the results of scientific and technological research, and encouraging joint research projects.

ARTICLE 9

The Contracting Parties shall encourage and facilitate diverse and close contacts and cooperation between the business communities of the two countries.

ARTICLE 10

1. In recognition of their respective centuries-old cultural heritages, the Contracting Parties shall promote the development of exchanges and cooperation in the fields of the arts, culture and education.

2. The Contracting Parties shall promote the development of exchanges and cooperation in the fields of the mass media, tourism and sports, and encourage the exchange of young people.

3. The Contracting Parties consider it a matter of special interest to increase the knowledge of each other's languages and cultures in the two countries. Each Contracting Party shall encourage and promote the establishment and activities of cultural and educational institutions for the purpose of providing all persons concerned with broad access to the language and culture of the other Contracting Party.

ARTICLE 11

Each Contracting Party shall, within its territory, recognize the rights of its nationals or citizens originating from Korea or Russia to enjoy their own culture, to profess and practice their own religion, and to use their own language.

ARTICLE 12

The Contracting Parties, deeply concerned about the growing internationalization of crime, shall promote effective cooperation in their efforts to combat organized crime, international terrorism, illegal traffic in drugs and psychotropic substances, illegal acts aimed against the security of maritime navigation and civil aviation, counterfeiting, smuggling including illicit transboundary traffic in articles of national, artistic, historical or archeological value as well as in animal or plant species under threat of extinction, or parts or derivatives thereof.

ARTICLE 13

This Treaty shall not affect the rights and obligations assumed by either Contracting Party under any international treaties and agreements currently in force and shall not be invoked against any third State.

ARTICLE 14

The Contracting Parties shall conclude treaties and agreements, wherever necessary, for the implementation of the purposes of this Treaty.

ARTICLE 15

1. This Treaty shall be subject to ratification and shall enter into force thirty days after the day of exchange of the instruments of ratification.

2. This Treaty shall remain in force for ten years and shall continue to be in force thereafter until terminated as provided herein.

3. Either Contracting Party may, by giving one year's written notice to the other Contracting Party, terminate this Treaty at the end of the initial ten-year period or at any time thereafter.

DONE at Seoul, this .... day of .... one thousand nine hundred and ninety-two, in duplicate, each in the Korean, Russian and English languages, all texts being equally authentic.

FOR THE REPUBLIC OF KOREA   FOR THE RUSSIAN FEDERATION

PUBLICATIONS OF THE DEPARTMENT OF INTERNATIONAL RELATIONS

CANBERRA STUDIES IN WORLD AFFAIRS:

Distributed by: Bibliotech, ANUTECH, GPO Box 4,
Canberra ACT 2601 Australia
(Fax order: (06) 257 1433).

The Department of International Relations is producing a new series of monographs which are published in association with and distributed by Allen & Unwin Pty Ltd, 9 Atchison St, St Leonards, NSW 2065, Australia. Titles are: